D1715285

Essays on
Industrial
Organization
in Honor of
Joe S. Bain

Essays on Industrial Organization in Honor of Joe S. Bain

edited by
Robert T. Masson
P. David Qualls

Ballinger Publishing Company • Cambridge, Massachusetts
A Subsidiary of J.B. Lippincott Company

International Standard Book Number: 0−88410−416−8

Library of Congress Catalog Card Number: 76−3610

Printed in the United States of America

Library of Congress Cataloging in Publication Data

Main entry under title:

Essays on industrial organization, in honor of Joe S. Bain.

Bibliography: p.
Includes index.
CONTENTS: Shepherd, W. G. Bain's influence on research into industrial organization.—Mason, E.S. Has the United States a dual economy?—Caves, R.E. and Porter, M.E. Barriers to exit. [etc.]
1. Industrial organization—Addresses, essays, lectures. 2. Bain, Joe Staten, 1912— I. Bain, Joe Staten, 1912— II. Masson, Robert T. III. Qualls, P. David.
HD21.E8   658.4   76−3610
ISBN 0−88410−416−8

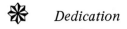 *Dedication*

To Joe

Contents

List of Figures

List of Tables

Foreword

"All successful scholarly careers are alike." What rot. Only this element of truth lies in this Tolstoyan paraphrase: scratch a professor and you find, usually in his vita, plenty of A's and honors. It is only after the rat race we call graduate study is over that the *summas* separate themselves into the creative and the competent.

So it was with Joe Bain. He took his A.B. (Phi Beta Kappa, with highest honors) from UCLA when it was just emerging from its cocoon as a normal school: as I can say about my hometown of Gary, Indiana, that UCLA Department of Economics was a good place for a Bain or a Domar to come from. Having an interest in the economics of accounting, Bain wisely chose to spend 1935–36 in graduate study at Stanford, where John B. Canning was taking an enlightened approach to that rather prosaic subject. The West Coast, with Canning at Stanford, and Hatfield, Staehling, and Mooritz at Berkeley, was then several time zones ahead of the East in the economic analysis of accounting–i.e., in accounting: they are really the same thing!

So when Bain arrived at Harvard in 1936, he was one up on us Eastern yokels–which included Schumpeter, Chamberlin, and Mason on the faculty, and in the student body such stalwarts as the two Sweezys, Musgrave, Bergson, Bourneuf, Stolper, Samuelson, Bishop, and Tsuru, as well as those soon to arrive such as Metzler, Lintner, Wallich, and other immortals. By taking surprisingly few courses, Bain completed his Ph.D. dissertation within three years: in those happy days, there was so little to learn in graduate school and so much time to think. (It was in Usher's economic history course that the Bains met: women then had to sit in the front rows and B came so high in the alphabet as to give Bain a chance to make contact, a privilege denied to us S's.) By the summer of his first year he had already published his first *Quarterly Journal* article, which must seem surprising in the modern age when an unusual student may submit his first article by his third or fourth year, and see it in print some two to three years after its formal acceptance.

The only pretense toward a Harvard meritocracy in those days was the statistics and accounting teaching staff for the pathologically shy Professor Frickey: along with R.A. Gordon, A. Bergson, W. Hance, L. Metzler, and G. Hauge, Bain prepared each October the June quizzes. Dr. Frickey ran a tight ship.

Berkeley, under the entrepreneurship of Robert Calkins, soon called. Bain replied and never looked back. For more than a third of a century—almost a dozen college generations—Bain pursued at Berkeley a research and teaching program in industrial organization. The learned journals and the library bookshelves testify to his fecundity in an area where it was not easy to be fecund. As a theorist, like Picasso, there is no afternoon when I cannot contrive a new gemlet. But in the study of real world markets, one must collect and analyze data for years in order to make relevant contributions.

Thoreau said that if, by forty, fame has not knocked at your door, forget it. Joe Bain could stop holding his breath early on, even before his classic analysis of barriers to entry and his independent discovery, along with Sylos-Labini, of the Bain-Sylos-Modigliani theory of oligopoly price as limited by potential entry.

This volume testifies that Joe Bain, although he is not your run-of-the-mill rotarian, has had profound influence on students and colleagues in the field of price theory. A pearl in his own right, he is also the clam shell around which pearls have formed. The students of his students will form a multiplier chain whose convergence to a finite sum is in doubt. No scholar can wish for more. And more his friends cannot wish for him.

Paul A. Samuelson
MIT
January 1976

Preface

Both we and the economics profession as a whole are greatly indebted to Professor Joe S. Bain for his major role in developing the
modern field of Industrial Organization from its beginnings to its
present status, and for laying the foundations for its future.

We are personally indebted to him for much more than just that. Joe Bain
was our teacher. And our gratitude and respect go well beyond that owed for
our training under his tutelage and his responsiveness and perspicacity as advisor
for our dissertation research. He is our close friend—one with whom we have
spent time fishing, playing softball, walking the Airedales, and relaxing at his
Savary Island retreat off the coast of British Columbia. He has helped us over
many professional and personal hurdles.

We thank our many colleagues who helped us anonymously review the papers
submitted for this volume and those authors whose works, owing to time constraints, could not be revised soon enough to meet the publication schedule for
the book. Finally, we would like to thank our wives and others, notably Theodore Keeler and Darius Gaskins, who were our major safety releases while we
planned the dinner honoring Joe at the 1974 AEA convention and undertook
the editing of this *Festschrift*.

R.T.M.
P.D.Q.
Washington, D.C., 1976

Essays on
Industrial
Organization
in Honor of
Joe S. Bain

Chapter 1

Bain's Influence on Research
ir   zation

W *Copy pgs*

1 - 17

' inside

Core 3

Book.

I. INTRODUCTION

It is a happy tradition in *Festschrifts* to define, admire, and celebrate the senior scholar's imprint on the field. If the scientific effect has been large, as in the present case, the writer's task is especially agreeable. Yet the form of the ultimate contribution can take many years to emerge, and that is also true in the case of Professor Bain's work.

To many of his students and colleagues, Joe S. Bain's contribution to the scientific study of industrial organization may seem to lie mainly in the concepts of entry barriers and limit pricing. I will suggest that his accomplishment has been larger, when one considers three levels at which research contributions can be made. Ultimately, Bain's legacy is likely to be the power of his exacting standards and scope of mind, rather than his stress on individual elements in that structure.[a]

I first summarize Bain's scientific work and then place it in context of the larger evaluation of the field. Next, I assess his scientific influence on three levels: (1) individual concepts and methods, (2) the framework of the field, and (3) standards of scientific rigor in theory and testing.

Bain's basic work on industrial organization is closely focused, and the main

---

[a]I deal here only with Bain's central work on the core of industrial organization. His broader writings on price theory, and his specialized studies of individual industries, are beyond my concern in this chapter. They are a large body of work, distinctive and varied. Though I suggest here that Bain has had a considerable scientific effect, this is not meant to belittle the many contributions of other major contemporaries of his. They have influenced scientific research into industry; they have also developed the many other parts of the whole field, including policy analysis (antitrust, regulation, and other), sector studies, international comparisons, and others.

ideas have become familiar to everyone who labors seriously in the field.[b] In trying to assess the scientific effect of the main lines of this work, I am not pretending to evaluate its "worth"; perhaps Bain would be the first to label my evaluation positive rather than normative. The question is, "How has Bain changed the scientific character of the field of industrial organization?" In this *Festschrift* we have a suitable occasion for a sympathetic appraisal.

Bain has always turned aside from fads and fancies in his pursuit of fundamental analysis. To appraise his effect is, in part, to take stock on the whole lasting framework and standards of the field. The field has evolved rapidly and in new directions in recent years. A review of Bain's contributions may help clarify the more basic concept and methods, at a time when many of them are under debate.

II. BAIN'S ANALYSIS, WITHIN THE EVOLUTION OF THE FIELD

Bain's Analysis

From the body of Bain's work one gains the impression that his primary effort has been to refine the analysis of the form and behavior of the oligopoly group within an industry. The industry is assumed to be definable, with established firms residing inside and others—including potential entrants—left clearly outside.[c] Technology determines the cost conditions and selling processes in the industry as a whole, though specific firms may also have specific "absolute" advantages.

Conditions affecting the entry of new competitors will influence not only the degree of concentration but also the resulting degree of monopoly and of monopoly profits. Bain gave various properties of this system an intensive analysis, especially economies of scale, entry barriers, and limit pricing. His analysis was also complete, embracing the emerging (and now conventional) three-level system in which technical factors determine structure, and then structure influences behavior and performance.

Figure 1–1 presents this set of relationships in the form that has become the consensus in the field.[d] The analysis is static; the given determinants shape the

[b]Several of his articles are collected in *Essays on Price Theory and Industrial Organization* (1972). The main books are *Barriers to New Competition* (1956), *Industrial Organization*, 2nd ed. (1968), and *International Differences in Industrial Structure* (1966). See References at end of book.

[c]Not all markets are neatly definable—in fact, most are not—as Bain recognized. His empirical work carefully selected industries that were relatively distinct. Yet his theoretical analysis does require a clear distinction between competitors inside the markets' edges and potential competitors outside.

[d]The structure-behavior-performance triad is often ascribed to Edward S. Mason. See Jesse W. Markham and Gustav E. Papanek, eds., *Industrial Organization and Economic Development, In Honor of E.S. Mason* (1970), and the references given there, including Bain's chapter. For recent restatements of it, see F.M. Scherer, *Industrial Market Structure*

Figure 1—1. The Structure-Behavior-Performance Triad

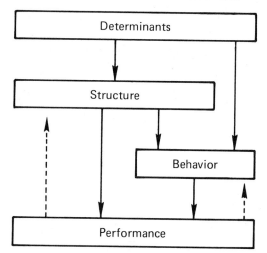

outcome. (They shape it within a range—in a probabalistic sense—not rigidly.) Bain's analysis is also mainly structuralist, though he also gave extensive—and creative—analysis of the behavior of oligopolists. Conduct included much variety, but its main forms and the range of its outcomes were shaped by structure.

Earlier Studies

Some of these concepts had been advanced and gained currency by 1900—for example, economies of scale (technical and pecuniary), varieties of pricing behavior, potential competition, and the normative properties of competition.[e] Empirical studies were less advanced. Yet official and unofficial studies and various antitrust cases had by 1930 created a rich store of evidence about leading American industries.[f] The dominant firm—both as a concept and as an industrial

---

and Economic Performance (1970), and W.G. Shepherd, *The Treatment of Market Power* (1975). The consensus now hypothesizes causality in both directions, though primarily downward in Figure 1—1.

[e]See the review article by Almarin Phillips and Rodney E. Stevenson, "The Historical Development of Industrial Organization" (1974). Bain's main precursors include the following: On oligopoly, F.Y. Edgeworth (1925) had treated the basic issues by 1897. On potential competition, John Bates Clark (1907) had stressed that dominant firms might be kept powerless by potential entrants. Charles J. Bullock (1901) showed that discussion of economies of scale was already advanced—though often misleading—by 1900. John Maurice Clark (1923) carried the analysis much further. The optimizing role of competition was, of course, standard fare in neoclassical works from 1870 on, including especially Alfred Marshall's *Principles of Economics* (1890). Important works by Bain's immediate predecessors include Edward H. Chamberlin, *The Theory of Monopolistic Competition* (1933); Joan Robinson, *The Economics of Imperfect Competition* (1933); E.A.G. Robinson, *The Structure of Competitive Industry* (1935); and P. Sargent Florence, *The Logic of Industrial Organization* (1933). For a valuable survey, see Robert E. Kuenne (1967).

[f]Among such "case studies" were the Bureau of Corporation's excellent work on the oil, tobacco, steel and farm machinery industries, among others. The FTC also produced a serie⁰

fact—was a major subject. Its extreme form, the supposed "natural monopoly," had become an important topic in its own right, as a focus for the study and regulation of "utility" firms.

But, during 1925–1940, as the field now known as "industrial organization" took form, attention shifted to the industry and the oligopoly group within it. In making this redirection, Sraffa, Robinson, Chamberlin (especially), Mason, and others profoundly changed the content of the field. By 1940 attention had shifted to oligopoly—the intermediate range of partial monopoly, with endless varieties of pricing and strategic behavior—as the central problem.[g] By 1950 Von Neumann and Morgenstern, and Fellner had extended the issues, increasing the preoccupation with group behavior.[h] The series of industry studies by Mason's circle of students at Harvard was well under way.[i] Two collective volumes neatly reflect the shape of the field as it had evolved by the early 1950s.[j]

Statistical tests of some hypotheses began in the 1930s, powerfully encouraged by new official sources of data on cost and concentration, covering a wide cross-section of industries.[k] Economies of scale, the rigidity of oligopoly prices, and the concentration-profits relationship were put to a variety of tests and much sharp debate. The Census disclosure rules helped to narrow the focus of attention to an industry basis, because the data for less than four firms were (and still are) locked up and the key thrown away. Scientific tests of hypotheses about concentration and its effects became technically much easier; studying dominant firms remained difficult and was soon neglected.

Bain's Role
In the 1930s Joe Bain entered a field which was in flux, rich in possibilities for giving new rigor to older concepts, for developing new ones, and for shaping

---

of studies beginning in the 1920s. There were also such broader sources as John Moody's *The Truth About the Trusts* (1904), and William Z. Ripley's (ed.) *Trusts, Pools and Corporations* (1916). Official investigations in the 1930s also generated a vast amount of material; the TNEC was only one among the largest of these.

[g]See the articles by J.H. Clapham, A.C. Pigou, F.H. Knight, P. Sraffa, and J. Viner, reprinted two to three decades later in G.J. Stigler and K.E. Boulding, eds., *Readings in Price Theory* (1952). J.M. Clark's, Robinson's and E.S. Mason's work did not narrow the focus to oligopoly, retaining instead a concern for a broader variety of market types.

[h]John von Neumann and Oskar Morgenstern, *Theory of Games and Economic Behavior* (1944), and William J. Fellner, *Competition Among the Few* (1949). G.J. Stigler, among others, remained sceptical of oligopoly analysis; see *Five Lectures on Economic Problems* (1950).

[i]Of course, on this list we find Bain himself with his three-volume study *The Economics of the Pacific Coast Petroleum Industry* (1945). Others have included Jesse Markham on the rayon industry (1952); Carl Kaysen on *U.S. v. United Shoe Machinery* (1956); Samuel Loescher on the cement industry (1959); James McKie on the tin cans and tin plate industry (1959); Morris Adelman on A & P (1959); Richard Caves on air transport (1962); and Merton J. Peck on the aluminium industry (1961). There are, of course, many other excellent industry studies, and Simon Whitney's two-volume survey of antitrust policies (1958) should be noted.

[j]E.H. Chamberlin, ed., *Monopoly and Competition and Their Regulators* (1954), and G.J. Stigler, ed., *Business Concentration and Price Policy* (1955).

the framework. That has been his main role and contribution. Though he did not create concepts, nor indeed the framework, he selected among them and carried their scientific analysis further than anyone else.

The analysis grew after 1940 in a series of articles and chapters, culminating in *Barriers to New Competition* in 1956 and *Industrial Organization* in 1959. Throughout, the scientific level was high and the approach objective. His analysis was verbal rather than mathematical. Theory was developed by an intensive discussion of the main elements in the system, distinguishing between normal and abnormal variants. Statistical tests, likewise, focused on simple and direct relationships rather than complex forms and advantages. Like a Ulysses S. Grant, Bain hammered relentlessly at the basic problems.

In the end, they have come to fit a distinctive and unified system that reflects his conception of the economic realities. That system relies, first, on categories. Bain began by drawing up lengthy classification systems for markets. His first outline, in 1942, was three pages long, including 126 entries arranged in five separate levels of detail. By 1951 his analysis of the conditions of entry ("other than that of easy entry") took this summary form:[1]

I. Conditions of entry which rest entirely or almost entirely on absolute-cost and product-differentiation advantages of established firms, with no significant economies of large scale.

   A. Where either the only or the greatest advantage is held approximately equally—by a few firms (entry being easy until they are in), and where

      1. The condition of entry, or excess of the entry-inducing price over minimal costs of these firms, remains the same through any progression of entry, and has
        a. A "low" value.
        b. A "medium" value.
        c. A "high" value.

      2. The condition of entry increases in value with a progression of entry because of differential advantages among potential entrants.

   B. Where either the only or the greatest advantage is held—approximately equally—by at least a moderately large but limited number of firms (entry being easy until they are in), and where the subcategories are as under A above.

II. Conditions of entry which rest almost entirely on economies of large scale, with no significant absolute cost or product-differentiation advantages to established firms—and where any advantage thus tends to

[k]For an excellent review of some of these early empirical studies, see G.J. Stigler (1955).

[1]At pages 85–86 of the *Essays* volume (1972), reprinting his main articles and chapters. This is a convenient source for citing as well as for reading.

be shared by all firms in the industry at any stage. (A provisionally assumed behavior-pattern is that all entrant firms retain their identity and share the market with previously established firms—i.e., there are no rationalizing mergers to counteract the effects of entry.)

. . .

Mixed cases will not be outlined in detail, but may be considered in conjunction with the simple cases.

Bain always recognized that the relationships were probably smoothly variable rather than cut into categories, and his more mature works rely less on such qualitative listings and divisions. Yet classifications remain important in his writings, especially in his empirical work on barriers, scale economies, profitability, degrees of concentration, and changes in concentration. And such taxonomy has value and force because it sets forth complete systems.

In 1949 Bain narrowed his focus cleanly to the limit pricing hypothesis.[m] The dominant firm(s) can choose to keep its market position by setting price just below the entry-inducing level. Ever cautious, Bain first limited his formal analysis "to oligopolies with relatively slight product differentiation," and later, mainly to oligopoly. Others have made this focus more rigid, treating pricing simply as something done by undifferentiated oligopolists (e.g., in steel, glass, chemicals, and similar industries). Yet Bain's initial discussion clearly included monopolies and dominant firms among those who might try variants of limit pricing.

Bain then turned to two empirical tests on his way to developing entry barriers and limit pricing as important concepts. One test covered technical economies of scale at the plant and multiplant level in twenty industries. A creative study requiring a mass of detail, this research pioneered the direct evaluation of scale economies. Its specific estimates are still of great value. The second test related industry structure (and especially concentration) to profitability. By 1951, then—when he was 39—Bain had formulated the main distinctive parts of his analysis and had begun testing their real world dimensions. (By this time he had also completed *Pricing, Distribution and Employment*, first copyrighted in 1948.)

Bain then prepared estimates of the height of entry barriers in the twenty industries, accompanied by an elaborate discussion of the phenomena he referred to as the conditions of entry. *Barriers to New Competition* in 1956 presented the finished system, combining the analytical and empirical parts. The emphasis on barriers was continued in the more comprehensive *Industrial Organization* (1959), which also devoted several chapters to policy issues.

Yet the range of theory and evidence in both books was much wider than barriers alone. It included scale economies, profitability, and other key concepts

---

[m] "Pricing in Monopoly and Oligopoly," *American Economic Review* (March 1949), reprinted at pp. 58–73 of *Essays* (1972).

and points of methodology. Even for those less engrossed in barriers and limit pricing, Bain offered a wealth of analysis and factual data, all fitting within a consistent system. This wider view was evident in Bain's later works, including *International Differences in Industrial Structure* (1966), where barriers were not treated separately as critically important.

Bain did not hesitate to draw policy conclusions. The most direct one was that actual concentration in many markets was greater than could be justified by technical economies of scale. This major set of findings—which was prepared and published in the 1950s, when a cult of bigness was flourishing—has not been shaken.[n] More recent studies have confirmed both Bain's methodology and his results.[o]

By 1959, Bain had selected and built up a distinctive set of concepts and tested them with an unusual intensity of detail. His objectives (as stated in 1972) were reflected in the work:[p]

> This development emphasizes applying economic analysis to empirical data, the origination and elaboration of related theory, its restatement in forms susceptible to empirical refutation, the empirical testing of resultant theoretical hypotheses, and a "wedding" of theoretical and empirical approaches to the study of firms and markets.

The system was thoroughly static, with some comparative statics. Change was only a frictional transition to equilibrium, rather than a process whose properties were of central importance. Preconditions determined the main lines of performance. Analysis consisted of logic and a mature good sense, applied intensively to a few basic propositions. Statistical evidence was grouped and compared, after Bain had given extensive effort to preparing the numbers themselves—often digit by digit.

There were none of the complex techniques, developed since the 1950s, which have sometimes applied strong apparatus to reams of weak data. Still, Bain had made oligopoly theory more operational for empirical research. Main elements had been singled out for testing by regression analysis. Instead of game theory indeterminacy, there was a set of testable hypotheses.

More Recent Study

Bain's contribution can also be evaluated in light of more recent work. The 1960s brought a growing mass of large scale econometric testing, some of it

[n]On the 1950s attitudes, see Mason's critical review, "The New Competition" (1957), and Kaysen and Turner (1959).

[o]See Scherer (1970), and Shepherd (1970). The most ambitious recent study follows much the same basic methodology as Bain's direct questionnaires and interviews. See F.M. Scherer et al. (1976).

[p]This passage is from Bain's *Essays* (1972), page vii, but the objectives are discussed, and are apparent, at many other places in Bain's writings.

sound and some not, and mostly relying heavily on concentration ratios.[q] More recently, younger specialists have begun exploring pure analytical modeling, which often yields clear-cut answers to major questions—e.g., the effect of vertical integration—but only within the compass of the model. This has provided interesting results on some dynamic questions.

A general rethinking of the elements of market structure is also now beginning. Some researchers have come to extend Bain's interest in barriers to a contention that they are exclusively the main element of structure. This in turn has invited a growing debate on the relative importance of market share, barriers, concentration, and other possible elements.[r] Since 1965, also, a hardy band of "Chicago school" analysts have begun an effort to establish (1) that market power does not exist, or at least does not last very long (unless it is officially supported); and (2) that all evidence relating structure to profitability really only reflects technical economies of scale rather than market power.[s]

None of this has really refuted Bain's work nor altered his basic contribution. The whole discussion has helped stir a rising interest in the process and rate of change in market structure, as distinct from conventional static conditions. This is probably the main present frontier for basic research in the field.

Finally, the scope of the field has broadened from the older manufacturing industrial issues to include—or reinclude—such other areas as utilities, public enterprise, externalities, and social enterprises (health care, education, etc.).[t]

Bain's work therefore has a certain vintage bouquet. Yet he treated the basic issues intensively, and it is these concepts of structure and performance which remain at the intellectual core of the field. It would take an upheaval in the very concepts of the topic to render obsolete Bain's specific additions to the field and his shaping of the frame work. Their vitality does not rest on his particular emphasis on barriers nor on the specific empirical findings he provided.

Bain entered a formative field in the 1930s; by the 1960s he had formed much of it. His special abilities—to explore basic concepts at length with both logic and a sense of reality, and to prepare evidence both creatively and painstakingly—fitted the peculiar needs of the field. From flux, Bain did much to impose order. In the process he set the standards of rigor, of objectivity and of balancing theory with facts that now give the subject coherence and quality. The

[q]See Leonard Weiss's review (1971) for an appraisal, especially, of profitability and technical change. Scherer's text (1970) also describes the research methodology and findings as they were in the late 1960s. See also my *Market Power and Economic Welfare* (1970).

[r]My reasons for refreshing the emphasis on the individual firm's market share rather than entry barriers or four-firm concentration ratios are given in Shepherd (1972, 1975).

[s]They are given generous space for debate in *Industrial Concentration: The New Learning* (Goldschmid et al., 1974). Their zeal and unity has no counterpart elsewhere among our colleagues, so their "findings" can be expected to gain prominence. In less professional quarters, such as *Fortune* Magazine and trade associations, they have already drawn much admiring comment for "revolutionizing the field" and "dispelling myths."

[t]The "public utility" literature had been particularly rich in the earlier period.

concepts, techniques, and evidence may all change, but much of the standards and wholeness of system will remain as Bain's contribution.

III. INDIVIDUAL CONCEPTS

So far I have discussed general points. To appreciate Bain's contribution properly, one must build up from more specific details. There are three levels on which Bain's scientific effect can be seen: (1) individual concepts, (2) the larger framework embracing those concepts, and (3) the methodology and standards with which concepts and framework are treated. I have suggested that the third level is the more enduring, for Bain and, generally, for all important scientists. The balance of this chapter presents more detail on these three levels, in order to define Bain's contribution carefully.

Bain's distinctive concepts—or areas of close study—include: (1) classifications of markets, (2) entry conditions and potential competition, (3) limit pricing, (4) scale economies, and (5) profitability. These were his selection from the abundance of elements and topics crowding in within the field. I will consider his treatment of them, and their lasting value, one by one.

1. Bain's *classification systems* were a natural response in the 1930s to the superabundance of conditions that oligopoly presented for analysis. The range of structures, behavior, and outcomes is virtually infinite. Needing, like all of us, to grasp and order the main conditions, Bain drew up some remarkably long taxonomic lists. This was an important first step to see the whole and its parts so that he could form priorities and concentrate on the more important elements. Having done that, Bain soon narrowed focus to scale economies, barriers, and limit pricing. Though classifications (including Bain's) are little used now in active research, they are an appropriate intellectual step for all specialists. Trivial analysis most often occurs when analysts have forgotten how complex the varieties can be.

2. *The conditions of entry* received Bain's most sustained examination. The basic idea is simple and direct. Barriers have three possible economic sources, which are, in Bain's own words (*Essays*, pp. 82–83):

1. Circumstances giving an absolute cost advantage to some or all established firms.
    a. Control of production techniques by established firms, via patents or secrecy, which permits exclusion of entrants from optimal techniques or the levying of a royalty charge for their use.
    b. Imperfections in the markets for hired factors (including materials) which favor established firms, or ownership or control by agreement of strategic factor supplies by such firms.

    c. Requirement by the entering firm of enough factors to cause their market price to rise significantly (linked to the need for large scale to gain efficiency).

    d. Money-market conditions imposing higher interest rates or severe rationing of investible funds on potential entrant firms.

2. Circumstances giving a product-differentiation advantage to some established firms.

    a. Patent control of superior product designs by established firms.

    b. The possible accumulative preference of buyers for established brand names and company reputations.

    c. Ownership or contractual control of favored distributive outlets by established firms.

3. Circumstances discouraging entry because of the size of an economical increment of entry.

    a. Real economies to the large-scale firm such that the optimal- and possibly smaller-scale firm will supply a significant share of the market.

    b. Strictly pecuniary economies of the same order. (The more steeply the scale curve falls toward the optimum level the greater the deterrent.)

4. Absolute legal prohibitions on entry.

Bain's elaboration of these conditions uses diagrams and explores a variety of real possibilities.

After an initial acceptance, barriers are under increasing debate.[u] All three categories of sources of barriers can be said to be efficiencies, which justify higher profits. Thus, in Figure 1–1, these determinants of structure would also have to be regarded as elements of performance (and possibly of structure itself). Yet how can cause also be effect? There is need for further analysis to disentangle causes and effects (and positive from normative criteria), if that is possible.

The definition of barriers as a single, unified, general phenomenon also needs work. "Sources" of barriers may proliferate so much that the concept of barriers loses unity. Since 1960, various new barriers "sources" have been proposed, such as R and D activity and vertical integration. One must apply Occam's Razor in

---

[u]Franco Modigliani showered them with praise in "New Developments on the Oligopoly Front" (1958). Bain incorporated them in *Industrial Organization* (1968). The obvious reality of some specific barriers (e.g., patents) helped smooth the way for acceptance of barriers as a general unified element of structure. Empirical studies have estimated the height of barriers and have provided some partial confirmation that they have effects on profitability. See Leonard Weiss's excellent, compendious review in *Industrial Concentration: The New Learning* (Goldschmid et al., 1974). My recent quantitative work provides a serious challenge to the primacy of barriers as an element (1972–1975). Yet this is negative "evidence" (a failure to confirm the role of barriers), so it cannot be conclusive. It may merely reflect the greater difficulty of measuring barriers—and thereby confirming their role—than other elements.

order to have a general concept. But what is to be included? If the sources proliferate, the concept of barriers could acquire just that ad hoc character which Bain frequently reproved in others' theories.

Measurement has also proved to be difficult. It requires a merging of disparate objective and subjective data about patents, cost advantages, capital requirements, advertising and other selling expenses, and the like. Also, the three or more sources of barriers may be reinforcing, or perhaps not; at some points Bain comments on this, but to no conclusion. This, too, remains an open issue. In short, the role and meaning of barriers are still open to a variety of interpretations and measures.

Still, Bain did treat barriers thoroughly, and he made strong efforts to estimate their height in a panel of industries. Ever cautious, he repeatedly pointed to the more complex surrounding issues that awaited analysis. Yet he may have carried the analysis of the basic ideas about as far as it can go.

3. *Limit pricing*, as Bain treated it, requires two parts: a firm or firms which consciously apply their strategy toward entry, and barriers for them to operate behind. Bain discussed the full range of strategies, from strict deterrence of entry to short term profit maximizing while inducing entry. It all hinges on long run expectations of the established firm(s) about entrants' behavior, and vice versa. The interactions among these expectations could grow very complicated. Bain focused on oligopolists as limit pricers. This is perhaps an improbable situation for analysis, for it assumes that collective strategy is adopted *and* that it is more important than the firms' own individual strategies. Yet oligopolists need not coordinate at all.

Also, Bain needed to assume that their attention and actions are directed primarily against such lesser threats as complete outsiders, rather than against smaller firms already in the industry, or against each other. Yet the analysis of limit pricing can easily cover individual dominant firms as well; indeed, it is more plausible in that direction. A single dominant firm with, say, 70 percent of the market, typically should have a more coherent policy than would four oligopolists with a combined share of 70 percent.

Bain drew the main conclusion clearly enough, and he pointed out the difficulties of empirical tests. In fact, estimation has been so difficult that the theory cannot be said to be established or "proved," nor perhaps can it ever be. "Limit pricing" actually defines a range of choice between short and long run profitability and market shares. It is a way of describing normal, rational, long run maximizing choices. One cannot *prove* that firms make such choices, though it seems likely that they do.

The subsequent theorizing by Baumol and many others about firm motivation, growth-profit choices, and the rest can help to clarify these choices.[v] Bain's

---

[v]Among this voluminous literature see W.J. Baumol (1959), and Oliver E. Williamson (1964), and references in those two sources.

"limit pricing" sets the scene, with strong assumptions that oligopolists set joint pricing policies and that barriers are important. Because it treats some of the most basic conditions, its continuing relevance is assured.

4. Bain's treatment of *scale economies* is distinctive in two ways. He measured them with great care, and he subsumed them in entry barriers. His measurement was pioneering, after an earlier series of cross-section tests by others. These earlier studies suffered from data problems and from a mingling of technical and pecuniary elements. Bain centered unerringly on technical economics. Thereby he gave the first solid normative basis for evaluating actual concentration.

The techniques were sound and the sample well chosen. With "only" twenty industries, Bain could go deeply into each one. By stratifying his group of industries, Bain included several leading cases (e.g., automobiles, oil, steel, cigarettes) as well as a variety of lesser types (e.g., fountain pens, canned fruits and vegetables). This gave study an especially close relevance for policy as well as for scientific importance.

By estimating "best practice" conditions of scale for new capacity, Bain neatly avoided the normative-positive confusion which infects cross-section studies of past costs and survivor tests of emerging sizes.[w] Bain's "engineering" estimates supply the normative basis for appraising how much concentration is socially "necessary." Actually, experienced executives may know efficient scale of plants and firms even better than their engineers. Bain used both as sources.[x] The whole exercise displayed a master's touch in welding concepts, opinions, and comparisons. The best subsequent work has used his methods, and has reached similar findings.

5. *Profitability* was also given a searching analysis by Bain. He focused on the patterns with normative content—several-year averages of returns on invested capital. Short of using multiple regressions (a laborious task in those precomputer days), Bain tried nearly every efficient method to factor out the concentration-profitability relationship. He averaged together the profitability of *all* firms in each industry, in line with his belief that oligopoly limit pricing behind entry barriers would set the degree of profitability for the entire industry.[y] This wide averaging has prevailed in many subsequent studies, though some research has also focused down to leading-firm groups and individual market shares.[z]

[w]See my "What Does the Survivor Test Show About Economics of Scale?" (1967), and Joe S. Bain, "Survival-Ability as a Test of Efficiency" (1972, pp. 158–165).

[x]Bain "supplemented" his direct sources with a mass of information from industry, financial, academic, and governmental studies. Never a prisoner of his methods, Bain artfully used all credible sources to reach mature findings.

[y]More precisely, his data usually centered on the larger firms, but the theory held that the price set by the leading firms would influence profitability throughout the industry.

[z]Weiss's survey in Goldschmid et al. (1974) is the most thorough recent appraisal of the many studies.

In his 1951 article (later extended in *Barriers*), Bain put the study of profitability on a firm scientific and normative basis. His findings of a step function, with a break at 70 percent for eight-firm concentration, has tended to be replaced in recent research by a continuously sloping concentration-profitability relationship.[aa] Still, Bain set the basis for all good later research on the subject. Moreover, his main conclusion—that concentration does yield excess profits—has been sustained by later work. It has also withstood the recent Chicagoite claims that (1) no such relationship exists, or (2) if it does, it only reflects scale economies.

These five are only the main concepts among many that Bain developed in putting the analysis of industry in a consistent form. His characteristic treatment included: (1) extended discussion of the basic analytical features of the concept; (2) estimation of the main empirical lines, using painstakingly prepared data; (3) a clear focus on normative content, as well as positive issues; and (4) caution in showing how much still remained unknown.

IV. BAIN'S CHOICES IN HIS FRAMEWORK

The way Bain combined these elements into his "system"—his architectural choices in using and emphasizing individual elements—also shows a distinctive personal touch. On this plane, three features stand out—the triad, the industry basis, and the stress on the oligopoly group behind an entry barrier.

1. Bain used and developed Mason's triad of structure, behavior, and performance with what may be called a "structuralist" emphasis. No bias has resulted from this focus; spirited work by the ranks of ardent "behaviorists" have seen to that. Indeed, Bain's stress on structure-performance connections helped to set the field firmly on the scientific analysis of measurable conditions. Here again, Bain's special interest and technical skills happily fitted the needs of the growing field. The triad can be adjusted, weighted, and made more sophisticated in many ways. Bain drove it deep into the bedrock of the subject. It can also be reduced to a mere cookbook formula for specific industry studies. Bain's own work is a standing reproach to such rote research. He used it as a broad set of concepts, by which the whole subject (theory, tests, policy lessons) is organized, not as just a format for individual cases.

2. Bain used the industry as the basic unit of behavior. This seemed perfectly natural in the new setting of the 1930s, but it was a choice that shaped the images and methodology in distinctive ways.[bb] It accords with the focus on

[aa]See Weiss in Goldschmid et al. (1974). Yet the true relationship could still be stair step, at least in some types of oligopoly if not in all.

[bb]Chamberlin's *Monopolistic Competition* (1933) was the obvious leader in this direction, as noted earlier, and the new abundance of industry data on concentration, etc., accen-

oligopoly and on entry barriers; indeed, these concepts are mutually dependent parts. If there are not clear, definable industries, then there can scarcely be a limit pricing stragegy toward potential entrants. It is the concept of the industry that permits one to speak of the barriers around it and of "potential entrants" as distinct from all "established" firms, large and small.

More recently, a number of us have found the industry basis confining. The firm is, after all, the most basic building block, and firms within industries often have strikingly different structural positions, behavior, and performance.[cc] Yet the field has benefited from Bain's stress on the industry. It gives correct form to many issues of market power, economies of scale, pricing behavior, and their effects.

3. The oligopoly group, setting limit price strategy behind an entry barrier, came to be a distinctive part of Bain's analysis. As of 1949–50, Bain regarded concentration as the key determinant of market power and profitability.[dd]

> The hypothesis in brief is that the average profit rate of firms in oligopolistic industries of a high concentration will tend to be significantly larger than that of firms in less concentrated oligopolies or in industries of atomistic structure. Firms in oligopolies of high seller concentration will tend to earn higher profit rates than all others.

Yet by 1951 he appeared to have shifted to barriers as the decisive element, which could be both necessary and sufficient to govern profitability. When barriers are absent then there could be no excess profits, even for a pure monopolist.[ee]

> In homogeneous-product markets with easy entry, established firms can never concurrently raise price above their own (identical) optimum-scale average costs without attracting entry; as a corollary, therefore, long-run excess profits cannot be earned without attracting entry. In

---

tuated it. Though Georgescu-Roegen (1967) notes that Chamberlin stressed the role of the firm in defining the product, the whole impact was instead to place oligopoly and its industrywide effects at the center of the analysis.

[cc]See my *The Treatment of Market Power* (1975), for discussion and evidence on the matter.

[dd]At page 31 of *Essays* (1972), "The major distinction, it may be emphasized, is not between industries of oligopolistic and atomistic structure, but between the more highly concentrated oligopolies and all other industries." (Note 5, 1972, p. 31).

[ee]In his paper for the International Economic Association collection (Chamberlin, 1954). The shift in emphasis must be read subjectively from the weights and treatment of these topics. In his article on the "Relation of Profit Rate to Industry Concentration" in 1951, he briefly mentions that the profit maximum to be attained depends upon the "conditions of entry" (*Essays*, p. 31). And on the third page of *Barriers to New Competition* he states that "actual competition among existing sellers is . . . of first importance as a regulator of business activity." But the primary focus of his view seems to shift during this period.

differentiated-product markets with easy entry, established firms can never raise their prices above the slightly higher-than-minimal average-cost levels . . . excess profits cannot be earned without attracting entry.

Conversely, if barriers were high, excess profits could arise regardless of the inner structure of the market:

The derived property of the existence of any or all of these barriers to entry is that established firms will be able to charge a price significantly above some or all of their own minimal average costs without attracting further entry, and may be able—in fact, probably will be able—at the same time to make an excess profit.

Bain elsewhere suggested frequently that barriers would be highly correlated with the degree of concentration. *In fact, all three sources of barriers—scale economies, product differentiation, and exclusive control of patents, mineral rights, or capital market advantages—are also sources of high market shares and concentration.* Do barriers shape the dominant firm's share, which then determines the degree of monopoly and profitability? Or do they operate jointly? If so, are they additive or parallel? The issues are partly a matter of definition, and partly of semantics; they also require care in hypothesizing cause and effect. The closer one analyzes them, the weaker grows the distinction between barriers and internal elements of structure.

Bain seemed at times to put barriers at center stage, but subsequent theory and testing have left their role more open. Some of Bain's younger colleagues have carried barriers further than Bain did. For them, nearly all industrial outcomes are determined by barriers, and the remainder is settled by "mutual dependence recognized." In response to this, a natural reaction has been to deny that barriers have primacy or, perhaps, even real content or measurability. This view may have a degree of validity. Barriers are not, after all, derived from conventional micro-economic theory. To focus on potential competition at the edges is to risk ignoring the main reality at the center—actual competition.

The issue is important and basic. Since 1950 the field has had an abundance of elements of structure. Mainly they have been concentration, barriers, and the older concept of the individual firm's market share.[ff] Bain has seen this clearly, and he has led in the effort to focus attention on the main elements. The growing efforts since 1965 to establish the priority among these elements may, if we are fortunate, clarify the true priorities on a scientific basis. As the research proceeds, one hopes that Bain's example of objectivity and care will prevail.

[ff]There has also been the growing effort by some to demonstrate that *no* structural elements are important. If this were true, the relative priority issue would not matter. But to test such absolute importance, one must use models that correctly fit the relative priorities. Therefore, the two issues are entwined, and "proofs" that no effect exists may be invalid because they center on the wrong individual elements. (They may also simply contain measurement error.) In short, the relative priority question is inevitably a basic one.

Any eventual resolution will probably assign barriers at least a significant role, thanks to Bain's stress on them. He put the concepts and relationships in testable form, and he began the testing of them. To a large extent he rescued the subject from a preoccupation with oligopoly interactions and games, and he gave it a strong framework.

All three of these architectural features—the structure–behavior–performance triad, the industry basis, and the stress on limit pricing and entry barriers—are likely to remain important. The natural process is for them to be modified as the field evolves. Indeed, there is already a growing variety of approaches in using these tools and in trying alternatives to them.

IV. RESEARCH STANDARDS AND METHODS

Bain's most durable contribution lies deeper, in the methods and research standards of the field. He entered a subject at its formative period, when it had an abundance of possibilities—some of them fertile, others barren or trivial—and a tendency toward woolly definitions, casual research, and the grinding of axes.

By 1960, and almost single-handedly, he had given it structure, precision, and high standards of research quality. Concepts were to receive extended analysis, with attention to their relative importance and real world plausibility. Empirical testing was to be rigorous, combining objective methods with care in preparing the data. Yet research was to be mature and artful, not chained to any single source or technique. Further, Bain's joinder of theory and practice was firmly set on normative foundations. Scientific research was directed toward the policy questions that mattered.

It would be hard to overstate the value of the contribution. The subject has such great real world importance that the flow of propaganda and paid "research" will always be strong; in some areas it is well-nigh overwhelming. The topic also seems to breed doctrinal zeal and fads. The number of researchers are small, the "facts" are often treacherous, and bright ideas abound. To contain these pressures toward anarchic confusion, the field needs selectivity, a clear framework, and rigorous research standards. It also needs a fairminded maturity of judgment.

That is precisely what Bain fixed firmly in the field of industrial organization. He selected the main concepts and relationships, gave them extended analysis, tested them, and drew policy lessons. The individual parts were firmly related within a framework of causation and performance. His theorizing went beyond the currently available data; that is another way in which a field develops and matures. In some cases Bain then proceeded to prepare new measures; in others, testing has come later or is still in the future.

Throughout Bain's work, inferior methods and data were rejected, problems and weaknesses were unsparingly brought out, and results were interpreted conservatively. At times Bain also evaluated others' work critically, but the main force of his quality standards was directed at his own tests. His example will continue to set the standard for subsequent theorizing and empirical studies.

His more specific methods and results have also continued to be valid *because* they met these standards. The clearest instances of this are his research into scale economies, entry barriers, oligopoly pricing, and the structure-profitability relationship. His tests were not the first nor the last, but their research quality is unlikely to be bettered.

Beyond the individual concepts and tests is the fact that they fit together in a system, and that this system was rigorously developed and tested. That is the way to scientific permanence. It is especially on this basic plane that we and our successors are lasting beneficiaries of Joe Bain's scientific contribution.

 *Chapter 2*

Has the United States a Dual Economy?

Edward S. Mason

The literature on the conditions of economic growth in less developed countries makes considerable use of the concept of economic dualism. In its original formulation, by Boeke (1953) and Furnivall (1948), dualism was seen as a cultural phenomenon.[a] One segment of society, the traditional segment, is characterized by values, motivations, institutions, work habits, and social interrelations quite different from those in the modern sector governed by western ideas.

In Boeke's view the techniques of economic analysis useful in the modern sector had little or no applicability in the traditional sector:

> . . . western economic doctrines are not, or are only partly, applicable in the East; money, capital, markets, price formation, division of labor, competition, the growth of trade and enterprise, of trade cycles, and so forth—in short all the important problems of western economic theory—do not present themselves, or at most do so only partly and imperfectly to eastern society (1953, p. 11).

Boeke's model was Indonesia in the period before World War II and the contrasting sectors were the traditional Indonesian society and Dutch colonial capital-

Most of the contributions to *Festshrifts* come from admiring young former students. This is from an admiring old former teacher. Perhaps this will become the fashion in an age of zero population growth, increasing longevity, and an impending gerontocracy. If this is so, I am happy to be an early trend setter. Joe Bain was one of the first of my graduate students and one of the best. He made his mark early and has continued to produce without visible diminution. It is to be expected that, in time, he will contribute scholarly essays in celebration of the retirement of his own graduate students.

[a]Boeke's theories were first presented in his doctoral dissertation in 1908.

ism. Furnivall's study contrasted the traditional Burmese sector with British capitalism.

Other writers have stressed a technological dualism emphasizing the distinction between capital intensive, technologically progressive methods of produc- in one sector, and traditional, labor intensive, relatively unchanging methods in another. To some, a fundamental distinction is between a self-sufficient production-for-use, nonmonetized area and a monetized, market dominated sector. But whether the emphasis has been placed on one or a number of differences, there has been general agreement that dualism is a significant economic phenomenon affecting not only the process of growth but the types of analysis relevant to the study of this process.

To Dudley Seers, neoclassical economics is the economics of a "special case," concerned with the behavior of advanced economies and applicable, if at all, only in part to the conditions of less developed economies: "The major inadequacies of conventional economics for those dealing with the typical case are that analysis focuses on the wrong factors, and the models do not fit at all closely the way in which non-industrial economies operate" (1963, p. 83). The theories of growth espoused by Arthur Lewis, Ranis and Fei, and a number of others envisage a modern, capitalist, market oriented sector of the economy expanding by drawing in surplus labor from the traditional sector where the marginal product of labor is, or is close to, zero. Adelman and Morris, in their study of the growth process in a large number of less developed countries (1967), make the impact of dualism one of the significant elements in their factor analysis.

> In classifying countries with respect to the extent of dualism, we have attempted to rank them on a scale, one pole of which is the largest agrarian society having an extremely small exchange sector and the other pole of which is the incipient stage of economic maturity in which continuous interaction between modern and nonmodern elements in the economic system is a pervasive phenomenon (p. 23).

There is, I think, general agreement among development economists that dualism, whether defined eclectically or with special emphasis on particular factors, is characteristic of a large number of less developed countries and that it has a significant bearing on the process of growth. Although there are significant differences of opinion among these specialists on the extent to which conventional economic analysis can be usefully applied in the traditional sectors of dual economics, there is no difference in the view that substantial modification and adaptation is required. At a minimum it can be said that in an economy in which factors are relatively immobile and the hold of custom is strong, demand and supply functions are apt to be much less elastic than in advanced economies.

The absence of well organized markets and sizeable enterprises and the existence of feudal land systems and social barriers of various kinds present a range of problems relatively unknown to conventional economics. We do not need to go as far as Boeke and Furnivall in denying the operation of economic incentives in the traditional sector to recognize that the differences between the traditional and modern are significant elements to be taken into account in any analysis of the growth process in less developed countries.

A number of writers have, during the last few years, advanced the proposition that there is at least an incipient dualism between the world of the large firm and the rest of the economy in the United States and perhaps in other advanced capitalist economies. Robert Averitt emphasizes "the distinction between center firms and periphery firms, the two disparate types of business organization comprising what I call the dual economy." And he goes on to say, "Center firms differ from periphery firms in terms of economic size, organizational structure, industrial location, factor endowment, time perspective, and market concentration" (1968, p. 1). In his view, a different type of economic analysis is needed to explain differences in the behavior of firms in these two sectors of the economy.

A segment of recent writing on the theory of the firm goes at least part way in this direction. Baumol, Marris, Penrose, and a number of others contrast the entrepreneurial controlled, profit maximizing firm of conventional theory with the large scale enterprise in which management pursues objectives other than profits. In their view the objective of corporate management is to maximize the rate of growth of the firm subject to a constraint imposed by the necessity of earning enough to sustain the position of the firm in capital markets. Others emphasize organizational differences and contrast the actions of the individual entrepreneur with the group decision making of the entrepreneurial firm.

As Winter points out, there are in effect two strands of thought in the attack on the conventional theory of the firm:

> The first, or "managerial," strand emphasizes the fact that the large size, diffused stock ownership, and market power of the modern corporation leave the management with significant freedom to pursue its own goals, which are not correctly represented as maximization of profits on behalf of the stockholders. The second, or "behavioral," strand emphasizes the orthodox theory's neglect of the character of the decision processes in individual firms, and argues essentially that this neglect is so serious as to make the theory unreliable for all but the crudest predictions (1971, p. 237).

Although these two strands lead in the same direction on a number of issues, they do not both support the claims of dualism. That is the prerogative of the managerial school. The behaviorists, on the other hand, see organization as affecting the actions of firms of all sizes. "Satisficing" is a rule for large and small. Rules-of-thumb decision making rather than the equating of marginal costs and revenues is a consequence of uncertainties and environmental complexities for all firms. As Simon put it:

> ... to predict the short-run behavior of an adaptive organism, or its behavior in a complex and rapidly changing environment, it is not enough to know its goals. We must also know a great deal about its internal structure and particularly its mechanisms of adaptation (1959, p. 250).

Size, to be sure, makes a difference in organization. But organization is too varied an element to be comprised in any concept of dualism. Only large multi-product firms, it is true, are apt to adopt the decentralized multidivisional form of organization so effectively analyzed by Chandler (1962). But many large firms do not operate under this form of organization. And, as Williamson (1971) rather persuasively argues, the decentralized, multidivisional type of organization, by lessening the area of discretion open to division managers, tends to create a central office primarily concerned with ownership interests.

The supposed gap between the behavior of the large firm and the conventional small enterprise may well be lessened rather than increased in this form of organization. It is the managerial strand of the attack on the conventional theory of the firm that points more directly toward dualism. Although he does not use the term, J.K. Galbraith has developed by far the most explicit formulation of such a dualistic hypothesis. In his *Economics and the Public Purpose* (1973), the world of the large firm is categorized as the "planning system" and sharply distinguished from the "market system" that comprises the rest of the economy.

The firm in the planning system is quite a different entity from the firm in the market system. It employs different technologies and operates on quite a different scale. Shaping the market for its product rather than responding to the market, relatively independent of external sources of capital, and assured of necessary inputs through vertical integration or long term contacts, it operates through management concensus rather than individual decision making, with the managerial group in control by virtue of a monopoly of the necessary information regardless of how concentrated the ownership. It is controlled by a management with interests of its own divergent from those of ownership; and behaves in ways that are not susceptible to explanation by conventional techniques of economic analysis.

If we can accept the Galbraithian description of the American economy as approximately accurate, it is indeed a dualism in the strict sense that the literature on the economic development of less developed areas uses the term. Two quite different and relatively separate sectors of the economy are discerned, each obeying its own and relatively distinct economic laws.

It is interesting that this concept of the American economy has begun to move into the textbooks. In his *Economics of the Firm: Theory and Practice*, Arthur A. Thompson, Jr. writes:

As things now stand in the ongoing development of American capitalism, the business sector has evolved into a composite of two essentially distinct sectors. On the one hand there is the sector populated with millions of small firms run by a single individual or family and producing a limited range of products for limited markets. On the other there is the sector made up of 750 to 800 massively capitalized, technologically dynamic, multi-million dollar corporations with thousands of employees, a complex organizational structure, and a diversified set of products (1973, p. 22).

He uses the Averitt terms "center" and "peripheral" for describing firms in these two sectors.

The question is, how much of this description can be accepted? It differs rather markedly from the more conventional view that there is a more continuous gradation from one-man enterprises to firms of the largest size, firms that are interrelated with each other in a complex variety of market and administrative arrangements. As Richard Caves puts it:

The gleaming glass and metal home of Union Carbide Corporation on New York's Park Avenue enfolds one kind of business important in the American economy; the elderly gentleman standing before it, selling roasted chestnuts from his pushcart, typifies another. Between the Davids and Goliaths of American private enterprise lie five million incredibly diverse individual business units (1973, p. 1).

Kaysen and Turner, whose study of antitrust policy (1959) concentrates on the world of the large firm, see plenty of diversity in this world. They distinguish national from regional markets, firms operating in the areas of manufacture, mining, and distribution, various degrees of structural concentration on both the sellers' and buyers' sides of the market, markets for investment goods, industrial material inputs, consumers durables and nondurables; and then they consider the consequences of various types of entry barriers and other relevant factors. If the dualistic thesis were to be taken seriously, the field of industrial organization to which Joe Bain has contributed so much and in which, at one time, I had a certain interest, would have to be considered irrelevant and immaterial. Perhaps that is one reason I react so strongly against the concept as a useful contribution to the analysis of the American economy. But I do not think it is the only reason.

There are, of course, useful distinctions to be made in analyzing the American or any other economy. The econometricians flaunt their two-sector, four-sector, and *n*-sector models. There are significant differences among the agricultural, manufacturing, public utility, and banking sectors, and economic specialization has emphasized—perhaps overemphasized—these differences. There are also differences between the behavior of large organizations and small organizations worth taking into account in all these areas. But these differences do not, in my view, add up to anything that could be appropriately described as a dualism. There is too much diversity within the large scale and small scale sectors, and too much similarity between them.

The impact of the large firm on economic analysis first surfaced in its effects of the structure of markets. Although Cournot, in his treatment of monopoly and duopoly, had talked of mineral springs rather than large firms, the significance of monopoly in the economy began to be seen only with the rise of the large scale corporate enterprise in the late nineteenth century. Under the guidance of Chamberlin and Robinson, monopoly elements were seen to be present in practically all markets, whether occupied by small or large firms, but oligopoly emerged as the characteristic market form for large scale enterprise. The Chamberlin-Robinson formulation led to numerous attempts to classify markets, in the course of which it became clear that the inclusion of *all* elements of structure that might affect business conduct was an unproductive task.

There emerged from these attempts a rough consensus on the elements that appeared to be of prime significance. Caves' summarization (1973), which differs little from that of other writers in the field, stresses seller and buyer concentration, product differentiation, barriers to entry, growth rate, and price elasticity of market demand. Other elements could be and have been added; Joe Bain has contributed more than anyone else to an operational definition and measurement of these elements.

In the meantime there developed that other necessary input to the field of industrial organization, the theory of the firm. R.A. Gordon (1945) and Berle and Means (1932) were the early innovators. The large firm was seen to be typically a unit, characterized by group decision making, with the possibility of fairly sharp differences in the interests and objectives of members of the group. The fragmentation of ownership and the use of various financial and managerial devices appeared to place control firmly in the hands of mangement. And the various ways in which large firms could be, and were, organized might well have a bearing on conduct. As noted earlier, a behavioral theory of the firm centering on questions of organization was developed, particularly at the hands of Simon, Cyert, and March. And a managerial theory resting mainly on the separation of ownership and control was shaped by a host of writers.

The large firm, then, enters industrial organization analysis as an entity characterized by fairly well established sets of possible external and internal relationships. In the manufacturing, mining, and public utility sectors, moreover, the conduct of these firms is typically influenced by a technology which is capital intensive and in which capital commitments are long term and relatively inflexible. But the use of this technology is by no means limited to firms of large size. And it is not characteristic of the large firms in the area of distribution.

What are the limits to this segment of the economy embracing the large firm? According to Schumpeter, economic progress in the United States "is largely the result of work done within a number of concerns at no time greater than 300–400 . . ." (1939, II, p. 1044). *Fortune* has its 500 largest American corporations and 300 largest international corporations. Thompson, following Averitt, mentions ". . . 750 to 800 massively capitalized technologically dynamic, multimillion dollar corporations. . . ." Williamson, who is not an exponent of economic dualism, puts 500 industrials, 50 utilities and 50 transportation companies in his "large firm universe," and 25 industrials, ten utilities and ten transportation companies in his "giant sized subset" (1971, p. 8). Other writers are less specific and content themselves with a figure of several hundred.

If economic dualism is to be a useful concept for economic analysis, three things are necessary: (1) it must be possible to define and distinguish clearly the contrasting sectors ; (2) there must be a substantial degree of uniformity in the behavior of the units making up each sector; and (3) an explanation of the differences in the behavior of these dual units must call for different types of analysis, or at least for substantial modification in one sector of the type of analysis used in the other.

I do not think that the world of the large firm meets these tests. There is no very clear distinction between the segment of the economy occupied by the large firm and the rest of the economy. A group of 500 large firms next to the largest 500 operate in similar markets and are subject to similar types of organization. As Caves put it, between the largest and the smallest "lie five million incredibly diverse individual business units."

Second, within the segment occupied by the large firm, diversity seems more striking than similarity to me. I once wrote that the "study of industrial organization can be said to offer a ticket of admission to institutionalism," meaning that it is extremely difficult to establish theoretically relevant generalizations in this field. And third, the instruments of conventional analysis in dealing with the behavior of the large firm do not seem to me to require that degree of modification or adaptation that would justify the term dualism. It is this aspect of the matter to which I now turn.

Those who consider the large firm to occupy a segment of the economy subject to laws of its own variously emphasize a number of particularities. The large firm is a planning unit relatively unresponsive to market forces. The large corporation not only has the power to shape demand for its products, but corporate salesmanship in the aggregate sustains an insatiability of material wants. It is controlled by a management with interests of its own divergent from those of ownership, and it is the primary source of technological change. Not all of those who tend toward a dualistic view of the economy emphasize all of these differences.

Perhaps only Galbraith embraces the whole of the unconventional wisdom. He is the exponent of dualism par excellence. No one else has gone as far as he in stressing the difference between the planned and the market segments of the economy, and no part of his analysis has been more vigorously attacked. Not many have been able to see how the activities of several hundred large firms could be coordinated without the services either of markets or of some central planning mechanism. As Meade objects:

> ... there is a great hiatus in his analysis of the economic system as a whole—or, perhaps more accurately, in his implied analysis of what the economic system as a whole would be like when virtually the whole of it was controlled by large modern corporations ... he never explains why and by what mechanism these individual plans can be expected to build up into a coherent whole.

Meade goes on to say that Galbraith

> ... believes that one can have either planning or the price system but not both. In fact "planning *and* the price mechanism" not "planning *or* the price mechanism" should be a central theme of every modern economist's work (1968, pp. 377, 392).[b]

Galbraith's reply to this criticism has been, first, a partial admission that he has not adequately dealt with this problem, and second, the citation of a number of failures of industrial coordination and the assertion that such failures cannot be avoided except under a system of central planning, hopefully controlled by Congress rather than by the Executive Branch. But he sees no useful role for the market so far as large firms are concerned.

Speaking of the powers and practices of the large firm, Galbraith says:

> But these efforts operate against the similar efforts of other firms—a process I have sketched although far from perfectly described—and against the increasing market resistance of the consumers and the increasing cost (as Professor Scott rightly observes) of a given increment of sales (1969, p. 501).

He also states:

> Nor did I identify sufficiently the problem, unknown to orthodox economics but endemic to planning, of matching performance in related parts of the economy and the consequences of failure to do so. From this failure come blackouts and energy crises of which we shall hear more before we hear less (1973, p. x).

Central planning, according to Professor Galbraith, is the only answer.

There seems little need to pursue this matter further except to offer a few

---

[b]For similar criticism see Lindbeck (1971, p. 38), Sharpe (1972, p. 45), and Scott (1968, p. 646).

observations on the relations between planning and the market mechanism in the industrial sector. To what extent do individual firms plan their activities and what differences are there between the planning of small and large firms? If we agree with Boulding that "Behavior governed by conscious expectations is what we mean by 'planning' . . . then, of course, all firms large and small are planners" (1953, p. XXIX). And indeed, as Meade surmises, the absence of control by a relatively small firm over inputs and prices "would increase, not decrease, the need for complicated engineering, personal and sales planning before large-scale resources could be wisely committed in an inflexible form. . . ." (1968, p. 382).

But large firms do have appreciable control over inputs, outputs, and prices, and can therefore engage in a type of "imperative" planning outside the competence of small firms. According to a much-quoted statement by Galbraith, "The size of General Motors is in the service not of monopoly or of the economies of scale but of planning. And for this planning . . . there is no clear upper limit to the desirable size" (1967, p. 76). It would seem to me more exact to say that the size of General Motors makes possible a type of planning outside the competence of smaller firms, rather than to hold that the opportunity to plan is the explanation for that size.

At any rate, a central issue in the field of industrial organization is the relation between planning and the market. There is no doubt that many large firms do have substantial control over inputs and outputs and use this control to stabilize prices and, to a certain extent, profits. But they operate within a complex of constraints established by the policies of their rivals, their customers, and their suppliers in an atmosphere of uncertainty that can be lessened but not eliminated by their own actions. It is this planning, guided and checked by expectations concerning the behavior of others, that characterizes industrial markets.

And the prices established in such markets serve the same purpose as indicators of appropriate courses of action and adaptation as in the rest of the economy. Coordination of economic activities is accomplished through market forces with the primary difference being that the behavior of the large firm is a distinguishable market force that needs to be taken into account by other buyers and sellers in the market. This is not true of small firms operating in competitive markets. But this difference hardly supports a respectable claim of dualism.

The imperative planning of large firms can go a fair distance in assuring sources of supply through backward integration, long term supply contracts, and the cultivation of satellite firms, though such devices cannot assure that these supplies will be available at expected costs. And most integrated firms still find it desirable to maintain a check on their own costs of production and fabrication by purchasing some of their supplies on the markets. Large firms can also go a fair distance in stabilizing the rate of growth and the prices of output by tacit understandings with rival oligopolistic firms, salesmanship, product adaptation, and by other means. But this stability is only relative—i.e., relative to the greater volatility of output and prices of firms operating in more competitive markets. It can be easily disrupted by product and process innovations, sizeable shifts in demand, and fluctuations in the economy as a whole.

The market limitations to the imperative planning of most large firms are very real. Many oligopolistic industrial markets have a large enough fringe of small competitors to constitute a serious check on market power. Large firms in other industries of this sort find it impossible to hold prices much above average cost because barriers to the entry of new firms are low. Although the short run demand for products may be inelastic, possibilities of substitution in the long run considerably increases demand elasticity for planning purposes. Power on one side of the market may be negated by power on the other side—a fact celebrated by Galbraith himself before he became convinced that planning is all. And the market uncertainties confronting even the largest firms suggests, in Caves' words, that "a significant portion of the potential profit latent in its position of market power is taken in the form of avoiding uncertainty . . ." (1970, p. 284).

All this is not to suggest that industrial markets are delicate self-regulating mechanisms. After all, a large literature in the field of industrial organization is devoted to establishing relationships between differences in market structure and the conduct of individual firms, and the effects of different combinations of structure and conduct on various welfare indicators of performance. And a number of writers have urged that the market power of large firms has permitted conduct that in the course of time can have a significant reciprocal effect on market structure (Jacquemin, 1972; Phillips, 1970).

It is clear that in oligopoly markets the response of firms to the market is only part of the story, the other part being the response of the market to the behavior of the firm. As Weston remarks:

> Broad environmental influences, combined with the constraints presented by existing products and firms in the market, lead the firm to develop adaptive policies with respect to product, quality, prices, sales methods, promotion efforts, service organization, and finance facilities (1973, p. 147).

The "adaptive policies" are part of the firm's planning activities and force similar planning activities on other firms. But the totality of their planning efforts do not exorcize the market, though they do shape its character. And industrial markets, however shaped, still serve as the principal coordinating mechanism in the world of the large firm as well as the world of the small. If an economic dualism is to be found, other considerations will need to be advanced.

Consumer Demand and Corporate Salesmanship

As I have suggested above, these other considerations have, in the main, been advanced as a difference between large and small firms in power to shape the demand for products; a difference between managerial and ownership control; and differences in the contribution of large and small firms to technological innovation.

To begin with the doctrine of consumer's sovereignty, no one, even in the benighted nineteenth century, believed that human beings come into the world with their tastes already formed. Demands for goods and services, even to satisfy physical needs, are formed through social processes. And the advertising and product variations undertaken by large corporations form part of those social processes. Upon that much we can all agree. If we want to get beyond that point, certain distinctions need to be made. The demand for producer goods is determined in a different environment from consumer goods; one in which salesmanship plays a relatively small role. And, as Bain points out, ". . . a majority of the value of shipments of manufactured goods output that passes through purchase and sales transactions consists of producer goods and is brought by producer buyers" (1972, p. 223).

In the consumption area, if services are included, a substantial majority of the sales are generated in industries of low concentration. This leaves an area of consumer goods industries in which concentration is relatively high and it is in this area that most of the large advertisers are found. And even in this area we should probably make a distinction between convenience goods—the corn flakes and soap flakes for which the different brands are close substitutes and where advertisers largely cancel each other's efforts—and more specialized products, the demand for which, at particular income levels, may indeed be substantially shaped by corporate salesmanship.

But there is a deeper question at issue. It is one thing to explain how consumer expenditure is distributed among the various goods and services offered for sale at a particular time and another thing to explain the marked shifts in consumer demand that take place over time. We all know from Engel's law that the share of income spent on food declines with rising incomes. But there are other drastic shifts in consumer expenditure, from clothing and housing to transportation, education, recreation, health, and other large areas of consumption. And, as we can observe from data on the decline in the length of the work week, perhaps the most drastic drift of all is from goods and services to leisure.

International comparisons suggest that these shifts in demand as income rises take place in all countries regardless of the organization of production and the volume and character of advertising. The pattern of expenditures appears to be related in much the same way to per capita incomes and relative prices. As Lindbeck notes, people in the Soviet Union queue up for much the same commodities that one would expect from observing what consumer demands are like, at similar income levels, in the United States (1971, p. 44).

I suppose it could be argued that demands created by corporate salesmanship in the United States—the country of highest per capita incomes—are imitated in other countries as their per capita incomes rise. But this seems a little far-fetched.

I tend to agree with Hession that it is not the corporate sector that has created the wants and values of American society, but the wants and values together with changes in technology that has spawned the large corporation (1972, p. 212).

We can assign to corporate salesmanship a considerable role among the social forces that determine at any particular time the distribution of consumer expenditures among competing goods and services without abandoning the proposition that, over time, large shifts in consumer demand take place because of changes in per capita income, technology, and relative prices. It is these shifts in consumer demand that are primarily responsible for changes in the structure of production. It can still be plausibly claimed that the ultimate purpose of economic activity is the satisfaction of consumer wants. It does not appear to be necessary for the explanation of large shifts in consumer expenditure over time, therefore, to accept a "revised sequence" in which corporate enterprise "shapes the social attitudes of those, ostensibly, that it serves" (Galbraith, 1967, p. 212). After all, Engel's law antedates by a considerable margin the rise of the large corporation.

But corporate salesmanship has laid itself open to a more serious indictment. While individual corporations are said to shape consumers' wants for the particular goods they produce, it is alleged that corporate salesmanship in the aggregate is responsible for the value system that sees in ever-increasing availability of material goods the essence of the good life. If material wants are indeed insatiable, this insatiability should, it is said, be laid at the door of corporate advertising. It is quantity rather than quality that characterizes this life style. The consequence of corporate salesmanship, according to Galbraith, is

> ... that while goods become ever more abundant they do not seem to be any less important. On the contrary it requires an act of will to imagine that anything else is so important. Morally, we agree that the supply of goods is not a measure of human achievement; in fact, we take it for granted that it will be so regarded (1967, p. 209).

In recent years there has been a sizeable revolt, particularly among the young and among intellectuals, against this "consumerist society" that the corporate system is supposedly fastening upon us. The numerous communes that dot the countryside, organic gardening, the sloppy Joes and Janes who grace college campuses, are all part of this phenomenon whose importance is celebrated in Charles Reich's *The Greening of America*. Although Reich greatly exaggerated its importance, it is an interesting phenomenon and many of the votaries are indeed searching for a quality of life that is not to be found in an increasing supply of material goods.

A question arises as to how so many have been able to escape the reach of corporate salesmanship. I think a part of the answer is to be found in high per capita incomes, for which the corporate system is partly responsible. If one looks at the development of American society, one cannot help but be struck by the obvious fact that the sway of material values has declined rather than increased over time. De Toqueville was one of the first of a series of foreign observers to be struck, early in the nineteenth century, by the extraordinary preoccupation of Americans with money making and material acquisitions.

John Stuart Mill's observations fell short of admiration. Commenting on life in the northern and middle states of the United States, he remarked, "They have the six points of chartism, and they have no poverty; and all these advantages do for them is that the life of one sex is devoted to dollar hunting, and of the other to breeding dollar hunters."[c] Perhaps the high point in the American worship of material things, if we are to believe Henry Adams and Henry James, was the period after the Civil War, long before the large corporation had begun to take form: the period of President Grant, Jim Fisk, Jay Gould, Diamond Jim Brady, and Chapters in Erie.

The view that corporate salesmanship is responsible for the obvious satisfaction that most Americans take in a high level of consumption hardly does justice to the cultural context in which large corporations operate. As one observer of the current scene puts it, ". . . given the success and status orientation of our culture, most of the avid consumers of durable goods are already 'sold' on the indispensability of such products for the good life even before the advertisers exert their promotional efforts" (Hession 1972, p. 212).

The fact is that the period during which nationwide corporate advertising came to the fore probably saw a lessening rather than an increase in the importance attached to material satisfaction. This is the natural result of the rise in per capita incomes. How else may we explain that the attacks on "consumerism" come almost entirely from intellectuals who enjoy a higher standard of living than they have ever enjoyed before and from students in Ivy League colleges who can count on a sizeable monthly check from home. Support for lower material standards of living obviously does not come from blue-collar workers. This growing interest in the quality of life was presumably what Keynes had in mind when he offered a toast at a dinner of the Royal Economics Society (1945) to "economics and economists, who are the trustees not of civilization but of the possibility of civilization."

Corporate salesmanship certainly has a signfiicant influence on consumer expenditures for the set of goods and services offered for sale at a particular point in time. But corporate activity, insofar as it contributes to a rise in per capita incomes, has over time an even more significant effect in broadening consumer choice among leisure, savings, and consumption, and the various large classes of goods and services. I see very little evidence of dualism in the performance of either of these functions. Consumer sovereignty, properly interpreted, is still a

[c]Quoted in Bowen (1855, p. VIII).

useful doctrine, and we can, I think, safely continue to assume that the primary test of the performance of an economy is how effectively it satisfies consumer wants.

Corporate Motivation and Behavior

I turn now to certain questions concerning the motivations and behavior of corporate managements and, in particular, to the question whether they act in the interests of owners or follow interests of their own. A tremendous literature has emerged in this area since the classic publications of R. A. Gordon, and Berle and Means. I cannot hope to do justice to this literature, but perhaps a few relevant points can be touched on.

The concept of the profit maximizing firm, attempting to equate marginal costs and revenues and choosing among investment opportunities on the basis of careful cost-revenue calculations, is central to conventional price theory. If firms maximize something else, or nothing in particular, it may make a difference to economic analysis. But more than economic analysis is involved. If there is a managerial class controlling the large corporation in its own interests, or at least in interests other than those of ownership, an important sociopolitical question of the locus of power in the economy and in society is involved.

I suppose everyone would agree that the only situation in which profit maximization can be precisely conceived is the textbook case of static equilibrium in which the firm deals with known demand and cost functions. The real live firm, whether small or large, confronted with uncertainty, is in a different situation. According to Solow (1971) it is impossible to answer specifically for a particular firm what it does maximize. "It may maximize nothing—different departments, committees and individuals may have conflicting interests. But even if it has a coherent policy it may be content with approximate solutions or rules of thumb" (p. 318). Yet, this same Solow defends the proposition that, in explaining how firms respond to changes in tax rates, investment subsidies, and the like it is useful to assume that they are guided by the profit motive. As Milton Friedman puts it, we may presume that corporations behave *as if* they were maximizing profits.

Whether or not the large corporation attempts to maximize profits is not the same thing as the question whether its management attempts to serve the interests of owners. Acting via a decision process that reflects the corporation's internal organization, and confronting uncertainty, a management may still attempt to serve the interests of owners even though it is incapable of maximizing profits. As Herbert Simon suggests, people may "satisfice because they have not the wits to maximize" (1959, p. 253).

To say that the internal organization of the firm defeats or modifies the objective of profit maximization is not to say that decisionmakers do not serve the interests of ownership. This is left to the managerial attack on profit maximization, and it is this attack that calls into question the conventional justification of ownership and raises the sociopolitical question of the locus of power.

The managerial strand derives from the Berle and Means doctrine of the separation of ownership from control and, in certain respects, from the earlier writing of Veblen in *Engineers and the Price System*. After the Berle and Means publication a number of voices were raised to ask the question what difference it makes to the conduct of the corporation even if management is in control? Since then this question has been answered, voluminously, by a host of writers including Baumol, Marris, Penrose, Burnham, Kaysen, Galbraith, *Fortune* Magazine, and others. To some the "managerial revolution" has meant the coming to corporate leadership of professionals concerned with the social function of maintaining an equitable balance of the claims of workers, stockholders, suppliers, and customers. (I tried to dispose of this thesis in an article I wrote called the "Apologetics of Managerialism" (1958).)

Baumol, Marris, and some others see management as having interests of its own, divergent from ownership, and better served by the size and rate of growth of the corporation rather than by attempting to maximize the present value of equity ownership. In their view the objective of corporate management is to maximize the rate of growth (variously defined) of the firm, subject to a constraint imposed by the necessity of earning enough to sustain the position of the firm in capital markets. All the expositors of managerial capitalism emphasize the importance of size. Indeed, in the view of some, a small number of large corporations (variously estimated as between 500 and 800) behave so differently from firms in the rest of the economy that strong support is offered to the concept of dualism.

Whether a firm attempting to maximize its growth rate subject to a capital market security constraint behaves differently from a profit maximizing firm depends largely on the tightness of the constraint. It may find it necessary to satisfy investors and potential investors with its earnings record if it is to grow at all. I suggest that this is the usual case in a world in which access to outside funds is both necessary to growth and difficult to sustain. A good many attempts have been made to distinguish differences in the behavior of owner controlled and management controlled firms on the basis of observed differences in the growth rates and relative stability of earnings.

These attempts have not been notably successful. Galbraith would presumably say that these studies are irrelevant since no very large corporation can be owner controlled unless the owners are in fact part of the management, with access to managerial information. As things stand, the case against the dominance of ownership interests becomes largely a series of assertions having to do with the presumed motivations of management. It is said to be interested in power, in prestige, in the fringe benefits of office space, rugs on the floor, silver pitchers on the desk, etc., and in the technological virtuosity of its performance.

All these things, it is said, are more closely related to the size and rate of growth of the firm than to the level and rate of growth of its earnings. But the evidence is scanty.

There are, moreover, at least two good reasons for doubting the validity of this relationship. One has to do with the character of executive compensation and the other with the dependence, even of large firms, on outside financing. A careful study of the relations of executive compensation to profits and to sales in large firms (Lewellen and Huntsman, 1970) has found a much closer relation to the former than to the latter. Most top executives, in addition to salaries and bonuses, receive compensation in the form of pension benefits, deferred pay, profit sharing, and stock options. The current value of these benefits depends closely on the earnings record, expected earnings and the market price of the stock and these benefits "frequently result in after-tax increments to executives' wealth that are of magnitudes many times the current salary and bonus awards" (p. 713). The authors conclude:

> Because the results of the study persistently indicate that both reported profits and equity market values are substantially more important in the determination of executive compensation than are sales—indeed sales seem to be quite irrelevant—the clear inference is that there is a greater incentive for management to shape its decision rules in a manner consonant with shareholders' interests than to seek the alternative goal of sales maximization (p. 719).

The second reason has to do with the fact that although large corporations—and smaller ones too—reinvest a sizeable fraction of their earnings, they also depend on the capital market for bond and stock issues, and, particularly in periods of depressed security prices, on short term borrowing from the banks as well. Somewhere near three-quarters of the debt securities of large corporations are held by institutional investors: insurance companies, trust departments of banks, and others. These are sophisticated lenders who are more impressed by a corporation's earnings record and prospects than by anything else. A majority, by value, of corporate stocks are held by individuals, most of whom everyone agrees have no part in managerial decision making. "Corporate liturgy," according to Galbraith, "strongly emphasizes the power of the Board of Directors and ultimately, thus, of the stockholders they are assumed to represent" (1967, p. 83).

I agree with him that, in ordinary circumstances, this is mere liturgy. But because stockholders, and even boards, do not participate actively in managerial decision making does not mean that the behavior of stockholders is of little concern to management. Stockholders can and do vote with their feet. And what this voting by actual and potential stockholders does to the price of equity securities is of primary concern to management. The frequency of recent disappearances of board chairmen and presidents of even very large corporations suggest that there are interests outside management that are concerned with how companies are run.

An increasing share of corporate securities, both equity and debt are held by pension funds usually administered, along with other funds, by the trust departments of large banks. A Senate Sub-Committee (1973) has recently published information on trust account holdings of 25 of the largest trust departments of American banks. These holdings are not only very large—the Morgan Guarantee Trust Company alone holds around $27 billion in corporate securities—but frequently represent a substantial share of the total stock of particular companies. The Morgan Company holds over 5 percent of the shares in twelve companies and over 10 percent in two. While there is little or no evidence that these trust holdings are used to exert managerial control, they do represent a substantial concentration of ownership interest. A corporate management that ignored these interests in favor of interests of its own divergent from the concern of ownership would, I expect, receive short shrift from institutional investors.

To sum up, I conclude that the growth of large enterprises has not led corporate managements very far from the conventional notion that the operations of an enterprise—even of a very large corporation—should be and are primarily in the interests of its owners. Obviously this does not mean that the management of a large corporation behaves in the same way as the owner-manager of a small shoelace firm. The market power enjoyed by large firms gives management what Williamson (1970) calls an area of discretion, a set of opportunities, not open to smaller firms. How this set of opportunities is used will depend not only on the internal organization of the firm but on preferences for risk acceptance or avoidance that, over time, may well reflect the attitudes of shareholders as well as management.

Market power permits a series of actions capable of reducing substantially the area of uncertainty confronting the firm. National advertising can expand the sale of products and stabilize the firm's share of the market. Vertical integration and long term contracts can assure continuity in the supply of inputs. Expansion into other product areas, through merger or other means, can lead to a pooling and diminution of risk. As Richard Caves puts it, ". . . a significant portion of the potential profits latent in a position of market power is taken in the form of avoiding uncertainty . . ." (1970, p. 284).

But this does not necessarily mean a sacrifice of ownership interest. As John Lintner observes, ". . . uncertainty and risk aversion in a profit-maximizing context may account for many of the phenomena so far ascribed in the 'revisionist' literature to other goals like sales maximization, as distinct from profit maximization, or management's concern with its emoluments and personal empire building" (1970, p. 241). The giant corporation is, in truth, a different kind of animal whose behavior has been examined extensively, if not adequately, in the literature on industrial organization to which Joe Bain has been so capable a contributor. But the managements of such corporations do not, in my view, have objectives so different from the management of smaller firms as to justify the thesis of dualism.

There remains the allegation that the world of the large firm is sharply distinguishable from the rest of the economy by reason of its near monopolization of the processes of invention and innovation. Are the 500 to 800 largest American corporations the primary source of technological change? The chief defenders of the affirmative proposition are Schumpeter and Galbraith. According to Schumpeter, invention has become the quasi-automatic product of the industrial laboratories of large corporations whose market power permits a desirable degree of protection for innovation. To Galbraith, the day of the small firm in technological change is over. Both these authorities make their case largely by assertion without bothering to undertake any very systematic empirical research.

But strong a priori arguments can be marshalled both for and against the proposition that large firms have particular advantages in invention and innovation. The question can only be answered by extensive empirical research. And, to a large extent, it has been answered: During the last few years a great deal of effort has been devoted to the study of the relationship between market structure and the scale of firms to the rate of technical change. A recent survey article by Kennedy and Thirwell in the *Economic Journal*, covering mainly British and American studies of size, market structure, and technical change, sums up as follows:

> As it stands, the evidence appears to be heavily weighted against the hypothesis that a necessary condition for technical change and progressiveness is that firms should be large scale and dominate the market in which they operate. From the very origins of technical change, in the work that is put into research, the commercial application of new knowledge, it does not appear that large firms or monopolistic industries are necessarily more dynamic or "progressive" or produce more fundamental technical change. After a certain threshold size there is even evidence that R and D activity and the number of patents issued appear to increase less than proportionately with size (1972, p. 61).

Patents issued are not necessarily a good measure of significant technical change, although Schmookler, a leading practitioner in this field, gives us reason to believe that they are a significant indicator. The only other general surrogate useful for interindustry and interfirm comparisons, the size of research and development expenditures, also presents difficulties. But the surveys using patents and R and D expenditures have been supplemented by numerous case studies of particular inventions that tend to support the proposition that important technical improvements come from firms of various sizes. One of the earliest and best undertook a careful study of some 50 significant innovations, and a second edition added ten more. Well over half of these 60 were the product of individual inventors or of relatively small firms (see Jewkes, Sawyers, and Stillerman, 1969).

It is true that in certain industries a very large scale of operation is desirable, if not necessary, for rapid technological innovation. Aircraft, office equipment (particularly computers), and chemicals may belong in this category. In these industries research and development expenditures, often heavily financed by government, are large, and as a result, the percentage of total employment represented by scientists and engineers is high. Vernon (1971, pp. 47–67) calls these "skill-oriented" industries and points out that not only do firms in these industries tend to be large, but the industries are highly concentrated, and strongly oriented toward export markets.

But in most industries, even those that are highly capital intensive, there seems to be no discernible relation between size of firms and technological progressiveness. By far, the most important innovation in the steel industry in the last half-century came from a relatively small firm, and this is by no means an isolated example. A careful study by Mansfield of technical change in five industries found that ". . . except for the chemical industry there is no evidence that the largest firms in these industries spent more for research and development, related to sales, than did somewhat smaller firms." And he goes on to say that, "In most industries, the productivity of a research and development program of given scale seems to be lower in the largest firms than in somewhat smaller ones" (1968, p. 43).[d]

After surveying the literature I am inclined to agree with Scherer that, "No single firm size is uniquely conducive to technological progress. There is room for firms of all sizes. What we want, therefore, may be a diversity of sizes, each with its own special advantages and disadvantages" (1970, p. 357). There does not seem to be much support for the dualism thesis in this area of business activity.

CONCLUSION

The fact that an hypothesis of dualism based on the distinction between the behavior of a few hundred large firms and that of the remaining five-million-odd enterprises in the American economy does not seem to be very illuminating does not, of course, mean that the large corporation has no special characteristics worthy of study. But both the internal decision making processes and the external market relationships of large scale enterprises are too varied to be embraced in a limited set of generalizations. The large corporation does have characteristic types of organization; its management does involve group decision making; its size and market position certainly gives it a degree of control over inputs and the demand for its product not available to small firms;

---

[d]These conclusions concerning the absence of a discernable correspondence between the size of firm and R and D expenditures, patents secured, and, presumably, of productivity of investment in R and D are shared by other researchers. See Scherer (1965, p. 109), Schmookler (1959, p. 628), and Nelson, Peck, and Kalachek (1967, pp. 66–67).

and its access to capital markets is usually more effective. If these characteristics are to be emphasized, the number of firms sharing them to some nonnegligible degree would have to be counted in the thousands rather than hundreds. And the differences in internal organization and external relationships among these thousands of firms need to be taken into account.

The enterprises included in this universe do engage to a degree in what may be called imperative planning, but they do so within the limits of a market structure that varies from industry to industry. They adapt their products, vary their prices, devise sales methods and promotional efforts, and undertake investments in response to changes on both sides of the market. Whether they maximize profits can only be interpreted in the light of their different time horizons and spectra of uncertainty. But the assumption that they do attempt to maximize the present value of their expected income streams provides a useful instrument of analysis in explaining market behavior. The market position of such firms usually gives managements an area of discretion within which various courses of action are possible, but there is no firm evidence that this discretionary potential is used in ways that run counter to the interests of ownership. The ownership interests of top management tend to be too substantial and the pressures of the capital market are too real.

Certainly a special type of analysis is needed to explain the activities of manufacturing and mining enterprises. But the rudiments, at least, already exist in the field of industrial organization, to which Joe Bain has contributed so much. This field is attached to the main stream of developments in theory on the one hand and on the other to the special institutional characteristics that differentiate manufacturing and mining activities from activities in other special fields of economic interest. It is still a relatively undeveloped area of expertise, but it offers more insight than is vouchsafed by the implausible assertions of dualism.

�֍ *Chapter 3*

Barriers to Exit

Richard E. Caves
Michael E. Porter

I. INTRODUCTION

Impediments to the removal of excess resources from an industry have long been a concern of American economists and economic policy. Destructive competition, whether actual or alleged, played an important part in motivating much of our present apparatus of direct regulation. The problems of income distribution and entrepreneurial uncertainty created by barriers to exit motivated much economic analysis and policy during the depression of the 1930s. Thanks to the greater success of macroeconomic policy since World War II the issues of destructive competition and excess capacity have slipped from view. Yet, as we shall argue, barriers to exit from an industry may retain a considerable significance for firm behavior in "normal" times, and hence for the general performance of markets.

Barriers to exit have traditionally been studied as a normative and ex post problem. We propose instead to consider them as an element of market structure and ex ante determinant of market conduct and (thereby) performance. Structural symmetries between barriers to exit and barriers to entry—the seminal concept that Bain did so much to establish—become apparent when we recognize the man-made component of entry barriers. After considering the sources of exit barriers and their implications for market conduct, we present some statistical tests of their implications. The normative implications of exit barriers in general and of our findings in particular are reviewed in the concluding section.

We wish to thank Dr. Sidney Schoeffler and the Strategic Planning Institute for allowing us access to the PIMS data base used in this project and financing the computations, and Catherine Donaldson Hayden for assistance with the statistical analysis. Other calculations were performed by Roger Bernstein, and John C. Gault and other Harvard students supplied helpful suggestions.

II. NATURE AND OCCURRENCE OF
EXIT BARRIERS

Exit barriers influence the behavior of firms through their power to inflict persistently subnormal profits. Their source is inputs that can become attached to the firm and then command persistently low earnings because they are *durable* and *specific* to an activity of the company. Such durable and specific assets (hereafter DSAs) may be specific to the particular business or productive activity, to the company employing them, to the physical location, or to any combination of these.

We are concerned with DSAs that are durably committed to the enterprise that employs them. The firm as a legal entity, or the entrepreneur as supplier of coordinating services, can move freely in geographic or product space. But DSAs can be attached to the firm through ownership or a nonterminable long term lease for the life of the asset—arrangements that differ only in collateral for holders of the firm's debt. They can also be annexed by rental for any period short of the life of the DSA, making the DSA's attachment to the firm one that is in fact freely variable in duration.[a] Inputs owned by the enterprise or on long term contract correspond financially to long term liabilities of the firm to the holders of its equity or debt, and shortfalls of quasi-rents earned by these inputs are shared among these creditors in accord with the terms of their claims on the firm's cash flows.

Tangible and Intangible Fixed Assets

The traditional image of the DSA is a piece of long-lived fixed equipment that is indivisible once installed and specialized to a single output; its user cost is a substantial proportion of the output's average unit cost. But the classic DSA is not the only source of specificity. Working capital includes inventories of partly and fully fabricated goods that have limited salvage value, even though their turnover is high. Intangible assets can be specific and durable and prove even more difficult for the firm to divest. True, intangibles can be traded through franchising arrangements, the sale of trademarks, etc., but their markets are limited. Franchising arrangements require special structures of local markets, and one's competitor already has a trademark of his own, and so forth. Impacted

[a]The distribution of ownership of DSAs between firms employing them and independent specialized owners can probably be explained economically. Specialized ownership is discouraged by the lack of a futures markets to permit the trading away of risk and by the specialized owner's inability to substitute his DSA for other inputs easily when its shadow price falls (the entrepreneur controls this substitution). Conversely, assets that are durable but nonspecific (e.g., computers) may well be acquired on lease because of economies in servicing, economies of knowledge concerning their operation and optimal replacement, and impacted information that makes it easier for the user enterprise to appraise the flow of services from such an asset than the physical asset itself. See Akerlof (1970), and McGugan and Caves (1974).

information deters the marketing of intangibles because of the difficulty of measuring their output of services, and they are probably often inseparable from the equity (goodwill) of the firm that produced or developed them. Tangibles, whatever their mobility, do not generally share that problem. Tangible DSAs can include inputs other than physical capital, notably labor with specific skills. Labor cannot be owned and seldom enjoys the protection of a long term contract (university professors excepted), but union agreements may preclude contracting work outside the firm.

Exit may involve substantial decision making and other one-shot costs. Because accounting data are designed for measuring the performance of going concerns, developing the information needed to weigh exit rationally may require special studies.[b] Furthermore, unlike the information required for other major business decisions such as capital budgeting, information needed for the exit decision is seldom routinely collected and thus is expensive to secure. Exit will also entail fixed costs of terminating employees (often substantial under collective bargaining agreements), pension settlements, costs of terminating contracts, retraining and transfer costs for employees, costs of maintaining service on discontinued products, legal costs, etc. (Lovejoy, 1971, chaps. 19–22). Some of these costs may be economically fixed, others may be imposed on the firm by contractual obligations. These fixed costs of making and executing the exit decision, variable from firm to firm, must be weighed as investments to avoid future losses, and thereby deter exit.

Of these structural sources of exit barriers only the role of tangible fixed assets is well documented in historical studies. Investigations of the problems of adjustment faced by various industries in the 1920s and 1930s confirm the power of durability and specificity to lock firms and factors of production into highly unprofitable activities. Bituminous coal is a well documented example (Fisher and James, 1955; Hendry, 1961). Cotton textiles was widely regarded as a distressed industry, but the industry suffered no heavy weight of DSAs, and exit was in fact substantial. An interregional shift in location was a major contributing factor (Reynolds, 1940; Alderfer and Michl, 1950, chap. 20). Innovations and reorganizations in the retailing sector provoked a powerful response in the political arena, but the changes were largely in organizational form, and the industry's tangible DSAs were not a major part of the problem (Hoffman, 1940).

Joint Production

DSAs' potential influence on the firm's activity depends not just on their proportional importance in its input structure but also on their linkage to other inputs through jointness and intertemporal dependence of profit streams. If the

---

[b]That these costs are substantial is supported by Lovejoy (1971, p. 113 and chap. 15), who bases his conclusions on a survey of divestment experiences in major companies. Hillman (1971) argues that the lack of appropriate data in accounting reports is an important reason why firms fail to exit from businesses that are part of a vertical chain.

physical productivity of durable input A depends on its joint use with semi-durable input B, it can pay the firm to replace B even when A's quasi-rents would not justify the initial acquisition cost or replacement of A and B together. As Lamfalussy (1961, chap. 7) has shown, a firm may rationally reinvest in the face of subnormal profits if its cash flow declines rapidly when any disinvestment or nonreplacement occurs. As an offset to subnormal returns on capital replacement outlays, the preserved cash flow can be invested at the market rate of interest. The replacement can thus be worth while at the margin because of the amount by which it stays the decline of the cash flow. This practice of "defensive investment" is more likely the longer-lived are capital goods (DSAs), the lower the breakup value of the firm, the lower the periodic replacement cost, and the shorter is the entrepreneur's time horizon.

Jointness of inputs and the conditions supporting defensive investment tend to amplify the power of durable and specific assets to keep an enterprise in a business earning subnormal returns. The multiproduct firm is apt to make joint use of fixed facilities such as distribution systems for multiple products, wherefore the persistence of production in low profit businesses could depend on the historical accidents of diversified development by companies engaged in that activity.

The cost of terminating a particular business should depend on its organizational relation to the rest of the enterprise and thus the degree of effective jointness in its costs. Abandoning a business whose product is complementary to others sold by the firm involves a potential loss of sales in excess of those of the exited business. Exit from a business can be more disruptive with customers and distribution channels if these are shared with the firm's other businesses.[c] And a business that is part of a vertical chain within the firm may be spared execution in order to avoid the transaction costs of new arrangements for the adjacent businesses.

Managerial Behavior and Exit Barriers

A firm's top management may acquire and possess specific skills that are of less value elsewhere. To the extent that managerial utility governs the firm's decisions, preserving the quasi-rents of its managers can become a barrier to the dispersal of its other inputs. The fact that management itself can comprise a DSA leads us to consider managerial motives and corporate control as significant factors determining what costs the firm treats as fixed (Porter, 1975).

Management can comprise a barrier to exit even if top management's skills are nonspecific, because poor performance of a firm may reduce its managers' mobility by acting as a signal of their competence to potential employers (who

---

[c]This point is repeatedly stressed in the managerial literature on strategies for divestiture. Secrecy in the analysis of divestment options is usually recommended for these reasons (Bettauer, 1967; Lovejoy, 1971).

wants a loser?).[d] Furthermore, management may derive utility from a large number of exit deterring factors—loyalty to a particular business or community, unwillingness to lay off employees, etc. (Gilmour, 1973; Hilton, 1972). This factor compounds the significance of specific managerial talents and calls for close attention to exit barriers in firms under managerial control. While checks imposed by stockholders, creditors, and the market for corporate control exert some disciplining force, there is evidence that they leave ample room for the effects of managerial control and utility maximization (Williamson, 1963; Palmer, 1973; cf. Hindley, 1970). Exit barriers are industry specific, but managerial control is of course specific to the firm. We cannot expect to explain interindustry differences in exit barriers just on the basis of industries' structural characteristics if managerial factors are important.

The typical management controlled firm is large and diversified, and diversification can have important effects on managerial exit barriers. The top management of the firm becomes a decision making group separate from the top management of its business in a given industry. Therefore the motivation and discretion of top management is important, and the significance of the firm's organizational structure is amplified. The effects of diversification on both managerial and structural exit barriers, however, can run in opposite directions.

On the one hand, diversification can remove or combat managerial sources of exit barriers. Multi-industry firms may be controlled by their top managements, but the evaluation and removal of managers of the firm's individual business units is the responsibility of top management. The lack of outside discipline over the firm may not transfer to its individual businesses. Top management may maintain an effective internal capital market, reviewing divisional performance internally and facilitating managerial changes or exit from the business when necessary. The possibility of internal placement of employees displaced from an extinguished business makes it easier for top management to wield the axe. And the greater the breadth and extent of the firm's diversification, the less threat does exit from one industry represent to its continuity, the more dispassionate can be the decision to exit.

But the pull of managerial utility can also augment barriers to exit in ways peculiar to the multi-industry firm. The diversified firm's resources may allow it to retain businesses in order to enhance managerial utility despite persistent losses. Its power to average these losses with the profits of other businesses in the diversified entity is said often to nullify any remaining capital market pressure to divest (Bettauer, 1967). Even when exit from a business does not directly threaten top managers' jobs, evidence suggests that the decision to exit is viewed as a sign of failure and mistaken judgment, so that a degree of stigma is attached to such decisions. To the extent that top management was involved in the deci-

[d]More formally, the market for managerial talent operates on limited information and may be unable to ascertain whether a business's failure was the fault of its manager or a drawing from the lower tail of fate's distribution.

sion to enter a business, managerial utility may call for remaining in the business and attempting a turnaround, and the willingness of a multi-industry firm to exit from businesses may depend on whether or not the current top management made the decision to enter (Hayes, 1972).[e]

Managerial utility may give negative weight to the dislocation of middle managers, or to the disturbance to continuity and the disruption of surviving operations associated with exit from an industry. The utility maximizing firm may be reluctant to exit from its "home" industry or the one that served as the original foundation for its success. Internally developed businesses may be carried longer than those entered through acquisition or merger.

Managerial utility maximization may interact with the jointness between the particular business and others of the multi-industry firm. For example, jointness and complementarity enhance the disruptive effect of exit on surviving operations, which managers may wish to avoid. Exit from a business that buys heavily from other units of the company may be opposed by the selling units' managers in their desire to avoid the exertions of selling in the external market. Managerial risk aversion may restrict the firm's willingness to rely on outside suppliers.

Exit Barriers and Entry Barriers

The structural bases of exit barriers can usefully be related to the sources of barriers to entry analyzed by Bain (1956). Although an industry can certainly experience easy entry and difficult exit (e.g., bituminous coal in the 1930s), exit barriers and entry barriers are connected in two ways. Technological factors that impede entry are likely to impede exit as well. And actions that going firms can take to deter entry also stay their own departure from the market.

Each source of entry barriers identified by Bain can also erect a barrier to exit by going firms. Absolute cost advantages accrue to going firms because they possess some specific resource that would cost the entrant more to acquire than its opportunity cost for going firms.[f] To fill this requirement the resource must be at least temporarily specific to the industry; otherwise going firms cannot enjoy control over these specific resources at favorable costs unless through ownership or long term contracts. The assets are unlikely to be scarce without also being durable; it is hard to think of an important input that is subject to a rising supply price and requires time for its fabrication or development that does not

---

[e]Gilmour (1973) conducted detailed case studies of three major divestment decisions by diversified firms. In all three cases he found that, despite persistent subnormal returns, the decision to exit was taken only when a new chief executive of the corporate parent was appointed.

[f]The two would of course be the same in a perfectly competitive market. Such markets are often imperfect because of fewness, uncertainties resulting from the dependence of expected quasi-rents on other firms' behavior, and information costs. If entry occurs and drives up the price of a scarce and specific resource, the remorse of going firms at the upward shift of their cost curves will be tempered by capital gains if they own the resource. The analysis of this paragraph does not apply to capital cost entry barriers.

also represent a durable asset yielding a flow of services over time. Therefore, going firms that enjoy an absolute cost advantage over entrants also find themselves owning DSAs that could comprise barriers to their exit.

Product differentiation barriers to entry stem from the established goodwill assets of going firms. Such assets may or may not result from identifiable historic investment outlays, but the structural barrier reposes in the outlay that the entrant must make to establish its own goodwill asset (and, in the process, impair the goodwill asset values of going firms). A goodwill asset is firm specific, not to mention industry specific, and has no expected salvage value for the entrant. Although goodwill assets can be transferred from firm to firm, an unsuccessful firm is unlikely to command a market value for its goodwill asset that will yield a normal return on the investment imputable to that asset. Therefore the entry cost involving expenditure on goodwill assets exposes the firm to a high risk of loss if it must exit; its specificity comprises a barrier to exit. Its durability should not be overemphasized, however, because of the high depreciation rates found in most studies of advertising investments.

Scale economy barriers to entry, and absolute capital requirements related to them, have no inevitable connection to exit barriers. However, substantial disadvantages for small scale units seem unlikely except where a production process somewhere along the line uses large scale physical capital equipment. On pragmatic grounds it seems unlikely that such equipment would be other than durable and specific, so that a correlation is expected between exit barriers and scale economy barriers to entry.

Entry barriers are not entirely structural, however; they also can result from investments in entry deterrence by going firms (Caves and Porter, 1975). The risk that product differentiation creates for the entrant similarly deters the going firm from investing in intangible assets that insulate it from entrants, if it too may face a possibility of exit. For instance, the extra cost fixity associated with vertical integration discourages its use as a way to enlarge economies of scale. Thus, although exit barriers and entry barriers spring from similar structural sources, increased exit barriers *ceteris paribus* can reduce the incidence of entry barriers by discouraging their fabrication.[g]

III. EXIT BARRIERS AND MARKET CONDUCT

In this section we examine hypotheses about how exit barriers affect firms' market conduct. One major conclusion about this influence is commonplace: that collusion is more likely where exit barriers allow adverse disturbances to

[g]Exit barriers also make liquidation of an unsuccessful firm a last resort, and thereby tend to lower the average price at which a new entrant can buy into an industry (Hayes, 1969; *Business Week*, 1970, p. 86; Lovejoy, 1971, p. 122). Because exit barriers both restrict the outflow of firms and deter the contrived elevation of entry barriers, they should tend to reduce seller concentration.

inflict serious losses ("if we don't hang together we'll all hang separately"). A casual review of antitrust history supports this view. The logical connection between premise and conclusion, however, needs to be examined, because it depends on specific attributes of the enterprises' cost structures and their attitudes toward risk.

How Exit Barriers Influence Market Conduct

The firm contractually saddled with DSAs necessarily faces an increased variance of its expected profit because the commitment enlarges its maximum possible loss in the event of failure. But exit barriers are also said to raise the profit variance by inducing sellers to maintain production even when only a small proportion of average total unit costs is covered. This latter effect of exit barriers is likely although not inevitable. The exact price-output response of a firm facing a reduced price or depressed demand depends on the shape of the short run marginal cost function at outputs below that for which capacity is optimal. The gap between marginal and average cost widens as output is reduced, but the size of the gap for any given percentage reduction depends on the exact form of the production function and not just on the percentage of costs that are fixed (Scherer, 1970, pp. 193–195).

We can say only that an enlargement of the proportion of costs that are fixed must reduce the integral of short run marginal cost up to any particular output. This proposition does not suffice to establish a perfect correlation between cost fixity and the proportional size of average-marginal cost gaps of different enterprises operating at the same rate (e.g., 90 percent) in the neighborhood of capacity. We shall assume in the following analysis that the correlation does indeed hold, but the assumption's validity is an expirical question.[h]

Given that exit barriers enlarge the variability of profits and the maximum size of losses, how should market conduct be affected? In particular, how could exit barriers affect the balance of firms' tendencies between interdependent conduct (recognizing their mutual interdependence) and independent action (neglecting rivals' reactions)? If fixed costs are sunk, profit maximization cannot be distinguished from loss minimization, and the hypothesis that firms maximize profits itself settles nothing about whether the largest expected profit derives from joining and adhering to an oligopolistic consensus, joining and then cheating, or not joining at all. A specific connection does emerge between exit barriers and conduct in oligopolistic markets, however, if we assume some form of risk aversion that we will characterize as a disproportionally high disutility of "dis-

---

[h]Some empirical evidence is at hand to support the assumption. If industries with higher exit barriers also exhibit steeper marginal cost curves in the neighborhood of normal capacity operation, their average level of capacity utilization should be higher than other industries. Esposito and Esposito (1974) indeed found a significant negative relation between industries' average rates of excess capacity and their assets-to-sales ratios, a variable that should be highly correlated with DSAs and exit barriers.

astrous" losses. This asymmetry becomes more potent as a predictor if we can apply it to accounting profits as well as internal (economic) rates of return.

There are various reasons why such an asymmetry might prevail. Conventional risk aversion on the part of the firm's owners or managers implies a subjective loss from a given shortfall of returns that exceeds the subjective gain from an equal windfall. Managers may experience great disutility from developments that threaten their job security. Suppliers of capital who must evaluate expected returns on very limited information may react sensitively to negative accounting profits even in a firm that has realized a satisfactory discounted-cash-flow rate of return over its lifespan, taking current accounting profits as a leading proxy for expected d.c.f. returns to incremental investments in the company (Monsen and Downs, 1965). These circumstances predict actions to limit short run slides in the rate of return that are in some sense asymmetrical to actions aimed at securing positive rents.

Collusive Arrangements in
Homogeneous Industries

Whether or not to take part in collusive arrangements is a choice that the oligopolist must necessarily make. Our seller considers the distribution of expected price-quantity outcomes in the market that he expects on various conjectures about the effects of collusive practices. He belongs, we suppose, to a group of (essentially) identical risk-averse firms surrounded by substantial entry barriers. Against increases in average profits through collusion he stacks the chance that his rivals might cheat on the collusive arrangement and divert profits toward themselves; he also weighs the expected cost if illegal collusion is found out and prosecuted. Collusion may or may not raise mean expected profits for him.

The firm that values avoiding disaster will find its preferences tilted toward collusive activity even though collusion per se need not reduce the variance of expected profit. So far as his rivals are believed to share his risk aversion, the potential adherent can hope that they will honor a commitment to maintain prices when disaster threatens. Where each firm holds this objective and believes it to be shared by its rivals, the chances of stabilization through cheating when profits are normal or less should in fact be reduced, and the chance of disaster reduced. Formal collusion then becomes a likely method of reducing profit variance, even if it should have only a modest effect on expected mean profits. The effect of collusion on profits may be largely to truncate the lower tail of expected outcomes, thereby raising the profit distribution's expected value.

We have established an incentive for an industry of identical risk-averse firms to collude in pursuit of more certain profits. Because exit barriers themselves expand the variance of expected profits, we can conclude that exit barriers raise the propensity of risk-averse firms to enter into collusive arrangements. But this conclusion based on expectational factors does not contravene the tendency of exit barriers (*ceteris paribus*) to impair the probable effectiveness of collusive efforts to elevate profits above normal. The value to any seller of an incremental sale or increase in market share depends on the margin between industry price and that firm's short run marginal cost. Where exit barriers are high and marginal cost steeply sloped in the neighborhood of the normal operating rate, colluding firms whose actual operating rates are distributed around the normal rate will display a high variance of ratios of price to marginal cost.

Hence, even without aggregate disturbances to the industry's demand or unit cost, a greater incentive to cheat exists for those sellers with the most to gain by cheating. Exit barriers thus reduce the probability of adherence to collusive efforts to raise profits above normal, and lower the survival probability of collusive arrangements in industries with high exit barriers.[i] In short, it appears that exit barriers raise the *demand* for collusive arrangements but also lower their probable *effectiveness* for elevating profits above normal. Their net effect on the allocation of resources becomes uncertain, and empirical evidence is predictably unclear (Hay and Kelley, 1974, p. 26).

How much collusion can improve the risk-return combination of an industry with high exit barriers depends on other elements of market structure. For example, the less elastic the demand curve facing the industry, the greater is the expected value of losses that can occur if price warfare or downward shift of demand forces price below long run average cost. The potential excess profits from successful collusion also are inversely related to demand elasticity. The probable willingness of firms facing exit barriers to enter into collusive arrangements is therefore increased when demand elasticity is low. It is also important that other structural elements are themselves affected by exit barriers; for instance, exit barriers probably tend to reduce seller concentration.[j]

Firm-Specific Exit Barriers and Parallel Conduct

So far as we have assumed that an industry's firms all face identical exit barriers, and furthermore that firms are symmetrically placed so that all disturbances affect them similarly. If that symmetry is absent, and exit barriers vary substantially among rival firms, the preceding analysis must be modified in several ways. Differing exit barriers imply differences in the competitors' cost structures and responses to disturbances, so that any given disturbance affecting them all will provoke diverse reactions. The likelihood of agreement on a collusive arrangement and the number of variables on which agreement is possible are

[i]Stigler (1964) supplies an economic model of the determinants of the ability to detect cheating, but its omission of structural explanations of the incidence of cheating and the effectiveness with which cheaters can be punished precludes its application here (Yamey, 1973).

[j]See footnote g. The direct effect of exit barriers on the mortality rate of firms that have run into adversity may be reflected in Shepherd's (1964, p. 206) finding that the rate of change in shipments is related very weakly to the change in concentration among shrinking industries.

both reduced because firms are apt to bring differing preferences to the bargaining table. And the agreement's likelihood of breakdown is probably increased by the rivals' asymmetrical reactions to common disturbances, although the presence of some rivals with low exit barriers does provide a safety net for the others in adverse times.

Are exit barriers likely to be firm specific, and thus diverse among competing sellers? Consider the stringent theoretical requirements for disturbances to affect all rivals in parallel. The industry must sell a homogeneous product requiring substantial inputs of DSAs. The product and the variable inputs are easily transported (or ubiquitous, in the case of the inputs). The firms' DSAs do not differ in productivity (e.g., capital goods of different vintages) or intrinsic quality (e.g., mineral deposits).[k] Even with these objective factors the same, managements must still be assumed to react identically to equal disturbances.[l] Disturbances affecting the industry's demand and cost conditions are only then likely to affect the quasi-rents of all firms in about the same proportion. The restrictive character of these conditions suggests the scope for firm specific barriers to exit.

This suggestion, that exit barriers are likely to be related to asymmetry in the positions of firms, implies that exit barriers are positively related to the variance of rates of return among firms in an industry—an empirically testable hypothesis. We attempted a statistical analysis of the determinants of the intraindustry profit variances calculated by Conrad and Plotkin (1968), but assorted deficiencies make the results unsuitable to report.

IV. STATISTICAL EVIDENCE

Because exit barriers have extensive implications for market conduct and performance, we undertook some statistical tests for their incidence and effects suggested by the preceding analysis. Two dependent variables served to anchor many of the hypotheses developed above about the effects of exit barriers.

1. Occurrence of Exit. As with entry barriers and actual entry (Orr, 1974), higher exit barriers should mean that firms exit from an activity less often. Is the actual occurrence of exit inversely related to the height (or presence) of exit barriers?

[k]Vintage and life cycle effects, which may appear in differentiated products as well, imply systematic movements over time in the accounting profits of individual firms and corresponding systematic patterns in the distribution of firms' profit rates at any given time. They may or may not also imply interfirm differences in economic or discounted-cash-flow rates of return.

[l]Managerial barriers may be particularly hard on the enforcement of consensus. Managers may make repeated attempts to turn a losing business around, in the process taking a short run view of coordination with other sellers and destabilizing the pattern of market conduct. A "managerial" firm stuck in a losing business may grow dissatisfied with its share of the market pie and attempt to force a revised understanding rather than to continue cooperation with its rivals.

2. **Prevalence of Low Profits**. Firms should continue to carry on low-profit activities only when exit barriers are present. Are unprofitable activities associated with exit barriers specific to the firm, or with barriers affecting all members of its industry, after we control for factors that might indicate low profits to be temporary?

These inquiries made use of an unusual body of data collected by the PIMS Program of the Strategic Planning Institute. Fifty-seven major North American corporations supplied disguised financial and market information on 556 individual "businesses" that they operate, whose outputs are characteristically confined within a single four-digit category of the Standard Industrial Classification. Data on the individual businesses for the years 1970–1973 were compiled by special allocations of existing company data, supplemented, for some items, by judgmental estimates supplied by operating managers of the company (Buzzell, Gale, and Sultan, 1975). The data provide a unique opportunity to study individual businesses without the bias introduced by diversification into published data based on the reports of enterprises. We utilized data on manufacturing businesses only, although PIMS also includes services.

Occurrence of Exit

A datum contained in the PIMS file is whether or not a competitor holding a market share of 5 percent or more exited between 1970 and 1973. The occurrence of exit can therefore be related to information on exit barriers in the reporting business, the company that operates it, and the industry in which it competes. Although the occurrence of exit is a logical (inverse) indicator of the presence of exit barriers, the PIMS data base for the most part informs us not about exit barriers and other conditions in the *industry* but rather about those in one competing firm. Furthermore, the competitor—the reporting business— *did not exit*, so there is a chance that its characteristics systematically misrepresent those of its industry, comprised of those that exit as well as those that carry on.

Therefore we proceed as follows. We take measurements of the reporting businesses and enterprises on the assumption that their characteristics typify the industry. But we also consider the statistical consequence if they prove systematically atypical, or if their traits reflect actions that the reporting firm took to evade whatever disturbance caused its competitor(s) to exit. To assume that the firm typifies its industry is evidently more sensible for some of its attributes than for others, and we shall note these differences as the variables are introduced.

The dependent variable in this analysis is a dummy equal to one if a major competitor (holding a 5 percent share) exited, zero otherwise. This qualitative dependent variable poses certain econometric problems, but ordinary least squares (used here) seems as satisfactory for binary choice analyses as the more sophisticated techniques that are available (Goldberger, 1964, pp. 248–251; Watson, 1974). Many businesses exit because of particular accidents and miscalculations unrelated to structural barriers to exit from their industries. To test the influence of these barriers on exit we therefore restricted our sample to businesses operating in industrial environments that offer a substantial incentive to exit. The sample was delineated as follows:

1. Rate of return on invested capital before taxes averaged less than 8 percent during 1970–1973. In the PIMS data the rate of return is measured before taxes on average investment allocated to the business. It is subject to random error in the allocation of joint capital costs. A pretax rate of return on total capital of 8 percent must be well below the opportunity cost of funds for most large enterprises. Our sample should include few businesses that would be yielding rates of return that their owners consider satisfactory on a long run basis.

2. The price-cost relation for the business, in the eyes of its management, compares at least reasonably well to those of its competitors.[m] This restriction excluded businesses earning low profits because of particular inefficiencies or adversities not characteristic of their industries.

3. The product was introduced by the company before 1965. We want to include only mature businesses with low accounting rates of return, because low profits in new ventures are likely to represent shakedown losses that the firm views as investments in learning or goodwill rather than as an occasion for exit. Inclusion of this class would inject undesirable random noise.

4. The products had matured sufficiently that the firm considered it beyond the introductory or growth stage of its product "life cycle" during 1970–73. Whatever the business's history within the firm, we excluded outputs sold in developing markets, because low profits could reflect shakedown losses. Also, there is an increased chance that conditions in reporting the firm would be atypical of conditions in the industry. The exit of firms from fast growing markets, furthermore, is likely to result from firm specific conditions.

These exclusions left us with a sample of 89 businesses. We proceeded to formulate a number of independent variables to explain the occurrence of exit by one or more competitors of these businesses. These fell into three classes: (1) indicators of exit barriers within the reporting firm, assumed to be characteristic

[m]The data base contains management's estimates of the output's selling price relative to those of its competitors, and of the business's costs relative to those of its competitors. Relative costs are in fact estimated separately for materials and labor, then weighted by their proportional importance to the business in question. We calculated a ratio of relative price to this index of relative costs, and excluded businesses for which the ratio was less than 0.9.

of its industry; (2) forces governing the incentive for firms to exit from the industry (other than those already controlled by excluding observations); and (3) indicators of the rate of "normal turnover" of businesses in the industry. The first group represents the core of our hypothesis; the second and third are included in order to make the model as complete as possible.

Whether or not a durable and specific asset exerts a fixed claim on the firm's revenues depends on the terms of its compensation, and outlays can be fixed contractually for the firm although the recipients of the income are not DSAs (Comanor and Wilson, 1971; Sherman and Tollison, 1971, 1972). Because our concern is with the behavior of the firm, we concentrate on the costs that it regards as fixed and the inputs that it cannot divest. What the firm counts as the capital committed to an activity should be correlated with the relevant tangible DSAs. Working capital is included because its inventory component is specific. We define as follows.

K/S Average investment of fixed and working capital (including the capitalized value of annual lease obligations), 1970–1973, divided by full capacity sales, 1970–1973. The denominator is constructed by dividing net sales by the average fraction of capacity utilized, as estimated by the respondents.

The heavier the weight of fixed investment (the higher is K/S), the less likely is exit (a finding reported by Marcus, 1967).

We also need a measure of the durability of major fixed assets committed to an activity. In the absence of specific information on the expected economic lives of fixed equipment, the best proxy is depreciation as a percentage of book value.

D/K Annual depreciation charge on major fixed assets, 1970–1973, divided by net book value of plant and equipment, 1970–1973.

The denominator inappropriately includes real estate. In a stationary steady state, depreciation divided by *gross* book value would provide an inverse measure of average capital durability whatever depreciation method the firm uses. Out of the steady state, however, wide discrepancies can occur between durability and current depreciation on gross assets. In particular, the faster the growth of either real activity or the price level, the more is our (inverse) proxy of durability biased upward if the usual sorts of depreciation schedules are in use. In a crude attempt to offset this bias we substituted net for gross book value in the denominator, because the faster is growth, the less accumulated depreciation (proportionally) do we subtract in going from gross to net. The variable should be positively related to exit.

As a complement to this treatment of depreciation we used a variable to indicate the newness of the business's plant and equipment.

NBV/GBV Net book value of plant and equipment, 1970–1973, divided by gross book value of plant and equipment, 1970–1973.

The newer an industry's plant and equipment, the lower its variable unit operating cost relative to what new competitors (or newly constructed facilities) can attain. Newer equipment makes an industry's sellers less likely to exit on account of either temporary adverse disturbances or the appearance of efficient new competitors (i.e., obsolescence). Note that the product of this variable and D/K is depreciation divided by gross book value. If all businesses were observed in steady state growth, that product would suffice to capture the influences of both longevity and newness. But the unsteadiness of actual states calls for factoring it into its components, as we have done.

Past outlays on intangible capital equip a business with durable and specific assets, even if they are not treated as capital in the accounts. We cannot measure the stocks of these assets, only the current flows of gross investment in the form of advertising and research and development outlays.

ARD/S Advertising and sales promotion expense plus product R&D expense, 1970–1973, divided by net sales, 1970–1973.

This proxy for the importance of intangible fixed capital should be negatively related to the occurrence of exit. Note, however, that disturbances causing a low rate of return to businesses in an industry are likely to impel both reductions in these discretionary expenditures and the exit of firms, so the predicted negative relation could be spurious.

A diversified firm is less likely to abandon an activity the more extensively it uses facilities shared with other outputs. This jointness can take numerous forms. Shared marketing channels as well as shared facilities and equipment can afford important elements of jointness. Disruption of these shared facilities is also a source of managerial disutility. Both tangible facilities and intangible organizational arrangements are likely to discourage exit when the activity in question is integrated with others carried on by the company, either backward or forward. The PIMS data base includes discrete or continuous estimates of each of these forms of jointness. The following variables should all be negatively related to exit.

SF Dummy variable, 1 if the business in 1973 shared 10 percent or more of its plant, equipment, and personnel with other components of the company.

SMP   Dummy variable, 1 if the business in 1973 shared more than 10 percent of its marketing expenditures (sales force, advertising and sales promotion programs) with other components of the company.

SDC   Dummy variable, 1 if the business in 1973 made 25 percent or more of its sales to customers also served by other components of the same company. (Common customers are taken as a proxy for common distribution channels.)

BVI   Backward vertical integration, measured by the percentage of total purchases of materials, supplies, etc., obtained in 1973 from other components of the same company.

SIF   Sales internal to the firm, percentage of sales by this business in 1973 made to other components of the company.

We also tested these variables in the following additive combinations:

$$JOINT = SF + SMP + SDC$$
$$LINK = BVI + SIF$$

The influences of each composite variable's components should be symmetrical in deterring exit from an unprofitable activity. Also, in the case of *JOINT*, the components do not seem conceptually independent of one another, and indeed they are highly correlated in the sample.

Some doubts intrude concerning the negative signs predicted for these variables—particularly the first three and *JOINT*. It is not clear that all firms active in a given business will employ the same joint arrangements, and thus that a single firm is an adequate proxy for its industry. Furthermore, jointness by itself can be a *response* to subnormal returns and a form of partial exit for the fixed facilities in question. Positive signs could indicate that the enterprise had diverted fixed facilities designed for an unprofitable activity to other uses, or had averted exit because its facilities were jointly used. The same unprofitability, if it affected the whole industry, could have caused the exit of other sellers, producing a positive relation. That is, the exogeneity of these independent variables is not assured.

Partly to test this last conjecture about the relation between jointness and exit, we included a measure of the diversity of the company in which the business is embedded. We might expect diversity to be related to exit for several reasons, and the predicted sign is ambiguous. On the one hand, diversification might comprise a reaction to subnormal returns suffered on part of a company's business, so that the diversion of resources to other activities represents a form of exit for any resources that are mobile within the company. This firm's exit through diversification would then be positively related to outright exit by other sellers, the dependent variable. On the other hand, the "managerial" hypothesis holds that diversified enterprises earning satisfactory rates of return overall may be softhearted about pruning unprofitable businesses, or better able to sustain losses in hope of an ultimate turnaround. The relation of diversity to exit would then be negative.

We used the variable:

DIV $\sum_{i} d_{ih} p_i$, where p_i is the proportion of the firm's total employment classified to industry i and d_{ih} is a weight indicating i's economic distance from the firm's home industry. The weight is determined from the Standard Industrial Classification (see Caves, 1975, chap. 4).

For reasons related to the inclusion of diversity, we entered a measure of the company's overall growth rate. For various reasons a company that is growing faster overall may be under less incentive to discard an unprofitable business. The high shadow price of funds characteristic of a fast-growing company argues against defensive investment, but satisfactory overall growth can also excuse a lack of managerial ruthlessness in severing the losers—a ruthlessness that a firm in an unsatisfactory position overall could not afford.

If the reporting firm's growth typifies that of others in the industry—a shaky assumption—we expect a negative relation between exit and:

COGROW Annual compound growth rate of the corporation's total sales, 1963–1972 (taken from *Compustat* data).

The industry's medium term growth rate should also influence the likelihood of exit. Current and recent growth of the market are no doubt a company's principal indicators of the future state of potential profits, especially where sellers are not very numerous. And expected future profits should have an important influence on the decision to exit after we control for current profitability (Marcus, 1967). Therefore we expect a negative relation between exit and

INDGRO Compound annual growth rate of industry shipments, 1963– 1972. Data are the firm's estimate of shipments by the relevant industry, if available, otherwise census data for the four-digit industry including the business.

The next variable bears on the inducement for firms to exit because sellers are squeezed by a strong upward trend in their costs. Other things equal, rising unit costs should be positively related to the occurrence of exit. We measured cost growth as follows.

CSTGRO Mean annual rate of increase of costs of labor and basic materials, 1970–1973, the components weighted by the average share of each in total costs over the period.

The remaining group of variables addresses the possibility that industries may vary in their "normal" levels of exit. Firms may go through life cycles, with life-spans varying from industry to industry. If some industries experience higher rates of generational turnover, perhaps due to greater frequency or amplitude of disturbances, they will show (*cet. par.*) more deaths *and* more births than other industries. Differences in exit barriers can be viewed as one factor explaining varying rates of generational turnover from industry to industry.

Also, our dependent variable signifies the *occurrence* of exit, not the proportion of going firms that departed, so we must control for the size of the population at hazard of death. Exit should be negatively related to

CONC Percentage of industry shipments in 1971 accounted for by the largest four firms in the four-digit Standard Industrial Classification category, or (where appropriate) in a weighted average of four-digit SIC industries.[n]

If industries vary in their rates of turnover, the occurrence of exit should be positively related to the occurrence of entry, with entry serving as a proxy for the unknown underlying forces that speed the generational turnover of sellers. With the rate of growth held constant we expect a positive relation between exit and

ENTRY Dummy variable, 1 if a major competitor (defined as one with at least a 5 percent market share) entered during 1970–1973.

One opportunity arose to delve into possible explanations for generational turnover rates differing among industries. Turnover should be speeded where production involves integrated process equipment that cannot be modernized piecemeal *and* where innovation often makes old processes obsolete. These conditions would inflate the proportion of firms finding themselves at any one time with inefficient plant requiring total replacement. Considering that our sample is confined to low-profit businesses, they would then face a strong incentive to exit. We felt that the joint presence of these conditions speeding turnover could be proxied by

[n]The PIMS data also include each firm's estimate of the number of competitors holding more than a 1 percent market share, but this variable is indicated only for broad ranges of values. Hence the concentration ratio, continuously variable in the data base, seemed preferable.

PROCRD   Expenses for process improvements to reduce the cost of manufacture, processing, and/or physical handling, 1970–1973, divided by net sales, 1970–1973.

It should be positively related to exit, on this reasoning. But process equipment
is also durable and specific, so *PROCRD* could measure a deterrent to exit (negative sign) rather than an inducement to exit.

Table 3–1 summarizes the regression results, which contain not a few sur-
prises. Significance is inferred from two-tailed tests, although definite sign predictions call for one-tailed tests of some coefficients. None of the exit barrier
variables related to tangible capital is significant. The capital-sales ratio is incorrectly signed but insignificant. *D/K* and *NBV/GBV* are both correctly signed in
most specifications, but neither is significant. The variable designating the importance of intangible goodwill capital (*ARD/S*), however, is correctly signed and
usually significant at the 1 percent level.

The variables measuring the linkage between the business in question and the
rest of the company turn in a peculiar performance. *LINK*, which combines
backward and forward integration, is correctly signed but not significant, its
coefficient only rising near the level of its standard error; disaggregating *LINK*
into its components *BVI* and *SIF* (equation 6) does not help. On the other hand,
JOINT and its components are wrongly signed and significant—*JOINT* at the 1
percent level, its components at the 5 percent level (equation 1). Apparently
JOINT and its components take up the role that we mentioned above as a possibility: adverse disturbances striking firms in an industry will induce a variety of
evasive measures, and some firms may exit while others avoid exit by using the
facilities required by the unprofitable business to produce and distribute other
lines of goods.

Two variables embodied hypotheses about managerial factors that might influence exit. Diversity (*DIV*) and the growth rate of the company (*COGROW*)
both increase the ability of an enterprise to sustain an unprofitable business and
reduce the pressure to eliminate it. Both carry the predicted negative signs, but
neither is significant. For both these variables, we are especially doubtful of the
assumption underlying our analysis that measures based on the firm are representative of the industry.

Variables measuring the inducement for firms to exit also display a mixed
performance. The expected inverse relation appears between industry growth
(*INDGRO*) and exit, and it is usually significant statistically. *INDGRO*'s performance contrasts with that of the firm's own growth (with which it is uncorre-
lated). *CSTGRO*, the upward trend in unit costs, is statistically significant and
incorrectly signed. For that curious result we can offer only this explanation
after the fact: If increase in input costs affect unit costs of members of an industry unequally, they relatively improve the lot of firms whose costs are under
control while they worsen the lot of firms with soaring costs. The competitors of

Table 3–1. Determinants of Occurrence of Exit of a Major Competitor, 1970–1973

Independent Variable	Equation					
	(1)	(2)	(3)	(4)	(5)	(6)
K/S	.0010 (.0013)	.0008 (.0013)	.0008 (.0013)	.0012 (.0014)	.0006 (.0016)	.0012 (.0014)
D/K	.0054 (.0078)	.0021 (.0078)		.0059 (.0081)	.0021 (.0091)	.0056 (.0082)
NBV/GBV	.0002 (.0036)	-.0011 (.0037)	-.0007 (.0033)	-.0016 (.0037)	-.0021 (.0042)	-.0018 (.0037)
ARD/S	-.0392[a] (.0105)	-.0359[a] (.0107)	-.0377[a] (.0100)	-.0385[a] (.0109)	-.0266[b] (.0122)	-.0384[a] (.0110)
SF	.2015[b] (.0911)					
SMP	.2045[b] (.1009)					
SDC	.2118[b] (.0990)					
JOINT		.1894[a] (.0390)	.2005[a] (.0374)	.2053[a] (.0407)		.2079[a] (.0414)
BVI						.0014 (.0019)
SIF						.0035 (.0047)

	(1)	(2)	(3)	(4)	(5)	(6)
LINK	-.0014 (.0016)	-.0010 (.0016)	-.0014 (.0015)	-.0018 (.0016)	-.0010 (.0019)	
DIV	-.1020 (.0807)	-.0854 (.0799)	-.0927 (.0765)	-.0305 (.0792)	-.0070 (.0906)	-.0223 (.0825)
COGROW		-.0020 (.0116)				
INDGRO	-.0260[b] (.0120)		-.0245[b] (.0112)	-.0214[b] (.0121)	-.0101 (.0136)	-.0220[c] (.0122)
CSTGRO	-.0568[a] (.0180)	-.0523[a] (.0178)	-.0569[a] (.0172)			
CONC	-.0054[b] (.0021)	-.0044[b] (.0020)	-.0052[a] (.0020)	-.0044[b] (.0021)	-.0067 (.0023)	-.0042[c] (.0022)
ENTRY	.1842[d] (.1248)	.2046[c] (.1221)	.1799[d] (.1168)	.1314 (.1234)	.2067[d] (.1404)	.1335 (.1242)
PROCRD	.0504 (.0398)	.0545[d] (.0405)	.0503 (.0391)	.0430 (.0416)	.0571 (.0475)	.0400 (.0425)
R^2	0.435	0.397	0.432	0.355	0.142	0.356
d.f.	74	76	77	77	78	76

Note: Standard errors appear beneath the regression coefficients. Significance levels are: a = 1 percent, b = 5 percent, c = 10 percent, all in two-tailed tests; d = 10 percent (one-tailed test). R^2 values are not corrected for degrees of freedom. Constant terms are omitted.

the latter firms are less likely to exit, whereas the competitors of the firms with slowly rising costs are more likely to exit. By implication, our sample is disposed toward businesses whose rates of return are low because their costs are out of hand.

The remaining variables control for factors reflecting the rate of normal turnover among firms in an industry. With our sample confined to low-profit and mature activities, we expect that exit and entry will be positively related. Thus *ENTRY* is correctly signed though weakly significant, usually 10 percent in a one-tailed test. Industry concentration (*CONC*) inversely proxies the number of firms in the market, controlling for the size of the population in which deaths might occur; it is significant. Finally, process R&D (*PROCRD*) turns in a weak performance, being correctly signed but only on the threshold of 10 percent significance in a one-tailed test.

We argued that the performance of *JOINT* (and its components) and *CST-GRO* indicates that these variables and the dependent variable reflect alternative responses of firms to common and unobserved underlying adverse disturbances. If that interpretation is correct, they do not belong among the causes of exit in the regression model. Therefore they are selectively deleted in equations 4 and 5. Their removal exacts a considerable cost in explained variance, and the deletion of *JOINT* proves fatal to the statistical significance of both industry concentration and industry growth. *CONC* and *JOINT* are the only relevant pair of variables with a high zero-order correlation, probably a reflection of the ability of high levels of advertising and product differentiation to promote concentration in certain classes of industries. The proportion of variance explained in equation 5, which omits these noncausal variables, is unimpressive at best.

In conclusion, we have found only weak evidence that tangible capital and linkages to other activities comprise barriers to exit. Intangible capital, however, does seem to create a significant exit barrier. We found evidence that exit is related to conditions portending continued low profits, and exit incentives induce a variety of evasive responses (transfer of potentially joint facilities to other uses, as well as outright exit). And we uncovered evidence of systematic differences in industries' rates of generational turnover.

Prevalence of Persistent Low Profits

In the preceding analysis we attempted to infer the presence of exit barriers from the absence of exits by leading competitors of a low-return business. Low-return businesses in the PIMS sample were used to identify industries from which exit would be indicated, on the assumption that the business's return was representative of those in its industry. Although we introduced a number of variables to control for possible differences between the PIMS business and its industry, the assumption remains a strong one.[o]

[o]For example, if a leading competitor of a low-return PIMS business *had* exited, the continued presence of the PIMS business made it questionable to infer that no exit barriers existed.

In view of this limitation, a complementary research design was employed that focused more directly on the association between exit barriers and the firm's presence in the market despite persistently low profits. What factors explain the continued operation (lack of exit) of businesses that had earned subnormal average returns over the period 1970–1973? In order to remove from consideration those businesses whose low current rates of return were probably temporary, we excluded from the sample all that were started within the five years prior to the period under study or were perceived by their managers to be in the introductory or growth phases of their product life cycle.[p] This screening yielded a sample of 310 businesses.

The dependent variable in the study was a dummy variable based on the average before-tax return on investment (ROI) of the business over the period 1970–1973:

$$LORETURN = 1 \text{ if ROI} < \text{cutoff value, 0 otherwise}$$

We utilized a number of ROI cutoffs ranging between 0 and 8 percent.[q] Many of the independent variables were taken over from the previous research design. Here, however, the measures of exit barriers defined from the firm's characteristics and the characteristics of its industry were tested for their influence on its business's own subnormal returns. The business's continuation despite subnormal returns was taken to signify the presence of exit barriers.

K/S, D/K and ARD/S were introduced as measures of the durability and specificity of the firm's capital as before, and a positive relation was expected to the low-return businesses' failure to exit for K/S and ARD/S, negative for D/K. In these tests we could correct K/S directly, using measures of capacity utilization for each business in the sample. The hypotheses linking DIV, $COGRO$, SF, SMP, SDC, $JOINT$, BVI, and SIF to the failure of low-return firms to exit are somewhat different from but complementary to those presented above. The four variables measuring the degree of jointness between the business and its parent's other businesses serve not only as potential measures of cost jointness and responce to exit barriers, as explained earlier, but also as measures of managerial exit barriers. The more extensive the jointness, the more likely is managerial utility maximization (or unwillingness to disrupt distribution channels, customers, etc.) to deter exit from a low-return business.

BVI similarly measures managerial exit barriers: the more of its inputs the business purchases from other units of the corporate parent, the less willing is

---

[p]Management's perception that a low-return business was early in its life cycle might be a rationalization to justify continued operations, but we have no way to discriminate between accurate perception and rationalization reflecting managerial exit barriers.

[q]Of the 310 businesses sampled, 94 had pretax ROIs of less than 8 percent; 69 had less than 5 percent; and 31 had less than 0 percent.

corporate management to exit from it.[r] High *SIF* may work in the opposite direction, however. A low-return business is likely to suffer from production inefficiencies or product quality inferior to its competitors. If it sells a large proportion of its output to other units of its corporate parent, their incentive to press for its exit would suggest a negative relation to the dependent variable.

The hypotheses about *COGROW* and *DIV* are the same as those outlined in the preceding section. Now we can introduce another measure of managerial exit barriers.

INYEAR   A dummy variable identifying the time period in which the business was entered: 1 if the business was entered prior to 1950; 2 if entered in 1950–1954; 3 if entered in 1955–1959; and 4 if entered in 1960–1964.

The longer the firm has been in the business, the greater may be the management's reluctance to exit from it. This hypothesis suggests a negative relation between the dummy and the prevalence of subnormal returns.

In addition to these relatively direct measures of exit barriers, several indirect measures are utilized in this analysis. Besides *NBV/GBV* and *INDGRO*, defined above, they include

CAPUTIL   Percentage of standard capacity used during the year, averaged over 1970–1973.
RELP/C   Ratio of management's estimates of its selling price relative to its competitors, and management's estimate of its relative costs.

We expect a business experiencing difficulty to go through a period of low capacity utilization. Chronically low utilization of capacity, however, signals the presence of exit barriers. In the absence of exit barriers, capacity would be reduced to match the new demand level in the medium to long run. Thus if persistently low utilization of capacity is associated with chronically low profits (a negative sign in our specification), we have evidence of exit barriers due to durable and specific assets.

A chronic adverse price-cost relation in persistently low-return businesses (negative sign) would also be associated with exit barriers. Because the price-cost ratio records management's own perceptions of its competitive deficiencies, a management in a persistently low-return business must be deterred from exit either by durable and specific assets or managerial exit barriers. *NBV/GBV*, a measure of the newness of plant and equipment, should be negatively related to

---

[r]A business with a high *BVI* might also earn low profits yet not be divested if it were charged inappropriately high internal transfer prices for the inputs it purchased internally. Internal transfer prices based on the market price are common practice in large U.S. corporations, and thus this possibility is deemed unlikely.

the presence of a business in the low-return group. Newness of plant would reflect recent reinvestment, unlikely in a poorly performing business or one with low potential.

INDGRO might be related to presence in the low-return group in a number of potentially conflicting ways. High industry growth generally means high profits, so a negative relation between growth and a business's presence in the low-return group may simply mean that it has failed to exit for reasons not captured by other independent variables. Undetected exit barriers may exist, or management may believe (rightly or wrongly) that slow growth is temporary. A positive sign for *INDGRO* could conceivably mean that some managements value growth and sacrifice profits to participate in fast growing industries.

Finally, three measures of the disturbance initially leading to the low returns were tested—*CONC, PROCRD* and a variable previously not defined:

> *TECHN* Dummy variable, 1 if a major technological change has occurred in the products or process of the business since 1967, and 0 otherwise.

Businesses in highly concentrated industries are unlikely to earn low profits. And if they do, management is unlikely to overestimate its ability to restore satisfactory profits. Each consideration suggests a negative relation between concentration and presence in the low-return group. Although atomistic industries may be associated with a greater probability of the business's earning subnormal profits in any year, a competitive environment does not justify its persistent presence in this group without exit.

PROCRD and *TECHN* are variables that attempt to measure the likelihood that the productive capacity of the low-return business is obsolete. Obsolete capacity deters sale of the assets, and interacts with their durability and specificity to discourage exit. *TECHN*, however, is an ambiguous measure of the likelihood of obsolete capacity because it measures both process and product innovation.

Table 3-2 presents the results of tests using these variables. Regressions are reported, taking 8 and 0 percent respectively as maximum ROI values for low-return businesses.[S] In each equation, *K/S, NBV/GBV, CAPUTIL,* and *RELP/C* all have the predicted sign and are highly significant. *D/K* and *ARD/S* always have the expected sign. Neither is significant in the 8 percent tests, but *ARD/S* becomes highly significant in the 0 percent tests, and *D/K* achieves a *t* value of approximately one.

[S]Tests were run with a cutoff value of 5 percent for ROI. The results were, as might be expected, intermediate between those reported for 0 and 8 percent. When the cutoff was elevated to 12 percent, the results deteriorated markedly, suggesting that businesses earning profits equal to or greater than their opportunity cost of capital had been included. The tests were also rerun using an earlier year of entry to exclude low-ROI businesses, with no effect on the results.

Table 3–2. Determinants of Failure to Exit from Low Return Businesses, 1970–1973

Independent Variable	Cutoff Maximum Rate of Return on Investment						
	8 Percent				0 Percent		
	(1)	(2)	(3)	(4)	(1)	(2)	(3)
Intercept	2.355^a (.506)	2.340^a (.465)	2.360^a (.499)	2.343^a (.484)	1.055^a (.326)	.8308^a (.3116)	1.067^a (.301)
K/S	.0048^a (.0011)	.0048^a (.0011)	.0051^a (.0011)	.0049^a (.0010)	.0029^a (.0007)	.0026^a (.0005)	.0031^a (.0007)
D/K	-.0023 (.0044)				-.0029 (.0028)		-.0028 (.0027)
ARD/S	.0085 (.0073)	.0075 (.0072)	.0068 (.0071)	.0066 (.0071)	.0139^a (.0047)	.0128^a (.0046)	.0132^a (.0045)
PROCRD	.0094 (.0303)		.0086 (.0298)		-.0046 (.0195)		
NBV/GBV	-.0045^b (.0023)	-.0039^b (.0021)	-.0041^b (.0022)	-.0038^b (.0021)	-.0025^b (.0015)	-.0020^c (.0013)	-.0027^b (.0014)
CAPUTIL	-.0073^a (.0018)	-.0077^a (.0017)	-.0076^a (.0018)	-.0077^a (.0018)	-.0049^a (.0012)	-.0033^a (.0011)	-.0049^a (.0011)
RELP/C	-.0155^a (.0044)	-.0155^a (.0042)	-.0158^a (.0044)	-.0155^a (.0043)		-.0074^a (.0028)	-.0074^a (.0027)
CONC	-.0004 (.0011)		-.008 (.0011)		-.0006 (.0007)		-.0008 (.0007)
SF	.1264^b (.0597)		.1162^b (.0553)	.1170^b (.0551)	.1274^a (.0384)	.1200^a (.0357)	.1242^a (.0347)

	(1)	(2)	(3)	(4)	(5)	(6)	(7)
SMP	.0086 (.0590)				−.0134 (.0379)		
SDC	−.0588 (.0627)				−.0114 (.0404)		
JOINT		.0196 (.0233)					
BVI	.0012 (.0011)	.0015[c] (.0010)	.0013 (.0011)	.0014[c] (.0010)	.0002 (.00007)	.0005 (.0007)	
SIF	−.0299[c] (.0208)	−.0037[b] (.0020)	−.0032[c] (.0020)	−.0032[c] (.0019)	.0005 (.0013)	.0002 (.0013)	
DIV	.0820[b] (.0444)	.0616[c] (.0411)	.0737[b] (.0425)	.0719[b] (.0416)	.0682[a] (.0286)	.0689[a] (.0269)	.0711[a] (.0268)
COGROW	.0035 (.0071)		.0029 (.0070)		.0029 (.0046)		
INDGRO	−.0414 (.0312)	−.0481[c] (.0325)	−.0411 (.0329)	−.0420[c] (.0327)	−.0138 (.0214)	−.0157 (.0212)	
TECHN	−.0066 (.0652)				−.0717[b] (.0419)		−.0632[c] (.0399)
INYEAR	−.0278 (.0347)		−.0261 (.0339)	−.0272 (.0336)	.0146 (.0223)	.0049 (.0218)	
R^2	.184	.167	.181	.178	.207	.191	.202
d.f.	291	299	295	298	291	298	299

Note: Standard errors appear beneath the regression coefficients. Significance levels (one-tailed tests) are: a = 1 percent; b = 5 percent; c = 10 percent. R^2 values are not corrected for degrees of freedom.

Of the measures of managerial exit barriers, only *SMP* and *SDC* yield unexpected signs, and neither is significant. *SF* is highly significant and has the expected positive sign in all equations. The coefficient of *DIV* is always positive and significant, suggesting that the net effect of diversification is to increase management's proclivity to remain in low-return businesses. *BVI* and *SIF* both have the expected signs and are significant in the 8 percent tests. They fall from significance in the 0 percent tests, *BVI* retaining the expected sign. Although *SIF* changes sign, its simple correlation with the dependent variable remains negative and its significance level is very low. *COGROW* has different signs in the two tests, though it is insignificant in both—perhaps reflecting the conflicting hypotheses for its effect. *INYEAR* takes the expected negative sign in the 8 percent runs, changing sign and losing all significance in the 0 percent runs. *INDGRO* is negative in all tests and significant in several 8 percent runs, where its better performance may be due to its positive effect on rate of return.

The disturbance variables are generally consistent with our expectations, with one important exception. *CONC* is always negative but not significant. *PROCRD* is positive as expected in the 8 percent runs, but not significant. Its sign changes in the 0 percent runs but it loses all significance. *TECHN* is negative in all runs, contrary to expectations, and it becomes significant in the 0 percent tests. In addition to the measurement error in this variable noted earlier, we can suggest an ad hoc explanation for this unexpected sign. The occurrence of a major innovation tends to raise short run profits for all businesses adopting it, keeping them out of the low return category.[t]

The results, in some contrast with the preceding analysis of the determinants of exit, lend strong support to most hypotheses advanced. Both the direct and indirect measures of exit barriers due to tangible capital are right signed and in general highly significant, as is the measure of intangible capital exit barriers. The variables describing the linkage between the business in question and the company's other businesses perform quite strongly. The general improvement in the results over those for the determinants of exit is consistent with the more direct character of the test and improved quality of the statistical specifications.

Further Statistical Tests

Some additional tests on the determinants of *LORETURN* are reported here, briefly and without statistical detail.

1. Our capital intensity variable (K/S) includes working as well as fixed capital. Working capital is partly specific and nondurable, so its influence might

---

[t]Readers may wonder why *ARD/S* did not emerge wrongly signed for the same reason, in view of its positive relation to industries' profit rates in previous studies. Our finding for the dummy dependent variable is consistent with a positive relation between ROI and *ARD/S* for profitable businesses. That relation does hold in the PIMS data, although it is not strong.

differ in strength from that of fixed capital. We replaced K/S with two variables, gross book value divided by sales, and working capital divided by sales. Each is highly significant, and the coefficient of working capital is actually several times larger than that of fixed capital. This result suggests a managerial factor: abundant working capital helps a firm trying to carry on in a low-profit business.

2. The longevity of fixed capital, measured inversely by D/K, should have greater influence where K/S is relatively high. We replaced D/K, with an interaction variable formed by dividing K/S by D/K. It is correctly signed and significant at the 12.5 percent level or better in the 8 percent sample, 5 percent or better in the 0 percent sample.

3. Jointness should deter exit only where one of the joint inputs is a DSA or where managerial exit barriers are in operation. Statistically, that consideration suggests that variables measuring jointness should be added only via interactions. We nonetheless reported additive specifications in Tables 3−1 and 3−2 because of uncertainty that our measures of structural and managerial exit barriers were correct and comprehensive. Interactions in fact did little to improve the performance of variables measuring jointness. Replacing the significant variable SF (shared facilities) by the interaction $SF*K/S$ raises the value of R^2 by about .015; but the performance of $JOINT*K/S$ is inferior, suggesting that the influence of $JOINT$ all reposes in its component SF. The importance of shared distribution channels and marketing programs should be augmented where advertising and product R&D are important; the interaction $ARD/S*(SMP + SDC)$ is rightly signed but significant only at 18 percent (0 percent sample, not at all in the 8 percent sample). No significant interactions were detected between jointness and the managerial variables.

V. STATISTICAL FINDINGS AND SUMMARY

Taken together, the two sets of results for the occurrence of exit and the persistence of low-return businesses offer some general conclusions about exit barriers. The presence of tangible DSAs is a strong determinant of the persistence of a low-return business, although not of the failure of competitors to exit. The influence of joint facilities and distribution is supported as determining a firm's persistence in an industry from which others exit, and it does not depend strictly on the presence of other measured exit barriers. The influence of intangible DSAs, perhaps unexpectedly, receives potent support from both statistical analyses, as do the variables indicating managerial barriers to exit.

If our empirical results dictate a major overhaul of received wisdom, it is to elevate the importance of intangible and managerial exit barriers relative to those linked to tangible assets. Another striking if incidental finding of the analysis of exit determinants is that industries—low profit ones, at least—display systematically differing rates of generational turnover. The scale of exit barriers must be regarded as one influence determining or modifying this turnover rate, along with elements of barriers to entry and the character of market conduct in the industry.

We have examined barriers to exit as a structural influence on market conduct and performance. They appear to deserve a place in our standard list of market structure elements. They alter conduct by expanding the risks that firms face, thereby shifting collective market conduct toward patterns—generally collusive— that might mitigate downside risk. But they also make collusion more difficult to sustain, especially because they permit disturbances to deal differing fates to the sellers in a market, and complicate the pursuit of consensus. Exit barriers interact with other elements of market structure. They share important affinities with the structural sources of barriers to entry. Our statistical analysis (summarized above) confirms the structural sources of exit barriers, but shows them unexpectedly associated with intangible capital and managerial factors. Elevated exit barriers thus may be an effect of the separation of control from ownership of large corporations.

Unlike pricing and other ongoing elements of firm conduct, the decision to exit from (or enter) a particular market is a one-time decision in which opportunities for learning, market feedback, and adjustments are limited if not absent. Although mistaken pricing decisions will rear their heads to prompt adjustments toward the maximizing price, decisions to exit are largely irreversible, and each decision is unique to its market context. Limited feedback and adjustment possibilities raise the importance of studying the decision making process itself, and not merely the structural determinants of its optimal outcome. Thus while one might argue that Carnegie Tech models of organizational decision making may not be important for understanding the firm's pricing behavior, they are clearly very important for understanding exit behavior. The importance of managerial barriers to exit, amply demonstrated in our statistical results, follows directly from this view.

We can now relate our results to the normative significance of exit barriers. They raise two classes of welfare issues.

1. Ex ante they are a source of social risk in decisions about resource allocation. The cost of that risk cannot be avoided, though it can be incurred more or less efficiently. Our analysis shows that the ex ante cost also includes an expanded incentive to collusion in oligopoly, though one that need not lead to increased *effective* collusion. On the other hand, exit barriers make some contribution to allocative efficiency in oligopolistic markets by discouraging the purposive elevation of entry barriers.

2. Ex post exit barriers can generate problems of income distribution and equity when durable and specific assets are truly sunk in their unremunerative

uses. They can also raise questions of market failure when DSAs can be converted to other uses through transformation (retraining or remodeling) and/or transportation.

Both conversions presume an investment in information followed by an investment in the transformation; both are risky, and efficient conversions may fail to occur because of information failures, capital rationing, or peculiarities of the preference functions associated with the affected factors (locational preferences, short time horizons, risk aversion). Our analysis raises the possibility that managerial barriers and the jointness of production in diversified companies may impede efficient allocations. Whether these barriers are "unnatural" and inefficient is too complex a question to address briefly, but we suggest they can induce market failures born out of managerial utility maximization, impacted information, and imperfections in the market for corporate control.

The policy implications of exit barriers also can only be sampled here. Among the complex arguments pro and con for restricting conglomerate mergers, an important negative factor is the social case for maintaining a free market in corporate ownership in order to facilitate efficient allocation of entrepreneurial talent and increase the liquidity of corporate assets. Our analysis suggests that high exit barriers amplify the case for a free market in corporate control, because a firm's market value, if sold as a going concern, can then greatly exceed its breakup value if no purchasers are available. Guidelines on mergers and applications of the failing business doctrine in merger proceedings should recognize this consideration and take account of its varying weight from industry to industry.

Although the apparent ability of the industrial countries to avert deep depressions has removed the most important consequences of exit barriers, we would nonetheless argue that the long run development process in the industrial countries is increasing their structural importance. The growth of income and productivity is associated with capital deepening in the economy at large. Even if this deepening occurs through shifts in activity among economic sectors rather than capital deepening within sectors, it can raise the economy's exit barriers in a weighted average sense.

Education may increase human flexibility, but much training is highly specialized, and much physical plant surely grows more product specific as it becomes more sophisticated and "automated." There is evidence that the division of labor among industrial countries has become increasingly fine since World War II, implying that plants and enterprises become increasingly specialized. There is also evidence that economies of scale in many settings are largely economies of specialization on closely specified activities. Whatever the present-day social significance of exit barriers for economic behavior, it seems likely to grow in the future.

✳ *Chapter 4*

Profits, Market Structure, and Portfolio Risk

James L. Bothwell
Theodore E. Keeler

It has long been hypothesized that industrial concentration and entry barriers should have an influence on profits. These hypotheses have been among the most extensively tested of any in the field of industrial organization, ever since Bain (1951, 1956) first developed and tested them. Relatively few studies, however, have incorporated risk into the market structure–performance relationship, despite the general belief that with risk-averse investors, even competitive, perfectly functioning markets will confer higher risk firms and industries. And those studies incorporating risk into this relationship have more often than not yielded insignificant or implausible empirical results.

This chapter integrates a relatively recent theory of portfolio risk into a market structure–performance equation (which differs from previous specifications in some important ways other than risk as well), and shows the results of estimation of this equation with two alternative sets of cross-section firm data.

The first section briefly surveys specification of the relationship between risk and return incorporated into previous market structure–performance studies, and then sets forth the more recent theory of risk and return from the capital asset pricing model of Sharpe and Lintner. The second section develops a new specification of the relationship between market structure and performance, including the effects of portfolio risk and of corporate profits taxes.

The third section describes the data used to estimate both portfolio risk for each firm and the market structure–performance equations. The fourth section

This work was largely funded by the Institute of Business and Economic Research at the University of California. We are very much indebted to Stephen C. Peck for his many useful comments on this work. Useful comments were also made by M.A. Adelman, J. Guy, R.T. Masson, and T.J. Rothenberg. In addition, we thank W.G. Shepherd, L. Weiss, and H.M. Mann for making data compiled by them available to us for this research.

71

discusses various estimation problems encountered, as well as presenting the results. The fifth discusses some recently raised challenges to the validity of the concentration-profits model, and the implications of our results for these challenges. The final section provides a summary of our results and conclusions.

I. RISK AND PROFITS

Previous attempts to quantify the relationship between risk and return have used one of three different measures as proxies to reflect variations in risk exposure faced by investors. The first measure is the standard deviation either of a firm's annual rate of return or of an industry's average rate of return over time. Empirical results incorporating this measure have been mixed. Within his sample of industries, Stigler (1963) finds no statistically significant relationship between average rates of return on assets and the standard deviation of annual rates of return for two periods, 1938-47 and 1947-54. For the first of the two periods, he in fact finds a negative relationship .

Fisher and Hall (1969), on the other hand, working with a sample of 88 firms, find a significant, positive relationship between firms' average rates of return on equity over the period 1950-64 and the standard deviation of firms' rates of return about a trend line. Fisher and Hall do not, however, control for other elements of market structure in their equation. Shepherd (1972), using the same measure of risk as Fisher and Hall, does control for other aspects of market structure, but with his sample of 231 firms for the period 1960-67, he finds a negative (and insignificant) relationship between risk and profitability.

A second measure of risk is based on the dispersion of rates of return among firms within an industry. Again, the evidence is mixed. Stigler finds no significant relationship between average rates of return and this measure of risk within his sample. On the other hand, Cootner and Holland (1970), with a sample of 39 industries, find a signficant, positive association between industry average rates of return and the standard deviation of firms' rates of return on the industry-wide average for each of the postwar years 1946-60. But again, they do not control for other elements of market structure.

A third measure of risk used is the variation in degrees of leverage among firms or, on average, among industries, the idea being that a firm or industry with relatively more borrowed capital represents a greater financial risk than one with relatively less debt. But the empirical evidence does not support the relationship here which the theory would predict. Stigler reports no significant relationship between rates of return and financial leverage within his sample.

Bradley Gale (1972), on the other hand, finds a significant, *positive* relationship between rates of return on equity and the ratio of common equity to assets for a sample of 106 firms. Hall and Weiss (1967) report similar results with their interindustry data. These last two studies would seem to have found results directly contradicting what the theory would suggest. In short, the results of previous studies of risk and firm profitability have been mixed at best. This may be the result of mismeasurement of risk on the part of previous studies.

In the past decade, a new theory of risk has been developed. This new theory of the relationship between risk and return is based on an intuitively plausible idea: if the investors can eliminate risk by diversifying their portfolio, they will do so. Therefore, the only measure of risk that matters for any given invetment is that which cannot be eliminated through diversification. It follows, then, that the cost of equity capital to a firm will be a function of the nondiversifiable risk associated with the return on that firm's stock. The foundations for this theory were laid by Markowitz (1959), and were extended by Sharpe (1964), Lintner (1965), Fama (1970), and others.

The relationship between risk and return was first developed rigorously by Sharpe and Lintner with a rather restrictive set of assumptions. It is assumed that every investor has identical subjective estimates of the means, variances, and covariances of the returns on all assets; that there are perfect capital markets, with no taxes, and riskless borrowing and lending opportunities; and that investors maximize expected utility over a single-period time horizon by selecting among alternative portfolios on the basis of the mean and variance of their returns. Under these assumptions, the equilibrium expected return on the j'th capital asset will be given by:

$$E(R_j) = R_f + [E(R_m) - R_f] \beta_j \tag{1}$$

where $\quad \beta_j = \dfrac{\text{cov}(R_j, R_m)}{\text{var}(R_m)} \quad$ is the "correlated," "nondiversifiable," or

"portfolio" risk of asset j (i.e., the stock of firm j),

$\quad E(R_j)$ is the expected return on the jth asset,

$\quad R_f$ is the riskless rate of interest,

$\quad E(R_m)$ is the expected return on a totally-diversified market portfolio, and

$\quad (E(R_m) - R_f)$ is the market risk premium.

(A complete derivation and explanation of this result may be found in Jensen (1972, pp. 358–363).) According to the Sharpe-Lintner model, then, the appropriate measure of risk is the value β, commonly called a "beta coefficient." It has not previously been incorporated into a market structure–performance equation, and it is our aim to do so.[a]

[a]Litzenberger and Joy (1973) do indeed make an interindustry comparison of profits correctly adjusted for nondiversifiable risk. But they do not incorporate market structure

Before developing the market structure–performance model, however, it is appropriate to consider briefly the evidence from previous studies shedding light on the validity of the Sharpe-Lintner model. Perhaps the aspect of this model most likely to incur skepticism is the apparent unrealism of its assumptions. A number of theoretical studies, however, have expanded on the model, relaxing its initial assumptions, and they show the basic model to be remarkably robust to variations in these assumptions. Fama (1970), for example, shows that under certain conditions, risk-averse investors seeking to maximize expected utility in a multiperiod world will make investment consumption decisions in the same way they would in a single-period model.

Another variant on the model (Brennan, 1970) drops the assumption of riskless borrowing and lending; the assumption of no taxes is also dropped and replaced by an assumption of positive, differential rates on dividends and capital gains. A significant conclusion of all these derivative models is that although the exact specification of the capital market equilibrium condition is slightly different in each of them, the major implications are the same—the market risk premium is positive, the relationship between risk and expected return is positive and linear, and no nonportfolio risk measure is related to equilibrium expected returns.

The Sharpe-Lintner model has been subjected to considerable empirical verification, as well as theoretical generalization. The work of Miller, Scholes, Black, Jensen, Fama, and others has subjected the model to extensive econometric tests using security price data and the evidence from capital markets has generally been found to be quite consistent with theory.[b]

II. THE MODEL

We wish to explain interfirm and interindustry differences in profits through differences in risk and in market structure characteristics. We turn first to the question as to what measure of profits is most appropriate for such a relationship.

Market power enables firms to set price above marginal costs. This simple fact, agreed upon by most economists, should be the starting point for any analysis of profitability as it relates to market structure. It is this notion that prompted Lerner (1934) to define a measure of market power, which he called the "degree of monopoly," in the following terms:

$$M = \frac{\text{price} - \text{marginal cost}}{\text{price}}$$

variables into their analysis; they do state, however, that portfolio risk explains only a small part of total variation in profits, and that further work would be necessary to analyze the other causes.

[b] Jensen (1972) provides a good summary of all this evidence up to the time his article was written.

Although this gauge of monopoly has some measurement problems,[c] we would argue that it comes closer to reflecting the market power a firm has than any other static measure. As it is written above, however, the measure cannot be used, because doing so would require finding price and marginal cost data for every product of every firm. If all the firms observed in our sample are operating in a region beyond minimum efficient scale, however, and if they are minimizing costs (i.e., are at or near their long run average cost curves), then marginal cost is equivalent to average cost, and the degree of monopoly is:

$$M = \frac{P - MC}{p} = \frac{P - AC}{p} = \frac{(P - AC)Q}{p \cdot Q} \tag{2}$$

$$= \frac{\text{total revenue} - \text{total cost}}{\text{total revenue}}$$

where Q is firm output per unit time. Thus it is possible to use the excess profits rate over sales as an estimate of degree of monopoly. Qualls (1972, 1974) has already used this measure in market structure–performance work, although his analysis does not incorporate risk and tax effects.

It is worth noting that in this model, "costs" include not only current operating expenses, but also debt and equity capital costs, the last being determined by the previously mentioned Sharpe-Lintner capital asset pricing model. We hypothesize that for each firm in our samples, this degree of monopoly is determined by a set of market structure variables, which we label:

$$X_1, X_2, \ldots, X_n$$

$$M_j = \frac{\text{total revenue} - \text{total cost}}{\text{total revenue}} \tag{3}$$

$$= \frac{S_j - E_j - r_j K_j}{S_j} = a_0 + a_1 X_1 + a_2 X_2 + \ldots + a_n X_n$$

where M_j is the degree of monopoly on average for all products produced by firm j;

S_j is total sales of firm j;

E_j is all costs other than equity capital costs of the jth firm (includes all interest and debt servicing payments);

K_j is the book value of common equity for the jth firm; and

[c]Most specifically, price-cost margins could appear quite different for different firms in the same industry—even if they were the same in reality—because of different degrees of vertical integration among different firms. Ths fact was pointed out to us by R.T. Masson.

r_j is the average cost of a dollar's worth of equity capital for the jth firm (assumed equal to its marginal cost of equity capital).

From the Sharpe-Litner model:

$$r_j = E(R_j) = R_f + (E(R_m) - R_f)\beta_j \tag{4}$$

where $E(R_j)$, R_f, $E(R_m)$, and β_j are as defined before.

Over a given (reasonably short) stretch of time, $E(R_m)$ and R_f may be taken as constants, so that:

$$r_j = E(R_j) = c_1 + (c_2 - c_1)\beta_j \tag{5}$$

Values for β_j, the beta coefficient for each firm in the sample, can themselves be estimated statistically from time series regressions of the monthly returns on the common stock of firm j upon the monthly returns on an index used as a proxy for the market portfolio:

$$r_{jt} = b_D + \beta R_{m,t} + e_{jt} \quad t = 1, \ldots, T \text{ months} \tag{6}$$

Substituting (5) into (3) yields:

$$M_j = \frac{S_j - E_j - r_j K_j}{S_j} = \frac{S_j - E_j - (c_1 + (c_2 - c_1)\hat{\beta}_j)K_j}{S_j}$$

where the hat on β is included to indicate it was estimated from (6). Rearranging the structure-performance equation so as to allow estimation of the cost of capital on the right-hand side of the equation yields the following relationship:

$$\frac{S_j - E_j}{S_j} = a_0 + a_1 X_1 + \ldots + a_n X_n + [c_1 + (c_2 - c_1)\hat{\beta}_j)\frac{K_j}{S_j}] \tag{7}$$

$$= a_0 + a_1 X_1 + \ldots + a_n X_n + c_1 \frac{K_j}{S_j} + c_3 \frac{K_j}{S_j}\hat{\beta}_j$$

where $c_3 = c_2 - c_1$.

It is this equation which we use to estimate the structure–performance relationship. However, as it stands, the equation does not deal with the effects of the corporate profits tax. One of the first things a microeconomics student learns about a profits tax is that it will have no impact on the price or output of a monopolist. However, the U.S. corporate profits tax is not simply a tax on economic profits; it also (to some degree) taxes the cost of equity capital. Common sense reasoning then tells us that from the viewpoint of a single firm (but *not* in a general equilibrium model), that component of the corporate profits tax that is charged against the cost of its capital will be passed on. If this is the case, the following equation summarizes the degree of monopoly from the viewpoint of a single firm j:

$$M_j = \frac{S_j - E_j - \frac{r_j}{(1-\tau)} K_j}{S_j} \tag{8}$$

where τ is the effective corporate profits tax rate on the firm. The equity cost, r_j, is divided by $1-\tau$ because for every dollar paid out to stockholders (or, in the case of retained earnings, for every dollar accruing as a capital gain), it is necessary to earn $1/(1-\tau)$ dollars in profits overall. (It must be emphasized that $S_j - E_j$ is profits *before* corporate taxes.)

Although rational profit maximizing behavior requires that a single firm pass on that part of the tax that falls on the cost of equity capital, it is worth repeating that our specification says nothing (and assumes nothing) about the tax in a general equilibrium setting: that is a function of the mobility of resources between the corporate and noncorporate sectors, and of the mobility of investors' supplies of capital between debt and equity. The degree of overall shifting will be shown by the extent to which the market return, R_m, shifts in response to a shift in τ. More specifically, with no shifting in a general equilibrium setting, $R_m/(1-\tau)$ will remain constant for any value of τ, and investors in equity capital will bear the full burden of the tax.

This study need not concern itself with the answer to such a general equilibrium question: since all our observations are from the corporate sector, it is of no consequence to our regressions whether resources have been shifted out of the corporate sector by the profits tax. The equation estimated is, therefore:

$$\frac{S_j - E_j}{S_j} = a_0 + a_1 X_1 + \ldots + a_n X_n + c_1 \frac{K_j}{(1-\tau)S_j} + c_3 \frac{K_j \hat{\beta}_j}{(1-\tau)S_j} \tag{9}$$

where all variables are defined as before.

It is worth nothing that equation (9) can be used to provide an independent test of the Sharpe-Lintner hypothesis, as well as estimating the structure–performance equation. More specifically, we know that c_1 should be equal to the return on a risk-free asset (often measured by the U.S. Treasury Bill rate), and c_3 is a measure of the risk premium attached to a fully diversified portfolio (i.e., where beta is one). Thus, $c_1 + c_3$ should be a measure of cost of capital for a fully diversified stock market investment.

Before this equation is estimated, consideration should be given to the market structure variables to be used. Despite the large number of market structure– performance studies made in recent years, there is by no means complete agreement as to what structure variables are most appropriate, what they mean theoretically, and how they should be specified (linearly or, if nonlinearly, what form). It is therefore necessary and appropriate to discuss the variables used here, as well as their theoretical justification.

The first and most obvious structure variable is concentration, and we use four-firm industry concentration (SC). The theory behind this, developed by Bain (1951), is well known: the smaller the number of firms that control a market, the more readily they will be able to coordinate their pricing activities so as to charge prices that exceed marginal costs. We shall discuss in the next section the method used to attribute a four-firm industry concentration ratio to each firm in the samples.

Although many studies have found correlations between concentration and profits, some recent studies, most especially those by Demsetz (1973) and Mancke (1974), have opened up to question just what such a correlation means. Specifically, they point out that such a correlation might stem from something quite different from the coordinative activity that Bain originally hypothesized. We shall deal with these objections, and with variations in specification of the equations in order to account for them, at a later time.

Along with concentration, barriers to entry represent the other most important element of market structure. In the manner of Bain, we use dummy variables to indicate the height of entry barriers. Industries are classified into three entry barrier classes: low to moderate, substantial, and very high. One dummy variable (SB) is 1 in value for substantial entry barriers and 0 for the other two classes, and another (HB) is 1 for high entry barriers and 0 for other classes (then, of course, the constant in the regression corresponds to the value of this coefficient for the low barriers industries).[d] Again, given that we are working with diversified firms and not industries, there are some problems attributing appropriate values for these variables to a given firm in the sample; these problems are discussed in the next section on the data.

These entry barrier variables may be thought to be somewhat arbitrary, for determining their values requires some judgment as to which category an industry belongs. However, these variables are preferable to most direct, quantitative entry barrier variables, for the theoretical justification of the latter type is often shaky. Consider, for example, advertising expenditures as a measure of entry

[d]These terms for heights of entry barriers are defined here as Bain originally defined them (1956, chap. 3–6). In fact, although the entry barrier data used here come from more recent sources than Bain (see the next section), they are consistent with Bain's earlier work, and are derived by the same methodology.

barriers from product differentiation. High advertising expenditures may either cause high profits or be caused by them; furthermore, advertising expenditures data take no account of how differentiable a product is in the first place. Qualitative variables of the sort developed by Bain provide a straightforward method of incorporating the effects of entry barriers into the model, with less likelihood of such problems.

It is now worth summarizing the basic equation to be estimated:

$$(10)$$

$$\frac{S_j - E_j}{S_j} = a_0 + a_1\,SC_j + a_2\,SB_j + a_3\,HB_j + c_1\,\frac{K_j}{(1-\tau)S_j} + c_3\,\frac{K_j\hat{\beta}_j}{(1-\tau)S_j} + e_j$$

where e_j is an assumed error term for firm j, and the other variables are defined as before. The hypotheses suggested by the theory as discussed so far would indicate the following:

(a)   From the market structure–performance hypotheses:

$a_1 > 0$

$a_2 > 0$

$a_3 > 0$

(b)   From the Sharpe-Lintner capital asset pricing model:

$c_1 \simeq \bar{R}_f$, the average riskless rate of return over the period.

$c_3 \simeq E(R_m) - \bar{R}_f$, the risk premium for an average risk stock.

This is of course not the only possible way of specifying the market structure–performance relationship. There are numerous alternatives, some of which are arguably at least as appropriate as the one shown here. For example, Bain, in his classic 1951 article, finds that there is a threshold effect of concentration on profits. At an eight-firm concentration ratio of around 70 percent, profits take a sudden jump, apparently reflecting a much greater ease of price coordination for firms in industries above the threshold in concentration. The appropriate specification to reflect this effect would be a dummy variable equal to zero when concentration is below the threshold level and one otherwise.

A more sophisticated variation on this theme (used by Bain (1956), Mann (1966), and Qualls (1974)) would allow different profit rates (or price-cost margins) in each of six different concentration and entry barrier classes. For example, one class would consist of firms in industries with high concentration and very high entry barriers; another would be low to moderate concentration and substantial entry barriers, etc. Yet another specification would subtract out the cost of capital completely from the left-hand side of the equation, leaving only conventional market structure variables on the right-hand side (this is done by Qualls (1974)). Fortunately our results are remarkably insensitive to alternative specifications.

All the specifications mentioned above were tried, and the results of each tell the same basic story as the simpler specification shown here.[e] Because of space limitations, only the results of specification (10) are shown here. But the results of a number of other specifications are shown in Bothwell (1976, chap. 3). The data used to estimate (10) are discussed in the following section.

III. THE DATA

The two overlapping samples of firm observations used in the present study are derived from previously published works. The first consists of 193 firms over the period 1956–62, and is a subset of a sample of 341 firms compiled by Hall and Weiss (1967). Basically, they selected firms from the *Fortune Directory* of the 500 largest industrial corporations which were within the top 400 for at least one of the seven years covered, and excluded those they believed were either below optimal scale, subject to regulatory constraint, or too diversified, and for which concentration or production indices were not available. The second sample consists of 158 firm observations over the period 1960–67 and is a subset of a panel of 231 firms taken from the 1967 *Fortune Directory* by Shepherd (1972: see the appendix to his article for a listing of his sample). Shepherd has excluded firms from this sample on the basis of inadequate market structure data, a high degree of diversification, a major merger during the decade of the 1960s, or the perceived existence of a major disequilibrium during the period.

In selecting subsamples from the Hall-Weiss and Shepherd samples, we used only two criteria. First, in order to compute the beta coefficients necessary to estimate the cost of equity capital, complete stock market data had to be available for each firm on the CRSP (Center for Research in Security Prices) tape, which is supplied by the University of Chicago School of Business and contains partial monthly returns on 2,085 common stocks over the period 1926–68. Also included on this tape is the monthly return on "Fisher's Arithmetic Index," an unweighted average of the return on all stocks listed on the New York Stock

---

[e]Although each of the alternative specifications tells the same basic story as that told by the specifications in Table 4–1 each alternative has certain disadvantages as well. The threshold concentration dummy (valued at one for four-firm industry concentration ratios over 55 percent) gave less explanatory power than the straight concentration variable used here. The equation allowing different price-cost margins for each of six concentration and entry barriers classes (estimated again by using separate dummy variables for each class, save for one class, which took on the regression constant) provided less reliable estimates of the relationship between concentration, profits, and entry barriers than do the equations in Table 4–1. This unreliability would appear to stem from the fact that some combinations of concentration and entry barrier classes have very few firm observations in them. Nevertheless, this specification yielded essentially the same results as those shown in Table 4–1. There is a rough tendency for firms in industries with high concentration and high entry barriers to earn high profits; risk variables have the same effects as in equation (10); and the inclusion of market share into the equation tends to weaken the effects of concentration on price-cost margins. Finally, keeping risk variables on the right-hand side of the equation has the advantage that it allows an independent test of the Lintner-Sharpe hypothesis on a set of data never used for those purposes before.

Table 4–1. Structure-Performance Regression Results

Equation	Data Sample	Dependent Variable	Intercept	SC	HB	SB	$\dfrac{K}{S(1-\tau)}$	$\dfrac{\hat{\beta}K}{S(1-\tau)}$	MS	R^2
(1)	1956–62	$\dfrac{S-E}{S}$	−.019 (.011)	.042 (.019)	.038 (.011)	.015 (.008)	.114 (.012)	−.022 (.012)		.570
(2)	1960–67	$\dfrac{S-E}{S}$	−.040 (.015)	.112 (.025)	.042 (.013)	.014 (.009)	.093 (.014)	−.016 (.012)		.591
(3)	1956–62	$\dfrac{S-E}{S} - \dfrac{.028K}{(1-\tau)S}$	−.006 (.012)	.058 (.021)	.043 (.012)	.017 (.009)		.042 (.008)		.295
(4)	1960–67	$\dfrac{S-E}{S} - \dfrac{.035K}{(1-\tau)S}$	−.025 (.016)	.117 (.026)	.053 (.014)	.022 (.010)		.023 (.008)		.401
(5)	1960–67	$\dfrac{S-E}{S} - \dfrac{.035K}{(1-\tau)S}$	−.015 (.014)	.037 (.027)	.055 (.012)	.024 (.008)		.021 (.008)	.186 (.032)	.504

Note: Coefficients for each of the variables are listed in columns below variables. Standard errors are shown in parentheses below the coefficients. For definitions of variables, see text.

Source: See text.

Exchange in each month, which may be used as a close proxy for the return on a market portfolio.

The second criterion for subsample selection was the availability of accounting data for the relevant firm on the Compustat tape (supplied by the Investor's Management Service). This tape was the source of data on total invested equity capital, effective tax rates, total expenses, and total sales. The effective tax rate, τ, was assumed for each firm to be average annual corporate tax payments divided by average annual profits for each of the two periods and for each of the firms.[f]

Estimates of average four-firm concentration ratios for both the 1956–62 and 1960–67 samples have been obtained from the data appendixes of Hall and Weiss (1967) and Shepherd (1972), respectively. They have both taken their raw concentration data from the Census of Manufactures on the basis of four-digit SIC (Standard Industrial Code) industries. However, SIC-defined industries do not correspond exactly to theoretical industries, and may thus be grossly over- or underinclusive. As a result, concentration ratios based on SIC estimates must either be screened or adjusted accordingly to insure that they correspond to measures of seller concentration within theoretically meaningful markets. This was done by the authors of both works from which the present data samples were taken. Another problem is caused by the diversification of firms. The concentration ratio of a diversified firm's primary industry does not accurately represent concentration in the markets in which it sells. Thus, one must either limit the sample to highly specialized firms (an increasingly impractical task) or calculate a weighted average of concentration in the markets in which a firm sells.

The latter approach was taken by Hall and Weiss and by Shepherd, although their procedures differed. When necessary, Hall and Weiss adjusted the raw four-firm, four-digit SIC concentration ratios supplied by the 1958 Census for both under- and overinclusion due to noncompeting subproducts, interindustry competition, and the existence of local and regional markets. Then, less diversified firms that could be assigned unequivocally to a four-digit industry were given the adjusted (if necessary) four-firm concentration ratio of that particular industry. In most cases, however, diversification prevented this and the firms were assigned to the broader three-digit SIC industry groups and weighted averages of four-firm, four-digit adjusted concentration ratios were computed with weighting done by the value of shipments for each of the component four-digit industries as reported by the 1958 Census.

In addition, four firms which operated in some but not all of the component four-digit industries, special weighted average concentration ratios were computed on an individual firm basis with the weight usually derived from gross

[f] An alternative method would be to leave $(1-\tau)$ out of the data completely, assume that it is constant, and estimate it in the regression. That was done for all the equations in Table 4–1, and the results were consistently the same as those shown. To save space, the results for these regressions are not shown, but are reported in Bothwell (1976).

employment statistics reported in the *1963 Fortune Plant and Product Directory.* With but one exception, all these concentration indices compiled by Hall and Weiss are accepted without revision. However, a Federal Trade Commission study has indicated that seller concentration in the drug industry is substantially higher than the Hall and Weiss four-firm ratio of .45, due to nonsubstitutability among most drug products.[g] Based on the FTC study, a higher (though still moderate) estimate of .75 is used for firms assigned to this industry.

The third procedure used by Hall and Weiss was uniformly employed by Shepherd in estimating concentration over the period 1960−67. That is, raw four-firm concentration ratios for four-digit SIC industries were first adjusted for over- or underinclusion and then used to calculate a weighted average based on either product line sales data or the gross employment statistics contained in the *Fortune Plant and Product Directory.*

Our data on entry barrier heights are based primarily on the previous work of Mann (1966) and Shepherd (1972). The barriers to entry dummy for each firm was determined on the basis of the most important industry in which that firm produced, using Mann's entry barrier estimates. For those industries for which Mann provides no estimates, the estimates of barriers data by Palmer (1973) are used. For the 1960−67 sample, Shepherd has already provided estimates of firm-by-firm dummy variables for entry barriers, and we have used them without revision for that sample, except where these estimates are inconsistent with the previous Mann classifications. The values of these variables are shown for each firm in the sample in Bothwell (1976).

IV. ESTIMATION AND RESULTS

Equation (10) was estimated with the two data sets discussed in the previous sections, and the results shown in Table 4−1. The results for the form of (10) specifically are listed as equations (1) and (2) in Table 4−1; the other specifications shown are discussed below. The market structure variables are all of the correct sign, and are significant, providing support for the structure−performance hypotheses. However, the coefficients relating to the cost of capital, c_1 and c_3, are disappointing. The estimated value of c_3 implies a negative risk premium; and the estimated value of c_2 implies a risk-free cost of capital of up to 11 percent after corporate taxes.

These implausible results would seem to stem from collinearity between $\frac{K}{S(1-\tau)}$ and $\frac{\hat{\beta}K}{S(1-\tau)}$. There is considerable variation in the equity-sales ratio; but on the other hand, beta coeffecients do not vary that much, and as a result reliable estimates of the separate effects of these two variables cannot be

---

[g]From U. S. Senate Subcommittee on Antitrust and Monopoly (1961). Our assumption of a ratio of .75 for drugs is consistent with Shepherd's later (1972) work.

had from the data. That this is the problem is confirmed by two pieces of evidence. First, the standard error on c_3 is extremely high, and the estimate does not differ significantly from zero at any reasonable level. Second, the simple correlation coefficient between these two variables is quite high (around .8 for each data set).

In the face of such a problem, the most appropriate procedure is to assign a prior value to one of the coefficients based on a priori information, and to estimate conditionally the value of the remaining coefficients.[h] Thus, by specifying $c_4 = \bar{R}_f$, in accordance with the Sharpe-Lintner model, it is possible to estimate more precisely the impact of portfolio risk on return and to test the hypothesis that the coefficient of $\dfrac{\hat{\beta}K}{(1-\tau)S}$ is equal to the average market risk premium for each of the two periods. To do this, we assume the risk-free cost of capital to be the three-month U.S. Treasury Bill rate, averaged over the periods of each of the two respective samples. Note, however, that because we are dealing with pretax profits, we must multiply this bill rate by $1/(1-\tau)$ before subtracting it from the left-hand side.

The results of these conditional regressions were shown in Table 4–1 (equations (3) and (4)). Now, all coefficients are highly significant and of the expected signs. Concentration, entry barriers, and risk all have the effects which one would expect them to have. If anything, the market structure variables are larger and more significant than they were in the previous regressions; this would indicate clearly that correctly adjusting profits for risk does not alter the basic relationship between market structure and market performance.

Although the risk variable is consistently of the right sign and highly significant, its coefficient in both samples is somewhat below the value that data based on stock returns would suggest. More specifically, Fisher and Lorie (1964) have found that the long term market return on a totally diversified portfolio (i.e., with beta of 1) is about 9 percent. Using the 1956–62 sample, the after-tax cost of capital for a firm with a beta of 1 is .028 + .042 = .07.[i] For 1960–67, the estimated cost of capital for a similar portfolio is .035 + .023 = .058. A confidence interval test would suggest that the 1956–62 result is within a 95 percent confidence interval around the actual market return; but for the 1960–67 data, it would appear that our estimate of the cost of capital for a diversified portfolio differs significantly from 9 percent at the 5 percent level.

How can this apparent downward bias in the estimate of the cost of capital be explained? There are at least two possible explanations. One possibility is that the beta coefficients that we have estimated from stock price data for individual firms are measured with error, so as to vary more than they "should" with

[h]For a discussion of this procedure, see Theil (1971, p. 49).

[i] .028 is tne average annual U.S. Treasury Bill rate for the 1956–62 period, and .042 is the coefficient of K/S $(1-\tau)$ in equation (3) in Table 4–1.

return. This likelihood has been pointed out by Miller and Scholes (1972). They recommend a method of solving this problem that involves grouping firms into portfolio groups that could be expected to have the same degree of risk, and estimating beta coefficients for groups instead of for firms. In the spirit of this suggestion, we reestimated beta coefficients for industry groups, rather than for firms; but this change had no impact on our results.

Second, it must be remembered that our profit and rate of return variables in these regressions are based on accounting data: book values of depreciation and rate base. Given all the errors of measurement that these accounting procedures could introduce, it is not surprising that our estimates are somewhat different from estimates of the same parameters made directly with data from capital markets.

Although our resulting estimates of the risk premium are lower than those deriving directly from capital market studies, nevertheless, they are of the right sign, the right order of magnitude, and it can be argued that in at least one (if not both) of the cases, the estimate of the relationship between risk and return from this sample is within a reasonable margin of error of estimate deriving from pure capital market data. The results, at the same time, support the market structure–performance hypotheses that we set out to test.

V. SOME OBJECTIONS AND REVISIONS TO THE STRUCTURE–PERFORMANCE HYPOTHESIS

The structure–performance hypotheses developed by Bain over twenty years ago have come under increasing attack in recent years. One line of attack is empirical, inasmuch as followers purport to find either no relationship at all (previously discussed), or an unstable relationship, wherein even when concentration and profits are high in a given industry for a given year, they tend to go down over time (see Brozen, 1971). The Brozen convergence hypothesis has been tested, using these data and methods, elsewhere (see Bothwell, 1976). Here we deal with another objection to the structure–performance hypotheses, one that is potentially quite damaging to it.

This line of attack, developed by Demsetz (1973, 1974), and Mancke (1974), asserts that the concentration-profits relationship is not one of cause and effect, but rather stems from outside variables which affect both concentration and profits at the same time. Thus, Demsetz argues that some firms are more efficient than others, and to the extent that this efficiency stems from characteristics unique, complicated, and unreproducible in a given organization, the benefits of this efficiency will be reaped mainly by the investors in this firm at the time(s) when these advantages are capitalized into share prices.

If one firm is indeed more efficient than others, it will be able to expand its market share relative to other firms, either by offering a lower price for its product, by offering a superior product, or by somehow offering superior services connected with that product (such as better maintenance and repair facilities, or a better distribution network). As a result, more efficient firms will at once achieve higher market shares and higher profits than less efficient firms. In industries dominated by such efficient firms, both concentration and profits will be higher than in industries which are not so dominated, and there will be a spurious correlation between concentration and profits.

Mancke's argument differs from that of Demsetz in that he places emphasis on chance and luck in influencing a firm's success. Thus a firm might have the good fortune to pursue a successful advertising campaign, to develop a new product for which there is substantial demand, or simply to produce an existing product for which demand rises in a given year. As a result of these random occurrences, firms with high market shares would also receive high profits, and industries with high concentration would earn high profits as well.

The Demsetz and Mancke arguments have in common the notion that the high profits that relate to high concentration stem not from the coordinating activity suggested by Bain, but rather from totally independent activity on the part of each firm. How can we distinguish between these hypotheses? And, to the extent that one or the other viewpoint on this question is correct, what are the implications for public policy? These questions lie on the frontiers of our knowledge in the field of industrial organization, and it is certainly beyond the scope of this chapter to resolve them completely. Nevertheless, the present methodology and data can shed some light on these questions, and some speculation as to their answers is appropriate here.

It has been suggested by Weiss (1974) that one possible test of these two alternative hypotheses is to include a measure of market share as well as concentration for each firm in the structure–performance equation. To the extent that market share explains profits instead of concentration, that would indicate that firms are earning high profits not because of coordingation among oligopolists but rather because each firm individually is getting both a higher market share and a higher profit than others through independent behavior. To the extent that concentration still emerges as positive and significant in such an equation, one can argue that the sort of coordination suggested by Bain is still occurring.

On the other hand, if market share emerges as dominant when it is included in the regression relationship, and if the effect of concentration disappears, then one has reason to believe that the other forces suggested by Demsetz and Mancke may be playing some role. The 1960–67 data compiled by Shepherd includes market share as a variable. Shepherd (1972), using a somewhat different specification, finds that market share does indeed emerge as positive and significant in explaining profits, and that the influence of concentration is relatively low when market share was included as a variable.

Equation (5) in Table 4–1 shows the results from including both concentration and market share in the structure-performance-risk equation (with the risk-free, after-tax cost of capital constrained to be the Treasury Bill rate). Market share does indeed "swamp" the effects of concentration in the equation, although after market share is included in the equation, concentration still emerges as positive, if not significant at the .05 level. On the other hand, risk remains of about the same importance as without market share, and, most interestingly, barriers to entry variables remain totally unaffected by the inclusion of market share in the relationship. Thus the relationship between barriers to entry and profits, as hypothesized by Bain (1956), is unaffected by the Demsetz-Mancke arguments, whereas the concentration-profits hypothesis is open to some question.

However, the theoretical interpretation of the market share variable is not totally straightforward. It simply says that firms which have market power above and beyond ordinary entry barriers make excess profits, but it says nothing about where this market power comes from. Dominant firms could indeed achieve their market power through a cost advantage, as suggested by Demsetz, through product differentiation (real or false), through patents, or through "luck" of the sort described by Mancke.

The antitrust policy implications of this relationship are not totally clear either. If, indeed, dominant firms gain their higher market shares solely through a Schumpeterian striving for greater efficiency and better products—and if, as Schumpeter (1947, chapter 7) suggested, such firms must always keep a step ahead of everyone else to maintain their high market shares—then antitrust policy that aims to break up large firms could be detrimental to economic efficiency. But these results do not suggest permissive antitrust policies regarding horizontal mergers. It is obvious that such mergers could quite easily allow dominant firms in industries with moderate or high entry barriers to earn excess profits over a long period of time with no real advantages in our economic efficiency or innovativeness. (Overall, our conclusions on this count are quite consistent with those of Weiss (1974, p. 232).)

To repeat, our conclusions deriving from the market share regression are of a tentative nature, because we cannot claim to know just how large, dominant firms achieve the high market shares and high profits which they have. That is most certainly a valid topic for further research.

VI. SUMMARY AND CONCLUSIONS

In this chapter we have integrated the risk-return relationship of the Sharpe-Lintner capital asset pricing model into the market structure–performance equation. In the process, we have developed a measure of market performance (degree of monopoly) which is superior to previous specifications also in that it incorporates the effects of the corporate income tax in a more theoretically meaningful way. The results of the model confirm both the capital asset pricing model and the market structure–performance hypotheses developed by Bain.

This suggests that correct incorporation of risk into the market structure–performance equation should improve the accuracy of estimates of this relationship, and it also provides one of the first confirmations of the Lintner-Sharpe model to be made with direct firm accounting data, rather than securities market data.

Some doubt is cast, however, on the validity of the concentration-profits relationship estimated here and elsewhere, by recent arguments of Demsetz and Mancke, who hold that the correlation is spurious. To test the Demsetz-Mancke hypothesis, we included another variable, market share, in the structure–performance equation, and it did indeed cast empirical doubt on the validity of the concentration-profits hypothesis as it is generally understood. The results would seem to suggest that dominant firms in highly concentrated industries earn high profits, not so much because they are able to coordinate prices with other firms, but rather because they possess independent market power indicated by their market shares alone.

What is it that enables these large, dominant firms to achieve these high market shares and profits? What are the appropriate antitrust policies to take against them? These questions are unanswered, and because of that the concentration-profits issue, first opened up by Bain over twenty years ago, remains an exciting area for further research.

 *Chapter 5*

Market Structure and Managerial Behavior

P. David Qualls

I. INTRODUCTION

Forty-four years have passed since Adolf Berle and Gardiner Means (1932) first propounded the thesis that a "managerial revolution" was taking place in American industry. In their view, the growing dispersion of stock ownership under the corporate form of business enterprise was conferring basic decision making control of the firm upon "hired" managers, whose behavioral motivations might not coalesce with the profit interests of stock owners. "Classical" economic theory was being rendered invalid owing to its crucial reliance on the role of the rapacious, decision making, risk taking, profit receiving entrepreneur, who no longer existed.

This view is still being debated today. If it is essentially correct, much of the work in the modern field of industrial organization adopting the structure-conduct-performance paradigm outlined by Professor Bain and relying implicity on a profit maximization assumption for business enterprises, may rest on a somewhat shaky foundation. This chapter critiques recent empirical tests of the managerial behavior hypothesis, distinguishes among alternative behavioral hypotheses, and presents some new empirical evidence.

II. SUMMARY OF RECENT EMPIRICAL STUDIES

Four recent empirical studies have explored the notion that decision makers in management controlled firms may not engage in profit maximizing behavior (Kamerschen, 1968; Monsen, Chiu, and Cooley, 1968; Larner, 1970; Palmer, 1973). These studies have looked at accounting rates of return on equity across

The views herein are the author's only, and do not necessarily represent those of the Federal Trade Commission.

samples of firms to investigate whether variations in this variable could be in part accounted for by differences in the type or source of enterprise control.[a] The argument is that if management-controlled firms exhibit lower profit rates, *ceteris paribus*, than do owner-controlled firms, the managerialist profit nonmaximizing hypothesis is supported. If not, the hypothesis is refuted.

The four studies report statistically significant negative impacts of management control on rates of return. Curiously, however, the authors of two of the studies conclude that their findings do not confirm the managerial hypothesis. Larner (p. 29) argues that since the magnitude of the coefficient that he estimates is small, management-controlled corporations exhibit nearly the same profit orientation as do owner-controlled corporations. Kamerschen (p. 443) states that in his multiple regression results, the management control dummy variable is "always statistically insignificant."

For this statement to be consistent with the *t*-values that he reports, he must have been thinking in terms of a .05 significance level for a two-tailed test. Actually, since the hypothesis being tested is one-sided, a one-tailed test is appropriate. With a one-tailed test, the management control dummy is significant at the .05 level in three out of seven regressions. In two others it is significant at the .1 level, and in the remaining two the *t*-ratios are greater than unity. In all the regressions the coefficient has the hypothesized sign.

The authors of the other two studies conclude that their empirical results provide strong support for the managerial hypothesis. Monsen, Chiu, and Cooley find a large and statistically significant difference between the average rate of return for 36 owner-controlled firms and the average for 36 management-controlled firms over a twelve-year period. Palmer, in a study of 450 of the 500 largest industrial corporations, finds that for firms operating in high barriers to entry industries, management-controlled firms, on average, report significantly lower rates of return on equity than do owner-controlled firms. Taken together at face value, the previous studies appear to provide strong support for the hypothesis that management-controlled firms exhibit a much weaker profit orientation than do owner-controlled firms.

It is my view, however, that the results of the previous studies should not be accepted at their face values. Each has several serious shortcomings. First, none of the previous studies adequately controls for variations in industrial market structures. Both seller concentration and barriers to entry have been shown to have important (although perhaps interactive) effects on market performance. Although Monsen, Chiu, and Cooley included an industry variable in their statistical tests, they did not distinguish between different industries with different structures. Larner included a concentration variable in his regression analysis, and Kamerschen included both concentration ratios and barrier to entry dummies in his.

[a]"Owner" control is indicated by a single party owning a large share of voting stock. "Management" control is indicated by wide dispersion of stock ownership.

However, as pointed out by Palmer, both these authors specified additive econometric formulations that implicitly assume that the effect of the type of control is the same for all varieties of market structure. This is inappropriate. Only in those market structural situations which give rise to discretionary monopoly power should a separation of ownership and control in the enterprise be expected to make a difference in operating behavior. An interaction between market structure and the type of control should be specified.

In addition, both Larner and Kamerschen utilize market structure observations only on the firm's leading industry. Structural aspects of secondary product markets of firms are not accounted for. Palmer accounts for barriers to entry in secondary markets as well as primary markets, and he allows for interaction effects between barriers to entry and the source of control. However, he does not control for differences in seller concentration; and concentration is important, along with barriers to entry, in determining the degree of discretionary monopoly power available to decision makers in the firm. Barriers to entry alone do not tell the whole story.

Last, but perhaps most important of all, is the fact that the profit rate of return to ownership equity is not really the most appropriate dependent variable. The statement by Kamerschen (p. 433) that "if managers act in the best interest of owners, they will try to maximize this rate," is insufficient as a justification for the use of the rate of return on equity. It is true that for a given firm with a given amount of ownership equity, behavior that maximizes total economic profit also maximizes the rate of return on equity. Moreover, it is true that for firms operating in competitive industries, competition will lead to an equalization (net of competitive risk differentials) of rates of return on equity in long run equilibrium. However, two profit maximizing firms with the same nonzero degree of monopoly power and with the same long run price–economic cost margins would not have the same rates of return on equity if they had different ratios of sales to equity. The one with the higher ratio of sales to equity would have a higher rate of return on equity. Conversely, two firms with monopoly power and with the same rates of return on equity would have different long run price-cost margins if they had different sales-to-equity ratios.

In order to illustrate this phenomenon, assume two pure monopolies with equivalent dollar-per-unit constant long run average (equals long run marginal) cost functions and facing equivalent demand functions for their products. If both maximize total economic profits, they will have the same economic-profit-to-sales ratios and hence the same price–economic cost margins. Even so, if one has lower stockholder equity, it will have a higher rate of return on equity. (Long run average cost incorporates the "interest" opportunity cost of equity capital.)

Sales-to-equity ratios vary across firms and industries. Therefore, if one firm has a higher rate of return on equity than some other, it does not necessarily follow that the first firm has a potential for making relatively greater monopoly profit, or that the first firm does a "better job" of extracting the monopoly profit that is potentially available. If the second firm is more equity intensive, it may actually be enjoying a relatively greater monopoly profit potential and extracting more of the potentially available profit, even though it yields a lower rate of return on equity.

Several years ago Professor Bain pointed out that the long run price–economic cost margin ("excess" profit as a percentage of sales) was the theoretically correct measure to use in market structure–performance studies.[b] In his famous study relating rates of return to industrial concentration in 42 manufacturing industries (1951), he took care to investigate the relationship between sales to equity ratios and concentration to see whether using the rate of return as a surrogate for the price–economic cost margin could have biased his results. He concluded that there was a bias *against* finding a significant positive relationship between rate of return and concentration since the ratio of sales to equity was negatively related to concentration.

Using the rate of return on equity as a surrogate for the price–economic cost margin in effect introduces a source of dependent variable measurement error, which biases statistical significance tests downward even if the "error" (arising in this case from the variation in sales-to-equity ratios) is randomly distributed with respect to the independent variables. If the sales-to-equity ratio is systematically related to the independent variable(s), an "errors in variables" type of phenomenon occurs that causes the estimated coefficients of the proxy variable (rate of return) regression to be biased estimates of the true variable (price–economic cost margin) regression. As indicated below, this is the case in the sample of firms used in the present study.

Recently I have suggested that this problem should be handled in market structure–performance studies by actually using excess profit (that over and above an imputed interest cost to ownership equity) expressed as a percentage of sales as the dependent performance variable (1972, 1974). This is of paramount importance for studies that look for differences in operating behavior between owner-controlled and management-controlled firms. The managerial hypothesis really predicts that with given degrees of discretionary monopoly power, management-controlled firms will have lower price–economic cost margins.

It does not necessarily predict *anything* about differences in rates of return on equity, however. As indicated by Scherer (1970, p. 34), a finding that management-controlled firms have lower rates of return on equity than do owner-

---

[b]"Excess" profit as a percentage of sales—i.e., accounting profit, minus the competitive "interest" opportunity cost of equity capital (total revenue minus total economic cost), all divided by total revenue (sales)—is equal to the difference between price and average cost divided by price, averaged across all products produced by the firm. Assuming that firms are operating above minimum efficient scale so that long run average cost is constant, and averaging over sufficient time to approximate long run relationships, it is equal to the famous Lerner (1934) measure of "monopoly": the difference between price and marginal cost divided by price.

controlled firms may indicate nothing more than that "the degree of owner control (is related to) financial structure (rather) than operating behavior." Other things equal, differences in operating behavior will be reflected by differences in the margins between prices and economic costs. Differences in rates of return on equity may merely reflect differences in capital structures and/or capital intensities. We are primarily interested in differences in operating behavior.

In analysis of either variance or covariance, with "owner" control defined as a "single party" owning more than a given predetermined percentage of voting stock, "owner"-controlled firms could show up as having higher average rates of return on equity, other things being equal, even though they might not have a higher price–economic cost margins. It is interesting to note that as between owner-controlled and management-controlled firms, Monsen, Chiu, and Cooley find almost no difference in accounting profit as a percentage of *sales*. The simple fact is that the managerial "profit nonmaximizing" hypothesis has not yet been fully tested.[c]

III. ECONOMIC PROFIT MARGIN IMPLICATIONS OF NONMAXIMIZING BEHAVIOR

There are at least three different types of profit nonmaximizing behavior that could have implications for long run price–economic cost margins. One has to do with constrained sales revenue maximization. A second is related to organizational slack and X-inefficiency, and a third (which to my knowledge has not been discussed in this context previously in the literature) concerns risk-averse behavior in a stochastic limit pricing framework.

Sales Revenue Maximization

For firms which enjoy some monopoly power there should be a tendency for management-controlled firms to have lower economic profit margins than owner-controlled firms, if the sales maximization hypothesis for management firms is correct. In a heterogeneous product industry, management firms should tend to charge lower prices relative to given costs than would owner-controlled firms in that industry. In either homogeneous or heterogeneous product industries dominated by management-controlled firms, industry price levels should be lower relative to given costs than those for other industries (of similar market structure) dominated by owner controlled firms.

Overall, across a large sample of industrial firms enjoying some market power, there should be a tendency for management-controlled firms to have lower economic profit margins than would owner-controlled firms. And the profit

[c]It is difficult to assess a priori whether the shortcomings of the previous studies, taken together, have biased the tests in a direction favorable to the managerial hypothesis or unfavorable to the hypothesis.

margin differences should be greater as market power, indicated by higher industry concentration and/or entry barriers, is greater. With higher achievable price–economic cost margins, the difference between achievable economic profit margins and the economic profit margins that result from sales maximization behavior should be greater, otherwise constrained sales maximization is not really behaviorally different from profit maximization.

The assumption here is that higher concentration and higher barriers to entry have positive and interactive effects with regard to firms' monopoly power and potential monopoly profits. A second assumption is that the minimum profit constraint is not systematically and significantly higher as concentration and barriers to entry are higher. If the profit constraint were higher for higher concentration and higher barriers, the profit maximization and constrained sales maximization assumptions would yield the same general predictions for price–economic cost margin performance in market structure analysis. The sales maximization assumption does not predict positive relationships of price–economic cost margins to seller concentration and barriers to entry unless it is assumed that the minimum profit constraint is higher for firms in more highly concentrated, higher barriers industries.

Organizational Slack

Another suggested result of management control is that of higher costs. With isolation from owner control, management may become less diligent with resultant X-inefficiency. Or managers may elect to allocate resources to "nonproductive" expenditures which yield some managerial utility.

With higher costs, management-controlled firms would tend to exhibit lower price-cost margins than would owner-controlled firms in the same industry or in other industries with similar market structures. Again, however, this would follow only for firms in industries whose market structures confer some monopoly power. In workably competitive industries, competition should prevent this for surviving firms. The higher the degree of seller concentration and/or entry barriers, the greater would be the cost increasing possibilities and opportunities for this organizational slack and the greater would be the expected difference in price–economic cost margins between management-controlled and owner-controlled firms.

Stochastic Limit Pricing

Limit pricing behavior is usually discussed in a context of certain knowledge regarding the new firm entry that will result from current pricing policy. However, firms may be able to assess only the *probability* of entry. In this stochastic framework a reasonable assumption is that established firms regard the probability of a given amount and "type" of entry (a minor amount of small firm entry or a major amount of large firm entry, for example) as being higher as current price is higher relative to cost. Risk-neutral firms would elect current pricing policies designed to maximize the expected present discounted value of present and future profits. In this context, a risk-averse firm would deliberately establish a current price lower than that which would maximize expected present value. This would be tantamount to sacrificing some expected present value for a reduced probability that the target expectation would be nonrealized as a result of entry.

A managerialist behavioral hypothesis might well argue that, in this sense, management-controlled firms would tend to behave in a more risk-averse fashion than would owner-controlled firms. To some extent, stockholders have the opportunity of balancing profit risks in their portfolio holdings. To the hired manager group, however, entry presents the prospects of declining market share, a smaller bureaucracy than otherwise and perhaps declining employment tenure probabilities. And managers do not have the same opportunity to balance this sort of bureaucratic employment risk as do stockholders concerned with the profit risks involved in stochastic limit pricing.

In short, a managerialist hypothesis would be that management-controlled firms will tend to establish lower prices relative to cost than will owner-controlled firms, given the same stochastic entry function. An important point here is that if this behavior occurs, one would expect it to be most clearly observed in industries characterized by moderate to high seller concentration coupled with only low to medium barriers to entry rather than high barriers. Limit pricing considerations presumably are relevant only where interdependent pricing policies are feasible—moderate to high concentration.

Moreover, an assessment of the barrier to entry as being "very high" quite likely also implies less uncertain knowledge concerning the entry function and less entry risk to be hedged. As a result of this sort of behavior, clearly observable differences in price–economic cost margins would be most likely expected, or larger differences would be expected, in moderately to highly concentrated industries in which barriers to entry are regarded as low to medium, rather than very high.

In order to attempt to shed some empirical light on these phenomena, the remainder of this chapter is concerned with the results of a statistical study of the hypothesized interactive relationships between long run price–economic cost margins and market structure and type of control in the enterprise.

IV. THE DATA SAMPLE

The data sample utilized here covers 205 large American industrial firms.[d] This is the intersection of the 231-firm sample studied by Shepherd (1972) and the 450-firm sample studied by Palmer (1973). For each of these firms, Shepherd calculated a concentration index as the weighted average of the adjusted four-

---

[d]Each of these firms was on the *Fortune* 500 list for 1965 and 1967.

firm concentration ratios in each of the industries in which the firm had significant operations.[e] For each firm, Palmer developed a barrier to entry estimate— "high," "medium," or "low"—as a weighted average assessment of the magnitude of entry barriers in each industry in which the firm operated.[f] Palmer designated each firm as "strong owner" controlled, "weak owner" controlled, or "management" controlled, depending on whether the largest block of voting stock held by any one "party" was equal to or greater than 30 percent, as great as 10 percent but less than 30 percent, or less than 10 percent of the firm's total voting stock, respectively.

In addition, I calculated excess profits as a percentage of sales (the price–economic cost margin) for each firm for 1960-1968. For each year, 6 percent times beginning of the year stockholder equity was subtracted from net after-tax accounting profit, and the difference—economic profit—was expressed as a percentage of net sales revenue. Averaging arithmetically over the nine-year period yielded the dependent variable observation for each firm.[g] Baa corporate bond yields averaged 5.4 percent over 1960−1968. Six percent seems to be a reasonable estimate of the opportunity cost of equity capital for these firms.

This 205-firm sample is superior to the larger 450-firm sample utilized by Palmer. The firms included in the Palmer sample, but excluded here, were deleted by Shepherd because of extensive diversification, government regulation, or substantial government contracting. For the very diversified firms, weighted average concentration ratios and barrier to entry estimates are probably less meaningful. With regard to regulated firms, it is not clear how their behavior relates to the hypothesis under investigation.

V. THE MODEL

Given the original Bain view that concentration and barriers to entry operate interactively—i.e., that either low concentration or low barriers to entry should lead to low long run equilibrium potential price-cost margins—the appropriate statistical approach for testing the managerial hypothesis is either interactive

[e]Shepherd adjusted some of the SIC four-digit industry concentration ratios for local or regional product market characteristics, and for industry product definitions that were too broad or too narrow.

[f]With regard to the barrier to entry assessments for the *industries*, Palmer placed heavy reliance on previous estimates by Bain (1956), Mann (1966), and Shepherd (1970). I made one change. In keeping with a previous argument (Qualls, 1972), I designated the barrier to entry in the liquor industry as "medium" rather than "high." This affected one firm (Seagram's) in the sample.

[g]As indicated above, this calculation approximates the Lerner measure of monopoly. For a full discussion of the mechanics and justification of this approach, see Qualls (1972). The raw data were taken from *Moody's Industrial Manuals* and Standard and Poor's Compustat tapes. The independent variable observations centered on 1963 and 1965, hence the selection of the time period 1960−1968.

analysis of variance (or its dummy variable regression equivalent) or interactive analysis of covariance, depending on whether concentration is treated as a discreet or continuous variable. The previous discussion indicates the nature of the interaction between market structure and the type of control.

Unfortunately, owing to an absence of observations in some cells, a formal three-way interactive analysis of variance could not be undertaken. In lieu of this, the observations are cross-classified by level of concentration and type of control in Table 5–1[h] and in Table 5–2 by barriers to entry and type of control. Cell means are presented. In Table 5–3 (below), a three-way cross-classification scheme is utilized so that one can observe, where possible, the effect of type of control, holding constant the level of concentration and the height of entry barriers and allowing for interaction effects between market structure and the type of control.

Following this, the hypothesis is tested by multiple regression–interactive analysis of covariance with concentration as a continuous variable–along the line suggested by Weiss (1971) for testing the "full Bain Model."

VI. EMPIRICAL FINDINGS

As indicated in Tables 5–1 and 5–2, the concentration and barriers to entry cell means conform to the traditional Bain hypotheses. Average price–economic cost margins are higher for "high" than for "medium" concentration, which are, in turn, higher than those for "low" concentration. Class means are higher for "high" barriers than for "medium" barriers, which are, in turn, higher than those for "low" barriers.

In the "medium" and "high" concentration classes and the "medium" and "high" barriers classes, the "owner" control class means are slightly higher, for the most part, than the "management" control class means (in the "high" barriers class the "strong owner" control average is less than the "management" average). This seems mildly supportive of the managerial hypothesis. On the other hand, the "strong owner" averages are slightly lower than the "weak owner" averages. This seems contradictory to the managerial hypothesis.

In order to calculate the class means tabulated in Tables 5–1 and 5–2 and to conduct statistical significance tests of differences between any two individual class means, the following dummy variable regressions were estimated from the 205-firm data:

$$PM = 1.774 + 3.777HC + 1.588MC \qquad\qquad (1)$$
$$(5.988) \quad (8.045) \quad\;\; (3.885)$$
$$R^2 = .243 \qquad F = 32.392$$

[h]Firms with Shepherd concentration indexes equal to or higher than 80 percent were placed in the "high" concentration category. The "medium" category contains firms with ratios from 60 to 79 percent, and "low" contains firms with ratios less than 60 percent.

Table 5–1.   Average Economic Profit Margin Percentages, 1960–1968: 205 Firms Classified by Concentration Level and Type of Control

Concentration Class	Type of Control				
	Management	Weak Owner	Strong Owner	Owner (Strong & Weak)	All Control Types
High, CR4A > 80, N = 50	5.1	6.2	6.1	6.2	5.6
Medium, 60 < CR4A < 80, N = 81	3.2	4.1	3.4	3.8	3.4
Low, CR4A < 60, N = 74	1.8	1.8	1.8	1.8	1.8
All concentration classes	3.1	4.0	3.5	3.7	3.3

Table 5–2.   Average Economic Profit Margin Percentages, 1960–1968: 205 Firms Classified by Barriers to Entry and Type of Control

Barriers to Entry	Type of Control				
	Management	Weak Owner	Strong Owner	Owner (Strong & Weak)	All Control Types
High, N = 47	5.0	5.9	4.8	5.4	5.2
Medium, N = 101	2.9	4.4	3.5	3.9	3.2
Low, N = 57	1.9	1.9	2.6	2.2	2.0
All barriers classes	3.1	4.0	3.5	3.7	3.3

$$PM = 1.753 + 3.378HC + 1.443MC + .093S + .030W + .831(HC{\cdot}S)$$
$$(4.780) \quad (5.616) \qquad (2.898) \qquad (.116) \quad (.037) \quad (.657)$$

$$+ 1.084(HC \cdot W) + .129(MC \cdot S) + .827(MC \cdot W) \qquad (2)$$
$$(.882) \qquad\qquad (.110) \qquad\qquad (.724)$$

$$R^2 = .255 \qquad F = 8.375$$

$$PM = 1.753 + 3.378HC + 1.443MC + .063(O) + .966(HC{\cdot}O) \qquad (3)$$
$$(4.812) \quad (5.653) \qquad (2.917) \qquad (.100) \qquad (.995)$$

$$+ .503(MC \cdot O)$$
$$(.571)$$

$$R^2 = .253 \qquad F = 13.498$$

$$PM = 1.995 + 3.188HB + 1.190MB \qquad\qquad\qquad (4)$$
$$(5.586) \quad (6.022) \qquad (2.665)$$

$$R^2 = .153 \qquad F = 18.240$$

$$PM = 1.869 + 3.168HB + .999MB + .771S + .006W \qquad (5)$$
$$(4.095) \quad (4.717) \qquad (1.792) \qquad (.735) \quad (.007)$$

$$- \quad .934(HB \cdot S) + .873(HB \cdot W) - .042(MB \cdot S)$$
$$(-.627) \qquad\qquad (.626) \qquad\qquad (-.034)$$

$$+ 1.519(MB \cdot W)$$
$$(1.266)$$

$$R^2 = .176 \qquad F = 5.238$$

$$PM = 1.869 + 3.168HB + .999MB + .327(O) \qquad\qquad (6)$$
$$(4.108) \quad (4.732) \qquad (1.797) \qquad (.446)$$

$$+ \quad .078(HB \cdot O) = .742(MB \cdot O)$$
$$(.071) \qquad\qquad (.791)$$

$$R^2 = .169 \qquad F = 8.078$$

$$PM = 3.089 + .429S + .878W \qquad\qquad\qquad (7)$$
$$(12.382) \quad (.760) \quad (1.610)$$

$$R^2 = .01 \qquad F = 1.399$$

$$PM = 3.089 + .663(O) \qquad\qquad\qquad (8)$$
$$(12.400) \quad (1.545) \qquad R^2 = .01 \qquad F = 2.397$$

PM is the price–economic cost margin averaged over 1960–1968. *HC* is a 0-1 dummy variable for "high" concentration and *MC* is a 0-1 dummy for "medium"

Table 5-3. Average Economic Profit Margin Percentages, 1960-1968: 205 Firms Classified by Concentration, Barriers to Entry, and Type of Control

Concentration	Barrier to Entry	Type of Control	No. of Firms	Economic Profit Margins (percent)	
High	High	Strong owner	6	5.5	
		Weak owner	8	6.8	6.1
		Management	18	6.0	
	Medium	Strong owner	2	5.6	
		Weak owner	2	6.1	4.2
		Management	12	3.6	
	Low	Strong owner	1	10.1	
		Weak owner	1	2.5	6.3
		Management	–	–	
Medium	High	Strong owner	–	–	
		Weak owner	2	2.4	3.5
		Management	9	3.8	
	Medium	Strong owner	10	3.7	
		Weak owner	10	4.0	3.3
		Management	41	3.0	
	Low	Strong owner	1	1.0	
		Weak owner	1	7.7	3.8
		Management	7	3.6	
Low	High	Strong owner	1	.5	
		Weak owner	–	–	2.2
		Management	3	2.7	
	Medium	Strong owner	4	2.2	
		Weak owner	2	4.6	2.3
		Management	18	2.1	
	Low	Strong owner	8	1.8	
		Weak owner	10	1.2	1.5
		Management	28	1.4	

concentration. HB, MB, S, and W are 0-1 dummies for "high" barriers, "medium" barriers, "strong owner" control, and "weak owner" control, respectively. O is a dummy variable that assumes a value of 1 for either "strong owner" or "weak owner" control and 0 for "management" control, and t-ratios are in parentheses.

The interactive dummy variable regression model was utilized rather than the two-way interactive analysis of variance model because the analysis of variance model is ill-suited to deal with cells containing different numbers of observations and to provide significance tests of contrasts between two individual cell means.

Otherwise the two models are equivalent. The estimated coefficients for the market structure dummy variables are all highly significant, whereas the estimated coefficients for the type of control dummies are not. Mostly their *t*-ratios are miniscule.

In Table 5–3, the firms are classified three ways—by concentration, barriers to entry, and type of control—and class means are presented. Unfortunately, there are some empty cells. Nevertheless, a couple of factors do stand out. First, there is no clear tendency for "owner" control averages to be higher than "management" control averages where concentration and barriers to entry are "high." Whereas the "weak owner" average is slightly above, the "strong owner" average is slightly below the "management" average. For the fourteen "owner" ("weak" plus "strong") firms the average is 6.2 percent as opposed to 6.0 percent for the eighteen "management" firms.

This contradicts the managerialist view that for firms with significant market power, management control will lead to distinctly lower prices with given costs, or higher costs with given prices, and strongly suggests that whatever slight overall tendency there is in the sample for price–economic cost margins to be higher for owner controlled firms cannot be explained by simple reference to sales maximization or X-inefficiency. Mostly, differences between "owner" and "management" class means seem to cluster in the "medium" to "high" concentration and "low" to "medium" barriers categories. This suggests that the slight overall tendency toward higher economic profit margins for owner controlled firms in the sample, if not the simple result of random variation, is more likely explained as management firms in concentrated, lower barriers to entry industries behaving in a risk-averse fashion and pricing lower relative to cost in order to increase the probability of entry preclusion.

All this was tested further by estimating the following three regression equations:

$$PM = -1.267 + .073(CR \cdot HB \cdot S) + .089(CR \cdot HB \cdot W) \qquad (9)$$
$$(-1.424) \quad (4.813) \qquad \qquad (6.223)$$

$$+ .082(CR \cdot HB \cdot M) + .073(CR \cdot MB \cdot S)$$
$$(6.445) \qquad \qquad (4.466)$$

$$+ .083(CR \cdot MB \cdot W) + .063(CR \cdot MB \cdot M)$$
$$(5.123) \qquad \qquad (4.481)$$

$$+ .079(CR \cdot LB \cdot S) + .070(CR \cdot LB \cdot W)$$
$$(3.561) \qquad \qquad (2.948)$$

$$+ .066(CR \cdot LB \cdot M)$$
$$(3.376)$$

$$R^2 = .275 \qquad F = 8.199$$

$$PM = -1.302 + .083(CR \cdot HB \cdot O) + .083(CR \cdot HB \cdot M) \qquad (10)$$
$$(-1.472)\ (6.528) \qquad\qquad (6.515)$$

$$+ .078(CR \cdot MB \cdot O) + .063(CR \cdot MB \cdot M)$$
$$(5.344) \qquad\qquad (4.544)$$

$$+ .074(CR \cdot LB \cdot O) + .066(CR \cdot LB \cdot M)$$
$$(3.732) \qquad\qquad (3.430)$$

$$R^2 = .268 \qquad F = 12.071$$

$$PM = -1.365 + .083(CR \cdot HB) + .069(CR \cdot MB) \qquad (11)$$
$$(-1.549)\ (7.089) \qquad\qquad (5.062)$$

$$+ .071(CR \cdot LB)$$
$$(3.858)$$

$$R^2 = .254 \qquad F = 22.852$$

Here, CR is the Shepherd individual firm concentration index (a continuous variable), M is a 0-1 dummy variable for "management" control, and LB is a 0-1 dummy for "low" barriers. The other variables are as defined previously. Given the theorized interaction between concentration and barriers to entry and between market structure and type of control, this interactive specification is appropriate.

The concentration slope coefficients are all positive and highly significant, providing strong support for the Bain concentration hypothesis. Holding the type of control constant, the coefficients are larger where barriers to entry are "high" rather than "medium"—i.e., the concentration–profit margin relationship is "steeper" with "high" barriers, providing support for the barriers to entry hypothesis.[i] Where barriers to entry are "high" there is no clear tendency for the coefficients to be higher for "owner" control than for "management" control. Where barriers are "medium" and "low" there does seem to be a tendency for the coefficients to be higher for "owner" control.

This can be seen most clearly in equation (10), where "strong" and "weak" are combined into a single "owner" designation. There the high barriers–owner

[i]The concentration–profit margin slopes are not greater for "medium" barriers than for "low" barriers. This can be seen most clearly in equation (11), where the type of control dummies are dropped out. There the "low" barriers concentration coefficient is slightly and insignificantly higher than the "medium" barriers concentration coefficient. This is consistent with the Bain view (1956) that many firms in highly concentrated, low barriers to entry industries may engage in entry inducing pricing. The "high" barriers concentration coefficient is greater than the "medium" barriers coefficient and the difference is significant at approximately the .01 level. The statistic used to test for significant differences in regression coefficients was $[(\hat{\beta}_j - \hat{\beta}_k)/S(\hat{\beta}_j - \hat{\beta}_k)] \sim t_{n-k}$. For an explanation of this, see Kmenta (1971, p. 372).

coefficient is exactly equal to the high barriers–management coefficient (when rounded off)–i.e., the concentration–profit margin relationship is no steeper for "owner" control than for "management" control. However, where barriers are "medium," the second pair of slope coefficients, the concentration–profit margin relationship is steeper for "owner" control. The difference between the two coefficients is statistically significant at the .01 level.

This again suggests that the slight overall tendency toward higher economic profit margins for "owner" control, if not the result of pure random variation, is the result of more risk-averse limit pricing behavior for "management" firms rather than simple sales maximization or X-inefficient behavior. If the latter were the case, the first slope coefficient in equation (10) should be significantly greater than the second.

Primarily for the fun of it, and secondarily to pacify one of my colleagues (who should be, but is not yet, convinced that excess profit as a percent of sales is a theoretically more appropriate variable than is the rate of return on equity[j]), I reworked all the empirical analyses substituting the rate of return on equity for the economic profit margin.

Since there is a weak but significant negative correlation between the ratio of sales to equity and CR across the 205-firm sample ($r = -.18$), and since the sales-to-equity ratios, on average, are slightly lower for higher barriers firms than for lower barriers firms and slightly higher for "owner" firms than for "management" firms, this substitution should work to "bias" the whole procedure in the direction of a greater likelihood of "significant" effects for type of control and a lesser likelihood of "significant" effects for market structure. Estimated market structure impacts are biased downward and estimated type of control impacts are biased upward.

The estimated impact and explanatory power and significance levels of market structure (concentration and barriers to entry) were reduced by the dependent variable substitution, but type of control did not appear to be distinctly more important than it had previously.

VII. CONCLUSIONS AND POLICY IMPLICATIONS

If the interpretation of empirical results stated above is reasonably accurate, the Berle and Means "managerial revolution" does not present much of a problem either for economic theory or public policy.

With regard to theory, the assumption of profit maximization appears to be virtually as meaningful (with perhaps one slight exception) for management-controlled firms as it is for owner-controlled firms. X-inefficiency seems to be no more of a problem for management-controlled firms than it is for owner-controlled firms. Market structure is important for market performance, but

---

[j]Leonard Weiss, who has previously used the rate of return on equity in his empirical studies, now appears to agree that "excess" profit as a percent of sales is the theoretically better variable. See his comment (1974, pp. 198–199).

whether firms are controlled by managers or owners doesn't really matter very much.

The only noticeable behavioral difference may be that management-controlled firms faced with serious but uncertain threats of potential entry, hedge against the entry risk to a greater extent by setting lower prices relative to cost than would owner-controlled firms in similar market structural circumstances. In a normative sense this may be regarded as *good* rather than *bad*. Although it may make for less actual entry and "turnover" overall, it means that in some cases potential competition may lead to more nearly competitive price performance where established firms are management-controlled rather than owner-controlled.

Finally, two recent studies (Lewellen, 1971; Masson, 1971) have concluded that executive compensation schemes provide financial incentive for managers to pursue the goal of profit maximization. The evidence presented here suggests that, by and large, managers behave in accordance with that incentive.

 *Chapter 6*

Industrial Structure, Scale Economies, and Worker Alienation

F. M. Scherer

I. INTRODUCTION

In economics there is a well developed tradition of empirical work on economies of scale—that is, measuring the systematic association between cost per unit of production (or some other aspect of the production-distribution sequence) and the scale at which a plant's or firm's operations are conducted. Professor Joe Bain has been one of the leaders in establishing this tradition (1956). My own research between 1970 and 1973 followed his footsteps (Scherer et al., 1975). Underlying such research has been the implicit value judgment that production inputs ought to be combined so as to satisfy consumers' product demands at minimum cost.

As nearly as I can tell from extensive reading in the scale economies literature, not much attention has been paid to the phenomenon of labor input as an aspect of consumption, i.e., as a utility enhancing or reducing activity in its own right. More specifically, those who have attempted to measure scale economies have not been concerned explicitly with the possibility that job satisfaction (or its approximate inverse, alienation) might be systematically correlated with the scale of production operations.

As this paper unfolds I shall argue that there are fairly compelling grounds for adopting the analytic approach followed by economists. At first, however, I should like to view the scale-alienation issue from a different perspective: that of psychologists and sociologists.

The views expressed in this paper are those of the author and not necessarily of the Federal Trade Commission. The help of Cheryl Williams in collecting and analyzing data is gratefully acknowledged.

II.   THE EVIDENCE ON ORGANIZATION SIZE
AND JOB SATISFACTION

An appreciable amount of psychological and sociological research on the structural correlates of job satisfaction exists. We therefore begin with a brief survey of the most recent literature. The difficulties an economist normally faces invading foreign disciplines are greatly reduced due to the availability of several good literature surveys, on which I initially rely heavily (Porter and Lawler, 1965; Thomas and Fink, 1963; Indik, 1965; Quinn et al., 1974).

The investigators in all scale-alienation studies had to resolve numerous methodological problems, of which two deserve immediate attention. First, how does one measure "job satisfaction" or "job alienation"? The literature appears to dichotomize on subjective measures, derived by asking a sample of workers how they perceive various facets of their job environment, and "objective" measures of such behavioral manifestations as rates of absenteeism and job turnover or the incidence of strikes.

Second, what is meant by a production organization must be determined—whether it should be an entire corporation, an individual plant, a department within a plant, or a narrowly construed "work group." Here investigators have often been unclear on the behavioral hypotheses affecting their preference for one organizational size definition over another, and sometimes this vagueness has been carried to the point of failing to reveal exactly what definition was being used, or scrambling plants and whole firms together in a single sample.

Despite differences in the resolution of these and other methodological issues, the results of the various industrial organization scale–job satisfaction studies are remarkably uniform and robust. The most comprehensive overall picture is provided in the survey by Parker and Lawler (1965) of some twenty relevant studies carried out prior to 1962. Among eight investigations that attempted to relate subjective indices of employee satisfaction to measures of firm, plant, department, or (in one case) work group size, seven concluded that job satisfaction *decreased* systematically with increasing organization size. In the eighth (concerning sales personnel at automobile dealerships) no significant correlation, positive or negative, was found.

Among twelve studies using absenteeism rates as a behavioral proxy measure of job satisfaction, ten exhibited positive absenteeism–organization size correlations, one a zero correlation, and one a curvilinear relationship (with the minimum absence rate occurring among medium-sized work groups). The correlation between job turnover rates and organization size was positive in three (partly overlapping) studies covered by the Porter-Lawler survey and zero in the fourth.[a] Two further investigations showed that the incidence of strikes or other

---

[a]See also Quinn et al. (1974, p. 25); and Burton and Parker (1969). The latter found, contrary to their prior expectations, an inverse relationship between firm size and quit rates, *ceteris paribus.*

labor disputes rose with factory and mine size.[b] Thus the psychological literature points strongly toward a conclusion that increased organizational scale
carries as a consequence decreased job satisfaction and other more active manifestations of discontent.

That these relationships persist at both the plant size level (which has been
the most common focus of scale economy studies) and the individual work
group level is noteworthy. However, it is not clear that the associations are entirely independent. As Porter and Lawler observe (1965, p. 39), "It may well be
that absenteeism is determined by work group size but because large work
groups are found in large factories and departments a spurious relationship exists
between absenteeism . . . and factory size." Little effort has been exerted thus
far to disentangle the observed effects.

Thomas and Fink (1963, p. 379) and Indik (1965, pp. 344–349) similarly
criticize the failure of previous investigators to isolate the role of such "intervening variables" as hierarchical structure, the degree of task specialization, the
degree of bureaucratic inflexibility, and varying communication patterns in the
size–job satisfaction relationship. They consider such intervening variables to be
potentially important from a social or managerial viewpoint, since if the internal
organizational and behavioral patterns that lead to low job satisfaction in large
units could be modified, the adverse size-alienation link might be broken. As
Indik asserts, the negative effects of large size are avoidable and not inherent.

My inclination as an economist is to ask, if changes in internal business organization and practice can break the link, why haven't they been implemented?
Reductions in absenteeism and turnover would surely be profitable if they could
be achieved through organizational changes of modest cost. And even the auto
assembly plant manager of Studs Terkel's *Working* fame (1974, pp. 177–181)
seemed to prefer having happy workers, all else equal (though his perception of
what his workers actually thought was remarkably distorted). One reason why
such changes have not materialized might be that the size–intervening variable–
satisfaction links are too poorly understood, despite decades of research on the
human factors in business organization. This is a sufficiently plausible conjecture
that further exploration of the links seems warranted.

It is nevertheless conceivable that there exist technological or organizational
imperatives that make it difficult or costly to mitigate the adverse psychological
effects of size. Among various possibilities, the question of how scale economies
affect internal work group organization appears particularly interesting and important. I confess to having given it only the most peripheral thought during
three years of field research on scale economies, so the most I can offer at this
juncture is speculation.

Prime sources of scale economies include (1) the scale-up of individual equip-

[b]More recent economic studies reaching similar (but mixed or weak) conclusions are
Eisele (1974) and Shorey (1975). Alexander (1962) found a tendency for days lost owing to
strikes to rise with seller concentration.

ment items or processes, (2) the specialization of equipment and operators to realize the productivity gains associated with increased division of labor, (3) pure automation (which may be economical only at high volumes), and (4) the replication of units to secure massed reserve economies or to spread the cost of indivisible complementary inputs. Scale-up and increased division of labor (especially as manifested in an assembly line) seem much more likely to increase the sizes of work groups than replication, although exceptions may exist—for example, when scaled up equipment embodies technological advances permitting operation by a crew of roughly constant size, or when assembly lines are reorganized in ways like those with which Volvo has been experimenting in Sweden.

The *type* of specialization or automation introduced—e.g., whether machines control the workers' activities or vice versa—undoubtedly makes a difference too.[c] Further research is plainly needed on how technology, man-machine relationships, and the organization of work groups interact to affect simultaneously the scale of operation required to achieve minimum unit costs and the satisfaction workers derive from their job environments.

Although it did not deal with the technology-scale interaction, recent research at the University of Michigan's Survey Research Center clarifies some aspects of the links between organization size and worker satisfaction (Quinn and Mangione, 1973). It also raises intriguing unanswered questions. The basic approach involved interviews of roughly 80 minutes' duration in 1969–70 and 1972–73 with some 1,500 to 2,150 civilian working adults throughout the continental United States. Respondents were asked general questions such as, "All in all, how satisfied would you say you are with your job?" and specific questions about their satisfaction with numerous facets of their jobs, such as how interesting the work was, how much operating freedom they had, how much job security they enjoyed, the competence of their superiors, and the like. Through factor analysis, the facet scores were consolidated into six largely independent dimensional indices characterizing satisfaction with job challenge, comfort, the adequacy of supporting resources, financial rewards, opportunities for advancement, and relations with co-workers.

Of the many interesting results, those that concern us here most directly come from a breakdown of 1972–73 survey responses by blue collar workers (other than self-employed and farm workers) classified according to the size of the establishments in which they worked.[d] One such tabulation took as its dependent variable a composite index of job satisfaction formed by averaging the mean normalized scores on 36 individual job satisfaction facets with the mean normalized scores on five questions relating to overall satisfaction. Despite its peculiar ad hoc formulation, the index was, among other things, significantly correlated with respondents' job turnover in the two years following a set of

[c]See, for example, Blauner (1964).

[d]The tabulation was supplied by Dr. Robert P. Quinn of the Michigan Survey Research Center.

pilot testing interviews. With high positive values of the index reflecting high overall job satisfaction, the mean blue collar worker satisfaction indices for various establishment size classes were as follows:

Establishment Size	Mean Index	Number of Respondents
Less than 10 employees	−3	128
10–49 employees	+7	145
50–499 employees	−23	224
500 or more employees	−29	156

In the larger establishments there is a marked and statistically significant adverse difference in overall job satisfaction.[e]

For three of the facet-related subdimensions of job satisfaction the average scores were as follows, with higher values connoting greater satisfaction:

	Workers' Satisfaction with		
Establishment Size	Job Challenge	Adequacy of Resources	Financial Rewards
Less than 10 employees	3.21	3.39	2.78
10–49 employees	3.17	3.43	2.91
50–499 employees	2.95	3.28	3.05
500 or more employees	2.79	3.21	3.24

For all three attribute categories, the size-correlated differences are highly significant statistically. Workers in the largest establishments were *less* satisfied on the average with the challenge afforded by their jobs and with the adequacy of the physical, informational, and managerial resources supporting their work, but they were *more* satisfied with the pay, fringe benefits, and security associated with their jobs.[f] Additional tabulations dealing with job comfort, opportunities for advancement, and relations with co-workers revealed no significant establishment size-correlated differences.

That persons employed in large establishments are relatively more satisfied with their financial rewards should not be surprising. Blue collar worker compensation does increase with plant size, at least in U.S. manufacturing industry, for which the richest data exist. Thus, for establishment size groupings identical to those analyzed in the Michigan survey, average 1967 manufacturing production worker wages per hour were as follows:[g]

Less than 10 employees	$2.49
10–49 employees	2.61
50–499 employees	2.59
500 or more employees	3.35

[e]For white collar workers a much less regular pattern appeared, although the lowest average satisfaction index coincided with the largest establishment size category.

[f]Similar but sometimes weaker associations were observed for white collar workers.

[g]Computed from U.S. Bureau of the Census (1970).

Table 6–1. Production Worker Wage Levels by Plant Size, 1967

Industry Sector	Plant Employment Range			
	1–4	*5–9*	*10–19*	*20–49*
All sectors	$2.38	2.57	2.68	2.58
Food products	2.31	2.28	2.28	2.33
Tobacco products	na	na	1.62	1.75
Textiles	2.25	2.38	2.30	2.20
Apparel	2.22	2.41	2.36	2.16
Lumber and wood products	1.79	2.03	2.21	2.25
Furniture	2.22	2.41	2.52	2.43
Paper and allied products	2.44	2.50	2.41	2.44
Printing and publishing	2.54	2.77	3.01	3.12
Chemicals	2.33	2.61	2.63	2.70
Petroleum and coal products	3.35	3.33	3.09	2.93
Rubber and plastics	2.40	2.46	2.42	2.12
Leather goods	2.03	2.02	2.15	2.07
Stone, clay, and glass	2.54	2.65	2.67	2.67
Primary metals	2.88	2.95	2.86	2.81
Fabricated metal products	2.56	2.23	2.86	2.78
Machinery	3.01	3.32	3.28	3.20
Electrical equipment	2.55	2.60	2.58	2.45
Transportation equipment	2.67	2.67	2.73	2.75
Instruments	2.58	2.85	2.80	2.75
Miscellaneous	2.19	2.47	2.45	3.20
Ordnance	na	na	2.66	2.92

Source: U.S. Bureau of the Census, *1967 Census of Manufactures*, "Size of Establishments," MC67 (1)–2.

Table 6–1 shows that this pattern is not attributable merely to the payment of relatively high wages in industries that happen to have relatively large plants. When 1967 *Census of Manufactures* data are broken down by two-digit industry groups, we continue to find the highest wages associated with the largest plants. The most common pattern is for wages to be roughly constant or to vary unsystematically in the smallest plant size groups, but for a distinct monotonic upward trend to appear above a plant size threshold somewhere between 20 and 250 employees. The main exceptions are the textile industry, where a negative correlation between wage levels and plant size appears; leather goods, where only the ten plants with 1,000 or more employees had appreciably higher wages; apparel, where the relationship is U-shaped; and furniture, where the pattern is particularly erratic.

It is worth noting that at least two and probably all four of these deviant industry groups are dominated by more narrowly defined industries in which large plant sizes are unnecessary to achieve all significant economies of scale.[h] This leads us to suspect that the higher wage levels in large plants are related at

[h] On textile weaving and shoes, see Scherer (1974).

Table 6–1. continued

		Plant Employment Range			
50–99	*100–249*	*250–499*	*500–999*	*1,000–2,499*	*2,500 and over*
2.54	2.55	2.65	2.87	3.29	3.74
2.43	2.53	2.71	2.88	3.39	3.85
1.79	1.91	1.83	1.82	2.85	2.98
2.12	2.07	2.06	2.11	2.11	2.10
2.01	1.87	1.82	1.91	2.25	2.90
2.26	2.39	2.57	2.71	(3.41	)
2.26	2.25	2.20	2.25	(2.57	)
2.53	2.79	3.08	3.32	3.41	3.28
3.24	3.26	3.42	3.65	3.82	4.25
2.80	3.02	3.31	3.41	3.53	3.66
3.21	3.48	4.04	4.12	4.31	4.47
2.35	2.39	2.58	2.81	(3.79	)
2.05	2.01	2.08	2.11	(2.47	)
2.72	2.84	2.97	3.13	3.38	3.71
2.90	3.01	3.28	3.48	3.70	4.00
2.78	2.82	2.98	3.19	3.38	4.19
3.14	3.01	3.13	3.27	3.48	3.78
2.41	2.43	2.49	2.66	3.10	3.39
2.76	2.77	2.90	3.23	3.74	3.88
2.60	2.59	2.65	2.68	3.20	3.49
2.18	2.25	2.36	2.50	(2.58	)
2.59	2.62	2.91	2.92	3.55	3.53

least in part to ability to pay, which in turn follows from the realization of scale economies and/or greater capital intensity.[i]

The existence of such a relationship by no means excludes the possibility that large plants must pay higher wages to compensate workers for less challenging and supportive working conditions. One link involves the demand side of the labor market, the other the supply side. Still, in the present state of knowledge we cannot exclude alternatives to the hypothesis that alienating work conditions force large plants to bid higher for their labor supply. Thus, larger plants are probably more strongly unionized; or they may draw their labor force from a wider geographic radius, all else equal, and hence must pay a wage premium covering higher commutation costs. Through the analysis of more disaggregated Census and survey data it might be possible to discriminate among these and other hypotheses contending to explain the positive correlation between plant sizes and wage levels.

The hypothesis that a "trade-off" exists between financial rewards and other job satisfaction (or dissatisfaction) components has been investigated by Nina Gupta and Robert Quinn, using 1969–70 University of Michigan survey data

[i]On the relationship of capital intensity to earnings in various labor skill categories, see Brogan and Erickson (1975).

covering 1,327 wage- and salary-earning workers.[j] They analyzed differences in the level of overall job satisfaction indices as a function of normalized and categorized differences in job challenge satisfaction scores and reported annual primary employment income. The resulting table revealed no consistent relationship between pay and job challenge, leading the authors to conclude that the various job facets did not substitute for each other and that "deficiency in quality of employment with regard to one job facet could only be compensated by providing a worker with better quality of employment *with regard to that facet alone* and not any other" (emphasis in the original) (Quinn and Mangione, 1973, p. 334).

To an economist this conclusion is strongly counter intuitive. Economists' intuition is not always correct. Yet it is also plausible that the failure of Gupta and Quinn to find a trade-off relationship stemmed from methodological deficiencies. No attempt was made to hold constant differences in education and other demographic traits that would put respondents on different trade-off surfaces. The tabular cell comparison technique used was primitive, and the authors' assumption of symmetric linear trade-offs followed from an inappropriate conceptual model. We should expect the trade-off relationship to be characterized better by a function of the Cobb-Douglas genre once differences in opportunity are held constant.

One is also stimulated by the Gupta-Quinn results to wonder what mental processes respondents go through when answering questions such as, "All things considered, how satisfied are you with your job?" and "How well would you say that your job measures up to the sort of job you wanted when you took it?" How do interviewees weigh the various facets of satisfaction, psychic and pecuniary, to reach a summary judgment?

What matters more, the absolute levels of satisfaction on diverse facets or the level in comparison with alternative attainable jobs? Might not respondents emphasize psychic over financial variables to a greater extent in answering a social science interviewer's questions than they do in making actual job choices?[k] And is it feasible to develop a set of measures that clearly differentiates the psychic and financial satisfactions from interviewees' jobs, so that the trade-off hypothesis might be tested with greater precision? These are issues into which one would like much deeper insight before attempting to resolve the general puzzle of job facet trade-offs and the specific question of how the higher wages associated with larger establishments are related to overall job satisfaction.

[j]"The Mirage of Trade-Offs Among Job Facets," in Quinn and Mangione (1973, pp. 321–334).

[k]For an exploration of whether interviewees' social attitudes affected job satisfaction responses, see J.T. Barnowe and Robert Quinn, "Social Desirability Response Set: A Possible Source of Bias?" in Quinn and Mangione (1973, pp. 161–189). Few strong associations were discovered.

III. JOB SATISFACTION, COMPENSATION, AND REVEALED PREFERENCES

Having let my economist's biases color my reading of the psychological survey results to an increasing degree, I now revert to full-fledged status as a card-carrying professor of the dismal science.

We have reviewed survey evidence that on certain plausible dimensions, workers' psychic job satisfaction is inversely correlated with establishment size. We have found that wages tend to increase (at least in manufacturing industry) with establishment size, and that workers appear to be more satisfied with their financial rewards in large establishments. The surveys also show that *overall* job satisfaction declines with establishment size, but on this we are more skeptical because it is unclear what mental processes underlie the responses. The inclination of a conventionally trained (i.e., bourgeois) economist is to suspect that this last observed association cannot be right in the sense of describing workers' actual job choices. For under the notion of revealed preference, the choices people make are those which, from the available set of opportunities, yield them the highest satisfaction.

Granted, individuals seldom behave quite as rationally as the pure economic theory implies. They make bad decisions, and sometimes they become committed through inertia (or pension plans) to those choices. Yet it seems highly implausible that there could be a *systematic* association between ignorance of one's real wants or the inability to distinguish more preferred from less preferred alternatives and the size of the plants in which workers are employed.

If a worker is not satisfied with the mix of relatively high financial rewards but low challenge and support he (or she) experiences in a big plant, he should switch to a smaller plant offering a different trade-off. If he does not so move, one must infer that he considers himself better off than he would be in an alternative position. If so, the higher wages he receives in the sizeable plant must be compensating him for the large plant's psychic burdens. Therefore the costs of size-correlated job dissatisfaction are reflected in firms' books of account, and it would be double-counting to say that plants which achieve lower unit money costs by expanding to a large scale may nevertheless be socially undesirable because they impose psychic costs upon their workers.

Needless to say, in this chain of reasoning there are many assumptions to which a reader might take exception. Noneconomists and Marxist economists may disagree, but I find only two caveats to be compelling. One is the possibility that psychic dissatisfaction spills over to affect not only the worker's own well-being but also the well-being of those with whom he comes into contact outside the work environment. A case in point is the articulate steel mill laborer of Studs Terkel's *Working* (1974, pp. xxxi–xxxvi) who, to maintain his onerous but relatively well paying job, represses his resentment at work and compensates by brawling afterward. Those who are intimidated or injured by the worker's bar-room behavior bear a cost that presumably appears nowhere in the steel mill's accounts. (Legal sanctions against brawling might internalize such costs, but the linking mechanism is so imperfect that skepticism is warranted.) It is also pos-sible—although I know of no evidence—that job dissatisfaction spills over into apathetic or destructive political behavior. In either case the external disecono-mies associated with alienation could deflect the economy away from welfare maximizing plant size and organization choices.

The other problem, and in my opinion the more persuasive one, stems from the fact that workers' freedom of choice is constrained by the industrial struc-ture within which they live. One might argue that the structure of the American economy is "wrong" in the sense that workers are offered an insufficiently attractive mix of choices between small and large establishments. To be sure, the number of job opportunities available in small establishments is far from mini-scule. In 1968, roughly half of the 54 million U.S. employees covered by Social Security worked in reporting units (usually establishments) with fewer than 100 employees (U.S. Bureau of the Census, 1970, p. 472).

If a conclusion is to be reached that workers' welfare has been impaired by inadequate opportunities for employment in nonalienating (presumably small) establishments, it must be based upon the premise that the present size distribu-tion is wrong in some absolute sense or, perhaps more operationally, that trends over time in the structure of the U.S. economy have significantly worsened the opportunity set. In either case, the impact of an excessive narrowing of psychi-cally satisfying small establishment employment opportunities would be a wid-ening of the pay differential between such establishments and large scale plants. That is, the terms of trade are worsened for the worker who would really like to work in a small shop environment—if only he could afford it.

The set of small plant employment opportunities could conceivably have narrowed through random growth of larger establishments or the deliberate ex-pansion of plants beyond sizes yielding all scale economies. That such a pattern would persist over a long time period seems implausible, however, since exces-sively large establishments enjoying no incremental scale advantages but forced to pay a wage premium should be relatively unprofitable and gradually disap-pear.

A more plausible scenario involves changes in the technology of scale econo-mies over time. It is illustrated in Figure 6–1. As technological change occurs, the transformation function relating output possibilities to plant size shifts out-ward from T_1 to T_2. The shift is biased, with an increase in slope over time re-flecting a rising productivity advantage for large scale production. What happens to average employment patterns depends upon workers' preferences, which are reflected in the social indifference curves I_1 and I_2. The indifference curves are upward\sloping and convex to the establishment size axis, connoting that work-

Figure 6–1. Effects of Technological Change on the Establishment Size-Correlated Wage Differential

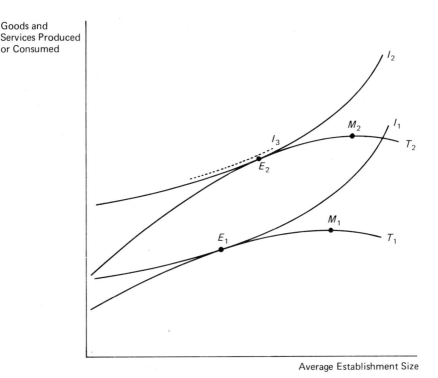

Average Establishment Size

ing in establishments of increasing size has increasing marginal disutility, *ceteris paribus.*

As the curves are drawn, market equilibrium occurs with increased average establishment size (at E_2) in the second period. The establishment size-correlated wage differential is shown by the slope of the tangent transformation and social indifference curves at market equilibrium. Given the assumptions of Figure 6–1, the wage differential has risen significantly with the shift from T_1 to T_2 and the equilibrium increase in establishment sizes.

The social indifference curves in Figure 6–1 have been constructed to be vertically parallel. If, however, the consumption of goods and services has diminishing marginal utility, all else equal, one might expect the curve slopes to steepen with rising real income. The effect of this increasingly adverse marginal rate of substitution between consumable income and establishment size would be to counteract the movement toward larger establishments and increase the establishment size-correlated wage differential even more as the production opportunity set shifts from T_1 to T_2.

On the other hand, if through mass education or otherwise, workers' aversion to large establishment employment were lessened, the slope of I_2 would be relatively flatter, employment in large establishments would increase even more, and the establishment size-correlated wage differential would rise less. In the limiting case of no establishment size aversion, the employment equilibria would be at points M_1 and M_2, where all economies of large scale operation are exhausted, and there would be no establishment size-correlated wage differential.

Note that at the second period equilibrium E_2 portrayed in Figure 6-1, workers are better off absolutely in addition to having chosen the best attainable trade-off between wages and establishment size. To be sure, they might be still better off if the transformation function had shifted to point E_2 but not increased in slope, for then indifference curve I_3 could have been attained. It is only in this last sense that we can infer from the orthodox analysis that technological progress was biased in a way that constrained workers' opportunity set.

Yet any comparison between average welfare levels at points E_1 and E_2 is rendered difficult owing to the substantial time interval which separates the two equilibria. One could construct a model involving changing aspiration levels over time, or interdependent consumer preferences, in which workers, if given the chance, would strongly prefer the ostensibly small shift (associated with a lessening of the establishment size bias in transformation function T_2) from indifference curve I_2 to I_3 over the biased progress-related shift from I_1 to I_2.

IV. HISTORICAL CHANGES IN SIZE STRUCTURE AND PAY DIFFERENTIALS

Has there in fact been a trend away from an economic structure characterized by small scale establishments? Table 6-2 provides a crude overview. The first and second numerical columns compare the fraction of all employed civilian workers plus farmers plus retail proprietors plus self-employed service tradespeople working in the economy's main branches between 1920 and 1967. The figures should be viewed as indicative rather than definitive, since several inconsistent data sources had to be spliced to permit a homogeneous comparison. The last numerical column presents the mean normalized overall job satisfaction indices derived by University of Michigan researchers from their 1969-70 nationwide probability sample, with the number of persons interviewed in a sector indicated within the subscripted parentheses.

The most striking employment decline occurred in agriculture. Its causes are well known—technological changes that rendered small scale farming increasingly uneconomic, with depressed incomes gradually driving farmers and farm workers into nonagricultural jobs, often following migration to the cities. Its impact on job satisfaction is not adequately portrayed by the average normalized index of +5 presented in Table 6-2. A further breakdown shows that farm owners and managers had an average satisfaction index of +28—higher than any other broad

Table 6—2.   Civilian Work Force Sectoral Structure and Job Satisfaction, 1920—1967

	Sectoral Employment Shares (percent)		Mean Job Satisfaction Index
	1920	*1967*	
Agriculture, forestry, and fisheries (including farm owners plus workers)	31.9	5.6	+5 (68)
Manufacturing employees	24.6	26.6	−3 (381)
Retail and wholesale trade (including an estimate of proprietors)	13.4	20.9	−17 (276)
Services employees plus estimated self-employed and professionals[a]	7.4	15.6	+8 (397)
Contract construction employees	2.0	4.6	+15 (123)
Mining employees	2.9	0.9	−2 (22)
Transportation and utilities employees	9.3	5.9	+16 (94)
Finance, insurance, and real estate employees	2.6	4.6	−2 (175)
Government employees	6.1	15.4	+2 (80)

[a]Professionals counted were physicians, dentists, pharmacists, lawyers, judges, and architects—a relatively high fraction of whom were believed to be self-employed in both periods.

Sources: U.S. Bureau of the Census, *Statistical Abstract of the United States: 1970; Historical Statistics of the United States: Colonial Times to 1957* (Washington: 1960); and Robert P. Quinn and Thomas W. Mangione, ed., *The 1969—1970 Survey of Working Conditions* (Ann Arbor: University of Michigan Survey Research Center, 1973), p. 148.

sector mean. Their numbers declined from nearly ten million in 1920 to 2.3 million in 1967. For hired farm workers, on the other hand, the population decline from 3.4 million in 1920 to 1.0 million in 1967 was probably accompanied by a net improvement in job satisfaction. Their average index in the 1969—70 Michigan survey was −56, the lowest of any occupational class.

Apart from government, whose "plant" and job structure is too heterogeneous to permit any global insights, the most substantial employment growth occurred in the service trades, which include hotels, sports, repair services, personal and domestic services, medical and legal services, and much else. Here modest establishment scale is more the rule than the exception. But job satisfaction is surely influenced by more than mere establishment size, and in western societies there appears to be a widespread belief that many kinds of personal service are demeaning. This may explain why the average job satisfaction index for the 146 service workers covered by the Michigan survey was −35.

On the other hand, for the 225 professional and technical personnel, many of whom would also be classified to the services sector, the mean index was +20. What this seems to imply is that, at least for those individuals whose education or skills are insufficient to gain the higher status service industry jobs, the availability of employment opportunities in small scale establishments may not constitute a particularly attractive alternative to depersonalized but well paying work in a sizeable factory.

The wholesale and retail trade sector is important both in absolute size and as a locus of considerable relative growth since 1920. Here too the small scale establishment, though on the wane, continues to command a significant position. Of all retail employees in March 1967, only 17.6 percent were employed in establishments with 100 or more employees and only 29 percent in establishments with 50 or more employees (U.S. Bureau of the Census, 1971, p. 3−1). In view of this, it is perhaps surprising that wholesale and retail employees had the lowest average overall job satisfaction index (−17) of any major industrial group.

One explanation could be an aversion to personal services jobs. It is also possible that an industrial organization variable not yet considered—the geographic separation of operations from ultimate managerial control in the multiplant or multistore firm—may adversely influence workers' sense of identification with their employer and the way operating unit heads relate to their staff. Thirty-five percent of all retail sales in 1967 were by establishments which belonged to firms operating four or more retail units (U.S. Bureau of the Census, 1971, p. 4−256). The comparable figure for 1929 was 21 percent. Twenty-three percent of 1967 retail sales were in establishments belonging to firms operating 51 or more units. A thorough investigation of the relationship between industrial structure and job satisfaction should take multiunit structure as well as individual establishment size into account.

We return finally to manufacturing, the largest single sector of the U.S. economy. It, more than any other sector, is the locus of the large scale operating unit. The trend over time has been toward increasing manufacturing plant sizes. In 1909, for example, roughly 31 percent of all U.S. manufacturing employees worked in establishments with 500 or more employees. By 1967 the comparable share had risen to 44 percent.[1]

Summing up, we find mixed evidence on whether U.S. workers' opportunities for securing employment in small, nonalienating establishments have on balance

---

[1]The 1909 data are from U.S. Bureau of the Census (1913, p. 183). Since establishments were classified by the number of wage earners in 1909 but by the number of all employees in 1967, an approximate adjustment was made in the 1909 data to achieve comparability.

been expanding or contracting over time. In farming, technological change has induced a sharp narrowing of those opportunities. There has been a modest decline in manufacturing. Meanwhile employment has expanded greatly in government, services, and trade. The service and trade sectors are characterized by small scale establishments, but the jobs they offer less-skilled workers may have additional features that detract from satisfaction, and in both the scale of operations has been rising over time.

My overall impression (and it cannot be dignified as anything more than that) is that there has been a modest contraction in the availability of satisfying jobs for nonprofessional workers over the past half-century. If workers do prefer a small unit, locally controlled employment environment, all else equal, and if that opportunity set has been contracting over time, we should expect to find the wage differential between small and large units widening. The only sector for which this hypothesis can be tested is manufacturing.

In Table 6−3 the annual earnings of production workers employed in establishments of varying size are summarized for 1939 and 1967. To facilitate comparison, the earnings levels have been converted to index numbers, with earnings of workers in establishments having 100 or fewer employees taken as the base. For both years, a consistent increase in earnings levels with rising establishment size is evident, mirroring the more detailed statistics for 1967 in Table 6−1. But more importantly, the size-correlated differential rises perceptibly over time. Relative to earnings in the smallest size group, the differential for workers in plants with 501 to 1,000 employees was 21 percent higher in 1967 than in 1939. For workers in the largest plant size group the differential widened by 17 percent.[m]

Table 6−4 compares the average wage differential patterns prevailing in 1947,

Table 6−3. Plant Size-Correlated Differential in All Manufacturing Production Workers' Annual Earnings, 1939 vs. 1967

(Earnings in Plants with 100 or Fewer Employees = 100)

Plant Size (Total Employees)	1939 Earnings Index	1967 Earnings Index
1–100	100.0	100.0
101–500	103.7	104.1
501–1,000	112.9	115.6
Over 1,000	135.7	141.8

Source: U.S. Bureau of the Census, *Census of Manufactures*, for 1939 and 1967.

[m]The observed annual earnings differentials could be associated with plant size-correlated differences in the number of hours worked as well as with wage differences. The data needed to disentangle these linkages were unavailable. In 1947, production workers in the smallest plants worked about 1.5 percent more hours than workers in the largest plants. Small plant employees worked 2.4 percent fewer hours in 1967.

Table 6-4.   Plant Size-Correlated Differential in All Manufacturing Production Workers' Hourly Wages: 1947 vs. 1967 and 1972

(Wages in Plants with Fewer than 100 Employees = 100)

Plant Size (Total Employees)	1947 Wage Index	1967 Wage Index	1972 Wage Index
1–99	100.0	100.0	100.0
100–499	106.4	101.2	102.3
500–999	115.5	112.1	114.3
1000 or more	129.1	138.5	145.6

Source: U.S. Bureau of the Census, *Census of Manufactures* for 1947, 1967, and 1972.

1967, and 1972. Again, a steady increase in compensation with increasing plant size is evident for all three years. For plants with from 100 to 999 employees, the size-correlated differential fell from 1947 to 1967 and 1972. But for workers in the largest plant size group, the differential widened by 32 percent from 1947 to 1967 and by another 18 percent from 1967 to 1972. Since other variables affecting the equilibrium structure of wages have not been taken into account, these patterns cannot be viewed as conclusive evidence that job opportunities in small, nonalienating establishments have been secularly declining, inducing a rising size-correlated wage differential. Still the evidence is at least consistent with that hypothesis, suggesting a possible time-related decline in satisfaction from the nonpecuniary facets of work.

V. CONCLUSION

It is fair to say that what we know about the relationships between industrial structure, scale economies, and workers' job satisfaction is dwarfed by our ignorance. One can see wisps of smoke, but we are going to have to break down some doors before we can tell whether a fire is raging. I should therefore like to suggest where the battering ram of scientific inquiry might be deployed most fruitfully.

A crucial question is whether there is in fact a trade-off between compensation and such psychic variables as job challenge as plant size increases. One way to resolve the issue would be to design a multi-industry sample that controls for the plant size–wage level gradient. Thus, industries such as textiles and leather goods, in which the size-wage correlation is negative or flat, would be matched against industries such as printing and chemicals, in which a monotonic positive relationship is observed. Survey methods could then be used to determine whether indices of job satisfaction fall more rapidly with plant size in the former as compared to the latter industry groups. Simultaneously, richer insights into the role of such intervening variables as hierarchical level, work group size, degree of unionization, and technology type would be sought.

Another structural variable that merits more careful study is the degree to which operating level activities are separated geographically from top management. In choosing a sample one would therefore want to ensure that an appreciable fraction of single-plant enterprises is included along with establishments belonging to multiplant firms.

Finally, the impact of market concentration—the industrial organization economist's oldtime favorite structural variable—deserves attention. Two main links suggest themselves. First, it is known that wage levels tend to rise with concentration as well as with plant size. Since plant size and concentration are in turn correlated, one needs an industry sample with considerable independent variation of the two to detect their separate effects on wages and ultimately on job satisfaction. Second, in the 1972–73 Michigan survey, the job satisfaction facet "resource adequacy" was negatively and significantly correlated with plant size. To the extent that concentrated industries earn supranormal profits, they should enjoy greater organizational slack than atomistically structured industries, and this slack might be utilized in part to provide superior equipment and staff support to help workers get their jobs done—an important component of the "resource adequacy" facet. On the other hand, no obvious a priori connections between seller concentration and other resource adequacy components such as availability of information, clear definition of responsibility, and the competence of supervisors come to mind. Our understanding of the business firm as a behavioral entity could be sharpened by a disentangling and clarification of these concentration—resource support—worker satisfaction relationships.

※ *Chapter 7*

Optimal Plant Size and the Extent of Suboptimal Capacity

Leonard W. Weiss

I. INTRODUCTION

One of the most influential and widely used products of Professor Bain's research is his pathbreaking estimates of minimum efficient scale in twenty industries (Bain, 1956). Among other things, he used these data in evaluating an element of industry performance, the extent of suboptimal capacity (Bain, 1966; Bain, 1968, p. 379). He concluded that:

> The proportion of industry output supplied by such efficient plants ranged, over the twenty industries, from about 70 percent at the minimum to 90 percent at the maximum. . . . The variation of the size of the inefficient fringe among industries (between 10 and 30 percent of industry output) did not appear to be especially related to the most prominent structural characteristics of the industries (seller concentration and conditions of entry), though the fringe did show some tendency to be larger in industries with strong product differentiation (p. 379).

This conclusion was important because of the traditional "dilemma of antitrust"—that we might lose economies of scale if we strenuously promote competition. He found little basis for that dilemma in the United States.

More recently, Scherer (1973) presented a model in which the dilemma seemed to reappear and tested it successfully using twelve industries in six countries. His conclusion seemed sufficiently important to warrant further testing. The purpose of this chapter is to reexamine Bain's earlier conclusions and Scherer's recent model using data which are now available on a number of additional industries, including some that I had developed myself and had not previously published.

II. THE THEORY

Economic theory offers mixed predictions with respect to the extent of sub-optimal capacity. In purely competitive long run equilibrium, no suboptimal capacity should exist at all. However, long run equilibrium is seldom if ever attained in the real world because of changes in technology, in input prices, and in demand. At any one point in time we must expect to find some suboptimal capacity in most competitive industries because of such changes.[a] In addition, some firms may operate with suboptimal plants initially because lack of capital prevents entry at minimum efficient scale (*MES*). Such cases seem common in agriculture and the service industries. Finally, some suboptimal capacity may exist in the short run because of entrepreneurial errors.

Once the assumption of pure competition is dropped, many complications arise. Some industries contain geographic markets so small that plants of less than *MES* would be optimal once transportation costs are taken into account. Similarly, markets for some specialty products may be so small that they can only support plants of less than *MES.*

A major concern of this paper is with the effect of concentration on the extent of suboptimal capacity. Traditional theory gives much less guidance here. If high concentration results in prices above minimum long run average cost, sub-optimal plants would be protected in the long run, especially if their cost disadvantage were mild. However, profit maximizing firms would still presumably seek to attain minimum efficient scale. They would only operate at suboptimal scale if some barrier prevented their expansion. Strong brand loyalties or capital rationing might be such barriers. These arguments suggest that the suboptimal fringe might be relatively large in the more concentrated industries.

On the other hand, Scherer proposes arguments that point toward a negative relationship between concentration and the extent of suboptimal capacity. The essential feature of his argument is that where additional sales are distributed over space or time, transportation costs or periodic excess capacity will limit the size of plant built, and these limits will be more serious, the smaller the firm's market share. Since average market share for leading firms is exactly proportional to concentration, this would imply that the extent of suboptimal capacity would be negatively related to concentration.

With respect to sales distributed over space, Scherer relied on a specification for unit transportation costs developed by Mohring and Williamson (1969).

[a]In sixteen industries which I investigated in 1965–67 (listed in Table 7–3), only cotton broad woven fabrics was reported to have experienced a decrease in minimum efficient scale (*MES*) since 1950. In addition, *MES* for tufted rugs was much smaller than for woven carpets, which tufted rugs were displacing in the 1950s and 1960s, though *MES* for tufted rugs itself was reported to have increased by 67 percent during the period. In two other industries—celulosic man made fibers and diesel engines—there had been no change in *MES.* All the other industries showed increases in *MES.* Taking all sixteen together, the value of 1965–67 *MES* ÷ 1950 *MES* ranged from .81 in cotton broad woven fabrics to 2.40 in cement, with a simple average of 1.59.

Assuming evenly distributed demand and circular markets, it implies:

$$\frac{dUTC}{dQ} = \frac{T}{3\sqrt{DM\Pi Q}} \tag{1}$$

where UTC is unit transportation cost of a firm selling more and more units at increasing distances from its plant.

Q is physical output

T is freight cost per mile

D is units of demand per square mile

M is market share.

It is easy to show that this implies that optimal scale considering both transport and production cost increases with M. Assume a simple long run total production cost function of:

$$PC = a + bQ \tag{2}$$

so that unit production cost is:

$$UPC = \frac{a}{Q} + b \tag{3}$$

Overall average cost is:

$$AC = UPC + UTC \tag{4}$$

$$\frac{dAC}{dQ} = \frac{dUPC}{dQ} + \frac{dUTC}{dQ} \tag{4a}$$

$$= -\frac{a}{Q^2} + \frac{T}{3\sqrt{DM\Pi Q}} \tag{4b}$$

Setting this equal to zero and solving for Q, minimum average cost is reached when:

$$Q = \sqrt[3]{\frac{9a^2 DM\Pi}{T^2}} \tag{5}$$

This implies that optimal scale considering both production and transportation cost increases with the steepness of the *UPC* curve, with geographical demand density, and with market share, and decreases with freight rates. The larger a firm's market share, the closer it will come to minimum unit production cost when it minimizes the sum of *UPC* and *UTC.*

Scherer's argument with respect to demand growth through time has to do with additions to plant. If firms attempt to maintain market shares in the face of a limited growth in demand, they have to choose between additions to plant of *MES* with long periods of excess capacity or suboptimal additions with less excess capacity. They would be more likely to build suboptimal plant if *MES* is large relative to the market, if long run *UPC* curves are flat, if demand growth is slow, and if market shares are small. (Although he does not mention it, the argument would also seem to imply more suboptimal capacity where fixed costs are low so that the costs of excess capacity are low.)

The alternative would be fluctuating market shares with firms alternating in their additions to plant—something that Scherer believes is unlikely short of legally enforced cartels because of mutual distrust among the oligopolists. Scherer acknowledges that in an atomistic market, concern with maintaining market share would not be relevant. His argument applies to oligopolistic industries which comprise the bulk of his sample of industries as well as of those covered in this chapter.

These arguments provide some theoretical basis for a negative relationship between concentration and the extent of suboptimal capacity that I found earlier and could not explain (Weiss, 1964). Scherer tested his hypothesis using twelve industries in six countries. A major purpose of this chapter will be to further test it using U.S. data and a more extensive set of estimates of long run *UPC* curves.

III. THE ESTIMATES

Tables 7–1, 7–2, and 7–3 show estimates of *MES* made by F.M. Scherer, by C.F. Pratten, and by me. The first column shows the absolute values of the estimates. All the estimates seem to have been made in 1965–1970.

Scherer's estimates appear to be extremely careful; Pratten's seem respectable. I have been skeptical about my own, which are summary estimates based on interviews with or questionnaires answered by officials of large numbers of firms (from three in textiles and transformers up to fourteen in petroleum refining). There was often a wide range of estimates received. The numbers shown in Table 7–3 are my judgments of the "best" estimates—usually averages after excluding inconsistent responses and responses that are extreme outliers. It does appear that my estimates are in the same ballpark with those of Scherer and Pratten where we made estimates for the same industries, except that Scherer's

Table 7–1. Minimum Efficient Scale and Costs of Suboptimal Plants Estimated by Scherer

Industry	MES	MES as a Percentage of U.S. 1967 Output	Percentage Increase in Average Cost at 1/3 of MES
2082 Beer brewing	4,500,000 bbl. per year capacity	3.4	5.0
2111 Cigarettes	36 billion cigarettes per year, 2275 employees	6.6	2.2
2211 Cotton and 2221 Synthetic broad woven fabrics	37.5 million square yards per year, 600 employees	0.2	7.6
2851 Paints, varnishes and lacquers	10,000,000 gallons per year, 450 employees	1.4	4.4
2911 Petroleum refining	200,000 bbl. per day crude input capacity	1.9	4.8
3141 Shoes (other than rubber)	1,000,000 pairs per year 250 employees single shift	0.2	1.5
3221 Glass containers	133,000 tons per year, 1000 employees	1.5	11.0
3241 Cement	7,000,000 bbl. per year capacity	1.7	26.0
3312 Integrated wide strip steel works	4,000,000 tons per year capacity	2.6	11.0
3562 Ball and roller bearings	800 employees	1.4	8.0
3632 Household refrigerators and freezers	800,000 units per year	14.1	6.5
3691 Storage batteries	1,000,000 units per year; 300 employees	1.9	4.6

Source: Scherer (1973, 1974).

estimated *MES* for beer is much larger than Pratten's or mine, and Pratten's estimated *MES* for cement is much larger than Scherer's or mine.

The third columns of the three tables show the estimate of *MES* as a percentage of United States 1967 shipments or capacity for four-digit Census industries. These percentages in Table 7–1 were computed by Scherer (Goldschmid et al., 1974, p. 26). Those in Table 7–2 were calculated on the basis of U.S. 1968 physical outputs reported by Pratten (Pratten, 1971, Appendix A) in a majority of cases, but on the basis of other totals in a minority of industries mentioned in

Table 7-2. Minimum Efficient Scale and Costs of Suboptimal Plants Estimated by Pratten

Industry	MES	MES as a Percentage of U.S. 1967–68 Output or Capacity	Percentage Increase in Average Cost at 1/2 of MES
2051 Bread	30 sacks of flour per hour	0.3	7.5 incl. delivery cost
2082 Beer	1,000,000 bbl per year	1.1	9 before tax
2211 Cotton spinning	60,000 spindles	0.3	less than 2
2211 Cotton weaving (used in regressions)	1,000 looms	0.4	less than 2
2824 Synthetic fibers: polymer production	80,000 long tons per year	5.5	5
2824 Synthetic fibers: yarn extrusion (used in regressions)	40,000 long tons per year	2.8	7
2841 Detergents	70,000 long tons per year	2.4	2.5
2911 Petroleum refining	10,000,000 long tons per year (about 180,000 bbls per day throughout)	1.7	5
3141 Shoes	300,000 pairs per year	0.05	2
3241 Cement	2,000,000 long tons per year (about 12,000,000 bbls)	3.5	9
3251 Bricks	25,000,000 bricks per year	0.3	25
3312 Integrated steel with wide strip mill	4,000,000 metric tons per year	3.0	8
3321 Iron foundries casting cylinder blocks	50,000 long tons per year	0.3	10
3511 Turbo generators	6,000 MW; 50% of UK Market	23	n.a.
3519 Diesel engines 1–100 hp	100,000 units per year	30	4
As a percentage of all 3519		9.2	
3541 Machine tools	300 employees	0.3	5
3573 "Electronic capital goods" (computers)	£200 million receipts per year	15.4	8
3621 Electric motors	60% of the U.K. market	15	15

Table 7—2. continued

Industry	MES	MES as a Percentage of U.S. 1967–68 Output or Capacity	Percentage Increase in Average Cost at 1/2 of MES
3632 Refrigerators and 3633 Washers (a firm with ten models)	500,000 units per year	9.7 for refrigerators 11.2 for washers	8
3711 Motor cars (a firm with three makes)	1,000,000 units per year	11.0	6
3721 Aircraft	More than 50 units per year	More than 10% commercial transports	20
As a percentage of all 3721		3.8	
3799 Bicycles	100,000 units per year	2.1	n.a.
As a percentage of all 3799		1.4	

Source: C.F. Pratten (1971), especially the table on pp. 269—277 for *MES* and percentage increase in cost at 50 percent of *MES* and the table on pp. 324—329 in computing the percentage of the U.S. market for the majority of industries. Other sources for U.S. totals were used for certain industries as follows: cotton spinning—20,519,000 cotton system spindles in place, July 1, 1967, from *Current Industrial Reports* M22P; cotton weaving—245,412 looms operating on cotton broad woven goods over 12 inches in width, July 1, 1967, from *Current Industrial Reports* M22T; petroleum refining—total capacity of 10,759,607 bbl per day, from API, *Petroleum Facts and Figures*; steel—total capacity of about 150 million tons, using an estimate based on the AISI 1967 *Iron and Steel Works Directory of the United States and Canada*; diesel engines—total shipments of 248,000 engines, from the 1967 *Census of Manufactures*; machine tools—total employment in industries 3541 and 3542 of 116,400, from the 1967 *Census of Manufactures*; automobiles—total registrations of 9,008,488, from the 1967 *Automotive News Almanac*; aircraft—total civilian transport aircraft shipments of 500 in 1967, from 1969 *Statistical Abstract*, p. 572; bicycles—total shipments of 4,871,200, from 1967 *Census of Manufactures*.

Note: A number of industries in Pratten were not included in this table for a variety of reasons. Some were excluded because they are only small parts of a four-digit industries and would not be usable in the rest of this chapter (they are ethylene, sulphuric acid, and dyes). Some were excluded because Pratten's statement of *MES* is too vague to permit an estimate of *MES* as a percentage of the U.S. market (these are newspapers, knitting mills and plastic products). Large marine diesel engines was excluded because there are no data on U.S. output. Books was excluded because the unit of observation is a title rather than an establishment.

Table 7−3. Minimum Efficient Scale and Costs of Suboptimal Plants Estimated by Weiss

Industry	MES	MES as a Percentage of 1967 Shipments or Capacity	Percentage Increase in Average Cost at 50 Percent of MES
2041 Flour mills	5886 cwt per day capacity	0.7	3
2082 Beer	5541 bbl. per day capacity	1.0	10
2092 Soybean mills	1423 tons per day capacity	2.4	2
2211 Cotton broad woven fabrics	94,000 yards per day	0.2	5
2272 Tufted rugs	64,000 square feet per week	0.7	10
2621 Paper: Printing papers	567 tons per day	4.4	9
Unbleached kraft	896 tons per day	6.2	13
Weighted average		5.2	11
As a percent of all 2621		1.2	
2631 Linerboard	850 tons per day	4.4	8
As a percent of all 2631		1.5	
2822 Synthetic rubber (SBR)	60,000 long tons per year	7.2	15
As a percent of all 2822		4.7	
2823 Celulosic man-made fibers filament	70,000,000 lbs. per year	9.8	5
rayon staple	125,000,000 lbs. per year	18.3	5
Weighted average		11.1	5
As a percent of all 2823		6.1	
2824 Nonceluosic man-made fibers Nylon	50,000,000 lbs. per year	5.1	12
Acrylic	42,500,000 lbs. per year	8.4	9.5
Polyester	40,000,000 lbs. per year	6.7	10
Weighted average		6.0	10.9
As a percent of all 2824		2.2	
2911 Petroleum refining	119,000 bbls. per day crude throughput capacity	1.1	3

Table 7-3. continued

Industry	MES	MES as a Percentage of 1967 Ship- ments or Capacity	Percentage Increase in Average Cost at 50 Percent of MES
3011 Passenger tires	16,500 tires per day capacity	3.8	5
As a percent of all 3011		1.8	
3241 Cement	6,000,000 bbls per year capacity	1.6	13
3312 Integrated steel mills with wide strip mill	4,000,000 tons per year capacity	2.7	10
3519 Diesel engines Automotive	$50,000,000 per year	21	28
Other diesels (50– 1500 hp)	$20,000,000 per year	5	10
Weighted average		11.1	16.7
As a percent of all 3519		1.4	
3612 Transformers Distribution transformers	$8,500,000 per year	2.0	7
Small power trans- formers	$12,400,000 per year	6.9	7
Large power trans- formers	$17,500,000 per year	7.1	10
Weighted average		4.9	7.9
As a percent of all 3612		1.5	

Source: Based on interviews with and questionnaires filled out by company officials. The number of responding companies ranged from three (in textiles and transformers) to four- teen (in petroleum refining). National totals are shipments from the 1967 *Census of Manu- factures* for a majority of industries. The questionnaires asked for optimal capacity and normal operating rates. *MES* shown in the table are physical capacities, but they were con- verted to annual values using values per unit derived from table 6A of the Census and multi- plied by normal operating rates before dividing by industry value of shipments.

the footnotes to Table 7-2. Most of my own estimates are based on the physical quantities reported as shipped in the 1967 Census of Manufactures.

In a few cases in Tables 7-2 and 7-3, the *MES* estimate applies to only a portion of a four-digit industry. Where this occurs, I have shown a second percentage, which applies to the entire industry. For instance, *MES* is 4.0 percent of 1967 linerboard shipments, but linerboard was only 36.5 percent of all shipments in industry 2631, paperboard; so *MES* as a percentage of all 2631 shipments was reported at 1.5 percent. In effect, this procedure assumes that *MES* for the other types of paperboard was of the same absolute size as that of linerboard. These four-digit percentages are on the same basis as four-digit concentration ratios with which they will be compared later in the chapter. In my interviews and questionnaires I asked for estimates of normal operating rates. The estimates of *MES* capacities were multiplied by these normal operating rates before computing *MES* as a percentage of 1967 shipments or capacity.

The last column of each table shows estimates of the extent to which average costs are elevated at one-third of *MES* in the case of Scherer's estimates and at one-half of *MES* for Pratten's and my estimates. My own experience is that these estimates are often quite rough. Many times they were stated in round numbers. Probably only the largest differences in estimated cost increases in Table 7−3 are meaningful.

The overall impression left by these tables is that plants of *MES* are consistent with quite low concentration in a majority of cases, but *MES* is 10 percent or more of U.S. output or capacity in the cases of major household appliances, diesel engines, turbogenerators, computers, electric motors, automobiles, and commercial aircraft.

IV. EVALUATING THE ESTIMATES

These estimates can be evaluated to some extent by comparing them with ad hoc proxies for *MES* that have been used in the past and by using them as variables in explaining concentration. This section attempts to do both.

The main proxies for *MES* have been the average value of shipments of plants accounting for the top half of industry shipments (Comanor and Wilson, 1967; Ornstein, 1973) and the estimated shipment size of the plant at the midpoint of the shipments distribution (Weiss, 1963; Scherer, 1973; Shirazi, 1974). Half of industry shipments are made by plants larger than this midpoint plant. Both proxies are really characterizations of plant sizes in an industry excluding the lower tail of the plant size distribution. Their use in the past has undoubtedly been based on the expectation that profit seeking firms will build plants of optimal scale where possible. One would surely expect a positive correlation between such indexes of actual plant size and estimates of *MES*. If none appeared, the estimates of *MES* would be very suspect. Still, the correlation can be expected to be less than perfect for all the reasons discussed in the theory section and the further reason that plants larger than *MES* can often be built with little or no cost disadvantage.

Table 7−4 shows coefficients of determination relating the two proxies with each of the three sets of *MES* estimates (expressed as percentages of industry

Table 7—4. $\bar{R}^2$ **(Corrected for Degrees of Freedom) Relating Direct Estimates of MES as a Percent of Industry Shipments to Two Common Proxies for Actual Plant Size**

	Number of Industries	Midpoint Plant Size	Average Size of Plant in Top Half of Shipments
Scherer Sample	12	.9033	.7671
Pratten Sample	19	.4338	.3808
Weiss Sample	16	.4414	.3974
Combined Samples			
Using Scherer's estimates where available	33	.5197	.4118
Using Pratten's estimates where available	33	.4531	.3471
Using Weiss's estimates where available	33	.5266	.4507

shipments) in the first three rows. The coefficients are corrected for degrees of freedom to make them comparable. The last three rows of the table show coefficients for three alternative groupings of data that will be used in subsequent regressions in this paper.[b] The coefficients in the fourth row were based on Scherer's estimates for all twelve of his industries, Pratten's estimates for industries where Scherer made none (eleven industries), and my estimates where neither Scherer nor Pratten made estimates (nine industries). The correlations in the fifth row used Pratten's estimates for all of his nineteen industries, Scherer's estimates where Pratten made none (five industries), and my own where neither Scherer nor Pratten made estimates (nine industries). The correlations in the last row used all of my own sixteen estimates, Scherer's estimates where I made none (seven industries), and Pratten's estimates where neither Scherer nor I made estimates (nine industries).

All the R^2s in Table 7—4 are significant at the one percent level or better. The correlation between Scherer's estimates and the midpoint plant size is remarkably close and that for the other proxy is quite high, confirming my impression that his estimates are extremely careful. Pratten's estimates and mine yield weaker correlations but still much more than would occur by chance. Of the two

[b]There are 33 rather than 35 observations in these cases because Pratten's estimates of *MES* for automobiles and computers apply to firms rather than plants. Pratten's combined estimate for 3632 (refrigerators and freezers) and 3633 (household laundry equipment) was treated as two observations.

proxies, the midpoint plant size is more closely correlated with the various estimates in all samples, perhaps because it is less likely to be affected by the largest plants in the industry which are often much larger than *MES*.

The second method by which the estimates may be evaluated is to use them as independent variables explaining concentration. In long run competitive equilibrium, *MES* would determine the minimum value of the concentration ratio, but of course concentration can (and ordinarily does) exceed that minimum value. One would expect a positive, but far from perfect, correlation between *MES* and concentration. In addition, in the imperfectly competitive real world markets, one might expect concentration to be lower in industries where suboptimal plants suffer only mild cost disadvantages. Finally, with a given long run average production cost curve, optimal scale will be smaller the higher the transportation costs. For both this reason and the fragmented markets involved, one would expect national concentration to be lower in industries where geographical markets are small.

Since the cost disadvantage for smaller plants is estimated at one-third of *MES* in Scherer's study and one-half of *MES* in Pratten's and mine, I have expressed all of these estimates as elasticities. A log-log *UPC* curve was fitted to two points for each estimate. One point was at *MES*, where both scale and average cost were given values of 100. At the other point, scale was assigned a value of 33.333 for Scherer's estimates and 50 for Pratten's and mine, and average cost was given a value of 100 plus the percentage increase in cost shown in Tables 7−1 to 7−3.[c] In effect, this procedure assumes that the long run average cost curve is linear in logs in the range below *MES*. Since the elasticities all have negative signs, their expected relationship to concentration is negative.

As a proxy for transportation cost I used the radius within which 90 percent of an industry's products were shipped in 1963 (Weiss, 1972). National concentration ratios should rise as this radius increases. No distance shipped data were available for bread, where most shipments are local, nor for aircraft, which of course is delivered under its own power. Bread was assigned an arbitrary radius of 50 miles, and aircraft one of 2,000 miles.

Regressions were run for the same groups of estimates used in Table 7−4. The elasticities of average cost with respect to scale were taken from the same sources as the estimates of *MES* as a percentage of industry shipments or capacity. That is, Scherer's elasticities were used where Scherer's *MES* estimates were used, and so forth.

The results are shown in Table 7−5. The coefficient of *MES* as a percentage of industry shipments or capacity is only marginally significant (at the 10 percent level) using Scherer's or Pratten's estimates by themselves, but it is highly

[c]Pratten makes no estimate of the percentage increase in average cost in suboptimal plants in the cases of turbogenerators and bicycles, so these industries have been deleted from the regressions in which the elasticity of average cost with respect to scale is a variable. On the other hand, computers and automobiles, which were excluded in Table 7−4, are included in Table 7−5.

Table 7–5. Regressions Relating 1967 Four Firm Concentration Ratios to Distance Shipped, to MES and to the Elasticity of Average Cost with Respect to Scale *(t-ratios in parentheses)*

Variable / Sample	Constant	MES as a Percent of Industry Shipments or Capacity	Cost Elasticity	Radius Within Which 90 Percent of Shipments Are Made	$\bar{R}^2$ and n
Scherer	41.48 (1.99)	3.40 (1.96)	52.09 (0.39)	-.0021 (-0.13)	.2475 12
Pratten	25.77 (1.93)	2.07 (1.99)	11.97 (0.97)	.0131 (1.30)	.3285 19
Weiss	24.73 (1.88)	9.64 (3.56)	42.42 (0.59)	.0081 (0.95)	.4104 16
Combined Samples					
Using Scherer where available	37.17 (4.00)	2.42 (2.92)	48.91 (1.04)	.0075 (1.06)	.2918 33
Using Pratten where available	35.66 (3.88)	2.55 (2.90)	46.70 (0.90)	.0088 (1.24)	.2834 33
Using Weiss where available	35.26 (3.89)	2.49 (3.08)	34.39 (0.73)	.0089 (1.28)	.3046 33

significant (at the 1 percent level) using my estimates or using any of the combined sets of estimates. Elasticity of average cost with respect to scale has positive coefficients although a negative sign was expected. However, the coefficients are never significantly different from zero. The radius within which 90 percent of shipments are made generally has the expected positive effect, but it isn't significant either.

These results are somewhat equivocal. The significant relation between the *MES* variable and concentration seems to indicate that the *MES* estimates are meaningful. But the weak relationship and wrong sign for the cost elasticity variable throws doubt on its accuracy. However, the theoretical basis for the excepted effect of elasticity was much weaker than for the *MES* variable. It may be that there simply is no relationship between concentration and the cost disadvantage of suboptimal plants.

V. THE EXTENT OF SUBOPTIMAL CAPACITY

A major purpose of this chapter is to estimate the extent of suboptimal capacity in the industries covered. These were computed using the estimates of *MES* as a percentage of total shipments or capacity from Tables 7−1 to 7−3. In most cases these percentages were multiplied by 1967 industry shipments to arrive at a value of shipments size for a *MES* plant. The Census employment size class in which the *MES* plant fell was determined by calculating the average value of shipments per plant within the Census size classes. The number of plants within that size class that were suboptimal and the value of their shipments was then estimated on the assumption that the plants in a class were arrayed in equal steps from the smallest possible plant in a class to the largest. The value of shipments of the minimum and maximum plant size in a class was estimated by multiplying the value of shipments per employee times the total number of employees per plant at the lower and the upper limit of the size class. The size of plants between these extremes was then estimated by dividing the difference between these extremes by the number of plants in the class and adding the resulting figure for each successive plant until *MES* was reached. The remaining shipments in that class were added to the shipments of any larger size classes to determine the total industry shipments from plants of *MES* or larger.

Where *MES* fell in the open-ended largest size class, other procedures were used. For petroleum refining 1967 capacities of plants of *MES* or greater were taken from the directory section of the *National Petroleum News Factbook*. For automobiles, new 1967 registrations by firm were taken from the *Automotive News Almanac*. Steel mill capacities were estimated from the American Iron and Steel Institute, *Directory of Iron and Steel Works of the United States and Canada* for 1967 on the assumption that one of two or two of three basic oxygen furnaces had capacities of 11,000 heats per year, that large electric arc furnaces had capacities of 1200 heats per year, and that basic open hearth furnaces had capacities of 850 heats per year. For computers, IBM was the only firm to attain *MES*. Its market share in 1967 was taken from Brock (1975, p. 21).

In other industries where *MES* fell in the open-ended class, estimates were made on the assumption that plants were distributed in equal steps so that they just exhausted the total shipments of the class. For instance, if there were four plants in that class, the smallest was assumed to have the minimum shipments in the class (shipments per employee times the minimum—M). The other three were assumed to have shipments of $(M + a)$, $(M + 2a)$, and $(M + 3a)$. As a result, total shipments in the class were $(4M + 6a)$. It was then a simple matter to solve for a by setting this sum equal to total shipments in the class.

The results of this exercise are shown in Table 7−6. The main conclusion to be drawn from Table 7−6 would seem to be that the extent of suboptimal capacity is far greater than Bain suggested. The majority of plants in virtually every industry covered are suboptimal, and the percentage of shipments or capacity that is from plants smaller than *MES* is often much more than 30 percent. This is true for each set of estimates. The simple average of shipments or capacity from plants equal to or smaller than *MES* is 58.2 percent for Scherer's estimates, 46.7 percent for Pratten's estimates, and 52.8 percent for mine. Some of the suboptimal plants undoubtedly serve small geographic markets or produce speciality items. However, even in those industries (footnoted) that seem to sell on very broad markets and where minor subproducts are of little importance, the majority of plants and much more than 30 percent of shipments are still suboptimal.

VI. THE DETERMINANTS OF SUBOPTIMAL CAPACITY

The obvious next question is what determines the extent to which an industry builds plant of optimal scale or greater. Scherer's analysis discussed in the first portion of this chapter led him to estimate a model where the midpoint plant size depended on:

    (i) the slope of the *UPC* curve;
    (ii) transport cost per dollar of fob mill product value over a standardized distance;
    (iii) population density per square mile times an index of real national product per capita;
    (iv) a concentration ratio;
    (v) domestic consumption divided by *MES*; and
    (vi) percentage growth in production per annum, 1950–1967.

Table 7-6.   Percentage of Shipments or Capacity in Plants of Less than MES 1967

	Industry	Scherer	Pratten	Weiss
		Using the Estimates of:		
2041	Flour mills[a]			50.6
2051	Bread		70.3	
2082	Beer	67.5	41.1	38.0
2092	Soybean mills			87.6
2111	Cigarettes[a]	44.7		
2211	Cotton textiles[a]	29.0	39.8	29.0
2272	Tufted rugs[a]			40.9
2621	Paper[a]			77.5
2631	Paperboard[a]			70.3
2822	Synthetic rubber[a]			42.6
2823	Celulosic man-made fibers[a]			32.3
2824	Noncelulosic man-made fibers[a]		18.3	10.6
2841	Detergents[a]		55.6	
2851	Paints, varnishes & lacquers	89.8		
2911	Petroleum refining	82.3	84.2	63.9
3011	Tires & inner tubes[a]			34.4
3141	Shoes (other than rubber)[a]	46.4	6.2	
3221	Glass containers[a]	69.8		
3241	Cement	92.2	100.0	92.2
3251	Bricks		6.4	
3312	Blast furnaces & steel mills	51.6	65.4	51.6
3321	Grey iron foundries		61.0	
3511	Steam engines & turbines[a]		100.0	
3519	Internal combustion engines[a]		74.3	25.9
3541	Machine tools, metal cutting[a]		27.1	
3573	Computers (based on firm market shares)		31.9	
3582	Ball & roller bearings[a]	33.0		
3612	Transformers[a]			22.6
3621	Motors and generators[a]		100.0	
3632	Refrigerators & freezers[a]	32.8	22.0	
3633	Household laundry equipment[a]		55.2	
3691	Storage batteries[a]	59.7		
3711	Motor vehicles (based on firm registrations)		3.0	
3721	Aircraft[a]		17.6	
3799	Transportation equipment NEC (mainly bicycles)[a]		9.7	
	Average	58.2	47.9	52.8

[a]Industries where transportation costs are relatively minor.

His form of the dependent variable was chosen to avoid bias in international comparisons. Since this chapter is concerned only with U.S. data, it will use the "percentage suboptimal" directly. Similarly, Scherer's demand density variable is used only to control for international variations in population and per capita *GNP* and is unnecessary here.

The slope of the *UPC* curve was represented by the elasticity of average cost with respect to scale so that estimates from the three sources used in this chapter could all be used. Since the elasticities have negative signs, the coefficient of this variable should be positive. A large negative elasticity means a steep cost curve and therefore relatively little suboptimal capacity. Instead of transportation cost, I have used a direct measure of geographical market size, the radius within which 90 percent of all shipments are made. This variable allows for other aspects of transportation cost besides freight rates—e.g., bulkiness, perishability, and the need for close consultation between suppliers and buyers. The coefficient of this variable should be negative. Concentration is measured by the 1967 four firm concentration ratio. My earlier a priori expectation was that concentration might have a positive effect on the extent of suboptimal capacity, but Scherer's model suggests a negative effect.

These four variables, together, can be used to test the portion of Scherer's model that depends on transportation cost. Scherer offered some arguments for both a linear and a log-linear specification, tried both, and found that the logarithmic form yielded a better fit. By contrast, the linear form yielded somewhat better fits for most of the samples and variables used in this chapter. The results for the linear regressions appear in Table 7−7. The results for log-linear regressions were similar in most respects, though they did yield stronger effects for cost elasticity and geographic market size in the smaller samples.

All the coefficients shown in Table 7−7 have the signs that Scherer expected except for the nonsignificant negative sign for cost elasticity using Scherer's own data alone. (That variable had a larger but still nonsignificant coefficient of the expected sign in the log-linear form using Scherer's data). Industry size relative to *MES* had a significant negative effect in all cases, as did concentration in all cases other than Pratten's sample. All variables had statistically significant coefficients in the combined samples, except for the geographic market size variable in the sample which used Pratten's data where available. It would appear that Scherer's transport model is well supported by the additional data.

An attempt was made to test Scherer's dynamic oligopoly argument by including the annual percentage rate of growth in industrial production, 1954−1967. According to his argument, this variable should have a negative effect on the extent of suboptimal capacity. In addition, the ratio of gross fixed assets to shipments was introduced in some regressions on the argument that high capital-output ratios would mean a relatively great increase in average cost with excess capacity so that firms would be more inclined to build suboptimal capacity as a result. The coefficient of this variable should be positive. These variables were introduced in both the linear and log-linear forms of the model using the three combined samples. One industry (3251, bricks) had to be excluded in the logarithmic form because its average annual growth rate was negative.

The growth rate variable had the expected negative effect in five of the six regressions but its coefficient was never statistically significant. The capital-

Table 7-7. Regressions Explaining Percentage of Shipments or Capacity in Suboptimal Plants,[a] 1967
(t-ratios in Parentheses)

Variable / Sample	Constant	Four-Firm Concentration Ratio	Industry Shipments ÷ MES	Cost Elasticity	Geographic Market Size	$\bar{R}^2$	n
Scherer	114.05 (5.18)	-.95 (-2.92)	-.97 (-2.96)	-18.59 (-0.16)	-.0012 (-.09)	.5246	12
Pratten	109.00 (5.00)	-.61 (-1.79)	-.043 (-2.76)	144.5 (1.70)	-.0064 (-.47)	.2763	19
Weiss	132.15 (8.77)	-.83 (-4.31)	-.11 (-3.10)	99.30 (1.57)	-.020 (-2.77)	.6907	16
Combined Samples							
Using Scherer's estimates where available	133.44 (9.81)	-.86 (-4.57)	-.13 (-4.55)	113.24 (2.06)	-.013 (-2.58)	.5227	33
Using Pratten's estimates where available	108.55 (8.23)	-.56 (-2.86)	-.043 (-3.62)	126.83 (2.19)	-.010 (-1.29)	.3918	33
Using Weiss's estimates where available	128.91 (8.90)	-.76 (-3.88)	-.12 (-3.96)	120.56 (2.62)	-.014 (-2.12)	.4803	33

[a]Suboptimal firms in industries 3573 (computers) and 3711 (automobiles).

shipments ratio had a negative coefficient in three cases and the expected positive coefficient in three cases. One of the positive coefficients was statistically significant. The coefficients of the other variables shown in Table 7−7 did not change much when these two were added. Scherer's dynamic oligopoly argument receives little support from the data in this study.

The general conclusions from Table 7−7 are those that Scherer suggested. The conditions for large percentages of output from plants of *MES* or larger are: (1) relatively concentrated industries, (2) steep cost curves, (3) industries that are large relative to *MES*, and (4) geographically large markets. The effect of concentration is perhaps the most troubling. In advance, I had suspected that much of the tendency for some unconcentrated markets to have large percentages of suboptimal capacity would be due to flat cost curves and/or geographically fragmented markets. These conditions might be expected to yield both low concentration and large amounts of suboptimal capacity. Moreover, if they did account for the relationship with concentration, the cost to society of such "suboptimal" capacity would not have been very great. As it turns out, however, the effect of concentration is enhanced when these variables are controlled for.

VII. CONCLUSION

To summarize: the recent estimates of *MES* are at least accurate enough to correlate well with the commonly used proxies for *MES* and to play a significant role in accounting for interindustry differences in concentration. They generally bear out Bain's conclusion that efficient plant scales are consistent with low or moderate concentration in a majority of industries. However, they do not bear out his conclusion that most capacity is as large as *MES* or larger. On the average, about half of total shipments in the industries covered are from suboptimal plants. The majority of plants in most industries are suboptimal in scale, and a very large percentage of output is from suboptimal plants in some unconcentrated industries.

The conditions for a large proportion of output in plants of *MES* or greater are markets where total output is large relative to *MES*, geographically large markets, steep long run average production cost curves, and high concentration. Only the last is much of a surprise. But the effect that Scherer found in twelve industries in six countries seem to be very robust. It holds up in a variety of additional industries using other sets of estimates and a number of variations in his model. He felt that the effect of concentration on plant scales was stronger in Europe than in North America, but it holds up very well with the U.S. data used here. It would appear that the traditional dilemma of antitrust still holds, even in the large U.S. economy.

※ *Chapter 8*

Advertising and Concentration: A Tentative Determination of Cause and Effect

J. A. Henning
H. Michael Mann

I. INTRODUCTION

Professor Bain, in his classic study, *Barriers to New Competition*, stated: "Perhaps the most surprising finding of our study—if previous casual comment on barriers to entry is taken as the standard—is that the most important barrier to entry discovered by detailed study is probably product differentiation" (1956, p. 216). This conclusion eventually inspired substantial research into the effect on the competitive process of product differentiation. One line of inquiry which has received considerable attention is whether advertising intensity, as a surrogate for product differentiation, is significantly related to market concentration.[a]

Empirical analyses treating the relationship between these two variables has been limited to that of establishing association (usually by correlation methods) between them. Any causal interpretation of the empirical results has always been disavowed, at least implicitly. Even where regression analysis was employed, the critical statistic was always the correlation coefficient. The necessary assignment of one of the two variables as independent (the "stimulus" or "cause") and the other as dependent (the "response" or "effect") was regarded as arbitrary.

Usually the direction of causation between two associated variables is clearly postulated by economic theory. As an illustration close at hand, consider the

The authors thank Lester Taylor for his comments, which substantially improved the chapter; Michael Magura, for his extensive research assistance; and James W. Meehan, Jr., for his interest and encouragement with regard to the project. None of the above, however, is responsible for any remaining errors.

[a]Two basic articles are Telser (1964) and Mann, Henning and Meehan (1967). Additional references may be found in ("Symposium on Advertising and Concentration," pp. 195–200), Cowling (1972), and Ornstein (1975).

relationship between concentration and profitability. Once the association between these two variables has been established by correlation (or other) methods, there is no need to disavow any causal interpretation of the observed empirical correlation because the conventional static micro-theory posits the direction of causation. With regard to the relationship between advertising and concentration, however, economic theory is rather indefinite. A plausible case can be made in support of each of the following propositions:[b]

1. Causation runs from advertising to concentration.
2. Causation runs from concentration to advertising.
3. Causation runs in both directions at once between advertising and concentration (i.e., joint determination).

All three predict a positive correlation between advertising and concentration.[c] Is there any way to discriminate empirically among the three causal hypotheses? As discussed below, we believe that under certain circumstances there is.

II. METHODOLOGY

The concept of causation used from here on is that of "causal priority." This avoids the hoary controversy surrounding the meaning of the statement "*X* causes *Y*" and confines the analysis to the corresponding statement, "*X* is causally prior to *Y*." The latter statement is unambiguously definable and is an hypothesis that is always testable in principle, and sometimes in practice.[d]

The statement that "*X* is causally prior to *Y*" is taken here as equivalent to the statement that "*Y* depends on *X*, but *X* is determined independently of *Y*." In the language of economic models, we would say simply that "*X* is exogenous to *Y*." The essential significance of such a statement is that a change induced in *X*, *ceteris paribus*, will be associated with a change in *Y*, whereas a change induced in *Y*, *ceteris paribus*, will not be associated with any change in *X*. In other words, if "*X* is causally prior to *Y*," a change can be effected indirectly by an induced change in *X*, but not vice versa. This is an implied hypothetical experiment, to which we shall refer later. The "induced changes" referred to here are accomplished by an appropriate hypothetical change in one or more parameters of the model determining *X* and *Y*. (See Simon, 1953, pp. 63–65.)

[b]See Mann, Henning, and Meehan (1967, p. 34, note 1). Greer (1971, pp. 19–23) contemplates the direction of causation and chooses joint determination as most plausible, a priori. We propose to choose on the basis of empirical evidence. No one to our knowledge has ever suggested that the two variables are independently determined.

[c]Although there is no unanimous agreement that this association has been established, we judge that the accumulated evidence does establish the existence of a positive and statistically significant association. The most recent work (Ornstein, 1975) with which we are familiar confirms this view.

[d]The notion of causal priority is associated primarily with Simon (1953). For a more applied approach, see Blalock (1964).

Consider now the problem of uncovering the direction of causal priority between two variables X and Y, taken to be endogenous in some otherwise unspecified model. (To avoid complicated qualifications, we assume nonstochastic linear relations among the variables.) Excluding the possibility that X and Y are determined independently of one another, there exist three possible causal relationships between these two variables: (a) X is causally prior to Y, (b) Y is causally prior to X, (c) X and Y are jointly determined. Suppose further that the variables Z_1 and Z_2 are taken to be exogenous. Each enters into the determination either of X or of Y, or of both. Given this, are there unique empirical implications of any specific causal relationships between X and Y? More precisely, how will X and Y, both known or given to be endogenous, depend on Z_1 and Z_2, both known or given to be exogenous?

For illustration, assume that the endogenous variable X is causally prior to the endogenous variable Y. To describe this same relationship, we say that Y is "causally posterior to X." In such circumstances we always observe that Y depends on both Z_1 and Z_2. This is so because Y is at the end of the line, so to speak, and must be affected by all the exogenous variables in the model, either directly or indirectly. A causally posterior endogenous variable will be found to depend on *all* the exogenous variables. A variable that depends on only *some* of the exogenous variables cannot be causally posterior.

Turn now to the variable X, which is causally prior to Y in our example. There are no restrictions on what we may find: X may be related to Z_1, or to Z_2, or to both. There is an extremely important difference, however, between the case where X is found to depend on only one variable (Z_1 or Z_2) and the case where X is found to depend on both variables (Z_1 and Z_2). In the former case, a researcher who did not know that X was causally prior to Y would be able to infer that fact, whereas in the latter case he could not. If he were to estimate regressions and find that Y depended upon Z_1 and Z_2, and that X depended upon only Z_2 and not on Z_1, he would conclude that X could not be causally posterior (because it depended on only some of the exogenous variables). X must be causally prior to Y. Equivalently, he might reason that such empirical findings would be impossible if Y were causally prior to X, or if X and Y were jointly determined, since in both cases X would have to be dependent on both Z_1 and Z_2.

There is another way of interpreting such a finding in terms of causal priority. In essence, the researcher has had a controlled experiment performed for him. He has varied X (through Z_2) and observed that Y varies, and he has varied Y (through Z_1) and observed that X does not vary. He has thus, in effect, performed the experiment referred to above. All this may be expressed in terms of the simple algebra of a pair of simultaneous equations. Suppose we write:

$$(1) \quad Y = b_1 Z_1 + c_1 Z_2 + d_1 X$$

$$(2) \quad X = b_2 Z_1 + c_2 Z_2 + d_2 Y$$

as a linear structure relating X and Y to each other and to the exogenous variables Z_1 and Z_2. We make no a priori zero restrictions on any of the parameters. Our problem is to determine empirically which parameters (our particular concern is with d_1 and d_2) are zero. The causal possibilities may be categorized in terms of zero and nonzero values for the coefficients d_1 and d_2 thus:

	$d_1 = 0$	$d_1 \neq 0$
$d_2 = 0$	$X\,I\,Y$ independent	$X \rightarrow Y$
$d_2 \neq 0$	$X \leftarrow Y$	$X \leftrightarrow Y$

where the arrows denote direction of causal priority, and the symbol "I" indicates independence. The reduced form for this structure, which itself may be a partially reduced form of some larger structure, is:

$$Y = \frac{b_1 + b_1 b_2}{1 - d_1 d_2} Z_1 + \frac{c_1 + d_1 c_2}{1 - d_1 d_2} Z_2 \tag{3}$$

$$X = \frac{b_2 + d_2 b_1}{1 - d_1 d_2} Z_1 + \frac{c_2 + d_2 c_1}{1 - d_1 d_2} Z_2 \tag{4}$$

The question to which we now turn is whether a knowledge of the reduced-form parameters (RFP), which can be estimated consistently, ever permits us to draw inferences concerning the direction of causal priority between X and Y— i.e., the values of d_1 and d_2. It is immediately apparent that if the four RFPs are found to be nonzero, then it is impossible to make any inferences concerning d_1 and d_2. Suppose, however, that one RFP, say that of Z_2 in the RF for X, is found to be zero whereas the others are nonzero. Then what we have are the inferences that:

(i) $c_2 + d_2 c_1 = 0$

(ii) $c_1 + d_1 c_2 \neq 0$

Excluding the possibility that $d_1 = d_2 = 0$ (independence) and recognizing that $c_1 = c_2 = 0$ in (i) is inconsistent with (ii), we are left with only two possibilities. One is that there exists a functional relationship among the parameters of the original structure, $d_2 = -\dfrac{c_2}{c_1}$ (all nonzero).[e] The other and only remaining

[e]This equality would imply that the value of $\dfrac{\partial Y}{\partial Z_2}$ in structural equation (1) happens to

possible explanation is that $c_2 = d_2 = 0$, which says that Y does not appear in the second structural equation (nor does Z_2).

The limitations of the method are, first, that it should be possible to assume that the two endogenous variables in question must somehow be causally related (i.e., not determined independently of each other—d_1 and d_2 are not both zero), and second, that the structural equation determining the causally prior variable must have at least one exogenous variable "missing." The first condition, which is convenient but not necessary (as will be explained below), obviously depends on the economic content of the model. Whether or not the second condition is satisfied is an empirical question.

To determine the direction of causal priority between the advertising-sales ratio and concentration, the procedure is simple and straightforward and follows the model just discussed. There is no need to specify the model beyond assuming that advertising intensity and concentration are somehow related to one another and that the independent variables selected (see the following section) are indeed exogenous.

First, we specify a set of variables taken to be exogenous to the system within which the advertising-sales ratio and concentration are determined. Admittedly, this is not—nor can it be—a complete set. Any conclusions we reach therefore are subject to possible revision if and when further exogenous variables become available. Second, we establish the empirical relationship between the advertising-sales ratio and the specified exogenous variables, and that between concentration and the same specified exogenous variables, by linear multiple regression methods. Third, we judge the presence or absence of exogenous variables in these equations, which is the core of the analysis, by conventional statistical tests.

The most we can expect to find is that one of these two variables is causally prior to the other. Since there are no possible results consistent only with joint determination, we cannot possibly demonstrate that this kind of relationship exists between the advertising-sales ratio and concentration. Similarly, no possible empirical results are inconsistent with independence; however, we shall formulate our conclusions *excluding* independence as a possibility (see footnote b above). This means that the effect of dropping our assumption that there is some kind of causal dependence between advertising and concentration is merely to add independent determination as a possible explanation of the results.

III. THE SAMPLE AND THE VARIABLES

The sample of industries used in this paper are the same ones employed in Mann, Henning, and Meehan (1967). The industry advertising-to-sales ratios are aver-

---

be exactly equal to that of $\dfrac{\partial Y}{\partial Z_2}$ in equation (2). It is, of course, conceivable that this is so.

In the present application, however, we can think of no reason why it would or should be so. The reader will have to evaluate for himself the likelihood of such an accident's occurring. For our part, we regard it as remote.

ages of the firm advertising-sales ratios reported in Appendix Tables I and II of Mann, Henning and Mechan (1967). Two sets of advertising data were used. One was provided by *National Advertising Investments*, which reports advertising expenditures for firms which spend more than $25,000 on 3 media. The other comes from *Printers' Ink* and *Advertising Age* figures for the 100 largest advertisers in several media. The measurement of and the sources for the other independent variables—new products per firm for each industry, economies of scale, and capital requirements—are as follows.

New Product Intensity

R.D. Buzzell and R.E.M. Nourse reported in their study that "... *about half of the total increase in large food processors' marketing expenditures since 1958 is attributable to higher rates of marketing effort devoted to distinctly new products.*" "Distinctly new products" are those "... developed wholly or in part by the processor which are substantially different in *form*, *technology*, or *ingredients* from other products previously marketed by *the company*" (pp. 25, 160).

This definition distinguishes a new product from a line extension (a new package size, a change in shape, etc.) and a product improvement (a change in ingredients, taste, texture, etc.). The distinction among these types is somewhat arbitrary, although Buzzell and Nourse gave us some guidelines (p. 26). A new product would be expected to have:

- Its own separate marketing plan or budget
- Its own separate advertising budget and distinct campaign
- Its own product manager, if applicable
- Its own profit and loss statement
- Its own brand name or product designation

Using these criteria, the annual reports of all the firms assigned to the fourteen industries used in Mann, Henning, and Meehan (1967) were scrutinized over the years 1952 to 1965. In addition, *National Advertising Investments*, which reports advertising expenditures by firm, broken down by the firm's particular brand, was examined in order to determine products given separate advertising budgets. These sources provided the information for tabulating a company's distinctly new product offerings over the period 1952–1965.

Since the advertising variable is in terms of intensity, the new-product variable was similarly determined. Thus an industry's new-product intensity was calculated by summing the new-product offerings of the firms assigned to the industry and dividing by the number of firms. This was done for each of the subperiods incorporated in the years 1952 to 1965: 1952 to 1956, 1957 to 1961, and 1962 to 1965.

Economies of Scale

The estimates of minimum optimal scale apply to plants only. The procedure assumes that 70 percent of the industry output is produced by plants that are at least of minimum optimal size.[f] The average plant size of the firms supplying 70 percent of industry output was divided by total industry output. (The measure of output was value of shipments, but the results varied only marginally if value-added or employment was used instead.) This gave the percentage of industry output contained in the average plant within this efficient range. This estimation technique was used for each industry for the years 1954, 1958, and 1963,[g] using the distribution of plant sizes by employee size classes as reported by the Census Bureau in the *Census of Manufactures*. A comparison of the estimates by the described procedure in 1954 with those of Bain for those six industries in common produced the following results:

Industry	Bain[h]	Present Study
Soap	5.0	3.3
Cigarettes	5.5	7.6
Tires and Tubes	2.1	3.3
Meat Packing	2.25	0.4
Liquor	1.5	3.0
Pens	7.5	7.0

The percentages are not identical, but they are tolerably close.

Capital Requirements

The capital requirements were estimated by calculating the average assets of the sampled firms for each industry in the selected time periods: 1952 to 1956, 1957 to 1961, and 1962 to 1965. The average of the firms' averages was the estimated capital requirement for the industry. This computation probably over-estimates the capital requirements for minor entry since it is based on the leading firms and is an average of their asset sizes. It does, however, indicate the financial wherewithal necessary to achieve the mean dominant position in the market—or, in other words, to make significant inroads against the leading firms.

IV. STATISTICAL ANALYSIS

The statistical analysis consists of multiple regressions with the advertising-sales ratio, for which we have two measures, one based on *NAI* data (AS_1) and the

---

[f]The 70 percent figure was chosen on the basis of Bain's finding that the proportion of the output supplied by the inefficient-sized plants reached no higher than 30 percent in the twenty industries he intensively studied (1968, p. 379). In some cases, more than 70 percent had to be used because of the way the data were tabulated.

[g]No estimate was made for canned fruits and vegetables in 1954. The revision of the standard industrial classification in 1957 reassigned about 30 percent of the pre-1957 *SIC* value added to new *SIC* codes established in the 1957 revision. (*Concentration Ratios in Manufacturing Industries, 1958*, Table 7, Pt. 2, p. 419.)

[h]These estimates are mean estimates. See Bain (1956, Table V, p. 76).

other based on *PI* and *AA* data (AS_2), and the concentration ratio (*CR*) as dependent variables; and with new products per firm (*NPF*), optimum plant size (*OPPL*), and average assets (*AVAS*) as independent variables.

The results reported here are based on the analysis of a linear model. We also estimated a model that was quadratic in the independent variables to allow for the possibilities of nonlinearity and/or interactions. This refinement merely reaffirmed the conclusions based on the simpler linear model. In addition, the exclusion of the new products per firm variable, which some might maintain is a surrogate for the advertising variable, did not affect our results. (We will be happy to supply any interested reader with the data used in the statistical analysis.)

The test for determining causal priority consists of comparing the set of independent variables which are statistically significant determinants of advertising-sales ratios with the same set for concentration. If we find that one of the dependent variables depends on only *some* of the independent variables, whereas the other dependent variable depends on all of them, then we infer that the former variable is causally prior to the latter. As demonstrated above, such a finding would be inconsistent with joint determination and with causal priority running from the latter to the former. It would be consistent with the only remaining possibility—that the direction of causal priority runs from the former to the latter.

As a first step, we set down in Table 8–1 the cross-section regression results for each of the three time periods for which data are available. We may now apply our test and exclude those variables that are not significant at 10, 5, and finally 1 percent. Table 8–2 summarizes the implied direction of causal priority for these significance levels.

In twelve of the eighteen cases presented, the results imply that the advertising-sales ratio (AS_1, AS_2) is causally prior to concentration (*CR*). In four cases, the conclusion is that AS_1 is independent of *CR* (not causally related to *CR* in any way). In two cases we draw the inferences that *CR* is causally prior to both AS_1 and AS_2. It is difficult to draw any general conclusions based on what might be called the preponderance of evidence (i.e., twelve out of eighteen artificially defined "cases") that the advertising-sales ratio is causally prior to concentration. The six instances where other inferences must be drawn are inconsistent with such a general conclusion. The results, therefore, must be regarded at this stage as suggestive but inconclusive.

Obviously, an important factor contributing to the erratic nature of our results is the very small number of degrees of freedom. Accordingly, our next step was to pool the data for all three years and run regressions of AS_1, AS_2, and *CR* on *NPF*, *OPPL*, and *AVAS*. The Chow Test was applied to test the hypothesis that there was no significant difference between goodness of fit when the regression coefficients were constrained to be equal for all periods (i.e., the pooled regressions), and when they were not so constrained (i.e., the separate

Table 8–1. Separate Regressions Relating CR, AS_1 and AS_2 to NPF, OPPL, and AVAS[a]

Independent Variables[b]	NPF	OPPL	AVAS	Constant Term	N	$\overline{R}^2$
Dependent Variables						
1954						
AS_1	1.388*** (.301)	.940* (.429)	−.184 (.164)	−.057	12	.665
AS_2	1.188* (.542)	1.646* (.771)	−.367 (.294)	1.751	12	.386
CR	8.835* (4.646)	2.303*** (.661)	.506* (.252)	25.727	12	.593
1958						
AS_1	.647* (.319)	1.293** (.532)	.169 (.153)	.032	13	.447
AS_2	.732 (.597)	2.254** (.994)	−.095 (.286)	2.481	13	.324
CR	7.354** (2.741)	2.512*** (.456)	.606*** (.132)	19.343	13	.818
1963						
AS_1	.777*** (.164)	1.134* (.507)	−.134 (.104)	.824	13	.714
AS_2	1.270* (.561)	3.793* (1.724)	−.565 (.366)	5.058	11	.466
CR	3.423 (2.187)	3.609*** (.675)	.210 (.139)	29.384	13	.753

[a]Standard errors in parentheses. [b]Independent variables have been scaled in order that coefficients have no more than four and no less than two significant digits. N is the number of observations. *Denotes significance at 10%; **denotes significance at 5%; and ***denotes significance at 1%.

Table 8–2. Implied Direction of Causal Priority

	10 percent Significance Level		5 percent Significance Level		1 percent Significance Level	
1954	AS_1 → CR		AS_1 I CR		AS_1 I CR	
	AS_2 → CR		AS_2 → CR		AS_2 → CR	
1958	AS_1 → CR		AS_1 → CR		AS_1 → CR	
	AS_2 → CR		AS_2 → CR		AS_2 → CR	
1963	AS_1 ← CR		AS_1 I CR		AS_1 → CR	
	AS_2 ← CR		AS_2 → CR		AS_2 → CR	

regressions of Table 8–1). The F-ratio was not statistically significant at the 5 percent level or even at the 10 percent level for the regressions with AS_1 and CR as dependent variables. The F-ratio for the regressions with AS_2 as dependent variable, however, was significant at the 5 percent level. Strictly speaking, therefore, the constancy of regression for this variable must be regarded as forced. The pooled regression results are set down in Table 8–3.

The conclusions to be drawn from the AS_1 and the CR regressions appear to be quite unambiguous; CR cannot be causally prior to AS, nor can these two variables be jointly determined. Under our assumptions, the only conclusion that can be drawn is that the advertising-sales ratio is causally prior to concentration. When NPF and $OPPL$ vary, we observe both AS and CR to vary; when $AVAS$ varies, however, only CR varies. This finding is consistent only with causal priority running from AS to CR. The AS_2 regression permits an identical interpretation although its quality is lower than the AS_1 regression because its coefficients are forced.

It might be worthwhile to recall at this point that either of two assumptions (maintained hypotheses) of our analysis, if invalid, could also explain our results: (1) CR and AS are independently determined; or (2) there happens to exist an equality of parameter values in two different and presumably independent structural equations (see footnote e). It has been pointed out to us that a reader who had doubts about either of these assumptions could argue that the risk of Type II error in our conclusion is greater than that entailed in the direct statistical conclusion that $AVAS$ does not appear in the reduced form for AS. Fortunately, even if we used a 50 percent confidence level in Table 8–3 (in order to reduce the risk of Type II error), the conclusions remain unchanged.

Finally, we explore tentatively the nature of the dependence of concentration on the advertising-sales ratio and on the exogenous variables. A regression of CR on AS_1, AS_2, NPF, $OPPL$, and $AVAS$ was estimated as follows (standard errors in parentheses; **significant at 5 percent; ***significant at 1 percent):

Table 8–3. Pooled Regressions Relating CR, AS_1, and AS_2 to NPF, OPPL, and AVAS[a]

Independent Variables	NPF	OPPL	AVAS	Constant Term	N	$\bar{R}^2$
Dependent Variables						
AS_1	.789*** (.133)	.105*** (.028)	.035 (.075)	.490	38	.591
AS_2	1.074*** (.355)	.223*** (.074)	−.018 (.020)	2.633	36	.332
CR	4.447** (1.732)	2.640*** (.362)	.036*** (.010)	29.865	38	.670

[a]Standard errors in the parentheses.   *Denotes significance at 10%;   **denotes significance at 5%;   and ***denotes significance at 1%.

$$CR = 30.534 + \underset{(2.430)}{5.727\ AS_1} ** - \underset{(.941)}{.689.\ AS_2} + \underset{(2.422)}{.240\ NPF} +$$

$$\underset{(.433)}{2.125\ OPPL} *** + \underset{(.010)}{.036\ AVAS} *** \ \overline{R}^2 = .691$$

This equation suggests that AS_2 has no effect on CR independently of AS_1, which is not surprising considering the indeterminate amount of overlap between these two variables. Furthermore, NPF has no independent effect on CR, and apparently affects CR only through AS_1. The significance of the $OPPL$ and $AVAS$ variables suggests that the two variables, on the other hand, do have powerful independent effects on CR.

A diagram of the network of causal priorities implied by our statistical analysis would be the following:

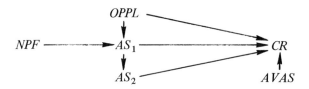

V. CONCLUSION

Our analysis suggests rather strongly that advertising intensity is causally prior to concentration. Since this is the first study to deal with this question, our findings must be regarded as tentative until corroborating evidence appears.

Chapter 9

Strategies and Structure: Majors, Independents, and Prices of Gasoline in Local Markets

Robert T. Masson
Fred C. Allvine

I. INTRODUCTION

In this chapter we discuss various aspects of gasoline supply, market structure, and pricing behavior in the decade preceding the energy crisis. We first analyze some structural aspects of the industry to show why independent marketing channels are an important element of competition in the industry. We show that the industry structure leads to a seemingly anomalous result: for the last fifteen years major oil companies have been both supplying much of the gasoline used by independent marketers, and concurrently fighting them in retail markets. We find that major sales to independents have increased and we present statistical support for the common (but disputed) assertion that majors cut their retail prices when they are located near independents. We demonstrate structure-performance links for a variety of possible market (or submarket) definitions, using both single time period cross-section tests and observed changes in market price dynamics and levels as a function of changes in market structure.

The format of this study is as follows: First we examine basic environmental

This chapter represents the authors' research at Northwestern University and is not intended to be and should not be construed as representative of U.S. Department of Justice opinion or policy. We would like to thank several research assistants who slaved away with us. Particular thanks go to Jon Castor, Mark Cronin, Debra Goldstein, and Lucian Piane, who found data, punched cards, and ran programs. Thanks are also due to Northwestern University for a faculty research grant that financed part of this study, and especially to Albert Page of Case Western Reserve for allowing us to use some of his data prior to the completion of his project on gasoline marketing; and to Darius Gaskins, Robert McGuckin, Robert Reynolds, Joanne Salop, and several others for comments and advice which we always thought about but didn't always take. An earlier version of this chapter was delivered at the Econometric Society winter meetings in 1973.

and structural conditions of the relevant markets. Second we give a brief sketch of a partial theory of oligopolistic competition for this industry. After that, we narrow the focus to analyze static and dynamic structural determinants of pricing behavior in various market areas.

II. BACKGROUND

Gasoline marketing is the final stage in a long series of activities in the petroleum industry: it is preceded by exploration, drilling, transportation of crude, refining, and transportation of product. Marketing itself has yielded a relatively low rate of return, often carried as a loss on the books of major oil companies. Since oil companies have reported substantial rates of return their rents were clearly being extracted at higher levels in the vertical chain. Our argument is that this was due to accounting conventions and that the profitability of retail operations was clearly demonstrated by continued investment in retail operations. Thus we feel that low stated returns for retailing did not imply there was no competitive problem at this level in the vertical chain.[a]

The industry nationally is dominated by about twenty highly vertically integrated firms which have been commonly called the "majors." The national twenty-firm concentration ratio has been high and slowly increasing since World War II.[b] And the high twenty-firm national concentration is reflected in high local-regional concentrations by four and eight firms. In our data, discussed below, there are generally less than eight majors in any defined submarket.

Outside of these (about twenty) largest firms we find the "independents." These firms are less vertically integrated and often independent marketers pur-

[a]The Temporary National Economic Committee found that for 36 firms, 25 rated marketing as the least (or tied for least) lucrative operation of the firm, with refining a close second. Twenty firms listed marketing as a deficit operation (*TNEC*, 1940, pp. 10040–10043). More recently Morris Adelman says, "We're often told that refining pays only 3% on investment. That's absurd. The companies have to pay 7% to buy the money. The figures they have are determined by accounting rules. They don't correspond to reality" (*Forbes*, March 15, 1972, p. 36). Similarly, we find *Business Week* saying, "Even in the best of times, the return on investment for a major oil company's retail operations will average only 3% . . ." (May 13, 1972, p. 135). The same rebuttal is still applicable. Short run accounting profits less than zero could be due to misplanning or competition, but even when Bain wrote his comprehensive study of the California petroleum industry there were net losses for retailing (1945, part II, p. 236). Misplanning for three decades is clearly unlikely and competition cannot yield long run profit rates below capital costs.

[b]Refining concentration by the top twenty has gone from about 65 percent in the 1920s to about 75 percent in the 1930s to 80 percent through much of the 1950s and later rose to the mid 80s (deChazeau and Kahn 1959, p. 487; U.S. Bureau of the Census 1971 Part I, p. SR2–21). Concentration in crude and in marketing are both lower. The concentration in domestic crude oil production for 1969 was 70 percent by 20 (up from 63 percent by 20 in 1960) and for gasoline marketing it was 79 percent in 1970. The *FTC* stated that 95 percent of proven domestic crude oil reserves are owned by the top twenty, but there are probable data biases in their study (U.S. Congress, July 12, 1973, pp. 13–14, 22). There is not a perfect correspondence between the majors and the "top twenty" at any one level of the industry.

chase much of their gasoline from the majors. Nationally 50 percent of the independents' gas supplies are refined by majors, primarily the ninth through the twentieth largest majors.[c] Although major refining concentration has been increasing, the retail sales of independents increased markedly from 5 percent of retail sales in the early post–World War II years to almost 30 percent in the early 1970s.[d] Independent private brand outlets tend to sell a different product—gas on a "price basis" rather than with a higher price with more service, advertising, credit cards, and so on.

Much of both the independent and major gasoline sold in the market is not refined by the company making the final sale. The independents buy gasoline and the majors operate by a complex system of reciprocal exchange agreements. These exchange agreements have apparently facilitated stability of refinery throughput in a market where high transport costs and uncertain locations of new sources of crude have led to companies having crude and refinery capacity geographically out of balance. Gasoline short run marginal cost curves have in the past been very steep after full capacity. Thus increased sales from any point near capacity would have rapidly created higher costs. Newer technologies have led to increased ability to change the output mix, making operations more flexible.

III. SOME THEORETICAL CONSIDERATIONS

With a homogeneous product, price competition in an oligopoly may lead to instability. In the oil industry we find a nearly homogeneous product and a steep short run marginal cost curve near full capacity. There are, in addition, potentially great adjustment costs if output levels are shifted rapidly in the short run. These factors allow for quick retaliation to price changes and make price competition futile in gaining a market advantage. Instead, some types of nonprice competition are resorted to.

For the theoretical discussion, assume for the moment that there are no independent marketers. Price competition is likely to be particularly costly where, as for gasoline, there are focal points one cent apart (for example, in the past retailers priced at 33.9¢ or 34.9¢, not at 34.3¢ per gallon). These customary one-cent differences are a high percentage of the actual gasoline wholesale price, which was, in the absence of price wars, generally 16¢ to 19¢ in the 1960s. As Richard Heflebower emphasizes, in such industries the decision to change one's price

[c]Only about 1 percent of their requirements are supplied by the top eight refiners, whereas close to half is supplied by the next ten or twelve, although the top eight supply quite a bit of gasoline to these next ten or twelve (U.S. Congress, 1973, pp. 9–10).

[d]Definitions, coverage, and accuracy of estimates differ. The *Wall Street Journal* quotes an industry source saying they had 15 percent in 1955 and 30 percent in 1962 (May 2, 1962, p. 1); the chairman of Gulf estimated the 1961 share as 25 percent [*Forbes*, December 15, 1961, pp. 14–15]; and Lundberg Surveys estimate a share of about 30 percent for 1973 (*National Petroleum News Factbook*, 1974, p. 109).

relative to one's rivals' prices is not taken lightly. The potential gains to be made from a lower price might be great if there were no reaction and no adjustment costs for increases in output. But there would probably be a swift reaction due to adjustment and opportunity costs of competitors and a homogeneous product. These reactions would offset any advantage that could be gained. Instead, firms compete by product differentiation, advertising, and related practices because ". . . devices other than price change do not often shift market shares rapidly" [1954, p. 127]. Hence, a change in advertising or station building policies may take six months to counter and may not be fully offset.

The logic employed is similar to kinked demand theory. Indeed we find for many of the markets we studied that, during the time period of the middle sixties, the average price of gasoline at (wholesale and retail) varied by less than one tenth of one percent for periods as long as a year. Many of these same markets started to gyrate wildly in the late 1960s. DeChazeau and Kahn are pointing out the same thing for our specific case when they say, "Nonprice competition is the hallmark of competitive [rivalous] markets . . . price is the easiest competitive weapon to parry and in such markets businesses search instead for advantages that are not so quickly matched in the eyes of the consumer" (1959, p. 279).

One type of nonprice competition that is emphasized in gasoline marketing is a heavy investment in building many stations, a profitable undertaking if prices are fixed above the marginal costs of existing outlets. As deChazeau and Kahn put it, this offers "precisely the security of not having to offer . . . a lower price to pick up additional sales of gasoline" (1959, pp. 380–381). This advantage may be easily seen through examination of the economics of market saturation competition in a nonprice competitive market. This model has a similarity to the case of airline competition except that price level is exogeneously determined in the airline industry.

The determination of the price level in gasoline may be endogeneously determined by a formal agreement, a tacit understanding, or simply enlightened self-interest. The price arrived at in the market may be "selected" to reduce entry from other firms and/or to not create too much "cheating" by majors supplying the market through the independent gasoline marketing channel. It suffices for our purposes that the price of gasoline is generally above the marginal costs of crude, refining, and marketing through existing outlets. We show some evidence of this below, but we do not directly examine all the processes that have led to this.

A model of nonprice competition may emerge both through advertising (services, and so on) and through station building. A key element to demonstrate is that *firms can benefit from not competing on price even if they compete in other ways.*

Considering station saturation competition first, we find that in the absence of price competition, monopoly rents would be earned on inframarginal units even with no restrictions on building of stations. This may be analyzed by looking at a simple model that assumes away most station location elements and then examining some spatial considerations.

Begin by assuming that gasoline stations have the same "L"-shaped cost curves (horizontal average and marginal cost curves beyond some moderate output level) and that they all offer the same product with the same services. In addition, assume that there are n most advantageously located gasoline station sites—in the sense that all other sites are less accessible to progressively more and more consumers. For example, no site is more accessible than one of the first n sites to any one consumer, but some consumers find the additional sites equally accessible. (This assumption allows us to ignore some important locational factors for the initial model.) Then if there are only stations at the first n sites, at a common price they will have equal shares of the customer population. If all sites have the same technologies, then in either a competitive solution or a blockaded entry barrier monopoly solution only stations at (a subset of) these first n outlets will be in operation.

But in an oligopoly, if by some mechanism the price of gasoline is fixed above the marginal costs of the first n outlets, then companies have an incentive to open less accessible stations. The first such new station will have a share of the market that is slightly below the total market divided by $n + 1$, and the first n stations will have slightly more than the total divided by $n + 1$, but less than the total divided by n. In general, each successive station opened will have slightly less of the market than the previous station will have after the entry. A company will open another station only as long as the profits from the outlet exceed the loss in profits to the company's already existing outlets due to the entry. This occurs if the price-average cost margin for the outlet times the outlet's output exceeds the price-cost margin times the reduced business attained by the company's inframarginal stations due to the building of the new station.

In the absence of other factors (goodwill and such), a company with a lower market share has a greater net gain from building a new station. If the last station built is built by a new entrant of equal efficiency (pricing at the fixed price) the outlet will only break even and operate on the declining portion of its average cost curve. If no new entrants exist, the last station will be built by the firm with the lowest market share and then even this last station will earn rents. In either case the inframarginal stations will all earn (higher) rents, with the highest rents going to the first n stations.

The rents on the inframarginal stations may be partly realized by the landowners and partly by the gasoline companies. But in any event even if all existing rents were realized by landowners, *if the price of gasoline changes, the total change in rents will accrue to the gasoline companies—not the landlords—on all existing long term leases or owned sites.* This means that as long as demand is not too elastic, at any time all integrated majors would have a mutual advantage in obtaining a higher price (and avoiding a lower price), even if they could not suppress station building competition and the rents on marginal stations were expected to fall to zero due to expansion. Noting that gasoline demand is inelastic, this is a key proposition since it establishes the value of obtaining higher prices even if nonprice competition cannot be curtailed.

Another question is how much of the rents that would result from a higher price would be captured by companies on their new leases. Clearly, some increment of rent must be expected or no new stations will be built. Thus, if the total rent of a station site exceeds the opportunity cost of the site, some rent will accrue to the gasoline companies. Furthermore, locational factors add to the rent attainable by the gasoline companies. For each set of sites (for example, four corners of an intersection), the rent attainable by a company is a declining function of the density of its own stations in the proximity of the site(s).

In general there will tend to be one company which can attain the highest rents from one of the sites. If the opportunity cost of the land in other pursuits is no higher (and in some cases less) than in gasoline, and if the various site owners compete, then the most advantaged company will be able to capture at least the difference between the total rents to a station at a site and the rents that would accrue (to landlord or company) by the building of a station by the next most advantaged company. But the key proposition of the model is that companies will gain all the rents from a higher price at their existing outlets and lose all the rents from a lower price at these outlets.

Advertising competition in general also would not cancel out the rents from setting a price above marginal production costs. If each firm assumes that each other firm's advertising budget is independent of its budget (a Cournot type of assumption), the final solution is characterized by rents. This proposition follows from the same logic as used in the Cournot quantity adjustment model as long as there are decreasing returns to advertising (and/or production). Diminishing returns fairly clearly characterize advertising, so rents should be attainable.

In the final solution the marginal costs of attracting *and* producing for the last customer are equal to the price (holding competitors' advertising budgets and price(s) constant), but the decreasing returns lead to rents on the inframarginal units sold. Thus, there remains a strong incentive to reduce price competition to a minimum even if advertising and market saturation competition is not in any way suppressed. In the absence of "cheating," then, the model would predict a long run result characterized by each firm trying to disperse its stations evenly in an urban area, with a central tendency towards equalization of market shares, since firms with larger existing market shares will find it less profitable to build new outlets.

One primary element of this framework as it relates to our work is that these same forces give gasoline firms an incentive to expand their sales by "cheating," price discriminating by selling some gasoline below the established price. Cheating cannot be accomplished by selling gasoline at one's own stations at lower prices, because these prices are virtually costlessly detected and will be quickly followed. But there is a niche in the market for selling through nonbranded outlets at a somewhat lower price. Stigler's "Theory of Oligopoly" (1964) brings out both the incentive to cheat and the fact that collusion will be more stable if sellers know other sellers' prices. In his model, as in ours, the value of "cheating" is a consequence of price discrimination. The lower price offered to some buyers need not transfer to an equally lowered price for other buyers. In Stigler's model this is a consequence of the price concession's being secret. In gasoline it is a consequence of some buyers preferring major gasoline and the consequent low cross-elasticity of demand between major and independent gasoline when their prices diverge by only a few pennies. In any such scheme the marginal revenue to be obtained through selling through the second mode is higher than the market marginal revenue of selling through only the first mode. This is akin to the second degree price discrimination case where the marginal revenue curve for the price discriminating firm is above that for the single price firm.

The firm may accept a noncompetitively high price on branded gasoline, but "cheat" by selling gasoline to independent marketers who are not "obligated" to sell at this noncompetitive high price. More generally, in industries with vertical integration the cheating on an oligopoly may arise at more than one part of a vertical chain. In this case the "cheating" comes at the wholesale level where interseller price detection is harder. Cheating on an intermediate product could be accomplished by vertical integration. An integrated firm could then, in effect, claim that lower final product prices were a consequence of superior efficiency of final production rather than a consequence of its quoting its own operations a lower (shadow) price.

The cheating will decrease, but not remove, inframarginal station rents unless it makes the branded gasoline price collapse. Cheating will be indulged in primarily by firms with lower market shares, for the same reasons given above. This and related locational factors probably provide part of the explanation of why although 50 percent of independent gasoline has come from the twenty major gasoline firms, only a miniscule proportion of this comes from the top eight major firms (U.S. Congress, 1973, pp. 9–10).

This cheating does lower rents on outlets located nearest to the independent outlets which generally are supplied by other firms. One way to reduce the cheating and the impact of the cheating where it occurs is to discipline the individual independent outlet operators with the intent of either bringing them into some parity with the noncompetitive branded price or, in some cases, eliminating them from the market.[e] This "price pocketing" around a station has been

[e]The "allowed" price spread in the early 1960s was about 2¢ per gallon in most regions (Allvine and Patterson, 1972, pp. 114–140). In seven West Coast markets that we studied for the period 1966–1972 we find the spread increased from 2 or 3¢ per gallon to an average of about 5¢ per gallon, with a range of about 3 to 8¢ per gallon. Albert Page has figures from the early 1970s on the major independent price spreads in Indianapolis, St. Louis, and Washington, D.C. These figures are based on five large sample surveys and the spreads ran from a low of 3.25¢ per gallon to a high of 5.81¢ per gallon, averaging about 4.5¢ per gallon (1974).

common in gasoline marketing, and, as explained below, most of the costs of this pocketing are generally borne by the supplying firms rather than the individual major outlet entrepreneurs or managers.

The problem majors cause themselves by supplying independents is exacerbated by the fact that during downturns consumers tend to experience an income effect, shifting their marginal rates of substitution between money and leisure. This leads them to shift their custom from major stations and drive slightly further or wash their own windshield to get a price break at an independent station. Exogenous fluctuations in market conditions, by affecting outlets assymetrically, then put a strain on market stability.[f] With this background we may look more closely at the form of nonprice competition and consequent price warring in the 1960s.

IV. GASOLINE COMPETITION IN THE 1960S

In the previous sections we developed the reasons why major gasoline companies will attempt to expand their retail gasoline sales through both branded and unbranded outlets, and why this expansion comes without active price competition among major marketers. Our theory leads us to believe that "cheating" through sales in the independent marketing channel must be policed or they will threaten the price level of the major brand gasoline.

Cheating may be inhibited by "price pocketing" and price wars. Price pocketing segments the market by dropping major outlet prices around individual independent stations without decreasing prices elsewhere in the market area. This retards the growth of the alternative marketing channel. Where independent growth is more rapid or their market shares are higher price wars may ensue. We find in particular that price wars appear to be most prevalent and severe where there are more independents, but that the conditions that cause price wars are at the discretion of major firms rather than independents. We examine first interlocational differences between prices and then price wars.

Interlocational Price Levels and Competition

The first step toward examining retail competition is to define retail markets. One approach defines markets by finding breaks in the chain of substitutes. Looking at large urban areas we find that large breaks are both difficult to find and hard to define. In fact, each station has an overlapping market with others, and by chainlinking all the stations might be lumped together in the same mar-

---

[f]*The Wall Street Journal* attributes the Gulf Oil offensive of the early 1960s at least in part to a shift in the driving population to more young and old drivers with less money and a higher price sensitivity (May 2, 1962, pp. 1, 22). And *The Oil and Gas Journal* attributes some price war activity and discriminatory pricing in the Mountain States to the high percent of defense workers in the area; given the ". . . employment cutbacks and other current uncertainties of defense industries, workers are especially economy-minded and tend to buy gasoline on price" (August 31, 1964, p. 24).

ket. And the chainlinking may not be of contiguous areas; for example, a station near a central city freeway ramp may be in competition primarily with stations in three different suburbs.

It would be misleading to assume that, since breaks in the chain are difficult to find within an urban area but do exist between urban areas, we must define a whole urban area as a market area. We shall attempt to define intraurban markets, (which we shall refer to as submarkets) in an empirically useful fashion. But we do feel that there is no single theoretically appropriate definition and have ourselves used multiple definitions.

By defining meaningful submarkets within an urban area and relating structure in these submarkets to competitive conditions within them, we accomplish two things that a cross-urban area study would not accomplish. If price differences between areas are related to market characteristics within areas, then we have verification that our submarket grouping is at least partially meaningful. Also, we have a distinct advantage in interpreting our results because intraurban groupings are within single supply areas. Thus, a company's delivered costs of gasoline to the station (although not necessarily the price) will not differ substantially in the area.

Our approach is to define a variety of different geographic submarket breakdowns, to cover (as much as possible, given data availability) all reasonable market definitions. In Table 9-1 we report the results of eleven different tests using five different types of market definitions. These tests were performed in six urban areas (two tests per area for five areas and only one test for San Francisco). The structure of the tests is described below. Five of these tests were run by Albert Page, who was kind enough to let us have his results prior to their final publication (Page, 1974).

In theory we could aggregate all eleven tests into a single analysis of variance model. We do not do so for three reasons. The first reason is that in all markets the price dispersion of majors in markets with independents is wider than in those without independents. Thus each individual t statistic is computed for unequal variances. The second is that with the different types of market definitions used the expected price differentials between markets should vary by market definition. And finally, the distribution-free binomial test we use for our aggregate test does not have to assume normality. (The price distributions are definitely skewed, a factor we do not take account of in our individual market t statistics.)

In all eleven tests, there was a positive relationship between prices *charged by majors* in an area and submarket station concentration. By the use of a binomial distribution or "zero test," the significance level of finding eleven such successes out of eleven tries is greater than 99 percent. But to use this test one must assume that all eleven observations are independent. Since some of these observations are for the same stations at different times, we may recalculate this test using only those tests that are known to be statistically independent. There are

Table 9—1.   Differences in Prices Charged by Majors Between Submarkets with High Major Market Concentration and Sub-markets with Low Major Market Concentration

Area	Market Condition	Percent Majors in Concentrated Group Is at Least	Cents Difference in Mean Price	t Statistic (calculated for unequal variances)	Sample Size
1. Indianapolis	between price wars	100	.2	3.44**	350
2. Indianapolis	price war	100	.06	.54	345
3. St. Louis	between price wars	100	.2	1.96*	635
4. St. Louis	price war	100	.5	4.17**	635
5. Washington, D.C.	stable	100	.7	7.38**	605
6. Washington, D.C.	stable	100	.9	5.47**	118
7. San Francisco	between price wars	100	.5	1.89*	178
8. Denver	between price wars	88	.6	1.82*	~ 500
9. Denver	between price wars	81	.2	.70	~ 500
10. Los Angeles	between price wars	92	.7	2.93**	~5000
11. Los Angeles	between price wars	95	.7	1.60	~5000

Sources cited in text.
* *t* significant at 95% level
** *t* significant at 99% level

six of these, and six successes out of six trials by the same test is still significant at the 98 percent level.

We feel that it is appropriate to interpret these pricing patterns as an element of major company policy rather than the passive result of individual dealer pricing. In part this feeling flows from personal discussions with people in the industry. It is somewhat strengthened, however, by our observation (discussed in more detail in the next section) that there are major oil company policies that lead to lower effective wholesale prices for retailers who are located near independents. The FTC has shown that during the period of our analysis companies had control over dealers' prices (FTC *News Summary*, November 1, 1972; *Wall Street Journal*, November 7, 1972, p. 5). For a Justice Department suit, see the *Wall Street Journal* (May 3, 1973, p. 2). Press stories report that the major companies' top executives generally denied such control, while local company representatives did quite the reverse, and news sources also claimed that most dealers felt that "suggested prices" were required prices (cf. *Wall Street Journal*, October 7, 1969, pp. 1, 19).

In addition, gasoline station dealers are charged "rents" that are frequently on a per gallon basis, which may not reflect the opportunity cost of the station sites and may be manipulated on the basis of market conditions (*National Petroleum News*, December 1966, pp. 52–53; U.S. Congress, 1971, part I, pp. 156–166). This means that dealer wholesale prices may be manipulated to reflect competitive conditions, influencing dealer prices without overt control of their pricing decisions. Of course, for our contention we need only recognize that the dealers themselves feel controlled and thus follow their "suggested prices." The fact that there are some areas where the dealers are hard to handle does not deny that most dealers in most areas are controlled. One such market of "mavericks" is Detroit, where if one company were to crack down it would lose outlets to others because they have all been traditionally lax. In an area where all companies have been more watchful, a dealer who loses his contract for rebellion may not find others willing to supply him as a branded dealer.

The tests summarized in Table 9–1 were run as follows.

Tests 1–5: These tests were performed by Albert Page [1974]. He examined stations on all the main roads in the greater Indianapolis and St. Louis areas, during both price war and nonprice war periods, and on the main roads in the greater Washington, D.C. area during a stable period. In each study he recorded the price charged for each grade of gasoline at each station and various other elements of their marketing mix. The service stations were all located on a map and groupings of stations were defined as clusters. These clusters were designated as homogeneous clusters (majors only) and heterogeneous clusters (both majors and independents); thus in Table 9–1 the concentrated group is said to have 100 percent majors. The mean price of regular gasoline charged by majors was computed for each of these two designations, and the significance test was based on a one-tailed t statistic computed for unequal variances. Page also conducted similar tests using other components of the marketing mix, which are not reported here. But his tests, plus additional regression tests we ran on his data, show little sensitivity of this result to the inclusion of other variables such as brand, station size, station appearance, and so on.

Test 6: A similar sampling technique was used during a long stable period in Washington, D.C. In this test we examined the pricing behavior of gasoline stations along four commuter routes into the city in an attempt to hold constant other variables affecting demand. These data were collected for an earlier study reported in Allvine and Patterson (1972, pp. 300–303) and were adjusted down by 1/2¢ per gallon at each station offering trading stamps.

Test 7: These data were collected by Allvine and Patterson in conjunction with their study, but much of it was not in fact used by them. Here we report the results of a study of the commuter road, El Camino Real, for its 48-mile length between San Jose and San Francisco. In this case, commuters are exposed to several miles of road and overlapping market areas. Majors located within a half-mile of independent outlets were differentiated from those that were further from independent outlets. The percentage of majors in the concentrated group (stations not within half a mile of an independent) is 100 percent. This study was done on the pump price and also on the pump price adjusted by 1/2¢ for each multiple of trading stamps given, since San Francisco stations often compete by the use of multiple trading stamps (up to ten times normal levels, in this sample). The results of the study reported in the table are not adjusted for stamps. When we adjust for stamps the differential is still positive at .33¢ and the t statistic is 1.38.

We also broke this sample into thirds of the road. Each third had between 85 and 87 percent majors. Where station density was higher the price was lower, holding constant the distance to the nearest independent. The t statistics on price for the three groups separately were 2.02, 1.11, and .25. Adjusting for stamps we have one wrong sign with the results of 1.69, −.24, and 1.14. Use of stamps as a competitive tool was most intense in group 3, where the station density per mile was lowest. Since the disaggregated figures adjusted for stamps yielded one wrong sign it may be argued that our test showing six out of six tries is biased. This argument for disaggregation (and independence) would break El Camino Real into three independent sections and for our aggregate test would yield a result of seven successes out of eight trials. This is significant at the 95 percent level using a binomial test.

Tests 8 and 9: In these tests a different market definition was used. This is a Denver market area breakdown used by a major oil company *for its own zone pricing decisions.* The criterion for dividing markets is in fact unknown to us, although we were supplied all the market boundaries. This company divided Denver into approximately 150 price zones to facilitate "feathering" during price wars. The practice of feathering is dropping prices in one area while charging slightly higher prices in contiguous areas and successively higher prices in further neighboring areas. If prices were dropped in a whole city it would cost too much to fight individual price cutters, and if they were cut by a single discount near the price cutter, then dealers just outside of the discounted area would lose customers and the discount area would spread. One study was run during a partial price war and the other the previous week while there was only limited price cutting. The data on prices come from a market survey corporation, Lundberg Surveys. In these two tests and in tests 10 and 11 we do not test differences between homogeneous and heterogeneous clusters.

Because of the wider market definitions used, we hypothesized that price would be higher when major concentration was above some critical concentration level. Having no a priori hypothesis as to this level, we used the following procedure. The zones were ranked from the zone with the highest percentage of majors down to that with the lowest. The zones were then broken into two groups—the ten zones with the highest percentage of majors and the 140 with the lowest, and the *t* value for the difference in their mean prices was recorded. Then the sample was cut again at the eleventh position, the twelfth, and so on. The largest *t* value was then identified. This *t* value is reported in Table 9−1. The figure reported in the third column is the percentage of majors in the least concentrated zone that is left in the more concentrated group where the *t* value was at a maximum.

Tests 10 and 11: These tests were done for two successive years on the widest market definition used in our study. The Lundberg Surveys for the greater Los Angeles area are broken up into 55 areas, such as Beverly Hills, Culver City, Burbank, Watts, Santa Monica, and so on. These areas were ranked by percentage of majors, and the two tests were run as for Denver. We also used linear regression, and our results are similar to those of Joe Bain's pioneering work on concentration [1951]. Despite significance using a step function we find linear regression to yield *t* values less than one for both time periods. This may be because, like Bain, we find that at the lowest concentration levels there are several high values of the dependent variable, with the lowest prices (in Bain's case, profit rates) at moderate concentration levels (Cf. Bain, 1951, p. 313).

The results of these tests strongly demonstrate that lower prices at major outlets are associated with the proximity of independent gasoline stations. The three tests in which positive but not statistically significant results are reported

may be due to errors in variables, random processes, or changing price align-
ments that are in the process of moving across an urban area. This latter explanation seems true in the case of Indianapolis, which was restudied within a few
weeks after the first study during a period of rapid change.

An average station's volume is about 30,000 gallons per month. Given mean
price differences of about .5 cents per gallon, this adds up to $150 per station
per month. Given the absence of a unique market definition, errors in variables
in these estimates probably understate true differentials. If there were a unique
"true" market definition with an exact one-cent differential, then any combination of approximate definitions would estimate a differential of less than one
cent, unless all of these definitions were based on subparts of individual true
markets.

It is worth noting that it is in Washington, D.C., the most stable of the markets studied, that the results of this study have both the highest statistical significance and the greatest differences between means. This may be due to deeper
pocketing, keeping prices more stable, or to market stability. A stable market is
likely to be characterized by less intensive consumer price search. This would
narrow the appropriate market definitions and give us better results. Our results
on Washington, D.C. are also consistent with results reported by Livingston and
Levitt, indicating that larger intraurban price differences are associated with
fewer price wars (1959, p. 127).

Gasoline station rents are in the area of $375−500 per month or 1-1/4¢ per
gallon.[g] Since the price differentials are substantial relative to station rents we
feel that they are not likely to be due solely to differences in station opportunity cost values. The results cited below reinforce this belief: they show, using
data for larger market areas, that prices fell in areas when there was more entry
of independent marketers.

The reasons for price pocketing are fairly clear. If majors did not use these
lower prices near independents, then even more independent entry and expansion would be forthcoming. If majors as a group used these lower prices throughout an urban area, then they would lose a great deal of money because of the
inelasticity of demand. Moreover, a unilateral price decrease would probably
bring retaliation. The similarity of customer appeal across the majors and the
competition by market saturation has led to a circumstance in which the majors

[g]Gasoline station economic land rents are hard to assess. The amounts that the majors
charge their dealers for rent are somewhat arbitrary, and can only be interpreted relative to
the tankwagon price the dealer pays, cf. [*National Petroleum News*, Dec. 1966, pp. 52, 53].
Often rents are adjusted like price protection to take account of localized price warring
[U.S. Congress 1971, part I, pp. 165–166]. One approach is to look at prices of station
sites. In the early 1960s these were running on average about 40 to 50 thousand dollars.
Using a common rule of thumb of 1% per month, we arrive at a monthly rent averaging
about $400 to $500 per month (cf. *Oil and Gas Journal*, April 29, 1963, p. 50). Another
approach is suggested by an article in the *National Petroleum News*. Here they surveyed
"banking circles" and found that majors are willing to pay 1-1/4¢ per gallon of projected
output for a fifteen-year ground lease (June 1962, p. 19)–e.g., $375 for an average station.

do not market as inexpensively as independent marketers. The current reversal of the trend in total number of service stations in the United States is probably in part a reflection of this.[h]

Price Wars and Competition

Our theoretical discussion leads us to expect majors and independent refiners to sell gasoline through independent channels, attempting to expand most rapidly where prices are higher. While independent concentration is low, their growth may be retarded by price pocketing. But after the concentration of independent outlets reaches some higher level, price pockets will tend to spread throughout an urban area. In a competitive world a greater concentration of independent marketers who purchase and sell gas for less should tend to lower the general level of prices, but it is not a necessary consequence that price wars would ensue.

Our results show that where there was more competition, prices were lower. This result in itself would be of little interest without the particular way competition is defined and the transitory nature of the price war phenomenon. Our definition of competition focuses on the *proportion* of independents, not the total *number* of gasoline outlets. We show that where independents had a greater proportional representation prices were substantiallly lower, but only during the price war periods in the early and late 1960s. A competitive hypothesis might explain price differences by adjustment costs and the total number (or rate of entry) of stations, not on the proportion of independents. Furthermore, what occurred during the decade presents a sharp contrast.

Almost all the price wars started abruptly at the same time and ended at the same time, which is not consistent with the competitive hypothesis with adjustment costs. When the price wars ended in March 1965, wholesale prices in the markets with high independent market shares rapidly converged to the national norm. When price wars reemerged in 1968, wholesale prices rapidly diverged from the national norm. Correlating this with the coincidence of price wars and majors' granting price protection, we have evidence suggestive of part of our primary theme—that price wars are a function of major marketing policies used to retard the growth of independent competition.

The theory that we pursue is that price wars are directed toward disciplining, slowing the growth of, and sometimes eradicating independent service stations. Because of the high proportion of independent gasoline supplied by the majors, this must be viewed in part as competition between major oil companies. The competition comes in part from major supply of independent marketers and in part from independent refiners. Both deChazeau and Kahn and Cassady agree that price wars would not have existed without independents acting either as a

[h]The total number of stations in the U.S. has been falling since 1970. Even when 1972 and 1973 are thrown out as atypical "energy crisis" years there is still a two-year reversal of a fairly long trend (*Business Week*, May 13, 1972, p. 138; *Forbes* January 15, 1973, p. 22).

catalyst or a trigger (deChazeau and Kahn, 1959, p. 457; Cassady, 1954, p. 275).

The basic concepts are easily explained. No major oil company should like nearby independents, but they must be tolerated as long as they play by the rules (for example, pricing 2¢ per gallon below the majors), rules dictated by major oil companies' policies. The target price differential has generally been small (although it increased in many markets over the time period of our analysis), leaving high margins for independent dealers and low margins for major dealers. Thus, at the same time independent dealers would like to be able to cut their prices, the major dealers would suffer negative returns if this were to happen.

This control over the decision about the "appropriate differential" is easily seen by statements from the major oil companies themselves.[i] An independent marketer who did not go along with these seemingly externally dictated prices often faced a price war. The dealers of the major oil companies were often glad to cooperate in chasing an independent down. They lost little in doing so and may even have gained by doing so because of "price protection": for every cent they followed one down they typically had their own wholesale price of gasoline decreased by .7¢.[j] It is important to note that the price war periods in almost all the markets studied coincided with periods where majors were nationally offering price protection to their dealers.

The object of the major marketers is to make any cutting from the targets an unprofitable undertaking for independents. When many of the independents raise their prices the majors' prices are restored. Often price wars were ended by the independent outlet's giving up and each restoring its price, hoping for a truce. Less often we found the major oil companies in the lead. We studied 241 price war restorations of 2 cents or more in twelve urban areas in the West, using weekly data collected by Lundberg Surveys, and found that the independents led the restorations in 31 cases and the majors led in only twenty cases. The remaining 190 cases were unable to be classified by the use of weekly data. This is not surprising, given that price war fluctuations are often less than a week in duration.

In cases where independents cannot be brought into line the major companies

---

[i]We find statements from officials of Sun, Shell, and Gulf in the early 1960s in which they threatened to decrease the major-independent differential, cf. Allvine and Patterson (1972, pp. 115–140). These statements foreshadowed the price war period that followed.

[j]A discussion of various types of price protection plans may be found in Allvine and Patterson (1972). Most companies dropped the wholesale price about .7¢ for a cent drop at retail over a wide price range at retail. Often after the dealer's margin per gallon fell to some level this margin was guaranteed, i.e., wholesale price was dropped cent for cent relative to retail. Industry sources often point out that price protection makes dealers more "trigger happy"—e.g., *Business Week*, May 29, 1965, p. 138; deChazeau and Kahn 1959, p. 456; *Oil and Gas Journal* June 17, 1963, p. 149. Sometimes it is alleged that some major dealers would start price wars when their tanks were empty and fill them with subsidized gasoline which they then sold after the price war was over; cf. testimony by the President of Derby (U.S. Congress, 1966, vol. I, p. 125).

either buy some independents out, drive some of them out, or give up. A market with single outlet independent dealers is easily dealt with, given their greater difficulty in obtaining financing. Markets with geographically dispersed independent chains are harder to deal with. In fact, the lessons of the early 1960s led to many mergers of geographically dispersed independents where geographic dispersion was explicitly sought to help by use of defensive cross-subsidization.[k]

The other key factor in price wars is the density of independent stations. If they are not dense, individual price cutters are easily dealt with; if they are dense, a retaliatory action against one dealer is likely to spread rapidly through the whole area. Furthermore, a price cut by one independent station that is not rapidly met by a price cut from the surrounding major stations becomes an invitation for all other independents to do likewise. Thus, price war activity that engulfs urban areas must be, at least in part, a function of the density of independent marketers.

The price wars of the early 1960s had several immediate causes. One of these cited most frequently by some industry sources was a general overbuilding of refineries and a condition of excess capacity that led to "excess supply." The popular conception that price wars occur because of short periods of excess supply is not borne out. As deChazeau and Kahn phrase it, "Price wars require continuing, substantial supplies of cut-rate gasoline, not just a single cargo. These will ordinarily be sold on long-term contracts, not in the spot market" (1959, p. p. 399). Thus we find one market, Los Angeles, with an average of one price war for every eight weeks and no lull of longer than six weeks over a period of seven years.:[1]

Excess capacity, it has been said, arose from "artificially high prices" in the 1950s (deChazeau and Kahn, 1959, p. 153). Excess capacity alone cannot account for the yo-yo pattern of prices, although it could account for low price levels. The excess supply hypothesis also does not account for high prices for a long period of time in one area with concurrent prices nearby below the costs of transport from the other area. We found wholesale prices that diverged by 10 or 15 percent over a period if several price war years which suddenly converged and stayed together in March of 1965. Since the price differentials are more than the cost of transportation between areas, this often led to jobber (wholesale

[k]The advantages of geographic dispersion can be seen by Chevron testimony that in the price war year 1963 only 1/3 of their market areas were depressed and about 1/12 were above normal (U.S. Congress, 1966, vol. 3, p. 719). Geographic and functional diversification followed the price wars in the early 1960s with many independents merging with others; cf. Allvine and Patterson (1972, pp. 175–175, 206–207).

[1]This is from weekly data from Lundberg Surveys on about 5,000 stations in Los Angeles for January 1966 to January 1973. We find 46 price wars in which the city average price falls by 2 or more cents (prior to August 1972) the longest stable period being six weeks. This was very unstable compared with greater San Francisco which (by the same data) held an average price within a quarter cent on a rising trend for almost eighteen months. When price wars finally hit San Francisco in January 1970 we find nineteen fluctuations of over a cent for the city average in less than three years.

agents) "moonlighting"–the practice of shipping gasoline to another area in violation of a supply contract.[m] And finally, as we discuss below, predictions of price wars or price stability by industry sources which have implicitly or explicitly used the "excess supply criterion" have performed miserably.

We may, on the other hand, view price wars as an excess supply phenomenon if we delve further. Prices elevated well above costs by an avoidance of price competition led to a great incentive to expand production, and this production had to find profitable outlets. One outlet was expanded sales to independents, which tended to damage market stability. Major oil companies needed to undertake programs to "shape up the market" and these yielded price wars in areas with high independent representation. Our results showing entry by independents and major versus major competition through supply of independent outlets may be interpreted as indicating a tendency toward a competitive result in the very long run. But they imply a very long span of short run results that are at wide variance with the competitive norm. In any case, adjustment is slowed by anticompetitive pricing and there is a welfare loss due to market power.

A brief historical sketch of the 1960s will help put the statistical evidence in perspective. In 1960 and 1961, Gulf, Sun, and some others introduced subregular brands of gasoline. These brands served essentially the same purpose as independent supply–they could be sold below the going price of regular to expand market share. What followed was a series of price wars in which the price of gasoline would sometimes fall below average variable costs, and at times even below the cost per gallon of crude oil.[n]

In some markets Gulf attempted to price its subregular (Gulftane) precisely at the price of independent regular gasoline, and in some of these areas Gulf's "Tane" prices were met on the nose by the prices of regular gasoline charged by other majors.[o] At the same time in California, Shell Oil was aggressively reducing

[m]This has led to cross-hauling in violation of contracts becoming common. One example reported in the *National Petroleum News* (December 24, 1962, p. 4) was a jobber in Buffalo, New York, who over a period of time sent his gasoline in highway tankers 300 miles to Connecticut, thus earning a profit over his protected price.

[n]One industry source (Chalfant of *Platt's Oilgram*) said that a typical price war yielded a refinery netback well below costs (*Business Week*, May 13, 1972, p. 138). A specific example of this is a city in Oklahoma, cited by Derby Oil's President in U.S. Congress, 1966, vol. I, pp. 125, 134. George F. Getty II, the president of Tidewater Oil, in the same volume of the hearings, said that prices sometimes even fell below the prices paid for the same volume of crude (pp. 48–49).

[o]According to R.V. Rodman, the Chairman of the Board of APCO Oil Corp., subregular gasoline production costs are probably 1/8 or 1/4¢ per gallon less than regular (U.S. Congress, 1966, vol. I, p. 92). Allvine and Patterson discuss the introduction of these grades of gasoline in their book (1972, pp. 141–178). An article in *Forbes* brings one of the reasons into focus, saying that Gulf ". . . drew a bead on the independents," and quoted Gulf's Chairman as saying that they couldn't let the independents continue to underprice them by 2¢ or 3¢ per gallon and that their policy was due to the increases in independent market shares since World War II. In fact, Gulftane was introduced in independent strongholds and was at first used to meet the price of independent regular on the nose (*Forbes*, December 15, 1961, pp. 15–15; *National Petroleum News*, September 5, 1961, p. 4; Allvine and Patterson, 1972, pp. 146–148).

the differential between the price of major branded regular and independent brands of regular to 1¢.[P] The aggressive tactics of Gulf Oil may have been in great part aimed at gaining a larger share of the majors' pie, but in part they were aimed at the independents. The one-cent policies and the subregular brands were explicitly aimed at independents (or in the case of Shell at major-owned independents), which had been entering for several years at the two-cent margin. Indeed the subregulars were sometimes referred to as "fighting brands" in the industry.

During these price wars the major dealers all used some variety of price protection, i.e., dropping their wholesale prices by about .7¢ for every 1¢ decrease in the retail price up to 7 or 8 cents and then often absorbing the decline penny for penny below this level. Price protection has been known to average over a cent per gallon for some majors' total operations for a whole year (Allvine and Patterson, 1972, p. 183).

One effect of price wars was to drive many independents out of business in some of the worst hit areas. For instance, in San Antonio, Texas, in the summer of 1961, there were 250 independents selling 50 percent of the gasoline. Then Gulftane price wars hit the market. By May of 1962, 100 independents had gone out of business and the remaining outlets were selling only 15 percent of the gas (*Wall Street Journal*, May 2, 1962, p. 1). In fact, much of the independent exit is traceable to buyouts or conversions (*Wall Street Journal*, April 8, 1964, p. 1). The use of buyouts for expansion is rational for several reasons other than just cheap acquisition of weakened stations. It is said to take about 5 percent of a market to justify a large ad campaign (*Wall Street Journal*, April 8, 1964, p. 16). If this is so, a rapid expansion is preferred. Many of the conditions that led majors to attempt to expand sales through independents also led to trying to trying to increase their branded outlets.

But in less depressed price war areas we still find evidence of positive margins and entry by independents and majors.[q] In fact, nationally, we find that in each

---

[P]Shell claimed that its one-cent policy differed from earlier attempts by Sun, Pure, and Union in that the earlier attempts were aimed at independents and this was aimed at major secondaries (major owned independent brands) (*National Petroleum News*, August 1962, p. 82). Texaco, Phillips, and Continental followed Shell with 1¢ plans of their own in other market areas, some where there were no major secondary brands. Phillips is reported to have had 200 markets on one-cent plans in 1964 (*National Petroleum News*, October 12, 1964, p. 1).

[q]Examples of independent entry in price wars include Provo and Salt Lake City, Utah (*National Petroleum News*, October 1963, p. 24), and much of Texas (*National Petroleum News*, August 1964, p. 68). Major expansion and building programs—not just buyouts—remained strong in some price war areas. In Florida's severely depressed markets American and Humble were in major expansionary phases and Atlantic, Gulf, and Phillips were building new stations (*National Petroleum News*, August 1963, pp. 90–94). In California, Gulf, Continental, and Humble were attempting to expand by buyouts of Wilshire, Douglas, and Tidewater, and Socal was concurrently expanding its refinery capacity in Richmond by 40 percent (*Business Week*, Feb. 22, 1964, pp. 84–86). During this period the profits for the 32 largest U.S.-based oil firms were rising at a record rate (*National Petroleum News*, November 1963, p. 60), and there were claims of profits still being made in depressed markets

of the price war years 1969, 1970, and 1971, the share of the market held by major marketers fell,[r] and that the primary periods of expansion of a large independent (Hudson) were during the price war years of the early and late 1960s (*Business Week*, May 13, 1972, p. 136). This suggests that the target prices were well above competitive levels.

During the latter part of this first price war period we find trade journals and industry leaders ascribing the price wars to (1) the "incremental barrel theory", (2) overcapacity, and (3) the use of price protection. The "incremental barrel theory" was the competitive expansion of output whenever firm (rather than industry) marginal revenue was above marginal costs (*Oil and Gas Journal*, May 27, 1963, p. 60; June 22, 1964, p. 104; *Business Week*, May 29, 1965, p. 138). Several industry leaders attacked this "theory" and advocated returning to a method of selling where prices for gasoline would cover all (average) costs including opportunity costs and concurrently allocating all fixed refinery costs to gasoline as the most valuable product. The implication in these writings is that if all firms would *return* to pricing above prices where firm marginal revenues equalled marginal costs, prices and profits would go up.

An observation from the history of the 1960s supports our interpretation. This is that near the end of the first price war period we find industry sources predicting excess supplies and price war activity for many years to come.[s] Shortly after this, in March 1965, Texaco led all the other major marketers in a policy of dropping price protection, nationwide. Within a month, a period of higher and very stable prices started that lasted until 1968, when renewed price war activity appeared. Curiously enough, during 1967 and early 1968 we find predictions of future stability based on the assumption that the industry "had licked" the overcapacity and oversupply problem (*National Petroleum News*, November 1967, p. 62; March 1968, pp. 66–69; May 1968, pp. 71–78). Shortly after the first price war period had ended, the chairman of the board of APCO Oil Corporation was asked why the price wars had stopped; he answered that it was because price protection had been withdrawn, directly after attributing the price wars to "oversupply" (U.S. Congress, 1966, vol. I, p. 113). It is clear that both geographically and across time, price wars seldom occur when and where

---

like Miami (*National Petroleum News*, August 1963, p. 96). Even during the price wars refiners were said to be *averaging* prices above marginal costs (U.S. Congress, 1966, vol. I, p. 125).

[r]This is derived from data reported in three issues of the *National Petroleum News Factbook* (1971, p. 127; 1972, p. 116; and 1973, p. 111).

[s]Two such predictions by industry executives (the President of Cities Service and a Vice President of American Oil) are reported in the *Oil and Gas Journal* of June 22, 1964, pp. 102–104, and in the *National Petroleum News* in April 1964, p. 84. A prediction based on discussions with "industry sources" is given by the *Oil and Gas Journal* in the same issue. In this article they further quote an "industry economist" as saying that it would take three to five years before "demand and supply" would yield stability, even without a new round of building that might also occur (p. 101).

the majors do not use price protection, and price protection is generally insti-
tuted or stopped in many markets contemporaneously.

Over this interwar period the marketing oriented majors—and particularly the
marketing oriented large independents—reaped significantly higher profits (*Oil
and Gas Journal*, April 24, 1967, p. 49). But these short run profits were bought
at the cost of allowing widening major-independent price differentials (*National
Petroleum News*, October 1965, pp. 44−45, and March 1968, pp. 66−69) and
entry of independents.

To study the end of the first price war period and the later movement into
the second price war period we gathered data from *Platt's Oilgram* on prices published monthly for 55 major urban markets. For the first period we located the
eleven markets with the highest and the eleven with the lowest standard deviations of tankwagon price (wholesale price exclusive of price protection). In the
last year before March 1965, the eleven unstable markets had mean tankwagon
prices, exclusive of price protection, that were about 3¢ per gallon below the
mean price of the stable group, which was about 16¢ per gallon (see Fig. 9−1).
The mean prices of those two groups for the whole price war period differ at the
99 percent significance level. In March 1965, when price protection was removed, the average price of the unstable group increased by 3¢ per gallon, and
the averages of the two groups over the next several months stayed about 1¢ per
gallon apart and then started converging again. By late 1967, *and during the second price war period*, these two groups were indistinguishable, with the prices
of the previously unstable group being frequently *above* those of the previously
stable group. If price wars were in fact used to decrease aggressive pricing by
independents, this is the result we would expect.

The same phenomenon (but in reverse order) appears if we break down the
sample by the most and least stable eleven markets in the second price war
period (see Fig. 9−2). The unstable markets during the second price war had
lower tankwagon prices (by on average 2¢), and again the difference is significant
at the 99 percent level. But in the interwar period the markets that were later to
be depressed were often slightly higher in price than the stable group, and during
the first price war period *they were higher most of the time!* This is suggestive of
a hypothesis that we test below: that the reasons why these markets had more
price wars in the second price war period is that prices elevated well above costs
in the earlier periods led to greater entry (and possibly major supply) of independents.

To test the hypothesis that entry of independents is a prime cause of this
shift, we used a crude measure of state market concentration reported in the
National Petroleum News Factbooks starting in 1966. In the 1967 and 1968
National Petroleum News Factbooks there is a listing of the number of service
station outlets by brand by state (1967, pp. 140−143; 1968, pp. 140−143).
Earlier issues did not give data for all states. All figures are supplied by a poll of
the companies involved. Six companies did not respond: these were Texaco,

Figure 9—1. Mean Tank Wagon Prices for the First Price War's 11 Stable and 11 Unstable Markets

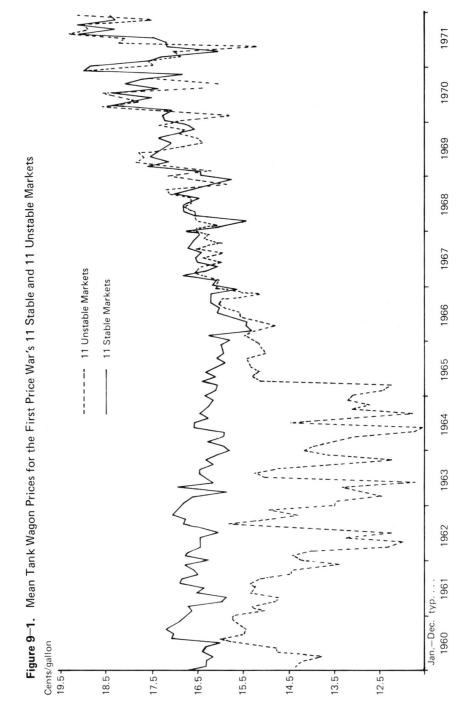

Figure 9–2. Mean Tank Wagon Prices for the Second Price War's 11 Stable and 11 Unstable Markets

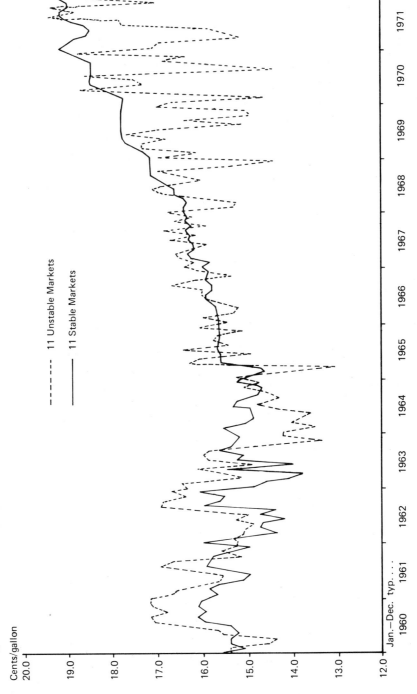

American BP, Chevron, Cities Service, and Sohio. In most of the states in our sample this meant that at most only two or three companies did not report if we judge this by more complete market share data collected by Lundberg Surveys and reported in the 1971 *National Petroleum News Factbooks* (pp. 127–133). To compute station concentration for these early years we assumed that the ratio between the excluded majors and three of the included majors remained the same over time and computed these ratios from the 1971 *Factbook* and projected them back to the earlier data.

We then broke our sample of 55 urban markets (by ranking in order of standard deviations) into those that were stable in each price war, those that were first stable then unstable, those that were unstable and then stable, and all others. We hypothesized that just before the second price war the stable-stable group would have had an even or rising percent of the market supplied by majors (contrary to the national trend) and that in the stable-unstable group majors would have had a declining market share. The cities were then identified by state. Because we had concentration data only by state, the states where there were cities in more than one of our groupings were dropped from the analysis.

The result was a correct prediction nine times out of twelve, which is significant only at the 90 percent level. (These tests are based on a binomial distribution and the assumption that if the null hypothesis (of no relationship) is correct each observation has a .5 probability of being of the correct sign.) One state, West Virginia, was obviously mismeasured in the sample. It was classified as a stable-stable state, but it appeared to have an unusually low and declining major market share in 1966–67. But suddenly in 1968 West Virginia's measured market share jumped radically, and this increase appears to be consistent with later observations (*National Petroleum News Factbook* for 1969, p. 152).

Market shares are not likely to have changed this rapidly. If they changed this rapidly toward major concentration (possibly by mergers) in a linear fashion over the year of 1968, and our test is, as it should be, about changes in concentration between 1966 and late 1968, then West Virginia should be registered as a correct prediction rather than an incorrect one. This yields even stronger results than those arrived at when West Virginia is simply dropped from the sample. Suspected measurement error, and the fact that if we based our test on 1968 data we found our hypothesis strongly confirmed, led us to drop West Virginia. We then have a score of nine out of eleven, which is significant at the 95 percent level.

Our hypothesis for the unstable-stable group was that it experienced independent exit during the first price war. Unfortunately, we could not find concentration measures for this period. We instead tentatively hypothesized that the unstable-stable group would not have experienced erosion of the major marketers' market shares just before the second price war period. Adding these results to our test, we correctly predict market structure changes in thirteen out of seventeen or thirteen out of eighteen cases (depending upon the inclusion of West Virginia), which are both significant at the 95 percent level. The results appear to confirm our hypothesis that changes in price war activity are associated with changes in market structure following higher net entry rates of independents rather than majors.

We were able to examine more closely the relationship of independents to price war activity in the second time period because we were able to construct a more refined measure of urban market concentration. We hypothesized that major marketers do indeed price in a consciously parallel fashion, and thus we felt that markets with high proportion of majors would have higher and more stable prices than those with lower proportions of majors.

Given constraints on our methodology, we instead tested the converse hypothesis. We selected the eleven least stable and eleven most stable markets for this second price war period from the group of 55 markets reported in *Platt's Oilgram*. In effect, the very similar wholesale prices of these 22 markets in the interwar period helped us to hold several supply conditions constant. The standard deviations of these groups were quite different (the highest of one group being .74¢ and lowest of the other group being 1.98¢), and their mean prices differed in the expected direction at the 99 percent level, with the tankwagon prices in the unstable markets averaging almost 2¢ per gallon below the average for the stable markets of around 18¢ per gallon.

To generate concentration data for these 22 markets we used 1971 phone book yellow pages and generated lists of stations with brand affiliations (cross-checked for multiple listings). A sample of 30−50 of the stations with no clear brand affiliation (generally 10 to 20 percent of an area's stations) were phoned and their brand assessed. These methods were supplemented in three cases by the use of survey data from Lundberg Surveys and Kent Surveys. The proportion of major stations in the eleven unstable markets ran from 51 to 90 percent with a mean level of 75 percent. For the stable markets the same figures ran from 65 to 96 percent with a mean of 88 percent. These means differed at the 99 percent level ($t = 2.53$), confirming our hypothesis.

The effect of these price wars has been to retard the growth of independents, but independents have not stopped growing despite the increasing concentration of majors in refining. We have related this to the classical oligopoly problem: if you can slow or stop competition of one type it will resurface in another guise. For a major company with a moderate level of market penetration it is an optimal policy to fight any competitively pricing independent that is located near one of its own stations while still selling gasoline to independents, and hoping, assuming, or assuring that little will end up next to its own stations. And indeed, the profitability of such a strategy is revealed by the degree of major supply to independent outlets.

The relative success of independents led to greater competition in the market.

Independent outlets were able to sell gasoline with low sales costs and were profitable outlets for major refined product leading to even more major competition. During the late 1960s and early 1970s, several majors started to use the independents' marketing techniques. Self-service and other low cost marketing arrangements started to expand and the emphasis on credit cards fell. As this competition increased, competition by maximizing the density of outlets started to reverse, and the total number of service stations even leveled off and started to decline (as our model would predict if the price level were to fall). More recently, even more radical changes in gasoline marketing practices coincided with price controls, an "energy crisis" and their aftermath, and it is misleading to analyze them in the same fashion.

V. CONCLUSIONS

In this chapter we have demonstrated strong statistical relationships between sublocal and local market structure and price behavior in gasoline markets. We have shown that both static and dynamic structure-performance links exist as we hypothesized. We have related these to a theory of nonprice competition. This nonprice competition between major oil companies successfully maintained prices above costs for long periods, but by so doing only opened the independent floodgates and fed the independent flood with major gasoline.

In our theory we argue that many majors in many areas found independents to be profitable outlets for their gasoline, "cheating" on the "going price," but that independent outlets located near major outlets were thorns in their sides. This, along with the fact that the major oil companies' branded marketing systems cost more per gallon to operate than the independents' (by an amount greater than the historically targeted price differential between branded and unbranded gasoline), led to tensions in the industry. The majors met these problems partly by charging lower prices when located near independents and partly by imposing discipline by the use of price wars and price war threats. This is not to say that they triggered individual skirmishes, but that they set the stage by the introduction of price protection and a hard line policy of major-independent price differentials. The interpretation is one of a market where non-price competition and avoidance of avoiding major versus major retail price competition has been moving the market toward the competitive result, but at a pace radically slowed by market conduct.

※ *Chapter 10*

Structural Effects of Regulation on Innovation in the Ethical Drug Industry

Henry G. Grabowski
John M. Vernon

I. INTRODUCTION

Professor Joe Bain has been very influential in promoting the use of structure-conduct-performance analysis in industrial organization research. Knowing the structure of an industry, of course, is essential in making predictions about its conduct and performance. In this study, we focus on what some have described as "basic conditions," and how changes in these basic conditions can affect industry structure.

In particular, we investigate the effects of increased product safety regulation on the innovative structure of the United States ethical drug industry. Since the passage of the 1962 Amendments to the Food, Drug, and Cosmetic Act, all new drug compounds must pass an extensive premarket regulatory review process. A by-product of this review process has been to make the research and development process riskier and more costly. Consequently, one hypothesis we examine is that increased regulation has led to increased concentration of innovation among the larger firms in the industry.

An important problem in the analysis is to determine to what extent increased regulation is the causal factor in affecting innovative structure and to what extent other factors may be at work. A leading alternative hypothesis is that new drugs are becoming more costly to invent because the underlying stock of research opportunities has declined. Since a depletion in research opportunities should operate worldwide, while increased U.S. regulation should affect only the U.S. industry, we also test our hypotheses using data on the United Kingdom ethical drug industry.

The idea that regulation may work to lessen competition is of course not a novel concept. Indeed, several industry case studies appear to provide concrete examples of this phenomenon, and Stigler (1971) has developed a theory that makes this the central rationale for government regulation. However, most previous investigations of this phenomenon have involved "traditional" regulatory situations in which entry and/or prices are directly controlled. Regulation of ethical drugs by the Food and Drug Administration (FDA) offers a much more limited form of regulation in which only product quality standards are controlled by the regulatory authorities. Given the recent rapid increase in this more limited type of product safety regulation throughout all sectors of the economy, investigations into the possible adverse consequences on competitive structure would seem especially warranted.

In the next section we present background information and summarize past studies on regulation and innovation in ethical drugs. In Section III an investment model of new drug development is constructed. Sections IV and V contain the empirical results of our analyses of the U.S. and U.K. industries, respectively. The final section offers some general concluding observations.

II. BACKGROUND

Past Studies of Innovational Activity in the Ethical Drug Industry

One of the issues that has received a great deal of attention by economists interested in the process of technical change is the so-called Schumpeterian hypothesis. While this hypothesis has been posed in a variety of ways, the most common approach from an empirical standpoint is to test whether innovational outputs (or inputs) in a particular industry increase disproportionately with size so that the largest firms tend to be its major innovators.[a] A number of a priori arguments, dating back to Schumpeter (1942) and others have been advanced as to why this might be so. These include the notion that the innovational process is costly, risky, and subject to economies of scale. The high degree of interest by economists in this question is tied to its obvious relevance to policy matters such as antitrust actions toward mergers and concentration.

Previous empirical studies by Mansfield (1964), Comanor (1965), Scherer (1965), Grabowski (1968), and Schnee (1971) have investigated the relation between firm size and innovation in the U.S. drug industry. These studies have used both output measures (e.g., new product sales) and input proxy measures (e.g., R&D expenditures) of innovation, and have employed data samples ranging from the top dozen or so firms to much larger aggregations. In general, these studies of the Schumpeterian question did not reveal any tendency for the larger firms to innovate proportionately more than smaller ones, at least over the size range of firms considered by these investigators.

---

[a]For a general discussion of this issue, see Scherer (1970, chap. 15). For a criticism of the methodology employed in some of these studies, see Fisher and Temin (1973). For a discussion of econometric issues and problems, see Grabowski and Mueller (1970).

Recent studies of innovation in the drug industry by Vernon and Gusen (1974) and Schwartzman (1975) have obtained results that appear to be more supportive of the Schumpeterian hypothesis. These studies not only have utilized samples from more current time periods but have also used somewhat different specifications than earlier writers. Because of this, it is not clear whether the differences in findings from earlier studies reflect differences in sample composition and research methodology or, alternatively, are the result of structural changes occurring in the industry.

One of the developments that might be expected to produce significant structural changes in the nature of the innovational process is the increased regulatory controls associated with the 1962 Kefauver Amendments. One might plausibly argue that such controls will make the research and development process both more costly and more risky in nature, and thus shift the structure of innovational activity in the direction of the Schumpeterian hypothesis.

The remainder of this section is devoted to a further discussion and development of the hypothesis. The various impacts of regulation on the innovational process are described in some detail and recent developments in the industry since 1962 are also discussed and analyzed. Much of this background information is then incorporated into the formal model of new drug development constructed in the next section.

The Nature of the R&D Process and Regulation in Ethical Drugs

The initial phase of drug research involves a team effort among chemists, biologists, pharmacologists, and the like, in screening various molecular structures of potential therapeutic value. The testing of a drug's pharmacological activity and toxicity is done exclusively on animals in this preclinical stage. As a result of the findings of tests on animals, some relatively small fraction of these drugs will be selected as sufficiently promising to warrant clinical testing on human subjects. Such clinical tests are divided into three phases. The first phase is directed toward examining a drug's possible adverse effects and is performed on healthy individuals under highly controlled situations. If a drug successfully completes this stage, it is then employed on a relatively limited number of patients to assess its effectiveness. It is then carefully evaluated from a therapeutic and marketing standpoint before entering a third phase. This final phase involves expanded studies in large patient populations with a substantial escalation in development expenditures.

The end point of all this clinical testing, when successful, is a new drug with therapeutic properties which have sufficient market value to warrant commercial introduction. Prior to 1938,[b] the developing firm could then proceed to com-

---

[b]The first law regulating drugs was the Food and Drugs Act of 1906, which prohibited adulteration and mislabeling of food and drugs sold in interstate commerce. Even within this narrow domain, implementation of this earlier law was plagued by a number of prob-

mercialization without any premarket regulatory approval. In that year, following the death of several people from consumption of the drug sulfanilamide, which was unfortunately dissolved in the poisonous substance diethylene glycol, Congress passed the Food, Drug, and Cosmetic Act. This established that all drugs undergo a premarket clearance process on the grounds of safety. At the same time, the new law prescribed some limits on the review process of the regulatory agency, the Food and Drug Administration (FDA). In particular the FDA had to reject a new drug compound within a limited period of time (180 days) or the new compound was automatically approved for commercial consumption.

In 1962, following the well known and tragic events associated with the drug thalidomide, which was cleared in several countries abroad but not in the U.S., Congress passed the Kefauver Amendments to the Food, Drug, and Cosmetic Act. This extended the mandate and regulatory control of the FDA in several ways. First, it required firms to provide documented scientific evidence on a new drug's efficacy in addition to the proof-of-safety required by the original law. In many instances this led to a substantial increase in the number of tests that had to be performed and included in new drug applications.

Second, the Amendments gave the FDA, for the first time, discretionary power over the clinical research process. Prior to any tests on humans, firms now are required to submit a new drug investigational plan (IND) giving the results of animal tests and research protocols for human tests. Based on its evaluation of the IND and subsequent reports of research findings, the FDA may prohibit, delay, or halt clinical research that poses excessive risks to volunteer subjects or does not follow sound scientific procedures. Third, the amendments imposed regulatory controls on the advertising and promotion of prescription drugs. In particular, firms must restrict advertising claims to those approved by the FDA for labeling and packaging inserts.

In addition to these new requirements, there is also evidence that FDA regulatory reviews of drug safety also became more stringent after the Amendments were passed. Contributing to this was the fact that the automatic approval clause of the original law was effectively repealed. Since 1962, various observers have noted that average total regulatory review times for clearance have significantly lengthened, and that many drugs in extensive use abroad have been kept in the regulatory popeline by the FDA for further evaluative tests of their toxicity properties.[c] The 1962 Amendments therefore appear to have resulted in a significant increase in the extent and degree of regulatory controls of ethical drugs.

Not only are regulatory reviews of safety more stringent, but the FDA also has become directly involved in the innovational process from quite early stages

---

lems and proved generally ineffective. For an historical discussion, see Wilcox (1966, pp. 587–589).

[c]A discussion of regulatory clearance times and comparison with other countries is undertaken by Sarett (1974). An extensive comparison of drugs cleared here and in the U.K. since 1962 has been performed by William Wardell (1973, 1974).

of development through the marketing of new drugs. These more stringent regulatory controls, put forth with the ultimate objective of protecting drug users from adverse situations, of course are not costless in nature. Some trade-off is to be expected between more stringent regulations for drug safety and efficacy and the supply of new drugs. That is, as development times and costs increase to satisfy stronger regulatory requirements, some potential drugs are eliminated from the development process because they no longer have expected rates of return sufficient to warrant development.

While some trade-off between development times and costs and the probability of a product's safety and efficacy seems unavoidable, various observers have suggested that the incentives operating in regulatory agencies like the FDA cause them to be excessively cautious and conservative in approving new drugs.[d] This reflects in part the narrow regulatory mandate of such agencies. The FDA is specifically responsible only for drug safety and efficacy rather than broader concepts of performance or welfare. Moreover, the effective reward structure tends to reinforce this limited objective function. Regulatory officials stand to bear a heavy personal cost if they approve a drug with unforeseen strong adverse effects, as occurred in the case of the drug thalidomide.

On the other hand, the costs of delays, expenditures, and a lessened rate of product introductions are less visible and are borne entirely by parties other than FDA officials. Furthermore, unintended side effects of drug regulation, such as long run adverse effects on the competitive structure of the drug industry, are also difficult to internalize in the regulators' decision making process, given the way the regulatory mechanism and mandate is now constituted.

Thus, the increased benefits resulting from more stringent regulation of product quality in a research intensive sector such as ethical drugs are also likely to entail substantial costs. A number of recent studies have observed structural shifts in the innovational process since the 1962 Amendments were enacted that appear consistent with this point of view.

Past Empirical Work on the Impacts of the 1962 Amendments

First, several studies have indicated rapid upward shifts in project development costs and gestation times for new drugs over the time period since the 1962 Amendments. For example, Dr. Lewis Sarett (1974) has recently indicated that average development costs per new chemical entity at Merck Laboratories have increased roughly tenfold from 1.2 million dollars in 1962 to 11.5 million dollars in 1972. New chemical entities (NCEs) represent drugs cleared by the FDA which have a new chemical structure rather than being just a new dosage

---

[d]For a discussion of incentives operating in regulatory bodies like the FDA, see various papers and comments in Landau (1973), especially the paper by Stigler entitled "Regulation: The Confusion of Means and Ends." For a comprehensive discussion of this issue, see also the survey article by Noll (1975).

form or combination of drugs already in use. Total development and clearance time for an NCE also now runs 7½ to 10 years as opposed to 2½ years in 1962. These large shifts in magnitude for development costs and times are supported in earlier independent investigations by Schnee (1971), Clymer (1970) and Mund (1970).

Second, there appears to be a corresponding increase in the attrition rate in drugs of IND status—more drugs fail to become new chemical entities. While the data for validating this are not generally available, Clymer (1970) and others have presented data from case studies and questionnaire surveys that indicate that the attrition rate of IND-investigated drugs is increasing.[e] Thus it appears that the risk and uncertainty associated with whether a drug will ever become a successful commercial product has increased along with development costs and time.

For the industry considered as an aggregate, the total number of new chemical entities approved for commercial use has also declined sharply over recent time periods. For example, if one calculates five-year averages for the annual number of NCEs, the number in the pre-Amendments period (1957–1961) was forty-eight, while in the first five years after the Amendments (1962–66) it was nineteen, and in the 1967–1971 period it had fallen to fifteen. These figures, combined with an upward trend in industry R&D expenditures over time, are the aggregate counterpart of the microeconomic trends in project development costs, gestation times, and attrition rates discussed above.

Of course, these adverse structural trends may be related to factors other than, or in addition to, more stringent regulatory controls. An alternate explanation, which has appeared in the literature, is that the underlying stock of research opportunities was depleted by the rapid rate of innovation that occurred in the earlier part of the post–World War II period.[f] Adherents of this hypothesis also tend to argue that any return to a rapid rate of drug innovation requires new research breakthroughs at a fundamental level, such as occurred in the antibiotic field prior to the new product explosion in this field in the 1950s.

Some formal analyses investigating the role of regulation and other factors in the decline of the supply of new drugs have been performed recently by both economists and noneconomists. Using models tested on aggregate time series

---

[e]Clymer (1970) surveys available information on this question and also presents some data based on case histories at Smith Kline and French. He estimates that prior to 1962, the attrition rate of drugs undergoing clinical tests was two out of three. His best estimate of the current situation is that less than one out of every ten new compounds entering IND trials become new products. Wardell and Lasagna (1974) have developed some new data on the attrition rate of new single chemical entities since 1962 through a questionnaire survey of fifteen large firms. Their work indicates that by 1974 only one out of twenty of the INDs filed after 1962 by these firms had resulted in FDA-approved new single chemical entities.

[f]See, for example, the testimony of FDA Commissioner Alexander Schmidt (1974, pp. 30–49) where some descriptive statistics on worldwide introductions are presented in support of this hypothesis.

data, Peltzman (1973) and Baily (1972) both found a statistically significant negative effect of regulation on the number of new product entities introduced in the post-1962 period. Baily also found support for the "depletion of scientific opportunities" hypothesis, using a moving average of past introductions to measure this phenomenon.

A basic problem with both the Peltzman and Baily studies is the possible confounding of the effects of regulation and the depletion of scientific opportunities in aggregate time series data. Using such data, at best one can measure these variables only in an indirect proxy fashion.[g] Given this measurement problem, a comparison of international trends and multinational movements in innovational resources might offer the best means for analyzing the relative role of regulation in dampening the level of innovation. This is because drug introductions in other countries also would be subject to a depletion of basic research opportunities but not subject to a change in regulations comparable to the Kefauver Amendments.

In a recent paper, we presented some new evidence on these alternative hypotheses based on a comparative analysis of the U.S. and U.K. (Grabowski, Vernon, and Thomas, 1975). In particular, we analyzed trends in R&D "productivity," defined as the number of NCEs discovered and introduced in each country per R&D dollar over the pre- and post-1962 periods. A principal finding of this analysis is that U.S. productivity declined by about sixfold between 1960—61 and 1966—70, whereas the corresponding decrease in the U.K. was only about threefold. Clearly some worldwide phenomenon, which might be labelled a "depletion of research opportunities," seems to hold for pharmaceutical R&D.

However, there is also strong support for the hypothesis that an additional factor apparently connected with increased regulation is at work in the U.S. industry. On the basis of an econometric analysis using these U.S. and U.K. changes in productivity, we estimate that the 1962 Amendments have roughly doubled the cost of an NCE. A similar estimate emerged from Baily's study of this question using domestic time series data and a very different measure of "research depletion."

In this chapter we also undertake parallel analyses of structural changes in the U.S. and U.K. to gain further insights into the relative impacts of regulation versus other factors. Before undertaking this empirical analysis, however, we develop a model in the next section that focuses on the expected effects of

---

[g]In the Peltzman study the effects of regulation are calculated as a residual difference between actual and predicted new entities in the post-Amendments period. The predicted level of NCEs in the post-Amendments period is determined using a "demand pull" type model estimated in the pre-Amendments period. Baily uses a simple time dummy (0 before 1962 and 1 after 1962) to measure the effects of regulation and a moving average of past NCEs as a proxy for the depletion of scientific opportunities. He estimates the effects of these variables on new drug introductions using a production function type of model.

increased regulation on various structural dimensions—including the number and concentration of firms producing new drug introductions.

III. A MODEL OF THE EFFECTS OF REGULATION ON THE STRUCTURE OF INNOVATION

Presumably, decisions on whether to develop a particular new drug are investment decisions and will be made in a decision making context that also considers expected returns from alternate investment opportunities. Given this, it would seem appropriate to examine the expected effects of increased regulatory controls within such a framework. In the discussion presented below, we develop such an approach.

Let us first consider an individual investment project involving the development of a new chemical entity. The expected return to development of a potential new chemical agent may be obtained from estimates of the time path of costs and revenues. In particular, the expected return to a new drug, r, is calculated from the relation:

$$C_0 + \frac{C_1}{(1+r)} + \cdots + \frac{C_m}{(1+r)^m} = p \frac{R_1}{(1+r)^{m+1}} + \frac{R_2}{(1+r)^{m+2}} + \ldots + \frac{R_n}{(1+r)^{m+n}} \qquad (1)$$

where

C_i = expected cost in period i

p = probability of regulatory approval by the FDA

R_i = expected net revenue in ith period after regulatory approval if the drug is cleared by the FDA

m = total number of periods necessary to develop and gain approval for the drug

n = total expected life span for the drug

Presumably there are trade-offs between development costs, development time, the probability and length of time for regulatory approval, and the expected revenues and product lifetime of a new drug. Let us suppose that the firm selects the values of these parameters that maximize the expected rate of return, and that the above formulation embodies these parameters and produces a maximum rate of return, r^*, for this project. This expected rate of return calculation abstracts from the interdependence among the various projects and does not consider possible differences in risk associated with different projects. Unless the firm is risk neutral, the expected return from each project has to be adjusted for risk.

The appropriate concept of risk for this kind of situation would seem to be some kind of portfolio risk, reflecting the contribution of each project to the variance in the returns (or expected probability of a loss) of the entire portfolio of projects. Similarly, an adjustment would also have to be made for interdependence among projects. The decision on whether to invest in this particular drug would then depend on whether this adjusted rate of return exceeded or fell below the firm's cost of capital, which reflects the opportunity cost of alternate investments for the firm and its shareholders.

Let us now consider how regulations of the type introduced by the 1962 Amendments influence the factors involved in this rate of return calculation. First, even if regulation is administered in an efficient manner, the additional tests and evidence required by the FDA will tend to increase development costs (the C_is) and gestation time, m, required to produce a new innovation. Moreover, tighter regulatory standards will mean a reduction in the probability of approval by the FDA, p, for many compounds under consideration. These effects seem straightforward in nature.

The influence of regulation on a product's expected revenues and product life, however, are somewhat more ambiguous. First, the firm will normally file for a patent on any new chemical entity that shows significant probability of leading to a commercial application quite early in the development process. Since the average time to develop and clear a drug now exceeds the time to obtain a patent, any increases in total gestation time caused by increased regulation standards will tend to lower the actual as opposed to the nominal patent life for a new drug. As a result, the expected values of future R_is and n may decline due to shorter periods for which a new drug will receive patent protection. In addition, the new constraints on drug labeling and advertising may also cause declines in R_i and n for some types of drugs, because these restrictions may produce reductions in a product's market size.

On the other hand, tougher regulation for new drugs might serve to increase general market acceptance of new products vis-à-vis older drugs. This could result from increased confidence in the safety and efficacy for drugs passing a more stringent regulatory process. This in turn would mean faster diffusion rates and greater market penetration for new drugs. Thus it is impossible to say on a priori grounds what the initial effects on regulation of R_i and n will be, although the factors producing an increase in these parameters appear to be somewhat more speculative in character.

Let us summarize these various effects. If we consider two states of the world, one where the pre-1962 regulations hold and the other where the post-1962 regulations hold, and we denote the latter state by ($'$), then, other things equal, we have:

$$C_i' > C_i; \; m' > m; \; p' \le p; \; R_i' \gtrless R_i; \text{and } n' \gtrless n.$$

If, as seems likely, increased regulatory controls cause a decrease in r^* for all or many projects, this will result in a curtailment of some projects that would have been undertaken without these controls.[h] The character of projects curtailed are likely to be those either involving smaller market sizes, or projects for which the costs of complying with newer regulations are particularly onerous. Among the former category, drugs that provide remedies for relatively rare diseases or ones that are essentially duplicative of existing therapies are among those likely to be significantly cut back due to increased regulation. In the latter category, drugs for which it is particularly costly and difficult scientifically to prove efficacy might be expected to bear a disproportionate part of the decline.

Thus far we have considered only the initial first order effects on the supply side of new drug innovation produced by increased regulatory controls. Over time, drugs that are approved will face much less competition from other new drugs. This lessened industry supply of new drugs will tend to mean higher prices and market shares for new drugs that receive FDA clearance. This is like the effect produced by a leftward shift in the supply curve. Moreover, as individual firms adjust to lower levels of innovational output for the industry as a whole, they will adjust upward their expected revenue and product life projections. This in turn will limit the size of the decline in innovational output triggered by an increase in regulatory standards.

What effects might these changes be expected to have on the number and size of firms producing product innovations? It is clear from the above discussion that the resource commitments that a firm must be prepared to make to develop a new drug increase as tighter regulatory standards and controls shift both costs and development times upward. In addition, higher costs and lower probabilities of FDA approval expose firms to more downside risks from innovational activity. While this may be accompanied by higher expected returns and life spans, as fewer drugs are approved under a more stringent regulatory environment, the overall variance in possible outcomes still increases.

As innovational projects become riskier and more expensive, the minimum scale at which R&D can be undertaken without exposing a firm to a high variance in earnings will also increase. In effect, a firm must pool a larger number of costlier projects to obtain a balanced total R&D portfolio that will provide security against the excessive risks of earnings fluctuations. Small firms with limited resource bases will have particular difficulty adapting to large shifts in costs and riskiness of R&D projects, unless they are especially confident about their comparative advantage in performing R&D. In addition, firms that are especially risk averse, or ones with relatively lower expected returns from R&D activities, are also likely to transfer resources out of new drug development.

Thus we would expect upward shifts in costs and risks produced by increased regulation to operate to concentrate innovation in fewer and larger firms. Over longer periods of time, this might be expected to have corresponding concen-

[h]Some empirical support for a decline in the expected rate of return from pharmaceutical R&D in the post-Amendments period is provided in studies by Clymer (1972) and Schwartzman (1975).

trating effects on total industry sales and assets. The importance and extent of these phenomena can of course only be ascertained through empirical investigation. This is the focus of our analysis in the remaining sections.

III. EMPIRICAL ANALYSIS: THE UNITED STATES

The model presented above suggests some a priori logical reasons why increased regulation in the post-1962 period might result in the concentration of innovational outputs in fewer and larger firms. In order to see whether this is consistent with trends in the industry, we assembled data on sales of new chemical entities (as classified by Paul de Haen) and total ethical drug sales for a sample of 53 firms over a period from the 1950s through 1971. These data are based on marketing audits of drugstore and hospital sales.[i] Our sample includes all firms introducing new chemical entities into the U.S. since 1957.

Concentration Of Innovational Output

In order to examine whether innovation is becoming concentrated in fewer firms over time, we have constructed concentration ratios of innovative output in the U.S. pharmaceutical industry over the three equal subperiods: 1957 to 1961, 1962 to 1966, and 1967 to 1971. Innovational output for each firm is measured by its sales over the first three years of all new chemical entities that it introduced during the particular subperiod. In effect, because new chemical entities are not homogeneous in nature, we use market sales weights here as an indicator of a new drug's value or quality.

This procedure has been employed in past work as well as weighting schemes of innovational quality based on the rankings of experts. In general, past investigations of the size structure of innovation in the pharmaceutical industry have not found that results are qualitatively altered when different measures of weighting NCEs are employed. For example, David Schwartzman (1975) used five different weighting schemes (a simple count of NCEs as well as weights based on sales, chemical novelty, medical importance, number of prescriptions, and number of patents) in such an investigation and found that his results were not highly sensitive to the method of weighting innovation. In this chapter we have used sales weights because they were readily available and have a somewhat more objective quality than some of the other measures used in the literature.

Our tabulations of innovational concentration are presented in Table 10−1. The first column shows the number of new chemical entities introduced in the

---

[i]Data on sales of ethical drugs were obtained from the publications of a marketing research firm, Intercontinental Medical Statistics (IMS). These data are based on a projection from a 1,000-drugstore sample to the population of all United States drugstores. The hospital data are based on a sample of about 10 percent of total hospital beds. Sales directly to other institutions, such as to the U.S. Government, are excluded here, but they account for less than 20 percent of U.S. ethical drug sales.

Table 10−1. Concentration of Innovational Output in the U.S. Ethical Drug Industry

Period	Total Number of New Chemical Entities (NCEs)	Number of Firms Having an NCE	Concentration Ratios of Innovational Output		
			4-Firm	8-Firm	20-Firm
1957−61	233	51	46.2	71.2	93.1
1962−66	93	34	54.6	78.9	97.6
1967−71	76	23	61.0	81.5	97.8

Innovational output is measured as new chemical entity sales during the first three full years after product introduction.

Data sources: List of New Chemical Entities in each year obtained from Paul de Haen *Annual New Product Parade*, various issues; all information on ethical drug sales obtained from Intercontinental Medical Statistics.

three periods under consideration. As previously noted, a sharp decline in aggregate NCEs was experienced in the post-Amendments period. The number of NCEs introduced in the 1967−1971 period was roughly one-third the number obtained in the 1957−1961 period. In addition, the second column shows that the number of individual firms producing at least one NCE also significantly declined over the three periods. In particular, the number of firms introducing NCEs in the last period is less than one-half the number doing so in the pre-Amendments period.

The last three columns of Table 10−1 show "concentration ratios" of innovational output in terms of the four, eight, and twenty leading firms (i.e., ranked in order of our measure of innovational output). The rather sharp increase in concentration of innovational output is clear. This is especially the case for the four-firm ratio, which increases over 15 percentage points between the first and last periods.

One minor qualification might be made to the results of Table 10−1. The four-firm concentration ratio in the final period is significantly influenced by the fact that one of the largest firms in the industry had a new product innovation in the antibiotic field in 1971 which captured a very large market. Nevertheless, even if we omitted the year 1971 entirely from the last period and just considered 1967−1970 to be the relevant time span, thereby eliminating the effects of the one extreme observation, one would still get a significant shift in the four-firm ratio (approximately 10 percentage points) between the first and third period. In this case, however, the eight-firm concentration ratio of innovational output would become larger than observed in the table (86.6% vs. 81.5%). Hence more of the increase would be distributed over the top eight firms rather than just the top four.

As one might expect, we generally found some sensitivity in the numbers observed to the particular choice of time period. Nevertheless, whatever convention we employed in this regard, a distinct upward trend in the concentration of innovational output over the range of the top firms was unmistakably observed.

The percentage of innovation accounted for by the top four and eight firms always increased significantly, irrespective of the time period convention utilized.

Innovation And Size

A further important question has to do with the relationship between the size of the firm (as measured by sales of ethical drugs) and its level of innovational output. Does innovational output tend to increase proportionately with firm size? And more importantly for our present purposes, has this relationship shifted over time?

In Table 10–2 the firms are ranked by size (i.e., their total sales of ethical drug products) instead of by innovational output and comparison is made of the largest four firms' share of industry sales to their share of innovational output over the three periods. This table also shows some dramatic trends over the three periods. In particular, in the pre-Amendment period, the largest four firms accounted for a slightly smaller share of total innovational output than their percentage of total sales (24% and 26.5%) whereas by the final period, they accounted for a substantially higher percentage of innovational output than sales (48.7% and 26.1%).

A different kind of analysis of the relation of innovational output to size is presented in Table 10–3. For each period linear, quadratic, and cubic regressions of innovational output on size were estimated. A possible statistical problem in the estimated equations concerns the presence of a significant number of zeros in the dependent variables, Y_{it}, for the equations estimated in Table 10–3. One means of adjusting for this is to use a Tobit Analysis. While this has not been employed here, it has been utilized by one of the authors in a similar context in a past study of drug innovation. The results were only moderately changed. (See the discussion of this procedure in Vernon and Gusen, 1974, pp. 300–301).

During the first two periods, the best relation is provided by a linear regression equation implying a proportional relation between changes in size and innovational outputs. While the estimated quadratic equation has a shift between these two periods in the quadratic term from a negative to a positive sign, both of these regression coefficients are statistically insignificant. Similarly, the cubic

Table 10–2. Percentage of Innovational Output and Total Ethical Sales Accounted for by the Largest Four U.S. Drug Firms, 1957–61, 1962–66, and 1967–71

Period	Four Largest Firms' Share of Innovational Output	Four Largest Firms Share of Total Ethical Drug Sales
1957–61	24.0	26.5
1962–66	25.0	24.0
1967–71	48.7	26.1

Data sources: See Table 10–1.

Table 10−3.   **Least Squares Regressions of Innovational Output on Firm Size in U.S. Ethical Drug Industry for Periods 1957−61, 1962−66, and 1967−71**
(Linear, Quadratic, and Cubic Regressions of the Form:
$$Y_{it} = a_0 + a_1 S_{it} + a_2 S_{it}^2 + a_3 S_{it}^3)$$

Period		a_0	a_1	a_2	a_3	R^2/F	N
1957–61	1)	359.35 (0.07)	0.74 (7.11)	−	−	.51/50.52	53
	2)	−701.19 (0.10)	0.85 (2.15)	$-.91 \times 10^{-6}$ (0.28)	−	.51/24.83	53
1962–66	1)	−2704.94 (0.67)	0.35 (5.57)	−	−	.39/31.12	53
	2)	2134.66 (0.44)	−.011 (0.53)	$.26 \times 10^{-5}$ (1.69)	−	.42/17.57	53
1967–71	1)	−11,467. (1.67)	0.94 (3.17)	$-.88 \times 10^{-3}$ (3.19)	$.25 \times 10^{-5}$ (3.81)	.63/27.07	53

"t" values in parentheses.

Innovational output, Y_{it}, is measured as the firms' total new chemical entity sales during the first three years after introduction; size, S_{it}, is measured by total firm sales of ethical drugs at midpoint of each period.

Data sources: See Table 10−1.

equations estimated for these periods had a lower F value than either the linear or quadratic cases and the cubic terms were statistically insignificant.

In contrast to the first two periods, the best fit in the last period is a cubic equation. In addition the coefficient of the cubic term, a_3, is positive and statistically significant at the 1 percent level. Moreover, the estimated coefficients of this equation imply that innovational intensity, Y/S, declines over the initial size range of firms, eventually reaches a minimum, and then begins to increase. Over the size range of firms in our sample, the largest value of Y/S is therefore estimated to occur for the largest firm (ranked by domestic ethical drug sales) in this third period.

Tables 10−1 through 10−3 taken together suggest there has been a strong shift toward higher rates of innovation by the very largest ethical drug firms. As noted above, an increasing relation between firm size and innovational intensity has not been characteristic of most industries in the U.S. It has been observed consistently only in the case of the chemical industry. Nevertheless, in the light of the large upward shifts in ethical drug development costs and times in the post-Amendments period observed by other researchers, this shift in the structure of innovation towards the larger firms is not really surprising. However, the sizes of such shifts are quite dramatic in magnitude, considering the relatively short time periods being analyzed.

MARKET CONCENTRATION IN ETHICAL DRUGS

What effect has increasing concentration of innovational output in the larger pharmaceutical firms had on concentration in the overall market for ethical drugs? In Table 10–4 we present industry time trends of four alternate measures of sales concentration—the usual four-firm ratio (the combined market shares of the four largest firms), the eight-firm ratio, the twenty-firm ratio, and the numbers-equivalent (N.E.). A major advantage of the N.E., which is the reciprocal of the Herfindahl index of concentration, is that it takes into account the *relative market shares* of the leading firms rather than simply the *sum* of shares of leading firms. The N.E. can be interpreted roughly as the number of equal-sized firms operating in an industry that would yield the observed degree of concentration (Adelman, 1969).

All four measures indicate a very mild tendency of decreasing concentration through the mid 1960s, and then a similarly mild tendency of increasing concentration through 1973. There is certainly no sharp increase in concentration which is clearly indicative of significant increases in market power. Of course, we are examining only total industry concentration, and it may be possible for concentration within certain therapeutic classes to be increasing quite sharply.

One of the interesting questions raised by these results is why the concentration trend in sales has been only mildly increasing while the concentration trend in innovative output has been sharply upward. This lack of change in industry sales concentration ratios could reflect a number of factors. In particular one might argue that this "concentrating" effect on industry sales may operate with

Table 10–4. **Concentration of Sales in the U.S. Ethical Drug Industry, 1957–1973**

Year	*4-Firm*	*8-Firm*	*20-Firm*	*N.E.*
1958	28.8	50.9	79.5	24.27
1959	26.8	48.0	75.5	27.32
1960	25.8	47.3	75.4	28.25
1961	25.8	45.6	75.3	29.07
1962	25.4	44.3	74.5	29.76
1963	24.5	43.5	74.6	30.40
1964	23.7	42.2	74.1	31.06
1965	23.4	42.3	73.7	31.25
1966	24.4	42.7	74.1	31.15
1967	24.5	41.8	72.3	32.70
1968	25.4	43.6	74.4	30.86
1969	26.1	43.9	74.4	30.12
1970	26.3	43.2	73.6	30.77
1971	26.5	43.7	76.0	28.99
1972	27.6	43.6	75.4	28.90
1973	27.8	43.5	75.7	28.65

Data sources: See Table 10–1.

a lag and cumulate only slowly over time. If this is so, it suggests that industry sales concentration would tend to increase in the future. A related point in this regard is that the tabulations in Tables 10–2 and 10–3 show that the increased concentration of innovational output in the largest firms only became pronounced in the last five-year period (1967–1971).

To gain some insight into the validity of the lag hypothesis, we estimated the following multiple regression of a firm's market share on past innovational output:

$$(1)$$

$$MS_{72} = 0.8 + .015 \, Y_{67-71} + .028 \, Y_{62-66} + .012 \, Y_{57-61} \, , R^2 = 0.72$$
$$\quad\;\; (4.89) \, (2.98) \qquad\quad (3.38) \qquad\quad (2.41)$$

where MS_{72} is market share of a firm in 1972 (measured in percent terms) and Y_{67-71}, Y_{62-66}, Y_{57-61} are levels of its innovational output (measured in million dollar units) over periods indicated ("t" values in parentheses).

The estimated equation explains 72 percent of the variation in the market shares of 53 firms in 1972, and all coefficients are statistically significant. It also indicates that there are indeed lagged effects of innovation in earlier periods on later year market shares. The lag pattern suggested by the estimated coefficients in equation (1) indicates that the average effect of new product introductions on market shares builds up to a peak somewhere between five to ten years after introduction and then begins to decline. Thus increasing concentration in innovational output would be expected to take a number of years to work its full effect on overall drug market sales.

On the other hand, there is a major factor dampening the concentrating effect of increased innovational output in the larger drug firms. This is the decline in output and total sales accounted for by new products in the ethical drug market. The first column of Table 10–5 again indicates the previously discussed sharp decline in the number of chemical entities over the three periods. Column 2 shows the average revenue per NCE introduced in each period. While the table does show that average revenue per NCE becomes successively larger in each of the three periods, the increase is little more than commensurate with the general rate of market growth experienced in the pharmaceutical industry over this period.

In this regard the third column shows the aggregate (annualized) value of sales for all the NCEs introduced in each of the five-year periods as a percentage of total sales of ethical drugs measured at the end of each period.[j] This provides a rough measure of the importance of new versus old drugs. This figure declines

---

[j]The following procedure was employed in calculating this ratio: we summed the average sales realized by each new entity during its first three years of product life over all entities introduced in the five-year period. We then divided this by total ethical drug sales in the last year of each period. This provides a rough measure of the relative importance, in terms of sales, of new products versus established ones in any given period.

Table 10—5. Number of Sales of New Chemical Entities in the Pre- and Post-Amendments Period

Period	Total Number of New Chemical Entities (NCEs)	Average Annual Sales per NCE (During First 3 Years)	Sales of NCE's as a Percentage of Total Ethical Drug Sales[a]
1957—61	233	$1,745,000.	20.0
1962—66	93	$2,657,000.	8.6
1967—71	76	$3,187,900.	5.5

[a]Average annual sales of all NCEs introduced during this period as a percentage of total ethical drug sales in the last year of the period.

Data sources: See Table 10—1.

from 20 percent in 1957 to 1961 to 5.5 percent in 1967—1971, a decline that is roughly proportional to the decline in the total number of NCEs (233 to 76) between the first and the last period.

Table 10—5 shows that innovational output has indeed become a much less significant factor in the total market for ethical drugs. Of course, equation (1) does suggest that the impact of new product sales is not realized for a number of years and therefore column 3 of Table 10—5 (based on only the first three years' sales) underestimates the eventual impact of new product innovations. Nevertheless, these declining percentage shares for new products do suggest that large increases in the concentration of innovational output might produce much smaller impacts on the concentration of total industry sales. Essentially, new product innovation has declined as a competitive factor in the total ethical drug market and a substantially greater portion of drugs being sold are "old" drugs.

Tables 10—1 through 10—5 taken together provide a composite picture of the strong shifts occurring in the structure of the competitive process in the U.S. ethical drug industry over the period from the late fifties to the early seventies. First, in accordance with the large shifts in development costs and times noted by other writers, innovational activity and output has indeed increasingly become the domain of fewer and larger drug firms. At the same time, the dominance of the competitive process by new product innovation, which characterized the earlier period, has considerably receded in recent periods. Thus the concentrating effects of innovation in a smaller number of firms to date has not tended to produce corresponding shifts in concentration in total ethical sales. Whether this will continue to be the case is, of course, conjectural and depends on whether the drug firms still actively engaged in large scale drug development will be able to develop and obtain regulatory clearance for drugs with significantly larger market shares in the future.

Up to this point we have confined our analysis to the examination of various structural shifts that have occurred in the U.S. drug industry. While all of the observed results are fully consistent with our theoretical predictions on the effects of the 1962 Amendments, the only basis up to this point for empirically linking them to the amendments is the timing of these shifts. That is, the Amendments provide a natural reference point (1962) for evaluating trends. This is obviously not strong from a methodological standpoint because, as noted above, other factors also have operated over this period to increase the costs and riskiness of pharmaceutical innovation. In particular, one might argue that these observed structural shifts are being caused primarily by "a depletion of scientific opportunities."

IV. ANALYSIS OF NEW PRODUCT INNOVATION FOR THE U.K.

In order to gain further insights into this question, we now turn to a parallel examination of developments in the U.K. over recent time periods. Given its much different and less stringent regulatory system since 1962, a comparative analysis of developments in that country provides some basis for assessing the relative importance of these different explanations for the above structural changes.

Regulatory Controls In The U.K.

The system of regulatory controls in effect in the U.K. over the period since 1962 differs in a number of ways from that in the U.S. In terms of formal requirements both systems do have a premarket review of all new drugs on safety grounds and both require the filing of an IND when a drug firm wishes to do clinical testing on human subjects. On the other hand, the U.K. did not require a formal proof of efficacy until 1971, a full decade after the U.S. requirement was put into effect.

Perhaps the greatest contrast between the two systems lies in the institutional characteristics of the review process. Sir Derrick Dunlop, who was the head of the British system for many years, provided a detailed comparison of the two systems in a recent conference on drug regulation. He notes:

> The main difference between the two systems is that ultimate power to license medicines in the United Kingdom rests with the Licensing Authority (the Ministers responsible to Parliament) acting on the professional advice of the Safety Committees. The decisions of these committees are taken by professional men whose careers in no way depend on their membership of the committees on which they serve part-time in a virtually honorary capacity as an altruistic chore. They are assisted, of course, by a small staff of expert professional civil servants who do most of the preparatory work, but the decisions are taken by the committees. It is probable that the experience gained from the eight-years' informal Safety of Drugs Committee will tincture their subsequenty official actions.
>
> In the United States, on the other hand, ultimate power rests with the full time professional civil servants of the FDA whose careers depend on

the correctness of their decisions, and who are subject to formidable grill-ings by Congressional Committees. The FDA has to work under fairly rigid rules by Congress which seem to rely more on animal experiments than is usual in the United Kingdom (Dunlop, 1973, p. 235).

The greater use of external professional advice in the U.K. apparently has pro-duced a regulatory incentive structure less prone to bias in the direction of cau-tion and delay. This has produced a regulatory system with shorter review times and lower development costs than has recently been the case in the United States.

One dimension in which the U.K. has apparently had much more stringent regulatory controls is in the area of postmarket surveillance. According to War-dell (1975), postmarket surveillance is rigorously enforced in the U.K., whereas it is relatively neglected in the United States. The British system therefore essen-tially combines a more liberalized, less bureaucratic premarket screening process for new drugs, with stronger postmarket checks on drugs once they enter the marketplace.

Wardell has attempted in a series of articles to assess the performance of the two systems over the period since 1962 in terms of their effects on medical therapy. He concludes:

> . . . it is clear that each country has gained in some ways and lost in others. On balance, however, it is difficult to argue that the United States has escaped an inordinate amount of new-drug toxicity by its conservative approach; it has gained little else in return. On the contrary, it is relatively easy to show that Britain has gained by having effective drugs available sooner. Furthermore, the costs of this policy in terms of damage due to adverse drug reactions have been small compared with the existing levels of damage produced by older drugs. There appear to be no other therapeutic costs of any consequence to Britain. In view of the clear benefits demon-strable from some of the other drugs introduced into Britain, it appears that the United States has, on balance, lost more than it has gained from adopting a more conservative approach than did Britain in the post-thali-domide era (Wardell, 1974, p. 90).

Wardell's studies have been widely cited, particularly in medical and phar-macological circles, and have played a significant role in the growing accep-tance of a U.S. "drug lag" by various members of these professional groups. Whatever the merits of this position, it would seem appropriate to compare the performance of the ethical drug industry in the two countries along eco-nomic dimensions, given the divergence of their regulatory systems since 1962.

Drug Innovation In The U.K.

The data on new product introductions and sales for the U.K. industry are more limited than for the U.S. We were able to gather new product sales data for only the two most recent five-year periods, 1962–1966 and 1967–1971. Furthermore, the sales data in the U.K. apply only to drugstores and exclude hospital or other institutional purchases.[k] For this reason, drugs used exclusively or primarily in hospitals (e.g., injections) have not been included. Finally, we lost a higher proportion of drugs in the 1962–1966 period (31 percent) than in the 1967–1971 period (10 percent) in large part because the data sources we used tended to exclude drugs introduced in the earlier period with low or zero current sales.

Subject to these data limitations, we performed analyses for the U.K. similar to those presented in Tables 10–2 to 10–5 for the U.S. In Table 10–6 some basic statistics on new product introductions in the U.K. are presented. Column 1 shows the number of U.K. new product introductions for which positive sales were observed in retail pharmacy outlets. Columns 2 and 3 show the average U.K. drugstore sales per NCE (during the first three years of product life) and the overall percent of total U.K. ethical sales in drugstores accounted for by the NCEs given in column 1.

The percentage of the drugstore market captured by NCEs in column 4 almost certainly significantly understates the percent of market captured by all NCEs introduced in the U.K. because of the data omissions discussed above. Nevertheless, despite these omissions, the estimated percentage of the U.K. market accounted by these NCEs is significantly greater than that obtained by the more comprehensive list of new product introductions in the U.S. market (as shown in Table 10–5). The situation in the U.K. in terms of the impact of new product sales appears to resemble much more the pre-Amendments situation in the U.S. than the post-Amendments periods.

In Table 10–7 data on the number of firms introducing new chemical intities in the U.K. and on the concentration of innovational output are presented. The

Table 10–6. Number and Sales of New Chemical Entities in the Pre- and Post-Amendments Period in the U.K.

Period	Total Number of New Chemical Entities (NCEs)	Average Annual Sales per NCE in pounds (During First 3 Years)	Sales of NCEs as a Percentage of Total Ethical Drug Sales[a]
1962–66	115	407,230	18.2
1967–71	95	744,550	25.6

[a]Average annual sales of all NCEs introduced during this period as a percentage of total ethical drug sales in the last year of the period.

Data sources: List of New Chemical Entities in each year obtained from Paul de Haen *Nonproprietary Name Index* and special reports by de Haen. All data on sales obtained from Intercontinental Medical Statistics.

[k]The data source on drugstore sales is the U.K. subsidiary of IMS and the data are quite similar to those collected for the U.S. discussed above. Data are based on the audit of 600 retail pharmacies in the U.K. and have been collected continuously since the early sixties.

Table 10-7. Concentration of Innovational Output in the U.K. Ethical Drug Industry

Period	Total Number of New Chemical Entities (NCEs)	Number of Firms Having an NCE	Concentration Ratios of Innovational Output		
			4-Firm	8-Firm	20-Firm
1962-66	115	48	63.1	76.6	94.1
1967-71	95	44	42.7	66.4	91.1

Innovational output is measured as new chemical entity sales in U.K. during the first three full years after product introduction.
Data sources: See Table 10-6.

trend between the two periods is quite different from that observed in the U.S. (Table 10-1). The number of firms introducing NCEs has remained fairly stable over time, and, in direct contrast to the U.S. situation, innovational output has become significantly less concentrated over time. The latter result is particularly surprising in light of the fact that R&D costs per NCE have been rising in the U.K. over time, although at a much less rapid rate than in the U.S.

Tables 10-8 and 10-9 present analyses of the relation of innovational output to firm size for the U.K. case. These correspond directly to the kind of analyses performed above on U.S. data (Tables 10-2 and 10-3). In contrast to the U.S. case, the estimates in Tables 10-8 and 10-9 clearly indicate a weakening of the linkage between innovational output and firm size. The results also suggest that this analysis is subject to more instability and unexplained variation (e.g., in the regressions of Table 10-9) than for the U.S. case. This can probably be traced in large part to the fact that the U.K. market is more interrelated with other economies than is the U.S. market, and that variables defined only in terms of the U.K. economy are less meaningful. Nevertheless, despite this fact, the trend toward larger firms accounting for proportionately less of U.K. innovational output is unmistakably clear. This is shown in Table 10-9 by the significant, negative coefficient of the quadratic term in the 1967-1971 period. This contrasts to the positive (but statistically in significant) quadratic coefficient observed in the earlier period.[1]

In Table 10-10, data on concentration in total ethical drugs sales is presented. As in the United States, the rate of change in this total market measure is quite small. Nevertheless, concentration of sales in the U.K. does exhibit more of a tendency to decline than was observed in the U.S. from the early 1960s to the present. Other things equal, one might have expected sales concentration to have increased at a significantly faster pace in the U.K. because the drug industry there was characterized by a greater number of mergers in the 1960s than its

---

[1]Cubic equations were also estimated in both periods but proved statistically inferior to the quadratic and linear equations.

Table 10-8. Percentage of Innovational Output and Total Ethical Sales in U.K. Accounted for by the Largest Four U.K. Drug Firms, 1962-66 and 1967-71

Period	Four Largest Firms' Share of Innovational Output	Four Largest Firms' Share of Total Ethical Drug Sales
1962-66	39.9	26.9
1967-71	14.5	29.5

Data source: See Table 10-6.

Table 10-9. Least Squares Regressions of Innovational Output on Firm Size in U.K. for Periods 1962-66 and 1967-71

(Linear and Quadratic Regressions of the Form: $Y_{it} = a_0 + a_1 S_{it} + a_2 S^2{}_{it}$ *)*

Period		a_0	a_1	a_2	R^2/F	N
1962-66	1)	10.57 (.03)	0.54 (3.66)	–	.19/13.4	60
	2)	75.26 (.20)	0.40 (.90)	$.27 \times 10^{-4}$ (.34)	.19/6.66	60
1967-71	1)	−53.3 (.15)	0.86 (3.90)	$-.60 \times 10^{-4}$ (2.94)	.24/9.19	62

"t" values in parentheses.

Innovation output (Y_{it}) is defined as firms' U.K. drug store sales of new chemical entities during first three years after introduction; size (S_{it}) is defined as total U.K. (drug store) sales of ethical drugs at the midpoint of each period.

Data source: See Table 10-6.

Table 10-10. Concentration of Sales in U.K. Ethical Drug Market and Percentage of U.K. Market Accounted for by U.S. Firms, 1962-73

Year	4-Firm	8-Firm	20-Firm	N.E.	Share of U.K. Market Held by U.S. Firms
1962	29.9	46.8	80.7	24.63	46.9
1963	28.9	45.8	81.1	25.44	47.2
1964	27.9	44.7	79.6	26.95	45.9
1965	27.0	44.0	78.2	28.57	45.9
1966	26.3	42.9	76.7	28.65	45.2
1967	28.0	43.0	75.1	28.74	44.0
1968	29.7	44.4	75.1	27.78	42.8
1969	29.5	43.9	73.2	26.52	40.1
1970	29.7	44.1	73.2	28.65	39.4
1971	30.1	46.9	76.1	26.25	38.1
1972	29.1	45.9	75.2	27.22	38.6
1973	28.8	45.5	75.3	27.56	38.4

Data source: See Table 10-6.

U.S. counterpart.[m] However, despite this increased merger activity in the U.K., concentration of ethical drug sales is actually less in 1973 than 1962, which is not true for the U.S. drug sales.

Perhaps the most interesting statistic concerning the U.K. ethical drug market for our current purposes is contained in the last column of Table 10–10. This is the share of the total U.K. ethical drug market accounted for by U.S. firms or their subsidiaries. This has steadily declined since 1962. Over the period 1962–1973, the U.S. firms' market share declined by 8.5 percentage points or almost one-fifth of their initial share in 1962.

An even more dramatic decline was experienced in the U.S. firms' share of U.K. new drug product innovation over this decade. U.S. firms and their subsidiaries accounted for 54 percent of total U.K. innovational output (as measured in Tables 10–6 through 10–8) in the period 1961–1966 and only 15 percent in 1967–1971. This sharp decline in innovative performance by U.S. firms would seem to explain in considerable part why total innovational output became less concentrated in the U.K. over the two periods.

Overall, the comparisons of the U.S. and U.K. ethical drug markets given in Tables 10–1 through 10–10 present a striking contrast in structural trends. In the U.K. the market share enjoyed by new chemical entities has remained at a relatively high level. In addition, the number of firms introducing new chemical entities has been stable and innovational output has become less concentrated in the very largest firms. In the U.S. the opposite trends have been observed in each instance. Furthermore, the position of U.S. firms in the U.K. market has steadily eroded since 1962. While these trends undoubtedly reflect factors in addition to regulation, it would seem difficult to escape the conclusion that regulation has been a significant force influencing both the level and structure of innovational activity in the U.S. economy.

Finally, it would seem important to note that there is some evidence that more stringent regulation by the FDA relative to other countries is producing other important structural effects. These include the stimulation of foreign investment in plant and equipment and the performance of R&D activity abroad by U.S. based firms. Prior to the 1962 Amendments, most new products discovered here were introduced first in the U.S. and then sold abroad through exports rather than being manufactured abroad. As long as drug regulations in this country were not excessively restrictive, this was a plausible strategy and conforms to the predictions of the trade cycle theory promulgated by Raymond Vernon (1971) and others. However, after U.S. regulations became much more stringent relative to those in other countries, this was no longer economically attractive.

---

[m]A few of the large U.K. firms such as Glaxo acquired a number of the smaller U.K. drug firms over this period. In addition, there were a number of mergers between various firms from other European countries. Such European firms typically account for a much greater share of the U.K. than the U.S. market.

This is because U.S. law prohibits the export of any drugs that have not received regulatory clearance by the FDA.[n] This probably accounts in large part for the decline observed in U.S. innovation and total drug sales in the U.K. and other countries from their formerly dominant position.[o] In effect, the traditional institutional arrangements utilized by U.S. firms with respect to foreign markets did not permit them to capitalize on their high research intensity, given the more restrictive regulatory climate that developed in the U.S. after 1962.

There are now various strands of evidence that these traditional institutional arrangements are experiencing significant changes. A cursory analysis of recent new product introductions by U.S. firms in this country suggests that these products are increasingly being introduced and manufactured abroad before they obtain FDA clearance in the U.S. market.

Some statistical evidence of this phenomenon is provided in a recent study by two German chemists (Reis-Arnt and Elvers, 1972). In analyzing world wide pharmaceutical discoveries and introductions over the period 1961 to 1970, they show the U.S. had been the country of initial introduction for 38 percent of all new drugs in 1961 but only for 8 percent in 1970. At the same time, the percentage of drugs first discovered in the U.S. declined from 40 percent of total discovered in 1958 to 28 percent of all discoveries in 1970. This indicates, therefore, that by 1970 a majority of drugs discovered here were being introduced abroad before becoming available in this country.

Given this movement abroad of research activities by U.S. firms in very recent periods, it has become increasingly difficult to establish the country of discovery for many new drugs. Many are the product of research activities in more than one country. However, if one focuses on introductions by U.S. based firms, and their subsidiaries, a strong trend toward introductions abroad first seems evident in recent years.

Moreover, sizable foreign investment by U.S. drug firms in the sixties and seventies has now provided U.S. firms with substantial manufacturing capacity abroad. In addition, U.S. firms apparently are performing more of their research and development and clinical testing in foreign environments. In a recent questionnaire study on this subject, Lasagna and Wardell surveyed the extent to which U.S. firms are first doing clinical testing abroad. Although the percentage of drugs for which this was true was negligible in the middle sixties, it had escalated to a majority of drugs being tested by these firms in 1972. Although their

[n]The importance of this factor in limiting the export sales of U.S. drug firms as well as in spurring foreign investment by these firms was first called to our attention by Harold Clymer.

[o]On the other hand, Roche, a Swiss firm, had outstanding success with its two U.S. developed tranquilizers, Valium and Librium, and increased its own U.K. market share by about 5 percentage points between 1962 and 1971. Concurrently, Roche increased its U.S. market share by about 4 points. Hence, at least part of the U.S. firms' decline cannot be attributed to tighter U.S. regulations.

results are based on a sample of only fifteen large firms, they suggest some strong shifts in this regard may be taking place.

The nature and extent of international movement of resources abroad by U.S. drug firms would seem to be a high priority for future research. If a significant transfer of technical and physical resources abroad by U.S. firms is now occurring as a result of a more stringent regulatory climate the decline of the position of U.S. firms in foreign markets may be arrested and turned around in the near future. On the other hand, such resource shifts, which would appear on logical grounds to be a plausible long run consequence of more stringent regulation by the U.S. relative to other countries, are not without costs to drug firms and consumers in this country. Therefore, they provide yet another example of an unintended side effect of regulation that would have to be weighed against the positive benefits of regulation.

V. SUMMARY AND CONCLUSIONS

One of Professor Joe Bain's most noted contributions was his work on the sources of entry barriers (Bain, 1956). The analysis presented above indicates that an unintended by-product of increased regulation in ethical drugs since 1962 has been increased entry barriers and concentration in the supply of new drugs. Given the rapid increase in product quality regulation in other U.S. industries in recent years, this would seem to be an important finding from a public policy standpoint. Further research on the effects of regulation on industry structure for other product areas would seem warranted.

From a methodological standpoint, the chapter demonstrates the value of comparative international analysis in the field of industrial organization. The different regulatory systems present in the U.S. and U.K. provided a natural analytical basis for examining recent structural developments. A pioneering work in international comparative analysis was, of course, Professor Bain's study of cross-country differences in industrial structure (Bain, 1966). In our opinion, this analytical approach should be fostered and encouraged in future research in industrial organization.

Chapter 11

The Economics of Potential Competition

Robert J. Reynolds
Barbara A. Reeves

I. INTRODUCTION

Recent Supreme Court decisions reflect a changing attitude toward antitrust law. Gone are the days when the Department of Justice could support its antitrust theories with an unbroken string of victories. Although the Supreme Court has not repudiated these theories, it has indicated that they must be accompanied by hard evidence of substantial economic harm, or, giving due deference to the Clayton Act, probability of substantial economic harm, if they are to prevail. With this in mind, we have set out to analyze the valid legal and economic grounds for one of the most ephemeral of all antitrust doctrines—potential competition—in order to determine whether it can and should survive the demands of current antitrust adjudication. Such an analysis is particularly appropriate at this time in light of the recent critiques of existing potential competition theory (Posner 1975, pp. 313–327; Steiner 1975, pp. 255–287).

Many Supreme Court cases have used the notion that a merger of a potential competitor with an existing producer may substantially restrain competition in a market in much the same way as do horizontal acquisitions.[a] Traditionally, there

The views expressed here do not necessarily represent the views of the Department of Justice. The comments of G. Hay, I.C. Jernigan, R. McGuckin, R. Masson, J. Preston, and B. Snapp, as well as anonymous referees on earlier drafts of this chapter, are all greatly appreciated.

[a]For example, *United States* v. *Marine Bancorporation*, 418 U.S. 602 (1974); *United States* v. *Falstaff Brewing Corp.* 410 U.S. 526 (1973); *FTC* v. *Procter and Gamble Co.*, 386 U.S. 568 (1967); *United States* v. *Penn-Olin Chemical Co.*, 378 U.S. 158 (1964); *United States* v. *El Paso Natural Gas Co.*, 376 U.S. 651 (1964). Note that *Penn-Olin* involved a joint venture of two potential entrants; however, it was assumed that in the absence of the venture one of the firms would have actually entered. For an excellent early exposition of the theory, see Turner (1965).

have been two rationales for using the antitrust laws to attack mergers between potential competitors: "waiting in the wings" and "deconcentration." The "waiting in the wings" rationale focuses upon procompetitive effects upon the conduct of market members exerted by a firm standing on the fringes of a market. These effects depend upon the perceptions and responses of the market members. The "deconcentration" rationale focuses upon the future procompetitive effects of a fringe firm's deconcentrating entry into the market. In each case, the hypothesized procompetitive effects are lost if the fringe firm–potential entrant enters the market by acquiring a large, established market member.

In this chapter we first critically review the notions of waiting in the wings and deconcentration, as accepted or at least as discussed by the Supreme Court to date.[b] In the process we determine the areas of their valid appearance and their dependence on "limit pricing." We then suggest an extension of the traditional theories to cover some additional anticompetitive mergers. We conclude with some remarks on the place of potential competition cases within the structure of antitrust law.

II. THE PERCEIVED POTENTIAL ENTRANT: WAITING IN THE WINGS

The waiting in the wings theory requires that the industry be practicing limit pricing in the following sense: that it is choosing a lower price than it otherwise would in order to reduce the expected entry rate.[c] Perceived potential entrants are defined as those firms which the industry believes would enter at prices only slightly higher than the prevailing price. (Firms whose entry inducing price is less than the limit price will be examined below.) Traditional potential competition theory focuses on the anticompetitive effects caused by the loss of one such potential entrant. If there are many potential entrants, the removal of any one of them has been assumed to have no significant effect on price. (See our discussion below on the effects of relaxing this assumption.) If, however, there are only a few, then the removal of one of them will encourage the industry to choose a new, higher limit price. If there are a few potential entrants, and if the

[b]For example, *United States* v. *Falstaff Brewing Corp.* 410 U.S. 526, 537 (1973); *Ford Motor Co.* v. *United States*, 405 U.S. 562, 567 (1972); *id.* at 587 (Burger, C.J., concurring in part and dissenting in part); *FTC* v. *Procter & Gamble Co.*, 286, U.S. 568, 580 (1967); *id.* at 586 (Harlan, J., concurring); *United States* v. *Penn-Olin Chemical Co.*, 378 U.S. 158, 173 (1964); *Columbia Steel*, 334 U.S. 499 (1948); *United States* v. *Continental Can Co.*, 378 U.S. 441 (1964). There is some dispute whether the Supreme Court has adopted or endorsed the deconcentration argument. Compare *United States* v. *Falstaff Brewing Co.*, 410 U.S. 526, 537 (1973) with *id.* at 544, 560 (Marshall J., concurring).

[c]I.e., it need not be pricing at the (strictly defined) limit price which completely forecloses entry, as in Bain, 1956, 1972. This usage is consistent with recent work (e.g., Kamien and Schwartz, 1971; Gaskins, 1971) indicating that optimal industry behavior under threat of entry may be to price above the limit price but below the short run profit maximizing price.

eliminated firm was the most likely potential entrant—i.e., the firm with the lowest entry inducing price—the incentive to set a higher limit price is clear.

The same holds true where there are a few firms with similar entry inducing prices, if before removal the existing producers were almost willing to raise price and accept entry and if the entry loss function is "well behaved." The extent to which the optimal industry price is changed by the merger will depend on the schedule of entry inducing prices of the remaining entrants and (positively) on the difference between the original price and the short run profit maximizing price. We explore the problem of the magnitude of the change in more detail below.

Such mergers arise in part because a firm gains by removing itself as a potential entrant through merger with one of the existing firms. (In what follows we write as if the potential entrant is the acquirer. Our analysis applies as well when the potential entrant is the acquired firm). The premerger level of noncompetitive return enjoyed by an existing market member will tend to be capitalized in the value of the acquired firm. Thus we expect that its acquisition would not be especially profitable for a nonpotential entrant. (Two provisos are that there may be true synergy effects from the merger, or that the stock market may not be completely capitalizing the firm's profit prospects. These are discussed below.)

There will, however, be capital gains associated with an acquisition of one of the largest existing producers by a waiting in the wings potential entrant. By acquiring a leading market member, the erstwhile potential entrant is in effect announcing his intention *not* to enter de novo if the market price rises above its entry inducing level; in effect, he announces a policy of noncompetition.[d] Instituting a policy of noncompetition—whether by contract or by acquisition—allows the industry to choose a new higher limit price and hence enjoy higher profits. Since this increment in the limit price would not have been capitalized in the value of the acquired firm, the acquiring firm realizes a supercompetitive return from its acquisition. Furthermore, since the new higher price yields a greater change in profits, the higher the acquired firm's output, the proportion of the industry's gains due to noncompetition that can be captured by a potential entrant is positively related to the market share of the acquired firm. The greatest capital gains will, therefore, be realized by acquiring the largest industry member.

If the potential entrant is a supplier or customer of the industry, it may already be receiving a "bribe" to not enter in the form of differential prices. The bribe may take the form of a purchase of any good or service at a noncompetitive price level, possibly a reciprocal purchase. However, this "bribe" may prove

---

[d] A toehold acquisition has a different meaning. Even if the industry were to gain from its removal, the potential entrant could capture little of this. The likely motivation is, therefore, the enhancement of the toehold's profits through rapid expansion. But this is procompetitive. Industrywide gains are, therefore, improbable.

insufficient due to such factors as uncertainty regarding the effectiveness of the entry threat or to "free rider" problems in the giving of the bribe. It should be noted that the conglomerate form provides broad opportunities for receiving such "bribes," and for this reason may have anticompetitive effects.

Presenting the potential competition theory in this form allows us to deal with some issues raised by Steiner. He argues that if an industry is tightly oligopolistic, the loss of a potential competitor will matter little, since the original price is likely to be close to the short run profit maximizing price (1975, pp. 258, 263). The closer the preacquisition price is to the short run profit maximizing price, or to the level of entry inducing price for the remaining potential entrants, the smaller will be the change in price and the more insignificant will be the welfare loss due to the acquisition. This argument, however, fails to recognize that if the change in price is small for the reason indicated, the capital gains produced will also tend to be insignificant. The potential entrant may be able to obtain a supercompetitive return by toehold entry, which it forgoes if it merges. In addition, insofar as the position of being a leading firm is correlated with corporate size, the evidence (e.g., Singh, 1975) suggests that leading firm mergers will not be easily effectuated. Hence, relatively few leading firm mergers with potential for only small capital gains will be attempted. It is likely, therefore, that *observed* leading firm mergers will produce significant capital gains and price effects.

Steiner also argues that a potential entrant acquisition of a leading firm may upset an original tight oligopoly. However, if a firm expected this result, it would be less likely to acquire. Thus the likelihood that leading firm acquisitions will upset tight oligopolies appears to be small. Steiner's analysis also rests on the idea that such an acquisition will indicate that entry is feasible and will lower the entry inducing price levels of remaining potential entrants (1975, p. 264). Actually, the converse would seem more likely, since the "demonstration" is that the "most likely" entrant had to "buy" its way into the industry. In any event, the acquiring firm must not expect Steiner's result, since it would tend to preclude the realization of the capital gains from the merger and thereby eliminate the acquisition motive. For the above reasons, Steiner's conclusion—that leading firm acquisitions by most favored potential entrants should not be presumed to lead to anticompetitive effects—is not warranted by his analysis.

Posner has argued that the observed potential competition mergers involving leading firms are not made by "most likely" potential entrants, because a "most likely" entrant will never pay the premium prices typical of such acquistions (1975, pp. 320–324).[e] According to this view, a truly strong waiting in the

---

[e]Posner qualifies his analysis by indicating that it "assumes" that existing producers misperceive the probability of entry (*Id.* at 321 n. 141). We find this "out" unsatisfactory for two reasons. First, while his assumption may produce the indicated result, it is not sufficient to do so. Second, he uses this analysis to argue that a ". . . more sensible presumption would be that the acquiring firm was *less* inclined than at least some other firms to enter the

wings potential entrant could approach a producer, make a threat of de novo entry, negotiate from a strong bargaining position, and accordingly buy at a discount rather than premium relative to the existing market value of the industry member. Since in those mergers that have been attacked under the potential competition doctrine, the acquiring firm has been the highest bidder paying a substantial premium,[f] it is argued that the acquiring firm must not have been the most likely potential entrant.

Unless the potential entrant was actually willing to enter, and had been so perceived, Posner's argument would not be valid, because the "threat" (unless it deceives the industry) would not cause the industry to change its limit price. Likewise, if the firm had and was perceived to have an entry inducing price below the limit price (i.e., it was an actual potential entrant), then its entry was already accepted and taken into account by the industry and the threat would be of no consequence. Contrary to Posner's argument, if the acquiring firm is the most likely potential entrant and has been exerting a waiting in the wings influence, it could pay a larger premium over capitalized value than any other potential acquirer and still make a supercompetitive return on its investment. Acquisition by any other potential entrant would tend to produce a smaller (or zero) capital gain, since the limit price would be very little (if any) higher after the acquisition.

For Posner's argument to be valid, a necessary condition is that the firm was not *perceived* as a potential entrant, but was an actual potential entrant. That is, the only way the threat strategy could work would be if the threat provided new information with respect to the firm's entry potential. In general, however, the "more likely" the potential entrant, the greater the care with which the industry will have previously evaluated its entry potential and the smaller will be the informational value of the threat. For these reasons we find no warrant for expecting discount prices to be paid in mergers between leading firms and most likely entrants.

Other factors also suggest the likelihood of an acquisition price premium. The acquired firm will attempt to extract some of the capital gains of the acquiring firm—i.e., to obtain a price for itself higher than its existing capitalized value. The magnitude of such potential extraction will be limited by (1) the entry potential of the most likely entrant compared to that of the next most likely entrant(s)—this determines how much the limit price will rise subsequent to the acquisition and, therefore, the total industry gains available; (2) the market share of the acquired firm—this determines the proportion of industry gains available to the acquired and acquiring firms; (3) the market share of the second leading

---

market by internal expansion" (*Id.* at 324). We do not believe that presumptions regarding the competitive consequences of mergers are well founded if they are fundamentally based on an assumption that firms have mistaken expectations.

[f]E.g., *United States* v. *Falstaff Brewing Corp.* supra; *FTC* v. *Procter & Gamble Co.,* supra; *United States* v. *El Paso Natural Gas Co.,* 376 U.S. 651 (1964).

candidate for acquistion—this determines the value of the next best acquisition alternative for the acquiring firm; (4) the costliness to the acquiring firm of a second method of acquisition—the "unfriendly" takeover; and (5) the returns that the acquiring firm might receive by entering de novo or by toehold acquisition—this also is a possible alternative strategy.

A separate factor affecting the amount of the premium is the elasticity of supply of the acquired firm's stock. The market value of the stock is equal to the offer price of the marginal investor. Inframarginal holdings will command a premium over market value, since they will reflect higher profit expectations, different risk premiums, etc., than those for the marginal investor. (See Gort (1969) and Steiner (1975, pp. 35–37).) This factor means that even in the case in which the threat conveys significant information, an acquisition premium may result (Cf. Posner, 1975, p. 321).

Thus, a bargaining game between the potential entrant and the existing firm(s) over the division of the gains from removal of the entrant (the noncompetition agreement) is likely to ensue, resulting in an acquisition price greater than the previous capitalized value. The above analysis indicates that the premium will be larger, the more significant the waiting in the wings influence, the smaller the number of potential entrants, the smaller the number of existing producers, and the larger the market share of the acquired firm. Thus the better the waiting in the wings potential competition case, the more probable and the larger the premium.

There are significant incentives to effectuate noncompetition agreements by merger between the waiting in the wings firm and the leading existing producer, since such agreements allow existing producers to raise price and profit thereby allowing the waiting in the wings firm to obtain supercompetitive profits from capital gains on its acquisition. Moreover, toehold acquisitions would tend to be preferred to leading firm acquisitions by the acquiring firm, unless the acquiring firm is one of a few most advantaged potential entrants, due to the apparent difficulty of digesting larger firms (e.g., Singh, 1975) and the profit opportunity arising from the ability to rapidly expand a toehold firm. Given these incentives, there is a rational economic basis for supporting antitrust policy attacking such mergers and insisting on de novo or toehold acquisitions.

It should be recognized that if an acquiring firm perceived real cost savings (synergism) it would also tend to buy large firms in the industry, if, as seems likely, their magnitude is related to the volume of production a de novo or toehold entry would delay realization of these economies. Inasmuch as the realization of these economies are delayed rather than foregone, the consequences of prohibiting a "synergistic" merger may not be excessively costly. Hence, claims for such cost savings should be scrutinized closely before allowing them to justify rejection of a potential competition case.

III. THE DECONCENTRATING
POTENTIAL ENTRANT

A second justification for attacking acquisitions by potential entrants is the so-called deconcentration theory. This doctrine would proscribe a potential entrant's market extension merger into an oligopolistic market on the ground that, regardless of the acquiring firm's waiting in the wings effect, such a merger would eliminate the possibility of deconcentration that would result if the acquiring firm entered de novo or by a toehold acquisition. A deconcentrating potential entrant is a firm whose entry inducing price (either now or in the future) is below the industry's price; such a firm will be referred to hereafter as an actual potential entrant. In order for the elimination of such a firm to have an anticompetitive effect, it is generally assumed that there must not be many such firms. We examine this assumption below.

While this deconcentration argument has been advanced in several antitrust cases, it has not yet been accepted by the Supreme Court.[g] Perhaps this has been mainly due to the theory's apparent dependence upon vague predictions of a diminution of future procompetitive effects. Although the courts have recognized that the prevention of conduct that may lead to increased market concentration and a more likely occurrence of future anticompetitive effects is a proper function of the antitrust laws, they have had difficulty accepting the idea that conduct that makes less likely the emergence of more competitive conditions and structure is also a proper subject of these statutes. We shall argue that such acquisitions may well produce anticompetitive effects and are closely akin to horizontal mergers, particularly in light of the viewpoint adopted by the Supreme Count in *General Dynamics* (415 U.S. 486 (1974)).

Consider an oligopoly industry pricing at a noncompetitive level, and assume that its present price is not a limit price. (The limit pricing case is discussed below.) If there are only a few actual potential entrants, the removal of one of them implies that the profits of present producers will be better sustained. De novo entry would depress industry prices and profits. Hence, members of the industry would be willing to pay a bribe for "noncompetition"—if they could identify the potential entrant and organize their behavior.

Although price and profits would not rise as a result of a merger, their decline would be diminished. Acquisition by an actual potential entrant benefits industry members by prolonging a noncompetitive market structure. The acquiring firm (the erstwhile actual potential entrant) could extract part of the acquired firm's share in the avoided profit reduction by paying less than the producer's present capitalized value. If the securities market had anticipated entry, then the acquiring firm might still pay a premium over capitalized value; although

[g]See *Falstaff*, 526, 537; *Marine Bancorporation*, 625, 639. Certain lower court cases embodying the deconcentration argument have been affirmed without opinion (*U.S.* v. *Phillips Petroleum*, 367 F. Sup. 1226, 1234 (D.D. Cal.), 418 U.S. 906 (1974)).

the acquired firm's profits would not rise as a result of the acquisition, its value would. Either way, there is a preference to acquire the largest firm in the industry.

This situation, therefore, is very similar to the "waiting in the wings" case. Had it recognized the firm as an actual potential entrant, the industry would have been willing to pay a significant bribe for a noncompetition agreement. The merger with a leading firm acts as a substitute for the bribe and produces similar anticompetitive effects.

If, alternatively, the present industry price is a limit price, the analysis is essentially the same as above; the merger will tend to diminish the fall in price that might have accompanied de novo entry. Moreover, if the limit price is chosen to reduce the rate of entry, such a merger may permit a higher limit price in all future periods.

The notion that the limit price may be chosen so as to delay entry is a generalization of our previous discussion, which viewed the limit price as simply (partially or completely) foreclosing entry. This generalization can be based on the following argument. Suppose that the more rapid the rate of expansion and entry, the higher the (present value) total costs of achieving a given size (the firm faces "costs of adjustment"). The firm must then decide on its rate of entry, trading off the higher costs of more rapid expansion against the fact that it will be in operation sooner and, therefore, generating profits earlier. If the price is reduced, then the foreseen profits are reduced, which changes this trade-off so that the firm chooses a lower rate of expansion, thereby reducing its rate of entry. Thus, a limit price which is not foreclosing may still delay.

In a deconcentration situation, unlike the pure waiting in the wings case, leading firm acquistion is not always the most profitable strategy. (If leading firm acquisition is most profitable, the incentive to buy the largest existing producer still holds). Since the acquiring firm could obtain a share of the (reduced) monopoly profits by de novo entry, leading firm acquisition vis-à-vis entry (or a toehold merger) will depend on whether entry profits are less than the share of industry profits obtainable by acquisition.

The industry's gains from removal of such an entrant will always exceed the profits that the entrant could make by de novo entry, since overall industry profits will fall due to that entry. However, the amount of the industry's gains obtained by the acquisition will not always exceed the profits available by de novo entry, since the amount captured will be at most the market share of the acquired (leading) firm times the industry's gain. (Note that a potential entrant—i.e., a firm whose entry inducing price is only slightly above the prevailing price—will never make noncompetitive returns by de novo entry. Hence for it, acquisition would always be preferable.) Thus, whether de novo entry or acquisition is the most profitable strategy will depend, inter alia, on the market share of the firm to be acquired and on whether the costs of the potential entrant are the same as those of the existing producers.

Although acquisition will be less attractive, *ceteris paribus*, the lower are the acquirer's potential costs relative to those of present producers, acquisition may still be preferred to de novo entry even if the entrant's potential costs are lower than those of established producers. In addition to entry costs, a firm must also consider the costs of attaining the desired market share. By acquiring a firm which already has experience in the field, the entrant may be able to combine its lower cost methods with the "learning curve" benefits enjoyed by the existing producer.[h]

The above analysis makes evident the similarity between a horizontal merger and such an acquisition by an actual potential entrant. The acquiring firm is not so much waiting in the wings as it is stepping onto the stage, because it is capable of profitably participating in the market, given the prevailing price. In acquiring a leading market member, the competitive element provided by its presence has been removed.

The appropriateness of prohibiting such an acquisition receives support from the Supreme Court's recent decision in *United States* v. *General Dynamics Corp.*, 415 U.S. 486 (1974). In *General Dynamics* the Court emphasized the importance in evaluating the effect of horizontal mergers on probable future competition, future market shares, and future ability to compete. A merger involving a stepping onto the stage firm is nothing more than an incipient horizontal merger.

IV. RELAXING THE ASSUMPTIONS OF TRADITIONAL THEORY

In this section we examine the effects of relaxing two assumptions: (1) that the industry is presently pricing a a noncompetitive level, and (2) that there are only a few equally qualified potential entrants. Relaxing the first assumption leads to an interesting extension of the law; relaxing the second does not delineate mergers with likely anticompetitive effects.

"Competitive Pricing" And Contingent Potential Competitors

Assume that an industry's structure is sufficiently concentrated so that it could support a price significantly elevated above the competitive level, but that current price and profits are competitive. Could anticompetitive effects emerge from the acquisition of a leading producer by a prospective entrant?

The answer is "yes" if the industry's competitive behavior is temporary (arising, for example, because very rapid technical progress has precluded effective

---

[h]"Learning by doing" has an interesting implication. Since entry barriers will tend to rise over time (as the costs of firms in the market fall relative to the initial costs of new entrants), a rise in the price-cost margin may become possible later. Thus the attractiveness of charging an entry *forclosing* price is greater. This heuristic argument appears to be supported by the model developed by Lee (1975).

collusion) and if, upon the establishment of a noncompetitive price level,[i] the acquiring firm will be one of a few prospective entrants whose entry including price is less than or only slightly above the industry's optimal premerger (limit) price. (We call such a firm a contingent potential entrant.) Under these conditions it is clear that the merger will produce anticompetitive effects, because if the industry were pricing noncompetitively, the merger would be either a valid waiting in the wings or a valid deconcentration case. (For the usual reasons, the entrant will wish to acquire the leading firm in the industry.) Thus, such "anticipatory" mergers by contingent potential entrants should be proscribed.[j]

The incentive to engage in such anticipatory mergers arises for four reasons. First, given antitrust enforcement, the firm may fear that the merger will be more difficult to effectuate after it becomes apparent that the industry is behaving noncompetitively. Second, insofar as the securities market does not completely capitalize these future profits, the acquiring firm, by virtue of the characteristics that make it a potential entrant, may have an advantage in recognizing these speculative possibilities. Third, if after effective collusion is established the industry chooses a price which at least retards this firm's entry, an anticipatory merger enables an earlier choice of a higher price. Fourth, the acquiring firm may believe that if it enters de novo, other firms will recognize the potential attractiveness of this industry and thus choose to enter themselves. Entry by acquisition, on the other hand, may signal other potential entrants that the market is too difficult to enter de novo, thus raising psychological barriers to entry. Therefore, it is not only rational but highly probable that the most likely potential entrant (and the one most likely to be perceived as such and to influence market behavior accordingly) will choose to enter by acquiring as large a market factor as possible *prior* to the market settling into oligopolistic behavior, even at the cost of paying a premium price.

The first reason offered is the most intriguing one since it indicates that anticipatory mergers may occur as part of an effort to avoid antitrust enforcement. Hence antitrust concern for the possibility of such anticipatory mergers will be more important as antitrust enforcement against the traditional types of potential competition mergers becomes tougher.

It may be argued by some that such contingent potential entrant effects are too speculative to justify action under Section 7 of the Clayton Act at the time of the acquisition. Such an argument overlooks the primary purpose of Section 7—the prevention of the emergence of conditions that substantially increase

---

[i]Steiner (1975, p. 263) has suggested that the timing of reaching a noncompetitive price may be influenced by the acquisition—i.e., the entrant may be able to offer the technical innovation of a more effective collusion scheme.

[j]The possibility of this type of situation was recognized by Justices Douglas and Marshall in *United States* v. *Falstaff Brewing Corp.*, supra, at 544, 560 n. 15, 569. Accord *Kennecott Corp.* v. *FTC*, 467 F.2d 67, 75–76 (10th Cir. 1972).

the probability of effective collusion. A merger that eliminates what was likely to have been the most effective restraint on future collusion and monopoly profits is a proper subject of the Clayton Act. Preservation of opportunities for competition is especially important in a market threatening to become oligopolistic, and it is well recognized that under the Clayton Act the government is not required to stay its hand until the market has reached an oligopolistic stage or condition.[k]

Once the anticompetitive potentialities of contingent waiting in the wings and deconcentration acquisitions are recognized, the "incipiency" orientation of the Clayton Act[l] provides a solid basis for attacking such acquisitions. Furthermore, failure to attack at the time of acquisition could lead to divestiture years later after the companies have combined their operations. The costs and difficulties of separating merged properties and technologies should be a strong factor favoring earlier rather than later antitrust challenges.

Numerous Potential Entrants

The above situations all involved actual or potential entrants which were among very few such firms. It is interesting to examine what the effect would be if the acquiring firm were one of many similarly situated firms. It has generally been assumed that entry by one potential entrant from a large class of potential entrants does not provide a basis for antitrust action. However, on occasion courts have struck down mergers on potential competition grounds where it was not clear that there were only a few probable entrants.[m] Accordingly, the assumption merits analysis.

Given that deconcentration due to de novo entry into an oligopolistic market tends to reduce price and profits in the market, entry by acquisition deprives the market of this procompetitive effect. However, this loss of competition is not substantial if there remain numerous other potential entrants. Further, when there are many potential entrants, each will tend to choose de novo or toehold entry. Since the acquiring firm will have to pay, in general, at least the capitalized value of the existing monopoly profits, and since its removal as an entrant will not allow a significantly higher price because of the existence of numerous other potential entrants, the acquiring firm can only expect to earn a normal return on the acquisition of a leading market member. On the other hand, if it enters de novo it can obtain a share of the (now reduced) monopoly profits. Since by entry it can earn a supercompetitive return, whereas by acquisition it

[k]E.g., *Brown Shoe Co.* v. *United States*, 370 U.S. 317 (1962).

[l]E.g., *S. Rep.* No 1775 at 5–6; 96 *Cong. Rec.* 11493, 16453 (1950); *Brown Shoe*, 370 U.S. 294, 315, 317–318 (1962).

[m]*Kennecott Copper Corp.* v. *Federal Trade Commission*, 467 F.2d 67 (10th Cir. 1972); *General Foods Corp.* v. *Federal Trade Commission*, 386 F.2d 936 (3rd Cir. 1967), *cert. denied* 391 U.S. 919 (1968); *United States* v. *Wilson Sporting Goods and Nissen Corp.*, 288 F. Supp. 543 (N.D. Ohio 1971).

can earn only a competitive return, such a potential entrant would prefer de novo entry. Anticompetitive returns will neither be the object nor the result of merger activity under these conditions.

There is one situation that may give rise to an exception to the conclusion that there is no basis for antitrust action given numerous potential entrants. If the market fails to capitalize the value of the industry's profits as foreseen by the potential entrant, the entrant would reap capital gains from an acquisition when the market realizes the profitability of the industry. The factors that qualify a firm as one which is objectively capable of entering may provide it with special knowledge about the industry's future profitability. (We note that preventing a firm from seizing such speculative bargains may, in general, produce no significant social losses. For an examination of some of these issues, see Hirshleifer (1971).)

If a significant number of the potential entrants recognize that the securities market is failing to capitalize the target industry's profits, then several acquisitions would take place. The number of potential entrants may be thereby reduced enough so that industry price and profits will rise substantially. Thus, while each merger would have no significant anticompetitive effects by itself and anticompetitive effects might not, therefore, be an aim of any party, the result of the set of mergers would be anticompetitive.

There are reasons to doubt the empirical importance of this possibility. Obviously if there are only one or two present producers, the number of entrants can be only slightly reduced. But if there are many present producers, it is unlikely that potential competition provides a significant restraint. It is doubtful that there are significant departures of stock values from capitalized profits when a number of firms realize them. Note further that the primary targets of such takeovers would tend, *ceteris paribus*, to be the leading firms in the market, since they potentially could provide the greatest acquisition profits. But if there is concentration on the leading firms, then the takeover price would tend to capitalize the speculative possibilities if there are several cognizant bidders. Similarly such departures are unlikely to persist as the market perceives takeovers in the industry taking place at superpremium prices. Further, the profit opportunities may be recognized by nonentrants. While entrants may possess, in general, some information advantages, some nonentrants may also recognize the gains, reducing the likelihood that the class of entrants will be significantly diminished.

Third, if there are a number of firms in the industry, then the "speculative bargain" must be firm specific rather than industry specific. If the bargain holds for the industry as a whole (industry specific), then the rational investment strategy is to buy a part interest in each firm rather than all of one, since a part interest in each can be obtained without significantly increasing the market price (by acquiring the marginal shares), whereas acquisition of one will require paying a significant premium over the previous market value, in order to acquire the inframarginal holdings. (This assumes that the strategy is not pushed so far that it itself raises antitrust problems.) Thus, the "bargain" must apply to only one or a few firms—i.e., be firm specific. Even if the stock market does not do a good job of arbitrating between firms in the same industry, the notion that a bargain is firm specific is in opposition to the assumption that there will be enough acquisitions to significantly reduce the number of entrants.

Fourth, if the entrant's entry inducing price is less than the present price, the capital gains must be greater than the profit from de novo entry, in order for it to be interested in an acquisition. The more efficient the capital market, the less likely this condition is to be fulfilled. The likelihood that the acquiring firm would have entered de novo and provided a deconcentration effect had the acquisition not been stopped by an antitrust action, thus appears to be small.

In sum, the requirement that an actual potential entrant be one of only a few such entrants in order to trigger antitrust liability on a deconcentration theory appears to be well founded.

V. CONCLUSION

In this chapter we have combined a flexible interpretation of limit pricing theory with the concept of noncompete agreements and the behavior of the capital market in order to develop and substantiate with legal and economic reasoning an expanded and cohesive theory of potential competition. We started with the assumption that firms in an oligopolistic industry may choose a limit price that does not foreclose all potential entrants, and argued that the merger of a potential entrant with a market leader reduced potential competition without increasing actual competition. We then examined the anticompetitive effects of the loss of potential entrants who are, to varying degress, foreclosed or not foreclosed by the prevailing price, upon an industry characterized by "tight" or "loose" oligopolistic conduct.

We have concluded that given an oligopolistically structured market, the elimination of one of a few objectively qualified potential entrants by leading firm acquisition will injure competition and increase oligopolistic behavior in the market. We have shown that those firms who are most likely potential entrants have strong incentives to enter by acquiring the largest market member in an industry.

The analysis in this chapter indicates that there is a reasonable basis for a potential competition approach to mergers. We would also argue that potential competition concerns are an important component of antitrust policy, in part because mergers that violate the standards of this paper may represent, to some degree, regulatory avoidance reactions to other antitrust tools. For example, in recent years antitrust activity against horizontal mergers and collusive arrangements has become more vigorous and effective (Stigler, 1966). Stronger enforcement against subsequent horizontal mergers and collusive arrangements may increase the perceived costs of allowing entry, reduce the optimal limit price

(Snapp, 1974)[n] and make larger the possible gains from a potential competition merger. Thus, such mergers are likely to be more frequent and the social costs of each will be greater. Antitrust theory and enforcement with regard to potential competition mergers will become more important.

However, much empirical work needs to be done in order to make the conclusions of this chapter workable tools for antitrust lawyers and judges. (Some first steps are represented by Gilbert (1974), and by Rhoades and Yeats (1972).) One especially crucial step is the identification of potential entrants. At the present time, identification of potential entrants requires a lengthy comparison between a checklist of manufacturing capabilities, research and development expertise, distribution similarities, and advertising complementarities for a long list of companies in related fields. One potentially fruitful area of study is the Department of Commerce, Bureau of Census SIC categories, in order to determine whether there is any worthwhile correlation between sources of entrants and industry codes. Without some such empirical work, the difficulties of defining a class of potential entrants may discourage further judicial development of the potential competition doctrine.

[n]A similar analysis, assuming relatively weak antimerger (horizontal) and anticollusion enforcement, may explain the behavior of the "early trusts" whose pricing conduct appeared to approximate short run profit maximization (Jones, 1922; Dewing, 1914).

Chapter 12

A Numerical Analysis of Bid Distributions in Sealed Tender Markets

Emil D. Attanasi
S. R. Johnson
David R. Kamerschen

I. INTRODUCTION

Numerous transactions by both public and private agents are conducted through sealed tender markets. For example, states and municipalities buy products as diverse as typewriters, water meters, asphalt, concrete, salt, and memo forms in this fashion. As a result of this activity and the fact that such markets have as a major function the maintenance of independence among bidders, they have come under more careful scrutiny by economists (Hay and Kelly, 1974). And as has frequently been the case over the last 30 years, Professor Joe S. Bain has cut a path through the jungle. While Professor Bain has not written extensively on the topic of sealed tender markets in particular, his general theoretical work on independent, collusive, and quasi-collusive market conduct is full of useful insights.

Attempting to apply the concepts of structure, conduct, and performance from the industrial organization literature in monitoring sealed tender markets, however, presents some special problems. In fact, except for a few studies—e.g., by Bain (1972), Stigler (1968) and Scherer (1970)—the accumulated theoretical developments and applied research on market structure and conduct are of limited value for studying the performance of these markets. A basic deficiency in the existing literature is that the implications of the theory of firm behavior have not been linked to bid distributions. As winning bids and bid distributions are major observable variables in sealed tender markets, the failure to develop systematic hypotheses connecting them has seriously hindered effective monitoring of performance.

One approach to extending existing results on market structure, conduct, and performance to the sealed tender markets is to provide a more structured basis for examining the behavior of firms and the attendant uncertainties associated with bidding. The purpose of this chapter is to present such a model and investigate its implications. Accordingly, in Section II, a firm bidding model is developed that provides for the incorporation of elements of market structure and conduct. After the firm model is presented, a procedure for using the results to derive market bid distributions is discussed in Section III. In Section IV, the design of the bid distribution experiments, along with methods for incorporating conduct and structure assumptions, are reviewed. In Section V, the experimental results supporting the implications of the model for monitoring bidding competitions are presented. A summary of the experimental results and implications in terms of the industrial organization literature is then presented in the concluding section.

II. FIRM BIDDING MODEL

Although the dynamic formulation of the firm model based on more primitive assumptions is investigated elsewhere (Kortanek et al., 1973; Attanasi and Johnson, 1975a), the static case is presented here. With firm pricing decisions emphasized, selling activities are structured and the production system is highly simplified. It is assumed that the firm submits sealed bids for the sale of a homogeneous product in n competitions. Contracts on which the firm bids are for q_j ($j = 1, 2, \ldots n$) units of the product.

Since the firm is selling in a sealed tender market, pricing decisions involve added uncertainty. Higher bids increase potential firm revenues but reduce the likelihood of winning the competition. To formalize these observations, let b_j represent the bid submitted in the jth competition. The conditional probability that b_j will be the winning (low) bid is $g_j(b_j | \cdot)$, a monotonically decreasing function. This implies simply that as the bid increases, the probability of winning decreases.

Variables assumed to condition the function $g_j(b_j | \cdot)$ describe industry characteristics, implying that the probability density function may shift between competitions, markets, and across industries. These shifts may be taken to be dependent upon structural variables—e.g., conditions of entry, number of firms bidding, the size distribution of firms, their capacity, and the like. Specifics of the conditioning process are discussed subsequently. However, this framework for representing the uncertainty of bidding competitions includes provision for the incorporation of market structure concepts.

Fixed production factors are assumed to provide a capacity constraint on the firm's bidding activities. This fixed capacity, K, determines the production services available for contracts won in the n sealed tender competitions. Variable and fixed factors are assumed to be related to output in fixed proportions over the relevant output range. If the firm is a price taker in the input markets, then the variable costs are constant. The cost of supplying a unit of the product to the

jth competition is d_j, with the competition identification rationalized on the basis of specialized marketing and/or nonproduction costs.

The firm described by these production and market characteristics is assumed to be an expected profit maximizer. Expected short run profits are given by the function:

$$E(\pi) = \sum_{j=1}^{n} g_j (b_j |\cdot) \; q_j (b_j - d_j) \; . \tag{1}$$

If the contract sizes (q_j) and variable costs (d_j) are taken as given, the expected profit for the firm is a function of the bids, b_j. This function is maximized subject to a number of constraints implicit in the previous discussion. First, the probabilities, $g_j(b_j|\cdot)$, must be restricted to the unit interval. This restriction is imposed by the inequality constraint:

$$\frac{1}{g_j(b_j |\cdot)} - 1 \geq 0 \; (j = 1, 2, \ldots, n) \; . \tag{2}$$

The fixed capacity constraint is conceptually more difficult to formulate. Clearly the uncertainty as to whether or not the firm wins other contracts suggests that the amount of available capacity is stochastic. This, in turn, implies that the capacity constraint, unless altered, is itself stochastic. Largely for purposes of simplicity, the capacity constraint is specified in expected value form:

$$\sum_{j=1}^{n} g_j(b_j |\cdot) \; q_j < K \; . \tag{3}$$

It is well known that stochastic restrictions for constrained maximization problems pose substantial difficulties (Dantzig, 1963). There are at least three alternatives for specifying such constraints deterministically: substituting expected values (as is done in the present analysis), using chance constraints, and artificially augmenting the constraints to permit additions to capacity. Algebraically, the latter two can be written as:

$$Pr(\sum_{j=1}^{n} q_j \leq K) \leq \alpha$$

and

$$\sum_{j=1}^{n} (q_j - k_j) \leq K$$

where α is a predetermined probability level and k_j is an artificial variable, which would also be entered in the objective function along with "price" as a cost. Although a capacity constraint of simple form is used, it is clear that the analysis could be extended to include the chance or augmented constraints. Although we have not proved it formally, we conjecture that the general tenor of our results would be similarly robust if the capital constraint were replaced by a rapidly rising marginal cost function.

If the firm faced with a set of bidding competitions is allowed some flexibility in delivery times, then operating subject to an expected capacity constraint may be plausible. Additionally, the possibility of subcontracting with firms not winning the contracts suggests this formulation as a reasonable proxy for the capacity constraint actually faced by the firm. Whatever the case, some care must be exercised in attaching an interpretation to the Lagrangian multiplier associated with the capacity constraint in the profit maximization problem.

The objective function (1) and constraints (2) and (3), together with a non-negativity condition on the bids, b_j, comprise a simple optimization problem. Applying the Kuhn-Tucker conditions to the problem formulated as a Lagrangian, and assuming the maximum occurs for $g_j(b_j|\cdot)$ in the unit interval, the first order conditions are:

$$(4)$$

$$g_j(b_j|\cdot)q_j + g_j'(b_j|\cdot)q_j(b_j-d_j) - \lambda g_j'(b_j|\cdot)q_j = 0 \quad (j = 1, 2, \ldots, n)$$

where λ is the multiplier associated with the expected capacity constraint. The prime is used to denote the derivative of $g_j(b_j|\cdot)$ with respect to b_j. Clearly the q_js can be divided out of the n equations represented by (4), a result that follows from the cost assumptions. Also note that each of the equations denoted by (4) is a function of bids on only one competition. An obvious extension would involve conditioning $g(b|\cdot)$ on bids of previous or other competitions. On simplifying and rearranging terms, an easily interpretable set of conditions for determining bids in the n markets is obtained:

$$\frac{-g_j'(b_j|\cdot)}{g_j(b_j|\cdot)} = \frac{1}{b_j-d_j-\lambda} \quad (j = 1, 2, \ldots n) . \tag{5}$$

The left-hand side of each of the equations in (5) is the failure rate function, whereas the right-hand side is the reciprocal of the per unit return in the jth competition minus variable costs and the implied opportunity cost associated with the capacity constraint. As the right-hand side is a monotonically decreasing function of b_j and the left-hand side is monotonically increasing, the optimizing condition specifies the firm's bids as the intersection of two functions (Attanasi and Johnson, 1975b).

If attention is restricted to a particular class of distributions for $g_j(b_j \mid \cdot)$, then the optimizing or equilibrium condition can be stated more explicitly. For the present analysis it is assumed that the conditional probabilities, $g_j(b_j \mid \cdot)$, are truncated normal. Under this condition, the failure rate can be approximated by a simple expression involving the bid, b_j, and the mean and variance of the conditioned distribution (Gnedenko et al., 1969)—i.e.:

$$\frac{b_j - \mu_j}{\sigma_j^2} = -\frac{g_j'(b_j \mid \cdot)}{g_j(b_j \mid \cdot)} \quad (j = 1, 2, \ldots, n) \tag{6}$$

where μ_j and σ_j^2 are the mean and variance, respectively. From this specializing condition, it follows from equations (5) and (6) that the firm's optimal bid for market j is the positive root of the expression:

$$b_j^* = \left\{ (d_j + \lambda_j + \mu_j) \pm \sqrt{(d_j + \lambda + \mu_j)^2 - 4\left[\mu_j(d_j + \lambda) - \sigma_j^2\right]} \right\} \tag{7}$$
$$(j = 1, 2, \ldots, n) .$$

Thus, the optimal bid is a function of costs, capacity, and parameters of the distribution $g_j(b_j \mid \cdot)$.

III. BID DISTRIBUTIONS

Bid distributions for individual competitions could, in principle, be derived by applying the optimal decision rule given in equation (7) to each of the rival firms. Such a procedure would require information on each firm's variable and opportunity costs as well as firm specific parameters for the probabilities $g_j(b_j \mid \cdot)$. Within the existing structure, parameters for the latter might be based upon different conditioning variables and weighting systems.

A more tractable approach to the derivation of bid distributions is to supply the required information in the form of distributional assumptions for the factors determining b_j^*. For example, instead of identifying a variable cost for each firm participating in the market, it may be more practical to assume that variable costs of the bidding firms are characterized by a particular probability distribution. This information, although less firm specific, is adequate for deriving market bid distributions. By addressing the bid distribution problem in this fashion, methods of analysis for bid data in applied situations can be developed. Whether through assumption or measurement, identification of industry distributions for the required characteristics seems more feasible than obtaining firm specific information.

Similar arguments apply to the parameters and variables assumed to define and condition the probabilities $g_j(b_j \mid \cdot)$. Although the process of assigning distributions representing industry or market variations between firms is obviously difficult, it does leave open possibilities for measurement. With measured cost information, observed industry bid distributions can be used to deduce these parameters, provided that a common distributional form and conditioning structure has been assumed. Alternatively, hypothesized distributional and conditioning structures can be used with observed cost data and market bid distributions to test various structural and behavioral propositions.

With distributions characterizing the factors on which the optimal firm bid is based, the process of obtaining a bid distribution for a competition is straightforward. In fact, were it not for the complexity of the transformation represented by equation (7), the market bid distributions could be obtained directly. The complexity of the transformation, however, means that only numerical methods are feasible for approximating market bid distributions based on the assumed distributions of the underlying factors.

These numerical methods involve sampling from the underlying distributions describing the firm and industry characteristics and then calculating an optimal bid. If the process is repeated a sufficient number of times, the resulting sample of optimal bids can be used to estimate a distribution corresponding to the parameter settings for the underlying factors. This capital intensive approach, although comparatively easy with high speed computers, presents two problems.

First, there is the problem of identifying the nature of the competition bid distributions implied by the model. As the transformation is complex, it is generally not possible to arrive at this decision deductively. Instead, alternative distributions must be fit to the sample of bids. Various statistical procedures can then be used to discriminate between classes of approximating distributions on the basis of the accuracy with which they characterize the sample data. The fact that the choice of an approximating distribution at one location in the design space (represented by particular values of the parameters of the distributions describing firm and competition variations) does not necessarily mean that it will be appropriate for other locations, makes this identification a problem of substantial dimension.

Second, in addition to identifying parameters of the market bid distribution for particular values of the parameters of the underlying distributions, it may be desirable to estimate the relationship over ranges suggested by alternative behavioral and structural assumptions. This can be accomplished by using response surface techniques (Kleijnen, 1975). A flexible functional form (usually a polynomial) is selected and an associated efficient experimental design for the underlying parameters or factors is structured. On the basis of repeated sampling at each of a set of design points, regression methods can be used to estimate relationships between parameters of the industry bid distribution and the specified characteristics of the distributions describing variations in the competitions. Although models for accomplishing this process have been available for some time in the statistical literature, they are only just beginning to be applied in economic analysis (Rausser and Johnson, 1975).

IV. BID DISTRIBUTIONS, STRUCTURE, AND CONDUCT

For application, the bid distribution generating procedure just described must be specialized for particular situations. As the specialization is rationalized in terms of the parameters of the underlying distributions, several comments about the probabilistic assumptions may be appropriate. First, attention is confined to distributions that do not admit negative values for the random variables. Such distributions are defined in terms of location and dispersion parameters. Although these parameters are not the means and variances as calculated for the more usual normal distribution, the characteristics described are interpreted similarly. Second, since assumptions are made with respect to several related random variables, the general distribution is multivariate. Assumptions concerning specific interrelationships between the random variables, however, will be restricted because of the interpretation difficulties.

Factors conditioning the optimal firm bids are variable costs, d_j; opportunity costs, λ; and the parameters of the function approximating the failure rate, μ_j and σ_j^2. The subscripts j indicate the several contracts and/or markets on which a bid is to be made. In isolating interfirm relationships and structure within a particular market, the market subscripts can be suppressed. A second subscript designating the firm making the bid must be added.

To avoid notational confusion, the subscript j is replaced with an i, indicating that the bid is from the ith firm ($i = 1, 2, \ldots, m$). Where the context is clear, subscripts are dropped. Keeping the competition distinction would permit the analysis of bidding behavior for firms operating in multiple competitions. The fact that the analysis goes through for several competitions suggests that the results subsequently obtained can be generalized to this situation. For highly concentrated industries selling in numerous markets, say to n cities, this generalization may be quite useful.

Costs

A reasonably straightforward interpretation can be afforded the necessary assumptions on variable and opportunity costs. The level of variable costs or location parameter for the cost distribution is probably more important in relative than in absolute terms. In relative terms it can be compared to levels of imputed costs and to characteristics of the distributions of the parameters approximating the failure rate. Associated interpretations relate to tracing out the effects of factor costs, increased opportunities for fixed resources, changes in productivity, and the like. The dispersion of variable costs among the bidding firms also can be linked to various structural characteristics. These might include factor prices, distances between firms or plants and markets, and variable production coefficients.

For opportunity costs, the interpretation again seems appropriately considered in terms of structure, but is somewhat more complex. Obvious factors related to both parameters of this distribution are capacity levels in the industry, inventories, delivery dates on contracts, and of course the firm's expectations concerning future prospects both within and outside the competition. The important characteristic about both cost distributions is that they appear to be potentially measurable and also rather directly attributable to technological factors, markets for inputs, and, more generally, the structure of the industry in question.

Failure Rate

The firm's perceptions of how conduct and structure influence the winning bid are embodied in parameters determining the failure rate function. Again, for experimental purposes the relative values of these parameters and specific characteristics of their distributions would seem more relevant rather than absolute values. To illustrate how parameters of the failure rate function are interpretable in terms of market variables, possible conditioning variables for μ_i and σ_i^2 are discussed briefly. Although this discussion outruns the numerical results, it may be useful in interpreting the modest experiments that follow.

For the individual firm, the estimate of the expected low bid, μ_i, determines the location of the subjective distribution for the winning bid. In turn, structure and conduct measures are assumed to condition μ_i. Subjective estimates of μ_i held by rival firms may then be assumed to be a function of competition variables and the relative sensitivity of the μ_is to specific competitive conditions, i.e.:

$$\mu_i = f(x_j \alpha_i, \sigma_\alpha^2, \mu_\alpha) \tag{8}$$

where x_j is a vector of structural characteristics describing the jth competition and σ_α^2 and μ_α are respectively dispersion and location parameters for the set of response parameters α_i. If for example this function were linear, the distribution of μ_i could be linked to values for the structural characteristics and the parameters σ_α^2 and μ_α.

Whereas the vector x_j is associated with structural features of the market, the parameters of the distribution of α_i seem more appropriately related to conduct. Specifically, the dispersion in the distribution of αs indicates the similarity or dissimilarity with which firms regard the existing structure. A small degree of dispersion may imply a conscious or unconscious similarity in the μ_is and hence the failure rates associated with particular bidding situations.

Alternatively, large variances would indicate that the firms react differently to the structural variables. In the limiting case, where μ_i is constant for all firms, differences in bids would be based upon parameters determining the distribution for σ^2 and other variables conditioning the industry competition. The distribution of the parameter σ^2 can be viewed as the result of various types of specification errors in equation (8). These specification errors might include omission of unimportant or unsystematic variables from the conditioning expression and omission of some dynamic factors.

If this rationalization is appropriate, then parameters of the assumed distribution for σ_i^2 may be viewed as reflecting both conduct and structure. Structural implications occur through the omission of possible conditioning variables. Conduct relationships would then enter as a result of misspecification of weights associated with market behavior. For example, if the number of firms bidding suddenly increased, the weights attached by firms to structural factors might become more diverse until a new appreciation for the structure adequately reflecting the presence of the new firms developed.

V. EXPERIMENTS

The numerical experiments are designed to compare and test sensitivities of alternative structure and conduct assumptions to properties of bid distributions and to relate these to commonly employed measures of performance. If a tight relationship can be established between properties of bid distributions and performance, then procedures for monitoring bidding competitions based on properties of observed bid distributions would appear feasible. Estimates of the bid distributions are generated from a log normality assumption for the underlying factors.[a]

In the first set of experiments two traditional measures of performance are related to costs, expectations measures and characteristics of the bid distribution. In the second and third sets of experiments, the variables identifying the competition are investigated under alternative structural assumptions. For each set of experiments, six factors at three levels were employed. A 3^6 full factoral design was used, resulting in 727 design points. At each design point 25 bids were generated.[b] Frequency functions were calculated on the basis of samples

[a] As indicated in Section IV, factors for the experiments are all parameters of underlying distributions and bounded above zero. As a consequence, a distributional assumption for the factors was required within which this property could be maintained. The log-normal distribution, which is bounded at zero, was selected largely because it is the more familiar of distributions with this required property. It however has the property of being unbounded above. As a consequence, other less familiar distributions—e.g., the beta distribution—might have been more appropriate. Such questions have empirical answers. The procedure being used can accommodate other types of distributional assumptions.

[b] The criterion for the sample reliability calculations is discussed in Hanson, Hurwitz, and Madow (1953). Sampling reliability for the estimates of the mean and standard deviations of the bid distribution were also calculated for smaller sample sizes. These calculations indicated a reliability of over 85 percent for sample sizes as small as 5 for the mean of the bid distribution but only 45 percent for the same sample size for the bid distribution standard deviation.

generated at widely varying design points and were compared to a number of probability density functions using goodness of fit tests.

Results of associated chi-square tests showed that the log-normal distribution closely approximated the true but unknown distribution of optimal bids. Finally, a number of preliminary experiments were conducted with different correlation matrices for the parameters of the underlying variables $(d, \lambda, \mu, \sigma)$ and for designs with different spreads and ranges in the possible parameter space. Response functions estimated on the basis of these exploratory experiments were quite stable, suggesting a possibility for generalization.

Bid Distributions and Measures of Performance

Properties of generated bid distributions are presented and compared to traditional measures of performance on the basis of these experiments. The analysis examines consequences of applying performance measures to static bid distribution data to ascertain their sensitivity to market considerations. In addition to relating the bid distributions and performance measures to the underlying experimental factors, an attempt is made to discover important interaction effects.

Table 12–1 contains estimated coefficients and associated t statistics for quadratic response surfaces.[c] These response surfaces are for parameters of the distributions of bids and performance measures. The first two response surface regressions are for the bid distribution mean and standard deviation. Reading Table 12–1 vertically, the estimated response functions for these variables indicate high explanatory power for the linear terms and a prominent role for the expectations related factors in determining both the mean and standard deviation of the bid distribution. The mean of the bid distribution is most sensitive to the mean of the expectations parameter, $m(\mu)$, whereas the standard deviation of the bid distribution is sensitive to the standard deviation, $v(\mu)$. The response surface estimate for the winning, or minimum, bid gives similar results. Estimated coefficients in this expression appear to be reflective of a combination of factors identified as important in the response functions for the mean and variance of the bid distribution.

Specifically, factor means and standard deviations influence the minimum bid in a more balanced fashion. This property was also observed for experiments in which the regressions were calculated using a transformation of the minimum bid (and the associated cost variable). For example, this pattern was observed when regressions of the mean and standard deviation of the distributions of price-cost margins and price–variable cost ratios were calculated and compared to those calculated on the basis of the minimum bid (and associated marginal cost) for each of the designs in Table 12–1.

[c]Design points for the response surfaces generated in Table 12–1 were the following: $m(\lambda)$, $m(d)$: 4, 7, 10; $m(\mu)$: 8, 14, 20; $v(d)$, $v(\lambda)$: 4, 7, 10; $v(\mu)$: 8, 14, 20. The cross correlations were $r_{d\lambda} = .5$, $r_{\lambda\mu} = .7$ and $r_{\mu d} = .5$. In this experiment σ^2 was assumed to be constant and equal to two.

These initial results show the sensitivity of properties of bid distributions to the underlying market assumptions. The related problem is to what extent do measures of market performance reflect these experimental factors. As a basis for some observations in this regard, the price-cost margin[d] for an individual firm in a competition is examined in the form:

$$pc_i = \frac{b_i^* - d_i}{b_i^*} . \tag{9}$$

Parameters of the associated response surface are also presented in Table 12–1. First, as expected, increases in the means of firm expectations, $m(\mu)$, and opportunity costs, $m(\lambda)$, positively influence the mean of the price-cost distribution, whereas their standard deviations $(v(\mu)$ and $v(\lambda)$, respectively), shift it in an opposite direction. Moreover, coefficient signs for the mean and standard deviation of direct cost $(m(d)$ and $v(d))$ have effects opposite to those of μ and λ.

The estimated response surface for the standard deviation of the price-cost margin distribution indicates statistical significance for parameters of both cost distributions and only the standard deviation of the expectations parameter. Comparison of the estimated price-cost margin response surface coefficients with those for the bid distributions shows a substantial reduction in the explanatory contribution of the expectations related variables. The increase in relative importance of the direct cost variables is not surprising given the structure of the bidding model and the fact that the expression is standardized for price. Perhaps, then, these experimental results emphasize the difficulty of relating price-cost margins to structure and conduct variables.

Much of the variation attributable to the expectations parameters appears lost or filtered out by the bid, b_i^*, in the numerator and denominator of the price-cost margin. In this context, the price-cost margin is highly related to cost determined structural parameters and thus a comparatively uninformative measure of conduct related performance. This result is corroborated by the available empirical work, in that even in normal market situations it has been argued that measurement of returns for the firm and industry should be based on capital, and that spurious correlations result if price-cost margins are regressed on variables such as concentration indices, which contain value of output (Weiss, 1971).

The last two columns of Table 12–1 contain response surface coefficients for the distribution of price–marginal cost ratios. These results also indicate a dominant role for cost factors. However, unlike the situation for price-cost margins, the results show that variables associated with the distribution of expectations

---

[d]Probably the most extensive empirical work attempting to relate the price-cost margin to structural measures has been carried out by Collins and Preston (1966, 1968, 1969). Saving (1970) has shown that under certain structural and market conduct conditions the price-cost margin bears a theoretical relationship to the concentration ratio.

Table 12–1.   Response Surface Experiments for Alternative Measures of Market Performance

	Regression Coefficients and Statistics					
	Bid Distribution					
	Mean		Standard Deviation		Minimum Bid	
Explanatory Variable[a]	Mean	"t"	Mean	"t"	Mean	"t"
$m(d)$	.132	18.4	−.061	11.6	.232	20.2
$m(\lambda)$	.138	19.1	−.053	10.0	.236	20.5
$m(\mu)$	.222	30.9	−.062	11.7	.291	25.3
$v(d)$	−.024	3.4	.057	10.8	−.136	11.8
$v(\lambda)$	−.040	5.6	.043	8.3	−.134	11.6
$v(\mu)$	−.026	3.6	.126	24.0	−.175	15.2
$m(d)^2$	.010	0.8	−.011	1.2	.060	3.0
$m(\lambda)^2$	.003	0.2	−.009	1.0	.038	1.9
$m(\mu)^2$	.006	0.5	−.018	2.0	.011	.5
$v(d)^2$	−.003	0.2	−.015	1.7	.038	1.9
$v(\lambda)^2$	−.001	0.1	−.010	1.1	.062	3.1
$v(\mu)^2$	.006	0.4	−.013	1.4	.084	4.2
$m(d)\,m(\lambda)$	−.004	0.4	.000	0.0	−.016	1.1
$m(d)\,m(\mu)$	−.069	7.9	.022	3.4	−.073	5.1
$m(d)\,v(d)$	−.005	0.5	.027	4.2	−.051	3.6
$m(d)\,v(\lambda)$	.003	0.3	−.003	0.5	.024	1.7
$m(d)\,v(\mu)$	.031	3.5	−.029	4.5	.075	5.3
$m(\lambda)\,v(\mu)$	−.090	10.2	.018	2.8	−.100	7.1
$m(\lambda)\,v(d)$	.002	0.2	−.008	1.2	.045	3.2
$m(\lambda)\,v(\lambda)$	−.003	0.3	.021	3.3	−.073	5.2
$m(\lambda)\,v(\mu)$	.030	3.5	−.010	1.6	.068	4.8
$m(\mu)\,v(d)$	.041	4.7	−.018	2.7	.078	5.5
$m(\mu)\,v(\lambda)$	.031	3.5	−.014	2.2	.068	4.8
$m(\mu)\,v(\mu)$	−.044	5.0	.040	6.1	−.131	9.9
$v(d)\,v(\lambda)$	−.001	0.1	.000	0.0	.010	.7
$v(d)\,v(\mu)$	−.007	0.8	.000	0.0	−.018	1.3
$v(\lambda)\,v(\mu)$	−.016	1.8	−.003	0.6	.044	3.1
R^2	.74		.65		.77	

[a] $m(\cdot)$ denotes the mean of the variate in parentheses, while $v(\cdot)$ denotes the standard deviation of the variate in parentheses.

Design points for experiment were: $m(d)$:   4, 7, 10 $v(d)$ 4, 7, 10
  $m(\mu)$:   8, 14, 20 $v(\mu)$: 8, 14, 20
  $m(\lambda)$:   4, 7, 10 $v(\lambda)$: 4, 7, 10

$r_{d\lambda} = .5$, $r_{\lambda\mu} = .7$, $r_{\mu d} = .5$ with σ^2 assumed constant

have significant explanatory power for both the mean and standard deviation of the price–marginal cost ratio distribution.

To conclude, these response surface results show that characteristics and structural aspects of bidding competitions can be related to bid distributions and price-cost performance measures. Unfortunately, they do not indicate the tight

Table 12-1. continued

	Regression Coefficients and Statistics						
Distribution of Price-Cost Margins				Distribution of Price-Marginal Cost Ratios			
Mean		Standard Deviation		Mean		Standard Deviation	
Mean	"t"	Mean	"t"	Mean	"t"	Mean	"t"
-.152	-86.2	.011	9.5	-4.26	-40.6	-5.69	-19.0
.056	32.0	-.028	-23.9	.57	5.7	.62	2.1
.064	36.2	-.001	-1.1	1.62	15.4	1.58	5.3
.043	24.4	.012	10.0	2.15	20.5	3.54	11.8
-.017	-9.6	.010	8.4	-.27	-2.6	-.51	-1.7
-.006	-3.6	.006	4.9	-.08	-.8	.09	.3
.021	6.8	-.017	-8.2	2.71	14.9	3.97	7.6
-.010	-3.3	.001	0.7	.12	.7	.29	.6
.005	1.8	-.008	-4.1	.39	2.2	.68	1.3
-.010	-3.4	-.000	-0.1	.35	1.9	1.00	1.9
-.002	-.8	.002	0.8	-.09	-.5	-.52	-1.0
.003	1.2	-.003	-1.4	.10	.5	-.56	-1.1
.018	8.3	-.001	-1.0	.41	-3.2	-.69	-1.9
.005	2.1	.015	10.5	-1.47	-11.4	-1.55	-4.2
-.001	-.0	.005	3.2	-2.34	-18.1	-4.16	-11.3
-.005	-2.5	.003	2.4	.25	2.0	.55	1.5
.001	.6	.005	3.2	.27	2.1	.49	1.3
-.029	-13.4	.001	0.5	-.20	-1.6	-.11	-.3
-.008	-3.7	.003	2.1	.29	2.3	.81	2.2
.002	1.0	-.002	-1.3	-.04	-.3	-.22	-.6
.009	4.1	-.004	-2.4	.22	1.7	.12	.3
.002	.0	-.001	-0.5	.77	5.9	.96	2.6
.012	5.6	-.002	-1.2	.14	1.1	.24	.7
.008	-3.7	.004	2.6	-.22	-1.7	-.51	-1.4
.005	2.2	-.006	-3.9	-.18	-1.4	-.66	-1.8
.003	1.3	-.006	-4.1	-.22	-1.7	-.59	-1.6
-.907	-3.1	.001	0.9	-.09	-.70	.03	.1
.94		.62		.82		.52	

connection between performance measures and bid distribution characteristics that had been sought. Apparently, both bid distribution and price-cost statistics must be studied under more restrictive conditions—perhaps of the type suggested by the discussion in equation (8)—before they can be more directly linked. However, the results provide a basis (i.e., norms) for comparing the distributions of bids and price-cost performance statistics across competitions with widely varying underlying structure and conduct assumptions. The following subsection, emphasizing the market portion of the model, offers results that seem empirically useful and somewhat less demanding in terms of required knowledge of the industry and competitions.

Bid Distributions and Structure

To concentrate the investigation on the relative importance (to bid distribution properties) of the variables σ_j^2 and μ_j that characterize a particular market, suppose there is a substantial degree of price interdependence among rivals. Also suppose that expectations of the price distribution are significantly in excess of costs. The design is centered so that the mean of the distribution of the low bid $m(\mu)$ is specified as twice that of costs $m(c)$ and the parameters for σ^2 and μ are allowed to vary over wide ranges. It is also assumed that random variables sampled from the distributions of σ^2 and μ are negatively correlated. The latter condition is suggested by the observation for an individual firm to maintain the same optimal bid according to equation (6), an increased variance must be offset by a reduction in the expected value of distribution of low bids, μ_j. In economic terms this implies that increased uncertainty tends to reduce the expected winning bid. Contrastingly, a decrease in the overall uncertainty is associated with an increase in the mean of the firm's subjective distribution of winning bids.

For the experiments presented in Table 12–2, the restrictions were placed on the standard deviations and means of costs (c), expectations (μ) and market variation (σ) to maintain a negative correlation of $-.2$ over a range of design points. With σ^2 and μ negatively correlated, there is a technical restriction on the degree of negative correlation imposed by the multivariate log-normal random number generator. Exploratory experiments were run with highly restricted coefficients of variation for the log-normal variates, but with higher negative correlations imposed than those presented in Table 12–2. In summary, these results (not shown) indicate that increasing the negative correlation tends to reduce the significance of σ^2 and increase the explanatory power of parameters associated with μ.

Consequently, caution must be exercised in interpreting the results because the standard deviations and means of the distributions of μ and σ^2 were varied independently. Had it not been for a restriction associated with the random number generator, it would have been desirable to run the experiments with correlations of perhaps $-.5$ or $-.7$. For designs A, B, and C respectively (see footnote in Table 12–2), the distributional parameters (means and standard deviations) of μ are equal to, greater than, and less than σ^2, with the cost distribution parameters always half the distributional parameters of μ at the center of the design. In design D, parameters of c, σ^2 and μ are equal, again at the central points of the design.

In the first of three experiments, the response surfaces indicate that the expected winning bid—i.e., location parameter of the distribution of low bids—dominates both costs and the variance term σ^2. It is also rather surprising that across all four experiments, with parameters of the distribution of σ^2 varying both in absolute and relative terms, the coefficients (in absolute terms) on the linear and quadratic terms for $m(\sigma^2)$ and $v(\sigma^2)$ change very little. Specifically, even when parameters of the distribution σ^2 are larger than μ, this variable does not explain much of the variation in the dependent variable.

To summarize, when attention is confined to situations where market variables are assumed to dominate firm pricing strategies: the parameters associated with μ explain most of the variation in the mean and standard deviation of the bid distribution. This also holds for response surfaces estimated with the minimum bid as the dependent variable. Accordingly, it would appear that additional refinement and development of the theoretical foundation for how firms arrive at μ_i would be important. One possible approach for making such refinements has been presented in Section IV. However, as the approach obviously requires a high degree of specialization to the situation in question, numerical response surface estimates so conditioned are not presented. The results obtained do show, by the importance of the expectations term, that such more specialized studies may have substantial potential in terms of discriminatory power among the alternative experimental hypotheses.

In the last experiment—design D in Table 12−2—the restriction of a pricing policy dominated by market variables is relaxed. Values of parameters associated with the cost distribution are made equal to the parameters for the market related distributions (σ_j^2 and μ_j). From the coefficient estimates it is apparent that the introduction of σ_j^2 and truncation of costs into a single variable increases the relative importance of the cost distribution. Thus parameters of the cost distribution now explain at least as much of the variation in the dependent variables as do the variables associated with the market side of the model. In economic terms, then, where costs approximate the firm's expectation of price—i.e., where $c\,(=d+\lambda)$ is close to μ—the introduction of σ^2 as a random variable induces a change in the relative importance of μ and c by increasing the significance of c in the response function as firms price according to average costs. Implicit in the results presented in Table 12−2 is that no changes occur in the nature of the bid distribution. This assumption was constantly being tested and it was found that the resulting distribution approximated a log-normal well.

As mentioned previously, a small degree of correlation between μ and σ^2 was imposed for the experiments presented in Table 12−2. To examine cases where μ and σ^2 have strong negative correlations, two related experiments were conducted with $\bar{\sigma}_i^2 = a/\bar{\mu}_i$ where a is a constant. Design points for the first experiment were chosen to represent a situation where the mean of the expected winning bid was approximated by the sum of the variable and opportunity costs, while the design points for the second experiment were chosen so that market expectations were one-and-one-half times the sum of direct and opportunity costs; thus simulating a situation where pricing was dominated by market conditions rather than firm costs.

For the first experiment, estimates for the minimum bid, mean, and standard deviation of the bid distribution are compared to results of similar experiments

Table 12–2. Response Experiments on Market Related Variables

	Regression Coefficients and "t" Statistics							
	Design A				*Design B*			
	Mean		*Standard Deviation*		*Mean*		*Standard Deviation*	
Explanatory Variable[a]	*Mean*	*"t"*	*Mean*	*"t"*	*Mean*	*"t"*	*Mean*	*"t"*
$m(c)$	.059	11.7	−.036	−9.4	.063	11.6	−.041	−10.4
$m(\sigma^2)$	.033	6.5	−.021	−5.5	.024	4.4	−.017	−4.4
$m(\mu)$	.247	48.7	−.047	−12.4	.268	49.5	−.058	−14.9
$v(c)$	−.008	−1.6	.041	10.8	−.010	−1.9	.045	11.5
$v(\sigma^2)$	−.006	−1.2	−.002	−.5	−.004	−.8	−.003	−.9
$v(\mu)$	−.032	−6.2	.167	43.6	−.041	−7.6	.177	45.4
$m(c)^2$	.003	.3	−.009	−1.3	.003	.4	−.009	−1.3
$m(\sigma^2)^2$	.002	.2	.007	1.0	.004	.5	.006	.9
$m(\mu)^2$	−.012	−1.4	−.009	−1.4	−.015	−1.6	−.010	−1.3
$v(c)^2$	.001	.0	−.005	−.8	.001	.1	−.005	−.8
$v(\sigma^2)^2$	−.010	−1.1	−.002	−.4	−.010	−1.0	−.003	−.4
$v(\mu)^2$	.000	0.0	−.019	−2.9	−.000	.0	−.022	−3.2
$m(c)m(\sigma^2)$	−.004	−.6	−.001	−.1	−.004	−.5	−.001	−.2
$m(c)m(\mu)$	−.040	−6.4	.021	4.5	−.047	−7.1	.026	5.5
$m(c)v(c)$	.002	.3	.016	3.4	.001	.1	.018	3.8
$m(c)v(\sigma^2)$	.002	.4	.001	.2	.002	.4	.001	.2
$m(c)v(\mu)$	.026	4.2	−.014	−2.9	.031	4.7	−.020	−3.7
$m(\sigma^2)m(\mu)$	−.019	−3.0	.003	.6	−.016	−2.3	.003	.6
$m(\sigma^2)v(c)$	−.002	−.3	−.001	−.1	−.002	−.3	−.001	−.1
$m(\sigma^2)v(\sigma^2)$	.003	.5	.001	.1	.003	.4	.001	.2
$m(\sigma^2)v(\mu)$	.009	1.4	−.009	−1.9	.009	1.3	−.008	−1.7
$m(\mu)v(c)$	.017	2.7	−.025	−5.2	.019	3.0	.029	−6.1
$m(\mu)v(\sigma^2)$	.009	1.4	.006	1.3	−.028	1.2	.007	1.5
$m(\mu)v(\mu)$	−.027	−4.3	.012	2.6	−.028	−4.2	.013	2.8
$v(c)v(\sigma^2)$	−.001	−.3	−.001	−.1	−.002	−.3	.000	.0
$v(c)v(\mu)$	−.007	1.1	.007	1.5	−.009	−1.3	−.009	1.8
$v(\sigma^2)v(\mu)$	−.005	−.9	−.007	−1.4	−.006	−.9	−.007	−1.5
R^2	.79		.77		.80		.79	

[a] $m(\cdot)$ denotes the mean of the variate in parentheses, while $v(\cdot)$ denotes the standard deviation of the variate in parentheses.

Design points for experiment:

A $m(c)$: 8, 12, 16; $m(\sigma^2)$; $m(\mu)$: 16, 24, 32; $v(c)$: 4, 8, 12; $v(\sigma^2)v(\mu)$: 8, 16, 24

B $m(c)$; $m(\sigma^2)$: 8, 12, 16; $m(\mu)$: 16, 24, 32; $v(c)$; $v(\sigma^2)$: 4, 8, 12; $v(\mu)$; 8, 16, 24

C $m(c)$: 8, 12, 16; $m(\sigma^2)$: 24, 36, 48; $m(\mu)$: 16, 24, 32; $v(c)$: 4, 8, 16; $v(\sigma^2)$: 12, 24, 36; $v(\mu)$: 8, 16, 24

D $m(c)$; $m(\sigma^2)$; $m(\mu)$: 16, 24, 32; $v(c)$; $v(\sigma^2)$; $v(\mu)$: 16, 24, 32

In all cases the following correlation matrix was assumed: $r_{c\sigma^2} = -.2$, $r_{\mu\sigma^2} = -.2$, $r_{\mu c} = .5$

reported in Table 12–1. They indicate that the introduction of σ^2 as a random variable tends to reduce the significance of expectations related variables by at least 30 percent. For the second set of experiments (those simulating a market where pricing policies are loosely tied to firm costs), introduction of σ^2 as a ran-

Table 12–2. continued

		Regression Coefficients and "t" Statistics					
	Design C				*Design D*		
Mean		*Standard Deviation*		*Mean*		*Standard Deviation*	
Mean	*"t"*	*Mean*	*"t"*	*Mean*	*"t"*	*Mean*	*"t"*
.057	11.8	−.033	−8.7	.155	32.0	.050	−14.0
.040	8.1	−.023	−6.2	.026	5.4	−.016	−4.5
.233	48.1	−.041	−11.0	.152	31.4	−.047	−13.2
−.007	−1.5	.039	10.3	−.022	−4.5	.096	26.8
−.007	−1.5	−.001	−.1	−.005	−1.0	−.002	−.4
−.026	−5.3	.160	42.4	−.008	−1.6	.116	32.2
.002	.3	−.009	−1.3	.011	1.3	−.005	−.8
.001	.1	.007	1.1	.005	.6	.002	.4
−.011	−1.3	−.009	−1.4	.000	.1	−.004	−.7
−.001	−.1	−.005	−.8	.001	.2	−.017	−2.7
−.010	1.1	−.002	−.3	−.006	−.6	−.003	−.5
.000	.0	−.017	−2.6	−.001	.1	−.005	−.8
−.004	.6	−.000	−.1	−.007	−1.1	.001	.3
−.035	6.0	.018	−4.0	−.066	−11.1	.016	3.7
.002	.4	.015	3.2	−.005	−.8	.031	7.1
.002	.4	.001	.3	.001	.2	.000	.0
.023	3.9	−.012	−2.5	.028	4.7	−.029	−6.5
−.020	−3.4	.003	.6	−.012	−2.0	−.001	−.2
−.002	−.3	−.001	−.2	.001	.2	−.005	−1.0
.004	.6	.000	.1	.002	.0	.000	−.1
.009	1.5	−.009	−2.0	.006	1.0	−.002	−.6
.015	2.6	−.022	−4.7	.029	4.9	−.035	−8.0
.009	1.5	.006	1.2	.004	.7	.007	1.5
−.025	−4.3	.012	2.4	−.021	−3.5	.019	4.2
−.001	.2	−.001	−.2	−.003	−.5	.001	.2
−.006	−1.0	.006	1.3	−.016	−2.8	.001	−.2
−.005	−.9	−.006	−1.4	−.003	−.5	.006	−1.3
.79		.76		.76		.77	

dom variable only slightly affected the significance of variables associated with $\tilde{\mu}_i$. That is, the response surfaces estimated for the bid distribution parameters showed that the variables related to μ strongly dominated the dependent variable even through σ^2 was introduced as an experimental factor.

Additional response surface analyses were carried out to investigate the relationship between the experimental factors and the competition price-cost margin (equation (9)) of the low bidder. Estimated coefficients were similar in sign and significance to the estimates presented in Table 12–1. Further, when σ^2 was introduced as an experimental factor, it produced a relatively small positive coefficient for the mean and nearly a zero coefficient for the standard deviation of $\tilde{\sigma}_i^2$. Variations in the parameters of σ^2, $m(\sigma^2)$ and $v(\sigma^2)$, had little direct influence on the significance of the other explanatory variables.

To summarize, the purpose of the response surface experiments was to determine both the relationship and sensitivity of the parameters of the bid distribution and market performance measure to underlying assumptions associated with market structure and conduct. Other experiments indicated the reported results to be fairly robust in terms of alternative design point locations. However, changes in the relative spacing of points, which can be interpreted in terms of conduct and structure, are reflected in the significance and relative values of coefficients of the response functions. In essence, the response functions provide a link between the observable bid distribution properties and performance indices with perhaps unobservable market conditions. Thus a basis is obtained for the formulation of hypotheses associated with conduct and performance which can be evaluated by using observed bids.

In the following section, which illustrates extreme cases, tests were carried out for diverse values of the underlying parameters. In particular, what changes in the bid distribution take place when the industry has either no cost variation, or all firms have exactly the same price expectations?

Bid Distribution Properties and Variability of Economic Factors

In the final experiments the bid distribution is examined as a function of the variability in the underlying factors. Therefore, tests conducted were different from previous experiments, which only examined changes induced by variations in factor levels. Space does not permit a description of the results in terms of response surfaces. Chi-square tests were performed to distinguish if significant changes in the nature of the generated bid distributions had occurred.[e] For each case that the test indicated a change in the generated bid distributions, other distributional forms were tested for identification of the appropriate new approximating distribution.

To summarize the results, the experiments indicated that no change in the bid distribution (i.e., log-normal) occurred when $\tilde{\sigma}_i^2$ changed from a log-normal distribution to a constant. However, when either the costs (λ and d) or the expectations were assumed to be degenerate, the nature of the bid distribution appeared to change from a log-normal to a gamma, where the gamma takes the form of a negative exponential density.

One interpretation for the case of a degenerate market expectations distribution is that of an extreme degree of market interdependence. Such interdependence could derive from the use of rules of thumb, focal point pricing, or covert activities of bidding firms. Establishing the latter would require information on the conditioning of the expectations distribution (Attanasi and Johnson, 1975b) as well as on firm costs. Appropriately qualified, this would suggest a difference

---

[e]While the chi-square test is relatively weak, it seems to minimize Type II errors, i.e., where the test implies that changes in the distribution have occurred, but the distribution has not really changed.

in the basic nature of bid distributions generated from collusive and noncollusive markets.

In the case where experimental results indicate that such differences are principally a function of the dispersion and higher order moments of the bid distribution, additional experimentation should identify a set of boundary points or a frontier in terms of the variability in μ, where a basic change in the distribution takes place. The empirical implications of this last set of experiments appear to be significant for applied work. First, the variability and functional form for the bid distributions was shown to be associated with the nature of the competitions and conduct. Observed changes in the form of the bid distributions can be the result of either of the two factors. It would seem that if costs were constant, with a degenerate distribution for all firms, this would be observable.

Alternatively, if it were clear from empirical observations that costs were not constant and a degenerate bid distribution resulted, a hypothesis of collusive conduct would be supported. Tests of conduct hypotheses, of course, would require supporting empirical information on costs, economic conditions, nature of capital requirements, industry excess capacity, and the like. The analysis of bid distributions might then be more useful in indicating suspect bid competitions than establishing the conduct that results in undue monopoly returns.

VI. CONCLUSIONS

The study derives several results useful to industrial organization theory and applications. First, while information from observed bid distributions reflects the structure, conduct, and nature of the industry, corroborating market information is required in order to interpret such properties. In addition, the analysis indicates how such economic information can be usefully combined with bid distribution data to suggest specific hypotheses about structure and conduct.

This observation must, however, be qualified by the fact that bid data derived within a static framework represents a weak basis for conclusions as to market performance. Market specific information which the regulatory agency frequently gathers through prequalification statements or other supervisory activities along with industry specific information is required for an accurate interpretation of static bid distribution information. Moreover, the static results might be advantageously supplemented by dynamic economic information and bid data. The experimental approach taken here is sufficiently general to accommodate a dynamic firm model.

Second, the analysis illuminates an important problem for applied studies that apply generally accepted measures of market performance to sealed tender markets. Values of these performance measures may be relatively insensitive to conduct and structure. Third, the combined interaction effects of structure and conduct tends to be greater than the effect of either factor alone. For example, the fact that introducing greater variability in the variance of the distribution $g_j(b \mid \cdot)$ influenced the relative significance of the mean of $g_j(b \mid \cdot)$ as an experimental factor is illustrative of this point. This observation, together with the structuring for variations in μ and σ^2 suggested in Section IV, would seem to indicate that conclusions regarding conduct should be made on the basis of bid distribution information only under highly controlled circumstances or where supporting market information is available.

Finally, the model appears most useful in applied situations where significant changes in the bid distributions have occurred between geographically dispersed bidding competitions with the same participants or in situations in which bid distributions have taken sudden shifts over time. In such circumstances, it would appear that with a minimum of quantitative cost information, many traditional as well as some new conduct hypotheses of market behavior could be investigated. Presently, the model and results have the most obvious utility as an initial step in the construction of more systematic monitoring systems for supervising conduct in sealed tender markets.

✳ *Chapter 13*

An Economic Analysis of Presale Exploration in Oil and Gas Lease Sales

Darius W. Gaskins, Jr.
Thomas J. Teisberg

I. INTRODUCTION

In considering the economic efficiency of production or consumption activities, economists typically focus their attention on the institutional context in which economic decisions are made. Unless this institutional context allows correct price signals and does not otherwise interfere with maximizing behavior, economic inefficiency is presumed to result.

In the case of oil and gas production, a number of institutions may distort price signals and/or interfere with maximizing behavior. These include price controls, production royalties, tax subsidies, "diligent development" requirements, and "maximum efficient production rate" standards. As economists have frequently pointed out, these institutions work against efficiency in the production of oil and gas.

We would like to direct attention to another potential source of inefficiency, not in the production of oil and gas, but in the actual sale of oil and gas properties, particularly as it occurs in federal oil and gas lease auctions. Federal oil and gas leases are very valuable, and there is a great deal of uncertainty about the true value of any given lease. Since models of bidding behavior indicate that a bidder with superior information can make profits in an auction, there is an incentive for prospective bidders for oil and gas leases to get a better idea of the true value of leases to be auctioned. Thus, as we in fact observe, there is considerable exploration activity which takes place prior to federal lease auctions.

This exploration activity has real resource costs. However, it is not clear to what extent the activity has corresponding real resource benefits. It is in fact

We owe a special debt to Robert Wilson for his theoretical work on bidding models, which he made available to us.

possible that presale exploration largely or wholely produces information that is useful in estimating the value of leases, but useless in actually realizing that value. To the extent that this is true, the production of information from presale exploration is socially wasteful.

The essential problem here is that there exists a strong private incentive to produce information that need not have any corresponding social value. This kind of problem has been recognized in other contexts as well. Two important examples are Hirschliefer (1971) and the literature on "screening," e.g., Stiglitz (1975). Hirschliefer notes the private incentive to produce information about future prices in order to reap speculative gains from this knowledge. The information produced may or may not have any real value to society. Similarly, the screening literature considers situations in which there is a private incentive to identify oneself as a productive worker, in order to receive a higher wage rate. This incentive also exists whether or not the identification of productive and unproductive workers has any real value to society.

In fact, the screening metaphor can also be applied to presale exploration in the oil and gas lease market, since this exploration in effect sorts leases according to their expected values. However, screening behavior in the lease market is different from that which would be expected in the labor market, because screening is done by the potential purchasers (rather than the owners) of an asset that is subsequently to be sold in a market. Whereas owners of an asset can expect to realize any gain, resulting from screening, in the asset's perceived value, potential purchasers of an asset can realize such gains only to the extent that the bidding process allows. This intervention of the bidding process makes the incentives for screening in the lease market more complicated than those in the labor market.

The remainder of this chapter is organized in the following way. Section II presents a description of the lease market and the presale screening of leases we observe in that market. Then in Section III we consider the private incentives for presale screening behavior, and the possible real resource benefits from such screening. We reach the general conclusion that the amount of presale screening is not optimal from the point of view of society, because the private incentives do not correspond to the possible real benefits.

Although actual presale screening is likely to be excessive in many cases, it is difficult to reach any general conclusions about the extent to which presale screening may be wasteful. However, models of bidding behavior suggest that there is an upper limit on the amount of presale screening which will occur. In some instances the bidding process, by sufficiently diminishing the payoff to screening, may result in too little presale exploration.

Finally, in Section IV, we consider policy implications of this analysis of presale screening. The policy problem is complicated by the sometimes incompatible public objectives of maximizing the real resource value of federal oil and gas properties, and maximizing the public return from those properties. Nevertheless, some conclusions can be drawn about particularly policies that are pursued or could be pursued in selling federal leases.

II. THE MARKET FOR OIL AND GAS LEASES

Federal offshore oil and gas leases entitle the lessee to explore for and produce any oil or gas which may be contained in the lease. The leases are sold in seal bid auctions, which appear generally to be quite competitive.[a]

Leases themselves are often very valuable. High bids for single leases have ranged up to $212 million in recent sales. (See Bureau of Land Management, *Oil and Gas Lease Data Reports.*) These high bids presumably reflect the expected value of net production revenues over the life of the leases. There is a significant degree of uncertainty about the actual value of the leases, however. For example, the set of leases on the Destin Dome—one of which received the $212 million bid—may in fact prove to have negative net revenues. Alternatively, the leases might have turned out to be worth many times the amounts bid for them.

Presale Exploration

Where an asset being offered for sale is very valuable, but the value is relatively unknown, there will be a strong incentive for prospective bidders to determine as accurately as possible what the true value of the asset will be. In fact, we do observe substantial efforts being undertaken by prospective bidders to assess the value of federal leases before lease sales are held. This presale exploration, moreover, appears to yield information about the true values of leases being offered for sale. In the December 1973 lease sale, for example, high bids for offered tracts ranged from zero to $212 million, with an average of $10 million. If presale exploration (or some other prior information) did not tell much about the relative values of leases, we would have expected all the high bids to be about $10 million, rather than spread over the range $0−212 million.

Presale exploration produces information of two different kinds. One is geophysical information. This category includes data from magnetic, gravity, and seismic surveys, as well as the interpretations which are produced from the basic data. On the federal OCS, most basic geophysical data (but not interpretations) is produced by geophysical exploration companies, who sell the data to anyone interested. In addition, however, prospective lease bidders sometimes produce additional geophysical data about prospects they are particularly interested in.

The value of the basic geophysical data by itself is apparently quite small. It is the interpretation of the data that produces useful information about lease values. We suspect that the bulk of the costs of geophysical information are

---

[a]Erickson and Spann (1974) cite the large number of potential bidders, the case of entry into the bidding auction, and an estimated rate of return of less than 8 percent as evidence of overall competition in OCS lease sales. It should be noted that this evidence doesn't preclude noncompetitive auctions for individual prospects.

244 Essays on Industrial Organization

those incurred as part of the interpretation of the raw data.[b] Finally, we also note that each prospective bidder is entirely free to initiate geophysical data gathering and interpretation independently of other prospective bidders' actions, and that the information gained from geophysical data interpretation is invariably a closely guarded secret for each prospective bidder.

The second kind of information produced as part of presale exploration is geologic data. Geologic data are data gained from actual drilling. Such data are most revealing about the area immediately surrounding the well; however, these data also can reveal general information about a much wider area. Usually, geologic information (or geologic coupled with geophysical information) will dominate geophysical information, at least in the immediate vicinity of a well.

Geologic information is produced as part of presale exploration in two ways. First, part or all of the motivation in drilling a test hole may be to gain geologic information about an adjacent or nearby tract which is to be offered for sale. This is known as a line hole, since it is often drilled on the line between tract A and tract B, where tract A is owned and tract B is to be offered for sale. Drilling line holes as a presale exploration activity is possible only in mature leasing areas where some tracts are already owned. Line holes are initiated at the discretion of the owner of the tract to be drilled, and the data obtained are kept secret from other potential bidders (at least under the existing information policy).

Geologic information is also produced by what are called stratigraphic tests, which are test holes drilled in the general areas of a lease sale, and which to date have been specifically placed off structure (where oil is unlikely to be found). Stratigraphic tests are now being conducted in several offshore leasing areas where little or no prior leasing has occurred. Stratigraphic tests are organized by one or more companies who solicit the participation of other companies, arrange for a drilling rig to be moved on site, and apply to the federal government for a drilling permit.

As the program is now organized, each of the original participants in a joint stratigraphic test share equally in the costs and the data produced. Others may also share in the data as late joiners, but they must pay a penalty by bearing some multiple of the cost born by original participants. As the stratigraphic test program is now organized, the decision to undertake a stratigraphic test is a joint decision of several prospective buyers. Moreover, the terms do not allow anyone to be excluded from sharing in the data; thus the data cannot be kept secret. In these respects, stratigraphic testing as a presale exploration activity is different from geophysical data gathering and interpretation, and line hole drilling.

---

[b]Geophysical Data can be purchased for less than $500 per line mile on exclusive contracts and for less than $50 for "group shoots." Intensive seismic exploration on a tract consists of a grid with lines spaced a mile apart and several tract specific lines. One major bidder spends an average of $50,000 per tract for all presale exploration while spending approximately $2,500 per tract for the acquisition of processed seismic data.

III. PRESALE EXPLORATION: PRIVATE INCENTIVES AND SOCIAL BENEFITS

Private Incentives for Presale Exploration

Where an asset with uncertain value is to be put up for sale in a competitive auction, any bidder who can obtain superior information about the true value of the asset will have a significant advantage in the auction. Suppose, for example, that an asset with value uniformly distributed between $0 and $100 were up for sale. A competitive auction among risk-neutral bidders would result in a winning bid of $50 for this asset. However, if one particular bidder knew exactly what the true value of the asset was, he could bid $51 if that value were $51 or greater, and he could bid nothing if the value were $50 or less. This bidding strategy would lead to the informed bidder receiving an expected profit approximately equal to $12 *if the uninformed bidders didn't modify their bidding behavior.* Obviously, then, there is a strong incentive to develop superior information about the worth of an asset to be auctioned.

Although we can recognize the existence of an incentive to find out the value of an asset to be auctioned, we cannot say much more about this incentive without specifying a more detailed model of the bidding process. The nature of the bidding process, and prior assumptions about information available to each bidder, will determine the ultimate payoff to bidders who do or do not have superior information. While the number of possible models is enormous, two special cases would seem to represent the most important possibilities that arise in OCS leasing. These are the case where one and only one bidder has perfect information, and the case where all bidders have exactly the same (imperfect) information.

We consider first the case of asymmetric information among the bidders. Both Wilson (1967) and Hughart (1975) have explored bidding models of this sort and both conclude that the informed bidder makes profits while the uninformed bidder makes zero profits.[c] The following model, which seems most directly applicable to the question at hand, was provided to the authors by Wilson in recent correspondence.

Specifically, assume that the value of the asset is uniformly distributed between $0 and $B. Now, let only one bidder know the true value of the asset (which could be any number between 0 and B) and assume this value is V. It can be shown that this informed bidder will bid $\frac{V}{2}$, and realize an expected profit of $\frac{B}{6}$. Since the prior expected value of the asset, $E(V)$, is $\frac{B}{2}$, the informed bidder's expected profit is $\frac{E(V)}{3}$. Thus the informed bidder realizes an ex-

---

[c]Hughart's paper on this subject is marred by analytic errors in determining equilibrium bidding strategies. These analytic deficiencies and Hughart's neglect of any potential social gain from presale screening obviate his policy conclusions.

pected profit from his superior information of 33 percent of the expected value of the asset being offered for sale. The uninformed bidders, on the other hand, are forced to follow a randomized (mixed) bidder strategy in this situation, and these bidders earn zero profits, no matter how many or how few of them there are in the auction.

The second case we consider is where all bidders have symmetric information (symmetric in the sense that they have similar stochastically independent samples drawn from the same distribution, which is conditioned on the unknown true value of the prospect). Bidding models of this sort have been considered by Vickrey (1961), Wilson (1969), and Rothkopf (1969). In this case, where all the bidders have the same imperfect information about the asset's value, each will make the same expected profit. Moreover, this expected profit will depend upon the number of bidders in the auction, and this profit will go to zero in the limit as the number of bidders becomes infinite.

For the special case of an asset which is known by all to have the Weibull distribution as a prior distribution, the relationship between the number of bidders and the expected profits of the bidders is shown in Table 13–1. (This is another example recently provided by Robert Wilson to the authors.)

The two bidding models provide a means to analyze the private incentives for presale exploration in two common kinds of situations that arise in OCS leasing. The first situation is that in which only one bidder has the opportunity to become (significantly) more informed than the other bidders. The bidding model where one bidder has perfect information can be applied here. That model shows that exclusive perfect information may be worth about one-third of the value of the asset. Therefore, we can infer that exclusive and significantly better information is worth at most about one-third of the value of the asset. This, then, is an upper limit on the incentive to develop superior information, where only one bidder has the opportunity to develop such information.

The second situation that arises in OCS leasing is that in which all bidders have relatively equal opportunities to become more informed. In this situation, we will assume for simplicity that only more informed bidders participate in the

Table 13–1. Relationship Between Number of Equally Informed Bidders and Profit as a Percent of the Asset's Value

Number of Equally Informed Bidders, n	Total Profit to be Shared Among Bidders, $\epsilon(n)$	Expected profit per bidder $\dfrac{\epsilon(n)}{n}$
1	100%	100%
2	25	12.5
4	10	2.5
8	4.55	0.57
16	2.17	0.14
∞	0	0

auction. With this assumption, we can specify the incentive for the nth bidder to enter the auction as follows:

$$I(n) = \frac{\epsilon(n)}{n} V \tag{1}$$

where $I(n)$ = the incentive for the nth bidder to become an informed bidder, if $n-1$ bidders are already informed,

$\frac{\epsilon(n)}{n}$ = the expected profit to each bidder as a fraction of asset value, if there are n informed bidders (see Table 13–1), and

V = the expected value of the asset.

To the extent that less informed bidders do actually participate, this participation is likely, if anything, to reduce the expected profits of the informed bidders. Thus, to the extent that less informed bidders do participate, the incentives to become an informed bidder, which are developed below, represent upper limits on such incentives.

It is natural to assume that the nth bidder will become informed if the incentive given by (1) exceeds his cost of becoming informed. Thus, bidders will become informed until

$$I(n^*+1) = \frac{\epsilon(n^*+1)}{n^*+1} V \leq C \tag{2}$$

$$\text{and} \quad I(n^*) = \frac{\epsilon(n^*)}{n^*} V \geq C$$

where n^* = equilibrium number of (informed) bidders

C = the cost of becoming informed, assumed for simplicity to be a constant.

Inequalities (2) are thus an equilibrium condition specifying the number of bidders n^*, for the situation in which all bidders have an equal opportunity to become informed. We note, in addition, that (2) implies upper and lower limits on the total expenditures to become informed, n^*C.

The upper limit is $\quad \epsilon(n^*) V \geq n^*C,$

and the lower limit is $\quad \dfrac{n^*\epsilon(n^*+1) V}{n^*+1} \leq n^*C.$

For simplicity we will usually assume that

$$n*C = \epsilon(n*)V \tag{3}$$

Thus, the total expenditure to become informed is assumed to be equal to the total profit to be shared among the $n*$ informed bidders, and this amount can be read from Table 13–1, for the case represented there. Finally, we also note that the costs of presale exploration are borne by the seller of the asset, through a reduction in the price received. Since the seller receives $(1 - \epsilon(n))V$, equation (3) indicates that the seller receives $V - nc = (1 - \epsilon(n))V$.

To conclude this section, we make four observations about presale exploration, based upon the models presented above. First, we have concluded that the total expenditure to become informed is approximately equal to the total gross profit to informed bidders, for the case where all bidders have an equal opportunity to become informed. However, for the case where only one bidder has access to superior information, he may spend much less than his total gross profit from superior information; yet his total gross profit is generally greater than the total profit in the equal access to information case. Thus, we conclude that there is *potentially* more expenditure on information when only one bidder has access to superior information, but we can be much less certain, a priori, about the amount that is actually spent in such a case. This amount can only be estimated by direct observation, rather than inferred from the number of bidders as is done in the equal access to information case.

Second, for the equal access case we observe that, *ceteris paribus*, less total expenditure as a percent of value is associated with greater numbers of bidders. This is true because the gross profit (= total expenditure) function, $\epsilon(n)$, can be assumed to have a negative first derivative. Not only is this a plausible assumption, but it is supported by the bidding models as well (see Table 13–1). However, we also note that the number of bidders tends to increase with the value of leases offered. Thus, in fact, leases with many bidders may have higher expenditures on information, because the values of these leases are higher.

Third, we observe that if the cost of information is low (C is small in equation (3)), then the equilibrium number of bidders will be higher, according to equation (3). Since a greater number of bidders implies less total expenditure on information, information expenditure would be reduced if the cost of information falls; and conversely, information expenditure would increase if the cost of information rises. What this means is that presale exploration techniques that provide good information at low cost are desirable, while techniques that provide good information at high cost are undesirable if the policy objective is to minimize presale exploration expenditure.

Last, we want to draw attention to the upper limit that the bidding process places on the amount of bidder expenditure which is justified in screening leases.

In the equal access to information case, this limit is 25 percent of lease value, or less, for two or more bidders; in the exclusive access case the limit is about 33 percent of lease value. These limits exist because the auction process will not allow a lease screener to capture all of any change in value resulting from screening. This is in contrast to the case of screening in the labor market. In that case, a worker who screens himself to show he is productive can capture all the resulting change in his wages, and there is no a priori reason why this change may not be a very substantial amount of his final wage.

Evaluating the Social benefits of Presale Exploration

The bidding models of the preceding section showed that the incentive to do presale exploration derives simply from the value of the asset being auctioned, and the possibility of developing more information about that value prior to the sale. It is of course possible that the information developed also is useful in other ways; for example, data that reveal the value of OCS leases may also be useful in the subsequent exploration program. However, this need not be true in order for the incentive to do presale exploration to exist. Thus, it is important to consider whether or not actual presale exploration does have real benefits, and whether or not the amount of presale exploration is optimal, given its benefits.

We can, in fact, identify some real benefits that could arise directly from presale exploration: presale exploration may reduce risks of lease acquisition, and if buyers are risk-averse, this provides a real benefit; presale exploration may produce information necessary in formulating or executing an exploration program. Finally, presale exploration may be the only feasible way of distributing leases to bidders who, because of lower costs or better exploration strategies, place the highest values on the leases.

Each of these potential real benefits in effect increases the value of leases at the time of their sale. Reduced risks, if firms are risk-averse, make leases more valuable; prior completion of a necessary step in exploring a lease makes the lease more valuable at the time of sale; and appropriate distribution of leases places each lease in the hands of a developer who can presumably realize the greatest value from development of the lease.

Another indirect kind of benefit could also arise from presale exploration, if such exploration led to a significant technological improvement in our ability to find oil and gas deposits. To the extent that the full benefits of such an innovation can't be captured by the innovator, the additional incentive to innovation provided by profit opportunities in presale exploration may be desirable.

We see, therefore, that presale exploration may have real benefits, and that the realization of such benefits can in most cases be thought of as increasing the value of the leases being sold. If it were true that the incentive for presale exploration derived from the change in lease value that results from presale exploration, then we could assume that the right amount of presale exploration might be induced. However, the incentive for presale exploration derives from the total value of leases, and this means that, a priori, we would expect the right amount of presale exploration to occur only by chance.

To illustrate some of the possibilities in the case of OCS leasing, we will present three very stylized models of presale exploration. These models use the equilibrium condition for number of bidders, which was presented in the preceding section: $V \epsilon(n^*) = n^*C$. For simplicity, we ignore the discrete nature of the number of bidders, n; and we retain the assumption that any potential bidder may become an informed bidder by performing an identical presale exploration program at fixed cost, C. We also retain the assumption that only informed bidders participate in the auction. Using this model, which determines actual presale exploration expenditure, we compare actual presale exploration to the optimal amount of expenditure, for three stylized assumptions about possible real benefits of presale exploration. The three models follow.

Case I—All Presale Exploration Is Wasteful. This is the simple case where the ultimate value of a lease does not depend in any way on presale exploration. The case might arise, for example, if holes are always drilled on leases in a known way, and the only uncertainty is that surrounding the amount of oil found by each hole. If lease buyers are risk-neutral there is no benefit to knowing, in advance of test drilling, the actual amount of oil contained in each lease. In such a case, all expenditure on presale exploration is wasteful. Thus, the social cost of presale screening would be n^*C in this case.

Since the cost of presale exploration is borne by the seller of the lease, any seller would be advised to prohibit presale exploration, if possible, in this case. The government, since it presumably is concerned about both its revenues and the total costs to society, should be doubly concerned in such a case.

Case II—Most Presale Exploration Is Wastefully Duplicative. This is the case where the real benefits of presale exploration justify its being done once, but duplication is completely wasteful. For example, the situation might be as outlined above, except that bidders are identically risk-averse. In this case the value of the lease to any potential bidder is increased by a risk premium δV if presale exploration reduces the variance of potential outcomes. Any individual bidder will be led to conduct presale exploration if his expected return from doing it, $\dfrac{\epsilon(n^*)(V + \delta V)}{n^*}$ is greater than the cost of presale exploration C.[d] However, since multiple presale exploration does not further reduce risks (by assumption

---

[d]In this case it is also possible that not enough presale exploration takes place. Neither the potential buyers nor the seller can capture the full benefit from reducing risk. The bidders collectively only receive a risk reducing benefit equal to $\epsilon(n^*)\delta V$, while the seller receives $(1 - \epsilon(n^*))(\delta V)$. Correct incentives concerning the socially optimal amount of presale exploration will obtain only if the costs are borne by all participants with the seller paying the bulk of the costs equal to $(1 - \epsilon(n^*))C$.

that presale exploration programs are identical), $(n^* - 1)$ presale explorations are wasteful.

Case II would also arise if buyers were risk neutral but a single presale exploration was necessary in formulating or executing an exploration strategy. Presale exploration then raises the value of the lease by the cost saving in exploration after the sale, which is just C. Thus, the net cost to society of presale exploration in this situation would be $(n^* - 1)C$.

Case III–Presale Exploration Is Productive. In this case we assume that presale exploration, even multiple presale exploration, is productive. This would be true if presale exploration distributed leases to buyers who placed highest values on them because of superior exploration strategies. This situation can be visualized, albeit in a stylized way, by considering the following story.

Assume that the quantity of oil to be discovered by each test well is known and fixed. However, there is only some probability–less than one–that each potential lease buyer will detect each possible test hole location. Thus, presale exploration might result in one buyer's seeing three test locations, another five test locations, and so on. Given these assumptions, the value of the lease is that corresponding to the maximum number of hole locations found by any bidder. The expected value of the lease therefore is a nondecreasing function of the number of bidders who screen the lease. Figure 13–1 illustrates this situation. $V(n)$ is the expected value of the lease as a function of the number of presale screeners. The socially optimal number of screeners is given by n^s, where $V'(n^s) = C$.

However, the number of screeners actually realized in the competitive auction is given by n^*, where

$$\frac{\epsilon(n^*) V(n^*)}{n^*} = C.$$

Figure 13–1. The Level of Presale Exploration: When Screening Is Socially Beneficial

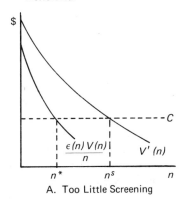

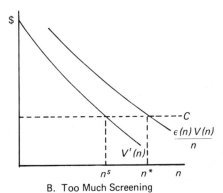

A. Too Little Screening

B. Too Much Screening

In this case the number of screeners will be determined by the ex ante expected value of the prospect. After screening a prospect will have a higher true value for some bidders than for others and therefore the bidding results presented in Table 13-1 are no longer directly applicable. The value of the prospect $V(n)$ cited above is always the prescreening expected value.

It is not possible to determine unambiguously whether

$$V'(n^*) \lessgtr \frac{\epsilon(n^*)V(n^*)}{n^*}$$

since $V'(n^*) < V(n^*)$, but $\dfrac{\epsilon(n^*)}{n^*}$ is always less than one. However, two possibilities can be specified. First, for small $\epsilon(n)$:

$$V'(n^*) > \frac{\epsilon(n^*)V(n^*)}{n^*},$$

and too little screening will take place. This is true because most of the value of screening, specifically $(1-\epsilon(n))V'(n)$, accrues to the seller. On the other hand, if $V'(n^*)$ is very small, then

$$V'(n^*) < \frac{\epsilon(n^*)V(n^*)}{n^*},$$

and screening will be excessive, since it has little real value.

It may be noted in this context that Case I and Case II above are instances where $V'(n) = 0$ for all n and where $V'(n) = 0$ for all n greater than 1. Thus, screening is excessive and wasteful in Case I, and screening is wasteful in Case II for any more than one bidder.

While the three models above are highly stylized, we believe that they do correspond to real possibilities that may arise in oil and gas leasing. For example, some anticlinal structures are relatively simple to identify, and exploration consists of little more than putting a few exploratory wells into the structures. This situation corresponds to Case I or Case II, and most presale exploration is probably wasteful in this situation. On the other hand, there are also much more complicated kinds of structures where it is not so obvious where or how deep to drill exploratory holes. Stratigraphic traps are an example of this kind of situation. Case III above partially describes these situations. The description is only partial because even where a major element of uncertainty is locating holes, the uncertainty surrounding the amount of oil at the bottom of each hole is always present. Thus, this situation is really a blend of Cases I and III. In general, we would expect this to be true; to some extent, any given oil and gas prospect will always contain elements of the whole range of possible cases discussed above.

Concluding Observations

In view of the above, what should be our policy toward presale exploration in federal lease sales? Specifically, if it were possible to prevent presale exploration, would this be a good idea? Unfortunately, we cannot offer any general prescription for policy toward presale exploration. However, we can make the following observations.

First, our analysis indicates that we cannot assume that the right amount of presale exploration will occur automatically. Thus, we are forced to look at the actual presale exploration that occurs, and to judge whether or not this presale exploration has real benefits which justify its costs. A useful way to approach this problem is to ask how much cost would be saved, and how much benefit sacrificed, if presale exploration were prevented. Viewed this way, we are led to the important observation that much presale exploration which has benefits in excess of its costs would be carried out as *postsale* exploration if it were prevented prior to the lease sale.

For example, presale exploration which is necessary in formulating an exploration strategy would be done after the sale, and it would be done only once, by the buyer of the lease. Similarly, it is possible that if multiple screening has benefits, as in Case III above, institutions would be developed to perform such multiple screenings by contract, for example, after the lease has been purchased. At worst, if the situation were as in Case III, leases could simply be resold in a subsequent auction in which presale exploration was not prevented. The only loss to society would be the delay associated with postsale multiple screening.

There is, however, an important exception to the conclusion that preventing presale exploration will have little or no ill effects. This exception arises from the possibility that risk reduction is one of the benefits of presale exploration. If this benefit exists, it can only be realized by making the value of leases less uncertain *before* the leases are sold. Only in this case is the risk (associated with the uncertain value) shifted to the government. Thus, the prevention of presale exploration would sacrifice any benefits of risk reduction that might have been gained from presale exploration. If, therefore, we admit the possibility that lease buyers may be significantly risk-averse, we are again forced to consider explicitly the costs and benefits of presale exploration, to determine whether or not such exploration is desirable.

IV. POLICY IMPLICATIONS

The preceding analysis has considered the problem of presale exploration primarily in terms of the social costs of allowing or preventing such exploration. We can briefly summarize the conclusions of that analysis:

1. Because the incentive for presale exploration depends only upon the value of leases, such exploration will occur whether or not it has real benefits.

2. However, we do recognize that there are potential real benefits of presale exploration.
3. We note that, with one exception, preventing presale exploration may not necessarily sacrifice the real benefits of such exploration, whereas it will prevent any waste arising from presale exploration.
4. A major exception is the real benefit of risk reduction. If this benefit is considered to be potentially significant, policy toward presale exploration should be guided by explicit consideration of the costs and real benefits of such exploration.

In considering policy implications we have to recognize that government policy is guided by two considerations. First, the government would like to eliminate any net social costs of presale exploration. Second, the government wants to maximize the return to the public from sale of OCS leases. Most of the time these objectives do not conflict. For the case of equal access to presale exploration opportunities, for example, we saw that the seller's return is simply the value of the lease, less total presale exploration costs. However, for the case where only one bidder has access to a presale exploration opportunity, a potential conflict of objectives exists. This would be the case if the government could somehow give all bidders access to the same opportunity. The result would be more competition, providing a higher return to the public; and more presale exploration, resulting in higher social costs.

Alternatively, the government might prevent the first bidder from exploiting his opportunity. This would also equalize information access, but it could either increase or decrease total expenditure on presale exploration, depending upon the new pattern of presale exploration which is induced. In considering particular kinds of presale exploration, therefore, we have to remain alert to the possibility of conflicts between minimizing net social costs and maximizing the public's return.

We now turn to a consideration of several particular kinds of presale exploration activities, and attempt to consider each with a view to its costs, potential real benefits, and effect on the public's return. Some of the activities are ones which presently are occurring: bright spot analysis (a geophysical technique), drilling of line holes, and off-structure stratigraphic test drilling. Two others are policies that might be implemented: on-structure stratigraphic drilling, and increasing the rate of leasing.

In considering ongoing private presale exploration activities, if it is possible to identify any of these as clearly wasteful, there are three policy instruments which may be applied: (1) prohibition of the presale activity; (2) mandatory public disclosure of data generated by the activities; and (3) direct data generation and public dissemination by the government.

Depending upon administrative feasibility in each case, the first and second policy instruments are logical tools to use to discourage presale activity that is primarily considered to be wasteful. On the other hand, where presale exploration has real benefits (e.g., because it reduces risks), or where unequal informational opportunities jeopardize the public's return, the government may want to become directly involved in data generation and dissemination, thereby replacing private presale exploration with public (and publicly available) presale exploration.

Bright Spot Analysis

Bright spot analysis is a relatively new geophysical technique that attempts to distinguish between the relative densities of subterranean strata. Because gas-filled rock is less dense than oil-filled rock, which in turn is less dense than water-saturated strata, an indication of lower density strata suggests the presence of hydrocarbons. The principal way that bright spot analysis affects presale evaluations of OCS tracts is to increase the probability that a given prospect contains gas and/or oil if the technique gives a positive indication (a bright spot). Unfortunately, a negative indication provides less information and typically will not condemn an otherwise favorable structure. It appears that bright spot analysis primarily provides information about the value of a promising prospect without affecting subsequent drilling decisions.

On the other hand, bright spot analysis is also applied to less promising areas. A bright spot on otherwise unattractive prospects may lead to additional holes being drilled as well as positive bids. There have been cases where bright spot analysis has been applied to already owned land before exploratory drilling. Bright spot analysis clearly has some real benefits in developing certain leases. Bright spot techniques are relatively inexpensive and are available to all potential bidders. The Geological Survey recently purchased bright spot analysis for approximately $500 for a 5,280 acre tract.

According to the bidding model previously discussed, we should anticipate that the loss in public return and the social cost of these geophysical techniques are therefore relatively small even when they are applied to the most promising prospects. Further, the application of bright spot analysis could lead to significant technological improvement in our ability to find oil and gas deposits. The application of bright spot analysis (or succeeding geophysical techniques) results in profits to the developers of these techniques. If potential innovators are otherwise unable to capture the full social value of new geophysical techniques, the "wasteful" application of these techniques to promising prospects could be socially beneficial. Our tentative conclusion is that while there are surely instances of socially wasteful use of bright spot techniques, no clear case can be made for any restrictive policy toward their use.

Line Holes

Line holes offer a significant contrast with bright spot techniques. Line holes are expensive, costing from $1 to $10 million, and typically can be drilled by only one or two potential bidders. Line holes, moreover, are certainly not likely to add anything to the technology of finding oil and gas that would not be added anyway by other kinds of exploratory or development drilling. Finally, while line holes may provide information useful in subsequent exploration, this information is certain to be inferior to that which would have been provided by a first well drilled after the sale in the optimum location on the previously unleased tract. About the only conceivable benefit from line hole drilling is a reduction of risk regarding the value of the unleased tract.

On balance, line holes appear to be a clearly undesirable form of presale expenditure. What then is the best policy instrument for preventing expenditures on line holes? A simple prohibition on line hole drilling would be difficult to enforce because it would be hard to establish when a hole has been drilled to gain information about an unleased tract. An ongoing program of government drilling with public data release may have some merit as a way of eliminating the incentive for line hole drilling (see on-structure stratigraphic drilling below). However, probably the most effective way to eliminate line hole drilling is required public disclosure of any data so obtained. But since it is extremely difficult to tell a line hole from any other hole, data disclosure would necessarily have to cover data from all holes in order to be effective.

This could raise other problems, though it is not clear how important they might be. One potential problem with requiring the disclosure of line hole data is that socially valuable information about neighboring tracts will no longer be owned by the driller. There may be instances of holes not being drilled even though the net social benefits of drilling exceed the costs under full disclosure of geologic data. It is also true that disclosure may be neither complete or timely. For example, a requirement to disclose data within 30 days may result in a spate of holes just prior to a lease sale.

Off-Structure Stratigraphic Tests

In many ways, off-structure stratigraphic test drilling is like drilling line holes. The stratigraphic tests are expensive—$1 to $10 million. They may help identify well locations, but they are inferior for this purpose to the first test well drilled after the sale in the optimum location (usually on-structure). Stratigraphic tests are unlikely to lead to any innovations in oil and gas finding technology. Finally, like line holes, the main potential real benefit of a stratigraphic test would be a reduction of uncertainty about the value of leases.

There is an important difference, however, between line holes and stratigraphic tests. The information gained from a stratigraphic test is readily available to all potential bidders. This means that drilling of a stratigraphic test tends to equalize information gathering opportunities, rather than being a way of exploiting differing opportunities as is the case with line holes. This aspect of stratigraphic tests has benefits from the point of view of the government, since its revenues will likely go up if information is equalized. Moreover, there could even be real resource benefits from this aspect of stratigraphic tests. By equalizing information gathering opportunities, stratigraphic test drilling might reduce the incentives for wasteful exploitation of differing opportunities. For example, if line holes were permitted by regulations, drilling of a few stratigraphic tests might lead to a reduction in the number of line holes drilled. There would be a net gain, as a result, so long as the number of stratigraphic holes drilled was smaller than the number of line holes prevented. Of course, it would probably be much cheaper simply to prevent line holes through a disclosure policy.

Off-structure stratigraphic testing is a difficult case to decide. It is certainly not clear that the real benefits of the program justify its costs. Therefore, increased rent to the government may be the main benefit of the program. Since we do not know the appropriate trade-off between government rent and present value of the resource, we will simply suspend judgment regarding off-structure stratigraphic testing, and move on to consider on-structure stratigraphic testing. With regard to on-structure testing, it is much easier to be unequivocal.

On-Structure Stratigraphic Tests

Stratigraphic tests drilled on-structure have the same characteristics as stratigraphic tests drilled off-structure, except in one all-important respect. If a stratigraphic test can be drilled at a location where a hole would in any event be drilled after the sale, there is no net cost of drilling the test before the sale. Thus a stratigraphic testing program need have no incremental costs if tests are drilled on-structure on a few selected sites where drilling is definitely expected after the sale. It is argued, however, that on-structure holes provide somewhat inferior stratigraphic information because strata sections are deformed by the existence of a geologic structure. Our recommendation is subject to the proviso that any such degradation in stratigraphic information is not serious.

If an on-structure stratigraphic test program can be essentially costless, then any benefits from risk reduction or prevented line hole activity are net gains to society. In addition, increased rent to the government can be achieved at no cost in terms of sacrificed present value of the resource. Thus, this is an additional clear benefit, regardless of the appropriate trade-off between government rent and present value of the resource.

In endorsing a program of on-structure stratigraphic testing, we want to emphasize two cautionary notes. First, the stratigraphic tests must be drilled only where holes would be drilled after the sale anyway. This probably means that the program should be limited to a few holes. The more holes that are drilled, the more likely it is that drilling will occur on prospects that would not necessarily be drilled after the sale. Second, it should be noted that even an on-structure stratigraphic testing program would not be costless if it led to delays in actual leasing. If delays did result, the testing program would be costless only if holes were drilled in the same placed *and at the same times* as they would have been drilled in the absence of the program.

While it is of course possible in principle to operate such a program, it seems very questionable that it would really turn out this way. Therefore, delays imposed by an on-structure stratigraphic drilling program would likely mean that the program would have costs. If so, these costs would have to be balanced against any real benefits of the program, and against any increase in government rent from the resource.

Increasing the Rate of Leasing

As the federal government's leasing program moves into frontier areas, it is sometimes suggested that a go-slow approach is desirable in order to develop more information about the area prior to any sales. While this might be a good suggestion insofar as environmental data are concerned, it is probably a bad idea in terms of oil and gas resources data.

If all potential bidders were equally uninformed about frontier area resource values, a rapid rate of leasing would minimize the opportunities to do presale exploration. To the extent that such exploration has net costs, therefore, a rapid leasing rate would reduce presale expenditures and thereby increase the public's return from the resource.

On the other hand, if some bidders now have an informational advantage which could be narrowed by a go-slow approach to allow others to catch up, then the conclusion would be somewhat different. A rapid rate of leasing would still minimize net costs of presale exploration. However, it might also result in lower returns to the public since sales would be less competitive. In this case, policy makers would again be faced with the difficult trade-off between social costs and the public's return.

References

CHAPTER ONE

Adelman, Morris A. *A&P: Price-Cost Behavior and Public Policy.* Cambridge, Mass.: Harvard University Press, 1959.

Bain, Joe S. *Barriers to New Competition.* Cambridge, Mass.: Harvard University Press, 1956.

Bain, Joe S. *Essays on Price Theory and Industrial Organization.* Boston: Little, Brown, 1972.

Bain, Joe S. *Industrial Organization,* 2nd ed. New York: John Wiley, 1968.

Bain, Joe S. *International Differences in Industrial Structure.* New Haven: Yale University Press, 1966.

Bain, Joe S. *Pricing, Distribution and Employment.* New York: Holt, Rinehart and Winston, 1948.

Bain, Joe S. *The Economics of the Pacific Coast Petroleum Industry.* Berkeley: University of California Press, 1945.

Baumol, W.J. *Business Behavior Value and Growth.* New York: Harcourt Brace Jovanovich, 1959.

Bullock, Charles J. "Trust Literature: A Survey and a Criticism." *Quarterly Journal of Economics* (February 1901): 167–217.

Caves, Richard E. *Air Transport and Its Regulators.* Cambridge, Mass.: Harvard University Press, 1962.

Chamberlin, E.H. (Ed.). *Monopoly and Competition and Their Regulators.* London: Macmillan, 1954.

Chamberlin, Edward H. *The Theory of Monopolistic Competition.* Cambridge, Mass.: Harvard University Press, 1933 (8th ed., 1962).

Clark, John Bates. *Essentials of Economic Theory.* New York: Macmillan, 1907.

Clark, John Maurice. *Economics of Overhead Costs.* Chicago: University of Chicago Press, 1923.

Edgeworth, F.Y. *Papers Relating to Political Economy.* London: Royal Economic Society, 1925.

Fellner, William J. *Competition Among The Few.* New York: Alfred Knopf, 1949.

Florence, P. Sargent *The Logic of Industrial Organization.* London: Routledge and Kegan Paul, 1933.

Georgescu-Roegen, Nicholas. "Chamberlin's New Economics and the Unit of Production." In *Monopolistic Competition Theory: Studies in Impact.* Robert E. Kuenne (Ed.). New York: John Wiley, 1967.

Goldschmid, Harvey J., H. Michael Mann, and J. Fred Weston (Eds.). *Industrial Concentration: The New Learning.* Boston: Little, Brown, 1974.

Kaysen, Carl. *U.S. v. United Shoe Machinery Corporation.* Cambridge, Mass.: Harvard University Press, 1956.

Kaysen, Carl and Donald F. Turner. *Antitrust Policy: An Economic and Legal Analysis.* Cambridge, Mass.: Harvard University Press, 1959.

Kuenne, Robert E. (Ed.). *Monopolistic Competition Theory: Studies in Impact.* New York: John Wiley, 1967.

Loescher, Samuel M. *Imperfect Collusion in the Cement Industry.* Cambridge, Mass.: Harvard University Press, 1959.

Markham, Jesse W. *Competition in the Rayon Industry.* Cambridge, Mass.: Harvard University Press, 1952.

Markham, Jesse W. and Gustav E. Papanek (Eds.). *Industrial Organization and Economic Development: in Honor of E.S. Mason.* Boston: Houghton Mifflin, 1970.

Marshall, Alfred. *Principles of Economics.* London: Macmillan, 1890.

Mason, E.S. "The New Competition." *The Yale Review* (Autumn 1953). Reprinted in *Economic Concentration and the Monopoly Problem.* E.S. Mason (Ed.). Cambridge, Mass.: Harvard University Press, 1957.

McKie, James W. *Tin Cans and Tin Plate.* Cambridge, Mass.: Harvard University Press, 1959.

Modigliani, Franco. "New Developments on the Oligopoly Front." *Journal of Political Economy* (June 1958): 215–252.

Moody, John. *The Truth About the Trusts.* New York: Moody, 1904.

Peck, Merton, J. *Competition in the Aluminum Industry, 1945–1958.* Cambridge, Mass.: Harvard University Press, 1961.

Phillips, Almarin and Rodney E. Stevenson. "The Historical Development of Industrial Organization." *History of Political Economy* (Fall 1974): 324–342.

Ripley, William Z. (Ed.). *Trusts, Pools, and Corporations.* Rev. ed. New York: Ginn and Co., 1916.

Robinson, E.A.G. *The Structure of Competitive Industry.* (1958 rev. ed.). Chicago: University of Chicago Press, 1935.

Robinson, Joan. *The Economics of Imperfect Competition.* London: Macmillan, 1933.

Scherer, F.M., *Industrial Market Structure and Economic Performance.* Skokie, Ill.: Rand McNally, 1970.

Scherer, F.M. Alan Beckenstein, Eric Kaufer, and R. Dennis Murphy. *The Eco-

nomics of Multiplant Operation: An International Comparisons Study. Cambridge, Mass.: Harvard University Press, 1976.

Shepherd, W.G. *Market Power and Economic Welfare.* New York: Random House, 1970.

Shepherd, W.G. "The Elements of Market Structure." *Review of Economics and Statistics* (February 1972): 25–37.

Shepherd, W.G. *The Treatment of Market Power.* New York: Columbia University Press, 1975.

Shepherd, W.G. "What Does the Survivor Test Show About Economies of Scale?" *Southern Economic Journal* (July 1967): 113–122.

Stigler, G.J. *Five Lectures on Economic Problems.* London: Macmillan, 1950.

Stigler, G.J. (Ed.). *Business Concentration and Price Policy.* Princeton: Princeton University Press, 1955.

Stigler, G.J. and K.E. Boulding (Eds.). *Readings in Price Theory.* Homewood, Ill.: Irwin, 1952.

von Newmann, John and Oskar Morgenstern. *Theory of Games and Economic Behavior.* Princeton: Princeton University Press, 1944.

Weiss, Leonard W. "Econometric Studies of Industrial Organization." In *Frontiers of Quantitative Economics.* M. Intriligator (Ed.). Amsterdam: North-Holland, 1971.

Williamson, Oliver E. *The Economics of Discretionary Behavior.* Englewood, Cliffs, N.J.: Prentice-Hall, 1964.

Whitney, Simon N. *"Antitrust Policies: American Experience in Twenty Industries.* New York: Twentieth Century Fund, 1958.

CHAPTER TWO

Adelman, Irma and Cynthia Taft Morris. *Society, Politics and Economic Development.* Baltimore: Johns Hopkins Press, 1967.

Averitt, Robert T. *The Dual Economy.* New York: W.W. Norton, 1968.

Bain, Joe S. "Technostructure, Revised Sequences, and the Locus of Power." In *Essays on Price Theory and Industrial Organization.* Boston: Little, Brown, 1972.

Berle, Alolf A. and Gardiner C. Means. *The Modern Corporation and Private Property.* New York: Macmillan, 1932.

Boeke, J.H. *Economics and Economic Policy of Dual Societies as Exemplified by Indonesia.* New York: International Secretariat, Institute of Pacific Relations, 1953.

Boulding, K.E. *The Organizational Revolution.* New York: Harper 1953.

Bowen, Francis. *Principles of Political Economy.* Boston: Little, Brown, 1855.

Caves, Richard E. "Uncertainty, Market Structure and Performance: Galbraith as Conventional Wisdom." In Markham and Papanek (1970).

———. *American Industry: Structure, Conduct, Performance.* Englewood Cliffs, N.J.: Prentice-Hall, 1973.

Chandler, Alfred D. *Strategy and Structure: Chapters in the History of Industrial Enterprise.* Cambridge, Mass.: MIT Press, 1962.

Furnivall, J.S. *Colonial Policy and Practice.* Issued in cooperation with the International Secretariat, Institute of Pacific Relations, Cambridge, England, 1948.

Galbraith, J.K. *The New Industrial State.* Boston: Houghton Mifflin, 1967.

_____ . "Professor Scott and the Close of the Galbraithian System." *Journal of Political Economy* (July/August 1969).

_____ . *Economics and the Public Purpose.* Boston: Houghton Mifflin, 1973.

Gordon, R.A. *Business Leadership in the Large Corporation.* Washington, D.C.: The Brookings Institution, 1945.

Hession, Charles H. *John Kenneth Galbraith and His Critics.* New York: New American Library, 1972.

Jacquemin, Alex P. "Market Structure and the Firm's Market Power." *Journal of Industrial Economics* (April 1972).

Jewkes, John, David Sawyers, and Richard Stillerman. *The Sources of Invention.* 2d ed. London: Macmillan, 1969.

Kaysen, Carl, and Donald F. Turner. *Antitrust Policy: An Economic and Legal Analysis.* Cambridge, Mass.: Harvard University Press, 1959.

Kennedy, C. and A.P. Thirwell. "Surveys in Applied Economics: Technical Progress." *Economic Journal* (March 1972).

Lewellen, W.G. and B. Huntsman. "Managerial Pay and Corporate Performance." *American Economic Review* (September 1970).

Lindbeck, Assar. *The Political Economy of the New Left.* New York: Harper and Row, 1971.

Lintner, John. "The Impact of Uncertainty in the 'Traditional' Theory of the Firm." In Markham and Papanek (1970).

Mansfield, Edwin, *Industrial Research and Technological Innovation.* New York: W.W. Norton, 1968.

Markham, Jesse W. and Gustav F. Papanek (Eds.). *Industrial Organization and Economic Development: in Honor of E.S. Mason.* Boston: Houghton Mifflin, 1970.

Mason, E.S. "The Apologetics of Managerialism." *Journal of Business* (January 1958).

Meade, James E. "Is the Industrial State Inevitable?" *Economic Journal* (June 1968).

Nelson, Richard, Merton J. Peck, and Edward D. Kalachek. *Technology, Economic Growth, and Public Policy.* Santa Monica, Calif.: The Rand Corporation, 1967.

Phillips, Almarin. "Structure, Conduct and Performance—and Performance, Conduct and Structure." In Markham and Papanek (1970).

Scherer, F.M. "Market Structure, Opportunity, and the Output of Patented Inventions." *American Economic Review* (December 1965).

_____ . *Industrial Market Structure and Economic Performance.* Chicago: Rand McNally, 1970.

Schmookler, Jacob. "Bigness, Fewness, and Research." *Journal of Political Economy* (December 1959).

Schumpeter, Joseph A. *Business Cycles.* New York: McGraw-Hill, 1939.

Scott, Gordon. "The Close of the Galbraithian System." *Journal of Political Economy* (July/August 1968).

Seers, Dudley. "The Limitations of the Special Case." Bulletin of the Oxford Institute of Economics and Statistics (May 1963).

Sharpe, Myron E. *John Kenneth Galbraith and the Lower Economics.* White Plains, N.Y.: International Arts and Sciences Press, 1972.

Simon, H.A. "Theories of Decision Making in Economics." *American Economic Review* (June 1959).

Solow, Robert M. "Some Implications of Alternate Criteria for the Firm." In *The Corporate Economy.* R. Marris and A. Wood (Eds.). Cambridge, Mass.: Harvard University Press, 1971.

SubCommittee on Financial Markets of the U.S. Senate Committee on Finance, 93rd Congress, 1973.

Thompson, Arthur A., Jr. *Economics of the Firm: Theory and Practice.* Englewood Cliffs, N.J.: Prentice-Hall, 1973.

Vernon, Raymond. "Organization as a Scale Factor in the Growth of Firms." In Markham and Papanek (1970).

Weston, J. Fred. "Pricing Behavior of Large Firms." In *The Impact of the Large Firm on the U.S. Economy.* J.F. Weston and S.I. Ornstein (Eds.). Lexington, Mass.: D.C. Heath, 1973.

Williamson, Oliver E. *Corporate Control and Business Behavior.* Englewood Cliffs, N.J.: Prentice-Hall, 1970.

――――. "Managerial Discretion, Organizational Form and the Multidivision Hypothesis." In *The Corporate Economy.* R. Marris and A. Wood (Eds.). Cambridge, Mass.: Harvard University Press, 1971.

Winter, Sidney G. "Satisficing, Selection and the Innovating Remnant." *Quarterly Journal of Economics* (May 1971).

CHAPTER THREE

Akerlof, G.A. "The Market for 'Lemons': Qualitative Uncertainty and the Market Mechanism." *Quarterly Journal of Economics* (August 1970): 488–500.

Alderfer, E.B. and H.E. Michl. *Economics of American Industry.* 2d ed. New York: McGraw-Hill, 1950.

Bain, J.S. *Barriers to New Competition.* Cambridge, Mass.: Harvard University Press, 1956.

Bettauer, A. "Strategy for Divestments." *Harvard Business Review* (March/April 1967): 116–124.

Business Week, August 15, 1970, p. 86.

Buzzell, R.D., B.T. Gale, and R.G.M. Sultan. "Market Share—A Key to Profitability." *Harvard Business Review* (January/February 1975): 97–107.

Caves, R.E. *Diversification, Foreign Investment, and Scale in North American Manufacturing Industries.* Ottawa: Economic Council of Canada, 1975.

Caves, R.E. and M.E. Porter. "From Entry Barriers to Mobility Barriers: Conjectural Decisions and Contrived Deterrence to New Competition." Harvard Institute of Economic Research, Discussion Paper No. 401, 1975.

Comanor, W.S. and T.A. Wilson. "On Advertising and Profitability." *Review of Economics and Statistics* (November 1971):408–410.

Conrad, G.R. and I.H. Plotkin. "Risk/Return: U.S. Industry Pattern." *Harvard Business Review* (March/April 1968):90–99.

Esposito, F.F. and L. Esposito. "Excess Capacity and Market Structure." *Review of Economics and Statistics* (May 1974):188–194.

Fisher, W.E. and C.M. James. *Minimum Price Fixing in the Bituminous Coal Industry.* National Bureau of Economic Research, Conference on Price Research, Price Studies, No. 5. Princeton: Princeton University Press, 1955.

Gilmour, S.S. "The Divestment Decision Process." D.B.A. dissertation. Graduate School of Business Administration, Harvard University, 1973.

Goldberger, A.S. *Econometric Theory.* New York: John Wiley, 1964.

Hay, G.A. and D. Kelley. "An Empirical Survey of Price Fixing Conspiracies." *Journal of Law and Economics* (April 1974):13–38.

Hayes, R. "Optimal Strategies for Divestiture." *Operations Research* (March/April 1969):292–310.

_____. "New Emphasis on Divestment Opportunities." *Harvard Business Review* (July/August 1972):55–64.

Hendry, J.B. "The Bituminous Coal Industry." In *The Structure of American Industry.* W. Adams (Ed.). 3d ed. New York: Macmillan, 1961.

Hillman, R.N. "How to Redeploy Assets." *Harvard Business Review* (November/December 1971):95–103.

Hilton, P. "Divestiture: the Strategic Move on the Corporate Chessboard." *Management Review* (March 1972):16–19.

Hindley, B. "Separation of Ownership and Control in the Modern Corporation." *Journal of Law and Economics* (April 1970):185–222.

Hoffman, A.C. *Large Scale Organization in the Food Industries.* U.S. Temporary National Economic Commission, Monograph No. 35. Washington, D.C.: U.S. Government Printing Office, 1940.

Lamfalussy, A. *Investment and Growth in Mature Economies: The Case of Belgium.* London: Macmillan, 1961.

Lovejoy, F.A. *Divestment for Profit.* New York: Financial Executives Research Foundation, 1971.

McGugan, V.J. and R.E. Caves. "Integration and Competition in the Equipment Leasing Industry." *Journal of Business* (July 1974):382–396.

Marcus, M. "Firms' Exit Rates and Their Determinants." *Journal of Industrial Economics* (November 1967):10–22.

Monsen, R.J. and A. Downs. "A Theory of Large Managerial Firms." *Journal of Political Economy* (June 1965):221–236.

Orr, D. "The Determinants of Entry: A Study of the Canadian Manufacturing Industries." *Review of Economics and Statistics* (February 1974):59–66.

Palmer, J. "The Profit-Performance Effects of the Separation of Ownership from Control in Large U.S. Industrial Corporations." *Bell Journal of Economics and Management Science* (Spring 1973):293–303.

Porter, M.E. "Please Note Location of Nearest Exit: Exit Barriers and Strategic and Organizational Planning." Harvard Business School, Working Paper 75–30, BP–7, September 1975.

Reynolds, L.G. "Cutthroat Competition." *American Economic Review* (September 1940):736–747.

Scherer, F.M. *Industrial Market Structure and Economic Performance*. Chicago: Rand McNally, 1970.

Shepherd, W.G. "Trends of Concentration in American Manufacturing Industries, 1947–1958." *Review of Economics and Statistics* (May 1964):200–212.

Sherman, R. and R. Tollison. "Advertising and Profitability." *Review of Economics and Statistics* (November 1971):397–407.

_____. "Technology, Profit, and Market Performance." *Quarterly Journal of Economics* (August 1972):448–462.

Stigler, G.J. "A Theory of Oligopoly." *Journal of Political Economy* (February 1964):44–61.

Watson, P.L. "Choice of Estimation Procedure for Models of Binary Choice." *Regional and Urban Economics* (October 1974):187–200.

Williamson, O.E. "Managerial Discretion and Business Behavior." *American Economic Review* (December 1973):1032–1057.

Yamey, B.S. "Notes on Secret Price-Cutting in Oligopoly." In *Studies in Economics and Economic History: Essays in Honour of Professor H.M. Robertson*. Marcelle Kooy (Ed.). London: Macmillan, 1973.

CHAPTER FOUR

Bain, Joe S. "Relation of Profit Rate to Industrial Concentration: American Manufacturing, 1936–1940." *Quarterly Journal of Economics* (August 1951):293–324.

_____. *Barriers to New Competition*. Cambridge, Mass.: Harvard University Press, 1956.

Bothwell, James L. "Profits, Market Structure, and Portfolio Risk." Ph.D. Dissertation, University of California, Berkeley, 1976.

Brozen, Yale. "Bain's Concentration and Rates of Return Revisited." *Journal of Law and Economics* (October 1971):351–369.

Brennan, M. "Investor Taxes, Market Equilibrium, and Corporate Finance." Ph.D. Dissertation, M.I.T., June 1970.

Cootner, P. and D. Holland. "Rate of Return and Business Risk." *Bell Journal of Economics and Management Science* (Fall 1970): 211–226.

Demsetz, H. "Industry Structure, Market Rivalry, and Public Policy." *The Journal of Law and Economics* (April 1973):1–10.

_____. "Two Systems of Belief about Monopoly." In *Industrial Concentration: The New Learning*. H. Goldschmid, H. Mann, and J. Weston (Eds.). Boston: Little, Brown, 1974.

Fama, E. "Multiperiod Consumption-Investment Decisions." *American Economic Review* (March 1970):163–174.

Fisher, L. and G. Hall. "Risk and Corporate Rates of Return." *Quarterly Journal of Economics* (February 1969):79–92.

Fisher, L. and J. Lorie. "Rates of Return on Investments in Common Stocks." *Journal of Business* (January 1964):1–21.

Gale, B. "Market Share and Rate of Return." *Review of Economics and Statistics* (November 1972):412–423.

Hall, M. and L. Weiss. "Firm Size and Profitability." *Review of Economics and Statistics* (August 1967):319–331.

Jenson, M. "Capital Markets: Theory and Evidence." *Bell Journal of Economics and Management Science* (Autumn 1972):357–398.

Lerner, A. "The Concept of Monopoly and the Measurement of Monopoly Power." *Review of Economic Studies* (June 1934):157–175.

Lintner, J. "Security Prices, Risk, and Maximal Gains from Diversification." *Journal of Finance* (December 1965):587–616.

Litzenberger, R. and O. Joy. "Interindustry Profitability Under Uncertainty." *Western Economic Journal* (September 1973):338–349.

Mancke, R. "Interfirm Profitability Differences." *Quarterly Journal of Economics* (May 1974):181–194.

Mann, H. "Seller Concentration, Barriers to Entry, and Rates of Return in Thirty Industries, 1950–1960." *Review of Economics and Statistics* (August 1966):296–307.

Markowitz, H. *Portfolio Selections: Efficient Diversification of Investments.* New York: John Wiley, 1959.

Miller, M. and M. Scholes. "Rates of Return in Relation to Risk: a Reexamination of Some Recent Findings." In *Studies in the Theory of Capital Markets.* M.C. Jensen (Ed.). New York: Praeger, 1972.

Palmer, J. "The Profit-Performance Effects of the Separation of Ownership from Control in Large U.S. Industrial Corporations." *Bell Journal of Economics and Management Science* (Spring 1973):293–303.

Qualls, D. "Concentration, Barriers to Entry, and Long Run Economic Profit Margins." *Journal of Industrial Economics* (April 1972):146–168.

――――. "Stability and Persistence of Economic Profit Margins in Highly Concentrated Industries." *Southern Economic Journal* (April 1974):604–612.

Schumpeter, J. *Capitalism, Socialism, and Democracy.* New York: Harper and Row, 1947.

Sharpe, W. "Capital Asset Prices: A Theory of Market Equilibrium Under Conditions of Risk." *Journal of Finance* (September 1964):425–442.

Shepherd, W. "The Elements of Market Structure." *Review of Economics and Statistics* (February 1972):25–38.

Stigler, G. *Capital and Rates of Return in Manufacturing Industries.* Princeton: Princeton University Press, 1963.

Theil, H. *Principles of Econometrics.* New York: John Wiley, 1971.

U.S. Senate Subcommittee on Antitrust and Monopoly, "Profits and Concentration in the Drug Industry." Reprinted in E. Mansfield. *Microeconomics: Selected Readings.* New York: W.W. Norton, 1975.

Weiss, L. "The Concentration-Profits Relationship and Antitrust." In *Industrial Concentration: The New Learning.* H. Goldschmid, H. Mann, and J. Weston (Eds.). Boston: Little, Brown, 1974.

CHAPTER FIVE

Bain, J. *Barriers to New Competition.* Cambridge, Mass.: Harvard University Press, 1956.

_____. "Relation of Profit Rate to Industry Concentration: American Manufacturing, 1936–1940." *Quarterly Journal of Economics* (August 1951): 293–324.

Berle, A. and G. Means. *The Modern Corporation and Private Property.* New York: Macmillan, 1932.

Kamerschen, D. "The Influence of Ownership and Control on Profit Rates." *The American Economic Review* (June 1968):432–447.

Kmenta, J. *Elements of Econometrics.* New York: Macmillan, 1971.

Larner R. *Management Control and the Large Corporation.* New York: Dunellen, 1970.

Lerner, A. "The Concept of Monopoly and the Measurement of Monopoly Power." *Review of Economic Studies* (June 1934):157–175.

Lewellen, W. *The Ownership Income of Management.* New York: Columbia University Press, 1971.

Mann, H. "Seller Concentration, Barriers to Entry, and Rates of Return in Thirty Industries, 1950–1960." *Review of Economics and Statistics* (August 1966):296–307.

Masson, R. "Executive Motivations, Earnings, and Consequent Equity Performance." *Journal of Political Economy* (November–December 1971):1278–1292.

Monsen, R., J. Chiu and D. Cooley. "The Effect of Separation of Ownership and Control on the Performance of the Large Firm." *Quarterly Journal of Economics* (August 1968):435–451.

Palmer, J. "The Profit-Performance Effects of the Separation of Ownership From Control in Large U.S. Industrial Corporations." *The Bell Journal of Economics and Management Science* (Spring 1973):293–303.

Qualls, D. "Concentration, Barriers to Entry and Long Run Economic Profit Margins." *The Journal of Industrial Economics* (April 1972):146–158.

_____. "Stability and Persistence of Economic Profit Margins in Highly Concentrated Industries." *Southern Economic Journal* (April 1974):604–612.

Scherer, F. *Industrial Market Structure and Economic Performance.* Chicago: Rand McNally, 1970.

Shepherd, W. *Market Power and Economic Welfare.* New York: Random House, 1970.

_____. "The Elements of Market Structure." *Review of Economics and Statistics* (February 1972):25–37.

Weiss, L. "Quantitative Studies of Industrial Organization." In *Frontiers of Quantitative Economics.* Michael D. Intrilagator (Ed.). Amsterdam: North-Holland, 1971.

_____. "The Concentration-Profits Relationship and Antitrust." In *Industrial Concentration: The New Learning.* H. Goldschmid, H. Mann, and J. Weston (Eds.). Boston: Little, Brown, 1974.

CHAPTER SIX

Alexander, Kenneth. "Strikes in Manufacturing, 1947–57." *Quarterly Journal of Economics* (February 1962):122–144.

Bain, Joe S. *Barriers to New Competition.* Cambridge, Mass.: Harvard University Press, 1956.

Blauner, Robert. *Alienation and Freedom: The Factory Worker and His Job.* Chicago: University of Chicago Press, 1964.

Brogan, Robert D. and Edward W. Erickson. "Capital-Skill Complementarity and Labor Earnings." *Southern Economic Journal* (July 1975):83–88.

Burton, John F., Jr. and John E. Parker. "Interindustry Variations in Voluntary Labor Mobility." *Industrial and Labor Relations Review* (January 1969): 199–216.

Eisele, C.F. "Organization Size, Technology, and Frequency of Strikes." *Industrial and Labor Relations Review* (July 1974):560–571.

Indik, Bernard P. "Organization Size and Member Participation." *Human Relations* (1965, No. 4):339–350.

Porter, Lyman W. and Edward E. Lawler III. "Properties of Organization Structure in Relation to Job Attitudes and Job Behavior." *Psychological Bulletin* (1965, No. 1):23–51.

Quinn, Robert P., Graham L. Staines, and Margaret R. McCullough. *Job Satisfaction: Is There a Trend?* Manpower Research Monograph No. 30. Washington, D.C.: U.S. Department of Labor, 1974.

Quinn, Robert P. and Thomas W. Mangione (Eds.). *The 1969–1970 Survey of Working Conditions.* Ann Arbor: University of Michigan Survey Research Center, 1973.

Scherer, F.M. "The Technological Bases of Plant Scale Economies in Twelve Manufacturing Industries." International Institute of Management Preprint I/74–6. Berlin: February 1974.

Scherer, F.M., Alan Beckenstein, Erich Kaufer, and R. Dennis Murphy. *The Economics of Multi-Plant Operation: An International Comparisons Study.* Cambridge, Mass.: Harvard University Press, 1975.

Shorey, John. "The Size of the Work Unit and Strike Incidence." *Journal of Industrial Economics* (March 1975):175–188.

Terkel, Studs. *Working.* New York: Pantheon, 1974.

Thomas, Edwin J. and Clinton F. Fink. "Effects of Group Size." *Psychological Bulletin* (1963, No. 4):371–384.

U.S. Bureau of the Census. *1967 Census of Manufactures.* "Size of Establishments." Washington, D.C., MC67 (1)–2, December 1970.

U.S. Bureau of the Census. *1967 Census of Business.* Vol. I, "Retail Trade–Subject Reports." Washington, D.C., 1971.

U.S. Bureau of the Census. *Thirteenth Census of the United States.* Vol. VIII, "Manufactures." Washington, D.C., 1913).

CHAPTER SEVEN

Bain, Joe S. *Barriers to New Competition.* Cambridge, Mass.: Harvard University Press, 1956.

Bain, Joe S. *International Differences in Industrial Structures.* New Haven: Yale University Press, 1966.

Bain, Joe S. *Industrial Organization.* 2d. ed. New York: John Wiley, 1968.

Brock, Gerald W. *The U.S. Computer Industry*. Cambridge, Mass.: Ballinger, 1975.

Comanor, W. and T. Wilson. "Advertising, Market Structure and Performance." *Review of Economics and Statistics* (November 1967).

Mohring, H. and H.F. Williamson, Jr. "Scale and 'Industrial Reorganization' Economies of Transport Improvements." *Journal of Transport Economics and Policy* (September 1969).

Ornstein, S. "Concentration and Profits." In J.F. Weston and S. Ornstein (Eds.). *The Impact of Large Firms on the U.S. Economy*. Lexington, Mass.: Lexington Books, 1973.

Pratten, C.F. *Economies of Scale in Manufacturing Industry*. Cambridge: Cambridge University Press, 1971.

Scherer, F.M. "The Determinants of Industry Plant Sizes in Six Nations," *Review of Economics and Statistics*, May 1973.

Scherer, F.M., "Economies of Scale and Industrial Concentration." In *Industrial Concentration: The New Learning*. Goldschmid et al. (Eds.). Boston: Little, Brown, 1974.

Shirazi, J. "Market Structure and Price-Cost Margins in U.K. Manufacturing Industries." *Review of Economics and Statistics* (February 1974).

Weiss, L.W. "Factors in Changing Concentration." *Review of Economics and Statistics* (February 1963).

Weiss, L.W. "The Survival Technique and the Extent of Sub-Optimal Capacity." *The Journal of Political Economy* (June 1964).

Weiss, L.W. "The Geographic Size of Markets in Manufacturing." *Review of Economics and Statistics* (August 1972).

CHAPTER EIGHT

Bain, Joe S. *Barriers to New Competition*. Cambridge, Mass.: Harvard University Press, 1956.

_____. *Industrial Organization*. New York: John Wiley, 1968.

Blalock, H. *Causal Inferences in Non-Experimental Research*. Chapel Hill: University of North Carolina Press, 1964.

Buzzell, R.D. and R.E.M. Nourse. *Product Innovation in Food Processing 1954–1964*. Division of Research, Graduate School of Business, Harvard University, 1967.

Cowling, Keith (Ed.). *Market Structure and Corporate Behavior*. London: Gray-Mills, 1972.

Greer, Douglas. "Advertising and Market Concentration." *Southern Economic Journal* (July 1971):19–32.

Mann, H.M., J.A. Henning, and J.W. Meehan, Jr. "Advertising and Concentration: An Empirical Investigation." *Journal of Industrial Economics* (November 1967):34–45.

Ornstein, Stanley. "The Advertising-Concentration Controversy." Unpublished paper, 1975.

Simon, H.A. "Causal Ordering and Identifiability," in *Studies in Econometric Method*. W. Hood and T.C. Koopmans (Eds.). New York: John Wiley, 1953.

Subcommittee on Antitrust and Monopoly, U.S. Senate. *Concentration Ratios in Manufacturing Industry 1958*. Washington, D.C.: U.S. Government Printing Office, 1963.

"Symposium on Advertising and Concentration." *Journal of Industrial Economics* (November 1969):76–100.

Telser, L. "Advertising and Competition." *Journal of Political Economy* (December 1964):537–562.

CHAPTER NINE

Allvine, Fred C. and James M. Patterson. *Competition, Ltd.: The Marketing of Gasoline*. Bloomington: Indiana University Press, 1972.

Bain, Joe S. "Relation of Profit Rate to Industry Concentration American Manufacturing, 1936–1940." *Quarterly Journal of Economics* (August 1951): 293–324.

Bain, Joe S. *The Economics of the Pacific Coast Petroleum Industry: Part II and Part III*. Berkeley: University of California Press, 1945.

Cassady, Ralph Jr. *Price Making and Price Behavior in the Petroleum Industry*. New Haven: Yale University Press, 1954.

deChazeau, Melvin G. and Alfred E. Kahn. *Integration and Competition in the Petroleum Industry*. Petroleum Monograph Series 3. New Haven: Yale University Press, 1959.

Federal Trade Commission. *News Summary*, November 1, 1972.

Heflebower, Richard B. "Towards a Theory of Industrial Markets and Prices." *American Economic Review* (May 1954):121–139.

Livingston, S. Morris and Theodore Levitt. "Competition and Retail Gasoline Prices." *Review of Economics and Statistics*, Part I (May 1959):119–132.

National Petroleum News, various issues.

National Petroleum News Factbook, various issues.

Oil and Gas Journal, various issues.

Page, Albert. "The Development and Testing of a Macro-Marketing Model of the Effect of Competition in Gasoline Retail Markets on the Degree of Consumer Choice." Unpublished Ph.D. dissertation, Graduate School of Management, Northwestern University, 1974.

Platt's Oilgram, various issues.

Stigler, George J. "A Theory of Oligopoly." *Journal of Political Economy* (February 1964):44–61.

Temporary National Economic Committee. *Investigation of the Concentration of Economic Power*, Part XVII–A. Washington, D.C.: U.S. Government Printing Office, 1940.

U.S. Bureau of the Census. *Census of Manufacturers, 1967*. Special Report Series: *Concentration Ratios in Manufacturing*, Part 2: Product Class Concentration Ratios, MC67 (S)–2.2. Washington, D.C.: U.S. Government Printing Office, 1971.

U.S. Congress, House. Hearings before Subcommittee Number Four of the Select Committee on Small Business. *FTC Industry Conference on Marketing of Automotive Gasoline*. Washington, D.C.: U.S. Government Printing Office, 1966.

U.S. Congress, Senate. Hearings Before the Subcommittee on Antitrust and Monopoly of the Committee of the Judiciary. *Marketing Practices in the Gasoline Industry*, Part 1. 91st Congress. Washington, D.C.: U.S. Government Printing Office, 1971.

U.S. Congress, Senate. Hearings Before the Subcommittee on Antitrust and Monopoly of the Committee of the Judiciary. *Marketing Practices in the Gasoline Industry*, Part 3. 92nd Congress, 2nd Session. Washington, D.C.: U.S. Government Printing Office, 1972.

U.S. Congress, Senate. Permanent Subcommittee on Investigations of the Subcommittee on Investigations of the Committee on Government Operations. *Investigation of the Petroleum Industry*, 93rd Congress, 1st Session. Washington, D.C.: U.S. Government Printing Office, 1973.

CHAPTER TEN

Adelman, M.A. "Comment on the 'H' Concentration Measure as a Numbers Equivalent." *Review of Economics and Statistics* (February 1969).

Baily, Martin N. "Research and Development Costs and Returns: The U.S. Pharmaceutical Industry." *Journal of Political Economy* (January/February 1972).

Bain, Joe S. *Barriers to New Competition*. Cambridge, Mass.: Harvard University Press, 1956.

Bain, Joe S. *International Differences in Industrial Structure*. New Haven: Yale University Press, 1966.

Clymer, Harold. "The Changing Costs and Risks of Pharmaceutical Innovation." In *The Economics of Drug Innovation*. Joseph D. Cooper (Ed.). Washington, D.C.: American University Press, 1970.

Clymer, Harold. "The Economics of Drug Innovation." In *The Development and Control of New Drug Products*. M. Pernarowski and M. Darrach (Eds.). Vancouver, B.C.: Evergreen Press, 1971.

Clymer, Harold. "The Economic and Regulatory Climate—U.S. and Overseas Impact Trends." In *Drug Development and Marketing*. Robert B. Helms (Ed.). Washington, D.C.: American Institute for Public Policy Research, 1975.

Comanor, W.S. "Research and Technical Change in the Pharmaceutical Industry." *Review of Economics and Statistics* (May 1965).

Cooper, Joseph D. *The Economics of Drug Innovation*. Washington, D.C.: American University Press, 1970.

de Haen, Paul. "New Products Parade, Annual Review of Drugs." New York: (mimeo).

Dunlop, Sir Derrick. "The British System of Drug Regulation." In Landau (1973).

Fisher, F.M. and P. Temin. "Returns to Scale in Research and Development: What Does the Schumpeterian Hypothesis Imply?" *Journal of Political Economy* (January/February 1973).

Grabowski, Henry. "The Determinants of Industrial Research and Development: A Study of the Chemical, Drug, and Petroleum Industries." *Journal of Political Economy* (March/April 1968).

Grabowski, Henry and Dennis Mueller. "Industrial Organization: The Role and Contribution of Econometrics." *American Economic Review* (May 1970).

Grabowski, Henry, John Vernon, and Lacy Thomas. "The Effects of Regulatory Policy on the Incentives to Innovate: International Comparative Analysis." Paper presented at Third Seminar on Pharmaceutical Public Policy Issues, American University, December 1975.

Landau, Richard L. (Ed.). *Regulating New Drugs.* Chicago: University of Chicago Press, 1973.

Lasagna, Louis and William Wardell. "An Analysis of Drug Development Involving New Chemical Entities Sponsored by U.S.-Owned Company, 1962–1974." In *Drug Development and Marketing.* Robert B. Helms (Ed.). Washington, D.C.: American Enterprise Institute for Public Policy Research, 1975.

Mansfield, Edwin. "Industrial Research and Development Expenditures: Determinants, Prospects, and Relation of Size of Firm and Inventive Output." *Journal of Political Economy* (August 1964).

Mund, Vernon A. "The Return on Investment of the Innovative Pharmaceutical Firm." In Cooper (1970).

Noll, Roger G. "Government Administrative Behavior and Technological Innovation." California Institute of Technology, Social Science Working Paper No. 62, 1975.

Peltzman, Sam. "The Benefits and Costs of New Drug Regulation." In Landau (1973).

Reis-Arnt E. and D. Elvers. "Results in Pharmaceutical Research: New Pharmaceutical Agents." *Drugs, Made in Germany* (15, No. 3), 1972.

Sarett, L.H. "FDA Regulations and Their Influence on Future R&D." *Research Management* (March 1974).

Scherer, F.M. "Size of Firm, Oligopoly, and Research, A Comment." *Canadian Journal of Economics and Political Science* (May 1965).

Scherer, F.M. *Industrial Market Structure and Economic Performance.* Chicago: Rand McNally, 1970.

Schmidt, Alexander. Testimony before U.S. Senate Subcommittee on Health of the Committee on Labor and Public Welfare. *Hearings on Legislation Amending the Public Health Service Act and the Federal Food, Drug and Cosmetic Act.* 93rd Congress, August 1974.

Schneed, Jerome E. "Innovation and Discovery in the Ethical Pharmaceutical Industry." In *Research and Innovation in the Modern Corporation.* Edwin Mansfield (Ed.). New York: W.W. Norton, 1971.

Schumpeter, J.A. *Capitalism, Socialism and Democracy.* New York: Harper, 1942.

Schwartzman, David. *The Expected Return from Pharmaceutical Research.* Washington, D.C.: American Enterprise Institute, 1975.

Schwartzman, David. "Research Activity and Size of Firm in U.S. Pharmaceutical Industry." Paper presented to Second Seminar on the Dynamics of Pharmaceutical Innovation and Economics. Joseph Cooper (Ed.). American University, 1975.

Stigler, George J. "The Theory of Economic Regulation." *Bell Journal of Economics and Management Science* (Spring 1971).

Stigler, George J. "Regulation: The Confusion of Means and Ends." In Landau (1973).

Vernon, John M. and Peter Gusen. "Technical Change and Firm Size: The Pharmaceutical Industry." *Review of Economics and Statistics* (August 1974).

Vernon, Raymond. *Sovereignty at Bay.* New York: Basic Books, 1971.

Wardell, William. "Introduction of New Therapeutic Drugs in the United States and Great Britain: An International Comparison." *Clinical Pharmacology and Therapeutics* (September/October 1973).

Wardell, William. "Therapeutic Implications of the Drug Lag." *Clinical Pharmacology and Therapeutics* (January 1974).

Wardell, William. "Regulatory Assessment Models Re-Assessed." Paper presented to Second Seminar on the Dynamics of Pharmaceutical Innovation and Economics. Joseph Cooper (Ed.). American University, 1975.

Wilcox, Clair. *Public Policies Toward Business.* 3rd ed. Homewood, Ill.: Richard D. Irwin, 1966.

CHAPTER ELEVEN

Bain, Joe S. *Barriers to New Competition.* Cambridge, Mass.: Harvard University Press, 1956.

Bain, Joe S. *Essays on Price Theory and Industrial Organization.* Boston: Little, Brown, 1972.

Dewing, Arthur. *Corporate Promotions and Reorganization.* Cambridge, Mass.: Harvard University Press, 1914.

Gaskins, Darius. "Dynamic Limit Pricing: Optimal Pricing Under Threat of Entry." *Journal of Economic Theory* (September 1971):306–322.

Gilbert, Gary. "Predicting *De Novo* Expansion in Bank Merger Cases." *Journal of Finance* (March 1974):151–162.

Gort, Michael. "An Economic Disturbance Theory of Mergers." *Quarterly Journal of Economics* (November 1969):624–659.

Hirshleifer, Jack. "The Private and Social Value of Information and the Reward To Inventive Activity." *American Economic Review* (September 1971): 561–574.

Jones, Eliot. *The Trust Problem in the United States.* New York: Macmillan, 1922.

Kamien, M. and N. Schwartz. "Limit Pricing and Uncertain Entry." *Econometrica* (May 1971):441–454.

Kamien, M. and N. Schwartz. "Cournot Oligopoly with Uncertain Entry." *Review of Economic Studies* (January 1975):125–131.

Lee, Wayne. "Oligopoly and Entry." *Journal of Economic Theory* (August 1975):35–54.

Posner, Richard. "Antitrust Policy and the Supreme Court: An Analysis of the Restricted Distribution, Horizontal Merger and Potential Competition Doctrines." *Columbia Law Review* (1975):282–327.

Rhoades, S. and A. Yeats. "An Analysis of Entry and Expansion Predictions in Bank Acquisition and Merger Cases." *Western Economic Journal* (September 1972):337–345.

Singh, Ajit. "Takeovers, Economic Natural Selection; and the Theory of the Firm: Evidence from the Postwar United Kingdom Experience." *Economic Journal* (September 1975):497–515.

Snapp, Bruce. "Mergers and Limit Pricing: The Optimal Response to Potential Competition." Ph.D. dissertation, University of Michigan, 1974.

Steiner, Peter. *Mergers: Motives, Effects, Policies.* Ann Arbor: University of Michigan Press, 1975.

Stigler, George. "A Theory of Oligopoly." *Journal of Political Economy* (February 1964):44–61.

Stigler, George. "The Economic Effects of the Antitrust Laws." *Journal of Law and Economics* (October 1966):225–258.

Turner, Donald. "Conglomerate Mergers and Section 7 of the Clayton Act." *Harvard Law Review* (May 1965):1313–1395.

CHAPTER TWELVE

Attanasi, E.D. and S.R. Johnson. "Sequential Bidding Models—A Decision Theoretical Approach." *Industrial Organization Review* (Spring 1975a):43–55.

Attanasi, E.D. and S.R. Johnson. "Expectations, Market Structure and Sequential Bid Pricing." *Southern Economic Journal* (July 1975b):18–32.

Bain, Joe S. *Industrial Organization.* 2d ed. New York: John Wiley, 1968.

_____. *Essays on Price Theory and Industrial Organization.* Boston: Little, Brown, 1972.

Collins, N.H. and L.E. Preston. "Price-Cost Margins and Industry Structure." *Review of Economics and Statistics* (May 1969):182–190.

_____. *Concentration and Price Cost Margins in Manufacturing.* Berkeley: University of California Press, 1968.

_____. "Concentration and Price Cost Margins in Food Manufacturing Industries." *Journal of Industrial Economics* (July 1966):226–242.

Dantzig, G.B. *Linear Programming and Extensions.* Princeton: Princeton University Press, 1963.

Gnedenko, B.V., Y.K. Belyayev, and A.D. Solovyey. *Mathematical Methods in Reliability Theory.* Trans. by Richard Barlow. New York: Academic Press, 1969.

Hay, G.A. and D. Kelley. "An Empirical Survey of Price Fixing Conspiracies." *The Journal of Law and Economics* (April 1974):13–38.

Hanson, M.H., W.N. Hurwitz, and W.G. Madow. *Sample Survey Methods and Theory.* Vol. 1. New York: John Wiley, 1953.

Kleijnen, J.P. *Statistical Techniques in Simulation, Part II.* New York: Marcel Dekker, 1975.

Kortanek, K.O., J.V. Soden, and D. Sodaro. "Profit Analyses and Sequential Bid Pricing Models." *Management Science* (November 1973):398–417.

Rausser, G.C. and S.R. Johnson. "On the Limitations of Simulation in Model Evaluation and Decision Analysis." *Simulation and Games* (June 1975):13–51.

Saving, T.R. "Concentration Ratios and the Degree of Monopoly Power." *International Economic Review* (February 1970):139–148.

Scherer, F.M. *Industrial Market Structure and Economic Performance.* Chicago: Rand McNally, 1970.

Stigler, G.J. *The Organization of Industry.* Homewood, Ill.: Richard D. Irwin, 1968.

Weiss, L. "Quantitative Studies of Industrial Organization." In *Frontiers of Quantitative Economics.* M.D. Intriligator (Ed.). Amsterdam: North-Holland, 1971.

CHAPTER THIRTEEN

Bureau of Land Management, U.S. Department of the Interior. *Oil and Gas Lease Data Reports,* 1954–1975. Washington, D.C., various years.

Erickson, E. and R. Spann. "The U.S. Petroleum Industry." In *The Energy Question on International Failure of Policy.* E. Erickson and L. Waverman (Eds.). Toronto: University of Toronto Press, 1974.

Hirshleifer, J. "The Private and Social Value of Information and the Reward to Inventive Activity." *American Economic Review* (September 1971):561–574.

Hughart, D. "Informational Asymmetry, Bidding Strategies, and the Marketing of Offshore Petroleum Leases." *Journal of Political Economy* (October 1975):969–988.

Rothkopt, M. "A Rational Model of Competitive Bidding." *Management Science* (March 1969):362–373.

Stiglitz, J. "The Theory of 'Screening,' Education and the Distribution of Income." *American Economic Review* (June 1975):283–300.

Wilson, R. "Competitive Bidding with Asymmetric Information." *Management Science* (July 1967):816–820.

Wilson, R. "Competitive Bidding with Disparate Information." *Management Science* (March 1969):446–448.

Vickerey, W. "Counter speculation, Auctions, and Competitive Sealed Tenders." *Journal of Finance* (March 1961):8–37.

Authors' Affiliations

Fred C. Allvine,
  Georgia Institute of Technology
Emil D. Attanasi,
  U.S. Geological Survey
James L. Bothwell,
  Tufts University
Richard E. Caves,
  Harvard University
Darius W. Gaskins, Jr.
  University of California, Berkeley
Henry G. Grabowski,
  Duke University
J. A. Henning,
  Syracuse University
S. R. Johnson,
  University of Georgia
David R. Kamerschen,
  University of Georgia, Athens
Theodore E. Keeler,
  University of California, Berkeley
H. Michael Mann,
  Boston College
Edward S. Mason,
  Harvard University

Robert T. Masson,
  U.S. Department of Justice
Michael E. Porter,
  Harvard University
P. David Qualls,
  Federal Trade Commission
Barbara A. Reeves,
  Munger, Tolles & Richershauser
  (Los Angeles)
Robert J. Reynolds,
  U.S. Department of Justice
F. M. Scherer,
  Federal Trade Commission
William G. Shepherd,
  University of Michigan
Thomas J. Teisberg,
  University of California, Berkeley
John M. Vernon,
  Duke University
Leonard W. Weiss,
  University of Wisconsin, Madison

About the Editors

Professor Joe S. Bain is widely recognized as the father of the modern interindustry methodological approach for the study of industrial organization. After receiving a Ph.D. at Harvard University, where he studied under Edward S. Mason and Joseph A. Schumpeter amongst others, he taught economics at the University of California, Berkeley, from 1939 through 1975.

The coeditors of this honorary volume received Ph.D. degrees at Berkeley, **Masson** in 1969 and **Qualls** in 1968, where they studied under Professor Bain. Masson has been a member of the economics faculty at Northwestern University and is currently an economist at the Antitrust Division of the U.S. Department of Justice. Qualls previously taught economics at the University of Maryland and is currently employed at the Bureau of Economics, Federal Trade Commission. Both coeditors have been visiting members of the University of California faculty.

The essay by **William G. Shepherd**, contained in the volume, outlines and pays tribute to the many substantive and fundamental methodological contributions of Professor Bain.